Taste of Home
Christmas

Taste of Home BOOKS

READER'S DIGEST —
REIMAN MEDIA GROUP, INC.

Taste of Home · Reader's Digest

A TASTE OF HOME/READER'S DIGEST BOOK
©2013 Reiman Media Group, Inc., 5400 S. 60th St., Greendale WI 53129. All rights reserved.
Taste of Home and Reader's Digest are registered trademarks of The Reader's Digest Association, Inc.

EDITORIAL

Editor-in-Chief: Catherine Cassidy
Creative Director: Howard Greenberg
Editorial Operations Director: Kerri Balliet

Managing Editor, Print and Digital Books: Mark Hagen
Associate Creative Director: Edwin Robles Jr.

Editors: Heather Ray, Jan Briggs
Art Director: Raeann Sundholm
Layout Designers: Catherine Fletcher, Nancy Novak
Editorial Production Manager: Dena Ahlers
Copy Chief: Deb Warlaumont Mulvey
Copy Editor: Dulcie Shoener
Content Operations Manager: Colleen King
Executive Assistant: Marie Brannon

Chief Food Editor: Karen Berner
Food Editors: James Schend; Peggy Woodward, RD
Associate Food Editor: Krista Lanphier
Associate Editor/Food Content: Annie Rundle
Recipe Editors: Mary King; Jenni Sharp, RD; Irene Yeh

Test Kitchen and Food Styling Manager: Sarah Thompson
Test Kitchen Cooks: Alicia Rooker, RD (lead); Holly Johnson; Jimmy Cababa
Prep Cooks: Matthew Hass (lead); Nicole Spohrleder, Lauren Knoelke
Food Stylists: Kathryn Conrad (senior), Shannon Roum, Leah Rekau

Photographers: Dan Roberts, Jim Wieland
Photographer/Set Stylist: Grace Natoli Sheldon
Set Styling Manager: Stephanie Marchese
Set Stylists: Melissa Haberman, Dee Dee Jacq

Business Analyst: Kristy Martin
Billing Specialist: Mary Ann Koebernik

BUSINESS

Vice President, Publisher: Jan Studin, jan_studin@rd.com

General Manager, Taste of Home Cooking Schools: Erin Puariea

Vice President, Brand Marketing: Jennifer Smith
Vice President, Circulation and Continuity Marketing: Dave Fiegel

READER'S DIGEST NORTH AMERICA

Vice President, Business Development: Jonathan Bigham
President, Books and Home Entertaining: Harold Clarke
Chief Financial Officer: Howard Halligan
VP, General Manager, Reader's Digest Media: Marilynn Jacobs
Chief Marketing Officer: Renee Jordan
Vice President, Chief Sales Officer: Mark Josephson
Vice President, General Manager, Milwaukee: Frank Quigley
Vice President, Chief Content Officer: Liz Vaccariello

THE READER'S DIGEST ASSOCIATION, INC.

President and Chief Executive Officer: Robert E. Guth

For other Taste of Home books and products, visit us at **tasteofhome.com**.

For more Reader's Digest products and information, visit **rd.com** (in the United States) or **rd.ca** (in Canada).

International Standard Book Number: 978-1-61765-219-6 (hardcover)
International Standard Book Number: 978-1-61765-087-1 (paperback)
Library of Congress Control Number: 2013931310

Pictured on front cover:
Festive New York-Style Cheesecake, page 210

Pictured in spine:
Decadent Brownie Swirl Cheesecake, page 229

Pictured on back cover:
Chocolate Peanut Butter Candy, page 272
Apple Cider-Glazed Ham, page 87
Crunchy Pomegranate Salad, page 142

Printed in USA
1 3 5 7 9 10 8 6 4 2 (hardcover)
3 5 7 9 10 8 6 4 2 (paperback)

Turkey Menu, p. 94

The 12 Tastes of *Christmas!*

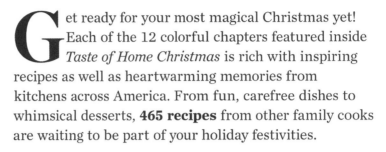

Get ready for your most magical Christmas yet! Each of the 12 colorful chapters featured inside *Taste of Home Christmas* is rich with inspiring recipes as well as heartwarming memories from kitchens across America. From fun, carefree dishes to whimsical desserts, **465 recipes** from other family cooks are waiting to be part of your holiday festivities.

In this extraordinary collection, you'll find more than **180 cookies**, **treats and homemade gifts** to charm friends and welcome any out-of-town guests—plus you'll discover **13 complete party menus**, **50 festive appetizers**, **dozens of brunch recipes** and enough **yuletide crafts** to help deck your buffet with holiday spice and everything nice.

PAGE 96

PAGE 95

icons

FAST FIX
Recipes marked Fast Fix can be made in 30 minutes or less.

MAKE AHEAD
Recipes marked Make Ahead can be prepared in advance.

TRY THIS CRAFT

Add a special touch with one of 10 holiday crafts throughout this book. (Custom Place Cards, page 97.)

PAGE 97

❝A small slice of this rich and fudgelike torte will go a long way to satisfy a sweet tooth. Chocolate lovers will thank you.❞

—**MARY CHOATE** SPRING HILL, FLORIDA

PAGE 118

PAGE 47

DO NOT OPEN
UNTIL
DECEMBER
25th

DO NOT O
UNTIL
DECEMBER
25th

PAGE 283

PAGE 116

LIKE US
facebook.com/tasteofhome

VISIT OUR BLOG
loveandhomemaderecipes.com

TWEET US
@tasteofhome

SHOP WITH US
shoptasteofhome.com

FOLLOW US
pinterest.com/taste_of_home

SHARE A RECIPE
tasteofhome.com/submit

PAGE 64

PAGE 222

PAGE 53

Contents

PARTY SHRIMP, PAGE 21

Festive Appetizers & Beverages

13

18

25

Beef Canapes with Cucumber Sauce

Homemade cucumber yogurt gives these tender slices of beef a fresh flavor. To save time, you can use 2 cups of plain Greek yogurt and skip the straining process.
—**TASTE OF HOME TEST KITCHEN**

PREP: 30 MIN. + CHILLING **BAKE:** 25 MIN. + CHILLING **MAKES:** 3 DOZEN

4 cups (32 ounces) plain yogurt
1 beef tenderloin roast
    (1½ pounds)
2 tablespoons olive oil, divided
1 teaspoon salt, divided
¼ teaspoon plus ⅛ teaspoon white pepper, divided
1 medium cucumber, peeled, seeded and diced
1 tablespoon finely chopped onion
1 garlic clove, minced
1 tablespoon white vinegar
1 French bread baguette
    (1 pound), cut into 36 thin slices
1 cup fresh arugula
    Sliced grape tomatoes, optional

1. Line a fine mesh strainer with two layers of cheesecloth; place over a bowl. Place yogurt in strainer. Cover and refrigerate for at least 4 hours or overnight.
2. Rub tenderloin with 1 tablespoon oil. Sprinkle with ½ teaspoon salt and ¼ teaspoon white pepper. In a large skillet, cook tenderloin over medium-high heat until browned on all sides. Transfer to a shallow roasting pan.
3. Bake at 400° for 25-30 minutes or until a thermometer reads 145°. Cool on a wire rack for 1 hour. Cover and refrigerate.
4. Transfer yogurt from strainer to another bowl (discard yogurt liquid). Add the cucumber, onion, garlic and remaining salt and white pepper. In a small bowl, whisk the vinegar and remaining oil; stir into yogurt mixture.
5. Thinly slice the tenderloin. Spread yogurt mixture over bread slices; top with beef, arugula and, if desired, tomato slices. Serve immediately or cover and refrigerate until serving.

Hot Buttered Rum Mix

I offered this comforting, hot drink to guests at one of my bunco gatherings. Everyone wanted a copy of the recipe. I like to keep a batch in the freezer for easy entertaining.
—**CAROL BEYERL** EAST WENATCHEE, WASHINGTON

PREP: 10 MIN. + FREEZING **MAKES:** 14-18 SERVINGS

1 cup butter, softened
2 cups confectioners' sugar
1 cup plus 2 tablespoons packed brown sugar
2 cups vanilla ice cream, softened
1½ teaspoons ground cinnamon
½ teaspoon ground nutmeg
1 teaspoon rum extract
**ADDITIONAL INGREDIENT
(FOR EACH SERVING)**
¾ cup boiling water

In a large bowl, cream butter and sugars until light and fluffy. Add the ice cream, cinnamon, nutmeg and extract. Transfer to a freezer container; freeze overnight. Yield: 3½ cups mix.
To prepare hot drink: *Dissolve 3-4 tablespoons of mix in boiling water; stir well.*

BACON-CHEESE BISCUIT BITES

Bacon-Cheese Biscuit Bites

PREP: 20 MIN. **BAKE:** 15 MIN. **MAKES:** 20 APPETIZERS

- 4   ounces cream cheese, softened
- 1   egg
- 1   tablespoon 2% milk
- ⅓   cup real bacon bits
- ¼   cup shredded Swiss cheese
- 1   tablespoon dried minced onion
- 1   large plum tomato, seeded and finely chopped, divided
- 1   tube (10.2 ounces) large refrigerated flaky biscuits

1. In a small bowl, beat the cream cheese, egg and milk until smooth. Stir in the bacon, cheese, onion and half of the tomato; set aside.

2. Cut each biscuit into four pieces; press each piece into a greased miniature muffin cup. Fill with cream cheese mixture; top with remaining tomato.

3. Bake at 375° for 14-16 minutes or until a knife inserted near the center comes out clean.

FAST FIX Brilliant Christmas Sunset Juice

When you pour orange juice over pomegranate juice or grenadine, the layers look like a sunset.
—RITA FARMER GREENDALE, WISCONSIN

PREP/TOTAL TIME: 5 MIN. **MAKES:** 4 SERVINGS

-     Crushed ice
- 4   tablespoons pomegranate juice or grenadine syrup
- 4   cups orange juice

Add ice to four glasses. Pour 1 tablespoon pomegranate juice or grenadine syrup over ice in each glass. Slowly add 1 cup orange juice. Stir if desired.

FAST FIX ## Calzone Pinwheels

Once you try these mini-sized calzones, you may never go back to the large ones. People love the cheesy, fresh taste.

—**LISA SMITH** BRYAN, OHIO

PREP/TOTAL TIME: 30 MIN. **MAKES:** 16 APPETIZERS

- ½ **cup ricotta cheese**
- 1 **teaspoon Italian seasoning**
- ¼ **teaspoon salt**
- ½ **cup shredded part-skim mozzarella cheese**
- ½ **cup diced pepperoni**
- ¼ **cup grated Parmesan cheese**
- ¼ **cup chopped fresh mushrooms**
- ¼ **cup finely chopped green pepper**
- 2 **tablespoons finely chopped onion**
- 1 **package (8 ounces) refrigerated crescent rolls**
- 1 **jar (14 ounces) pizza sauce, warmed**

1. In a small bowl, combine the ricotta, Italian seasoning and salt. Stir in the mozzarella cheese, pepperoni, Parmesan cheese, mushrooms, green pepper and onion. Separate crescent dough into four rectangles; seal perforations.

2. Spread cheese mixture over each rectangle to within ¼ in. of edges. Roll up jelly-roll style, starting with a short side; pinch seams to seal. Cut each into four slices.

3. Place cut side down on greased baking sheets. Bake at 375° for 10-15 minutes or until golden brown. Serve warm with pizza sauce. Refrigerate leftovers.

top tip ## Bite-Size Buffets

For an appetizer buffet that serves as a meal, offer five or six different appetizers (including some substantial selections, such as the Honey Garlic Ribs, p. 15) and plan on eight to nine pieces per guest. If you'll also be serving a meal, two to three pieces per person is sufficient.

Mushroom Cheese Bread

Savory slices of cheesy, aromatic French bread are lifesavers when you need a last-minute appetizer or brunch item. I also like to serve this as a side with soups and salads.

—LORI STEFANISHION DRUMHELLER, ALBERTA

PREP: 25 MIN. **BAKE:** 20 MIN. **MAKES:** 16 SERVINGS

- 6 cups sliced fresh mushrooms
- 1 tablespoon butter
- 4 green onions, chopped
- 1 loaf (1 pound) French bread
- 1 carton (8 ounces) spreadable garlic and herb cream cheese
- 2 cups (8 ounces) shredded Italian cheese blend
- 1 cup mayonnaise
- 1 cup grated Parmesan cheese

1. In a large skillet, saute the mushrooms in butter until tender. Add onions; cook and stir until liquid has evaporated. Set aside.

2. Cut French bread in half lengthwise and then widthwise; spread cut sides with cream cheese. Combine the Italian cheese, mayonnaise and Parmesan cheese; spread over bread. Top with mushroom mixture.

3. Place on a baking sheet. Bake at 350° for 20 minutes or until cheese is melted. If desired, broil 4-6 in. from the heat for 2-4 minutes or until golden brown. Slice and serve warm.

FAST FIX Cranberry Chili Meatballs

PREP/TOTAL TIME: 30 MIN. **MAKES:** ABOUT 6 DOZEN

- 1 can (14 ounces) jellied cranberry sauce
- 1 bottle (12 ounces) chili sauce
- ¾ cup packed brown sugar
- ½ teaspoon chili powder
- ½ teaspoon ground cumin
- ¼ teaspoon cayenne pepper
- 1 package (32 ounces) frozen fully cooked homestyle meatballs, thawed

In a large saucepan over medium heat, combine the first six ingredients; stir until sugar is dissolved. Add meatballs; cook for 20-25 minutes or until heated through, stirring occasionally.

66 My sister passed this sweet-and-spicy sauce recipe along to me. I use it to coat store-bought meatballs for festive gatherings. My friends look forward to them every year. 99

—AMY SCAMERHORN INDIANAPOLIS, INDIANA

Veggie Quiche Bundles

My advice to you is to make a bunch of these bundles because they will be gone fast. I like to seal the tops with a light twist so they look like pretty packages.

—LORRAINE CALAND SHUNIAH, ONTARIO

PREP: 25 MIN. **BAKE:** 20 MIN. **MAKES:** 1 DOZEN

1 cup chopped fresh mushrooms	½ cup milk
½ cup diced zucchini	1 tablespoon prepared pesto
¼ cup chopped red onion	¼ teaspoon coarsely ground pepper
1 tablespoon plus ⅓ cup butter, divided	½ cup crumbled feta cheese
1 plum tomato, seeded and diced	½ cup shredded part-skim mozzarella cheese
3 eggs	12 sheets phyllo dough (14 inches x 9 inches)

1. In small skillet, saute mushrooms, zucchini and onion in 1 tablespoon butter until mushrooms are tender; stir in tomato. In small bowl, whisk eggs, milk, pesto and pepper. In another bowl, combine feta and mozzarella.
2. Melt the remaining butter. Place one sheet of phyllo dough on a work surface; brush with butter. Repeat with three more sheets of phyllo, brushing each layer. Cut phyllo in half widthwise, then cut in half lengthwise. (Keep remaining phyllo covered with plastic wrap and a damp towel to prevent it from drying out.)
3. Repeat with remaining phyllo dough and butter. Carefully place each stack in a greased muffin cup. Fill each with 4 teaspoons vegetable mixture, 1 tablespoon cheese mixture and 4 teaspoons egg mixture. Pinch corners of phyllo together and twist to seal.
4. Bake at 325° for 20-25 minutes or until golden brown. Serve warm. Refrigerate leftovers.
Make Ahead Note: *Freeze cooked and cooled bundles in freezer container, separating layers with waxed paper. To reheat, place pastries on baking sheet in 325° oven until heated through.*

FAST FIX **Layered Shrimp Dip**

This is even better than shrimp cocktail, and it's not your average layered dip—it's a win-win.

—SUE BROYLES CHEROKEE, TEXAS

PREP: 15 MIN. + CHILLING **MAKES:** 12-16 SERVINGS

- 1 package (3 ounces) cream cheese, softened
- 6 tablespoons salsa, divided
- ½ cup cocktail sauce
- 3 cans (6 ounces each) small shrimp, rinsed and drained
- 1 can (2¼ ounces) sliced ripe olives, drained
- 1 cup (4 ounces) shredded cheddar cheese
- 1 cup (4 ounces) shredded Monterey Jack cheese
- Sliced green onions
- Tortilla chips

1. In a small bowl, combine cream cheese and 3 tablespoons salsa; spread into an ungreased 9-in. pie plate. Combine cocktail sauce and remaining salsa; spread over cream cheese.
2. Arrange shrimp evenly over top. Sprinkle with olives. Combine cheeses; sprinkle over top. Add onions. Chill. Serve with tortilla chips.

Mini Chimichangas

My family raves over these south-of-the-border bites. There's nothing like green-chili-infused beefy snacks to liven the fiesta!

—**KATHY ROGERS** HUDSON, OHIO

PREP: 1 HOUR **COOK:** 15 MIN. **MAKES:** 14 SERVINGS

- 1 **pound ground beef**
- 1 **medium onion, chopped**
- 1 **envelope taco seasoning**
- ¾ **cup water**
- 3 **cups (12 ounces) shredded Monterey Jack cheese**
- 1 **cup (8 ounces) sour cream**
- 1 **can (4 ounces) chopped green chilies, drained**
- 1 **package (1 pound) egg roll wrappers (14 count)**
- 1 **egg white, lightly beaten**
  Oil for deep-fat frying
  Salsa and additional sour cream

1. In a large skillet, cook beef and onion over medium heat until meat is no longer pink; drain. Stir in taco seasoning and water. Bring to a boil. Reduce heat; simmer, uncovered, for 5 minutes, stirring occasionally. Remove from the heat; cool slightly.

2. In a large bowl, combine the cheese, sour cream and chilies. Stir in beef mixture. Place an egg roll wrapper on work surface with one point facing you. Place ⅓ cup filling in center. Fold bottom third of wrapper over filling; fold in sides.

3. Brush top point with egg white; roll up to seal. Repeat with remaining wrappers and filling. (Keep remaining egg roll wrappers covered with waxed paper to avoid drying out.)

4. In a large saucepan, heat 1 in. of oil to 375°. Fry chimichangas for 1½ minutes on each side or until golden brown. Drain on paper towels. Serve warm with salsa and sour cream.

FAST FIX Tomato Pizza Bread

My husband loves to add sliced ripe olives to this appetizer before baking. We think it's best when served hot and fresh out of the oven.
—**KIMBERLY MASON** BROKEN ARROW, OKLAHOMA

PREP/TOTAL TIME: 30 MIN. **MAKES:** 8 SERVINGS

- 1 tube (13.8 ounces) refrigerated pizza crust
- 2 garlic cloves, minced
- ½ teaspoon dried oregano
- 1 cup (4 ounces) shredded part-skim mozzarella cheese, divided
- 1 plum tomato, halved lengthwise and thinly sliced
- ½ teaspoon Italian seasoning, optional

1. On a greased baking sheet, roll pizza crust into a 12-in. x 8-in. rectangle. Bake at 425° for 6-8 minutes or until the edges are lightly browned. Sprinkle with garlic, oregano and half of the cheese.

2. Arrange tomato slices in a single layer over cheese. Top with remaining cheese and, if desired, Italian seasoning. Bake 6-8 minutes longer or until cheese is melted and crust is lightly browned.

FAST FIX Pomegranate Martini

PREP/TOTAL TIME: 5 MIN. **MAKES:** 1 SERVING

- Ice cubes
- 2 ounces pomegranate juice
- 1 ounce vodka
- ½ ounce triple sec
- ½ ounce club soda
- ½ teaspoon lemon juice
GARNISH
- Pomegranate seeds

Fill a shaker three-fourths full with ice. Add the pomegranate juice, vodka, triple sec, club soda and lemon juice. Cover and shake for 10-15 seconds or until condensation forms on outside of shaker. Strain into a chilled cocktail glass. Garnish as desired.

66Shake up the holidays with a crimson cocktail promised to make spirits bright. This deliciously smooth martini will be the talk of the party.**99**
—**TASTE OF HOME TEST KITCHEN**

Honey Garlic Ribs

I've been reluctant to reveal my recipe for honey-garlic sauce, but something as good as this needs to be shared.

—LILY-MICHELE ALEXIS LOUISVILLE, KENTUCKY

PREP: 15 MIN. **BAKE:** 2¼ HOURS **MAKES:** 24 SERVINGS

- 6 **pounds pork baby back ribs, cut into two-rib portions**
- 2 **cups water, divided**
- ¾ **cup packed brown sugar**
- 2 **tablespoons cornstarch**
- 1 **teaspoon garlic powder**
- ¼ **teaspoon ground ginger**
- ½ **cup honey**
- ¼ **cup reduced-sodium soy sauce**

1. Place ribs bone side down in a large roasting pan; pour 1 cup of water over ribs. Cover tightly and bake at 350° for 1½ hours.

2. In a small bowl, combine the brown sugar, cornstarch, garlic powder and ginger. Stir in the honey, soy sauce and remaining water until smooth. Drain fat from roasting pan; pour sauce over ribs.

3. Bake, uncovered, for 45 minutes or until meat is tender, basting occasionally.

Chili Ham Cups

I like to entertain a lot and have used these tasty cups on several occasions as an appetizer. I appreciate how easy it is to switch around the ingredients to give them a different flavor.

—LAURA METZGER YORK, PENNSYLVANIA

PREP: 15 MIN. **BAKE:** 20 MIN. **MAKES:** 10 SERVINGS

- 1 **package (3 ounces) cream cheese, softened**
- 1 **cup finely chopped fully cooked ham**
- 1 **cup (4 ounces) shredded cheddar cheese**
- 1 **can (4 ounces) chopped green chilies, drained**
- ¼ **cup sliced ripe olives, drained**
- 1 **tube (10.2 ounces) refrigerated biscuits**
  Salsa and sour cream, optional

1. In a small bowl, combine the cream cheese, ham, cheese, chilies and olives. Separate dough into 10 biscuits; press each biscuit onto the bottom and up the sides of a greased muffin cup. Fill with ham mixture.

2. Bake at 375° for 20-25 minutes or until cheese is melted and crust is golden brown. Let stand for 2 minutes before removing from pan. Serve warm. Garnish with salsa and sour cream if desired.

top tip — Keep Ribs Hot

Hold ribs until serving time or transport hot cooked ribs to a party by placing them in heavy-duty foil and then in a brown paper bag. The ribs can stand this way for up to 1 hour.

OLIVE BRUSCHETTA

FAST FIX Olive Bruschetta

I like to make this convenient bruschetta several days in advance so the flavors have a chance to blend together. It's best served at room temperature with toasted French bread or crackers.
—**LINDA AUSTIN** LAKE HOPATCONG, NEW JERSEY

PREP/TOTAL TIME: 30 MIN. **MAKES:** 2½ DOZEN

- 2 cups grape tomatoes, quartered
- 2 celery ribs, chopped
- ½ cup shredded carrot
- ¼ cup sliced ripe olives
- ¼ cup sliced pimiento-stuffed olives
- ¼ cup minced fresh flat-leaf parsley
- ¼ cup chopped red onion
- 1 teaspoon minced garlic
- 3 tablespoons olive oil
- 2 tablespoons balsamic vinegar
- ¼ teaspoon salt
- ⅛ teaspoon pepper
- 1 loaf (1 pound) French bread baguette, sliced and toasted

In a large bowl, combine the first eight ingredients. In a small bowl, whisk the oil, vinegar, salt and pepper; pour over vegetables and toss to coat. Serve on toasted baguette slices.

MAKE AHEAD Black Forest Ham Pinwheels

When I served this at my annual Christmas party, people really liked the smokiness of the ham and sweet surprise of the cherries.
—**KATE DAMPIER** QUAIL VALLEY, CALIFORNIA

PREP: 20 MIN. + CHILLING **MAKES:** ABOUT 3½ DOZEN

- 1 package (8 ounces) cream cheese, softened
- 4 teaspoons minced fresh dill
- 1 tablespoon lemon juice
- 2 teaspoons Dijon mustard
  Dash salt and pepper
- ½ cup dried cherries, chopped
- ¼ cup chopped green onions
- 5 flour tortillas (10 inches), room temperature
- ½ pound sliced deli Black Forest ham
- ½ pound sliced Swiss cheese

1. In a small bowl, beat the cream cheese, dill, lemon juice, mustard, salt and pepper until blended. Stir in the cherries and onions. Spread over each tortilla; layer with ham and cheese.
2. Roll up tightly; wrap in plastic wrap. Refrigerate for at least 2 hours. Cut into ½-in. slices.
Make Ahead Note: *Wrapped in plastic wrap, the roll-ups can be stored in the refrigerator up to 2 days. Slice before serving.*

Honey Barbecue Wings

This is my family's favorite way to eat chicken wings. My grown son and daughter request them when they visit home. It's a fantastic appetizer, but we sometimes eat them as a main dish.

—DIANE ACORD SAVAGE, MINNESOTA

PREP: 40 MIN. + MARINATING   **BAKE:** 25 MIN.   **MAKES:** 3 DOZEN

- 2 garlic cloves, minced
- 1 tablespoon canola oil
- ½ cup honey
- ¼ cup ketchup
- 2 tablespoons orange juice
- 2 tablespoons lemon juice
- 2 tablespoons reduced-sodium soy sauce
- 2 teaspoons ground ginger
- 2 teaspoons cider vinegar
- 1 teaspoon Worcestershire sauce
- 1 teaspoon Dijon mustard
- ¼ teaspoon pepper
- ¼ teaspoon hot pepper sauce
- 18 whole chicken wings (about 3¾ pounds)

1. In a small saucepan, saute garlic in oil until for 1 minute. Stir in the honey, ketchup, juices, soy sauce, ginger, vinegar, Worcestershire sauce, mustard, pepper and hot pepper sauce. Bring to a boil. Reduce heat; simmer, uncovered, for 15 minutes. Remove from the heat; cool to room temperature.

2. Cut chicken wings into three sections; discard wing tip sections. Place wings in a large resealable heavy-duty plastic bag; add ¾ cup cooled honey mixture. Seal bag and turn to coat; refrigerate for 2 hours. Cover and refrigerate remaining honey mixture for basting.

3. Drain and discard marinade. Place chicken wings on a greased rack in a large baking pan. Bake at 400° for 10 minutes on each side, basting occasionally with honey mixture.

4. Broil 4-6 in. from the heat for 2-3 minutes or until browned and juices run clear.

Sticky Chicken Wings: *Omit marinade. Cut chicken wings as directed. Combine 1 cup brown sugar, ¾ cup soy sauce, ½ cup teriyaki sauce, ½ cup melted butter, 1 tablespoon Creole seasoning and 1 teaspoon ground mustard. Marinate and cook chicken as directed.*

Editor's Note: *Uncooked chicken wing sections (wingettes) may be substituted for whole chicken wings.*

FAST FIX ## Bacon Cheese Spread

Each year, I share Christmas cheer by setting up a buffet at my family's hardware store. This cheese spread is always a biggie!

—SHARON BICKETT CHESTER, SOUTH CAROLINA

PREP/TOTAL TIME: 15 MIN.   **MAKES:** 4 CUPS

- 1 package (12 ounces) bacon strips, chopped
- ½ cup chopped pecans
- 4 cups (1 pound) shredded sharp cheddar cheese
- 2 cups mayonnaise
- 1 small onion, chopped
- 2 tablespoons finely chopped sweet red pepper
- ⅛ teaspoon cayenne pepper
  Assorted crackers

Cook bacon until crisp; drain. Meanwhile, in a large bowl, combine next six ingredients. Stir in bacon. Serve with crackers.

FAST FIX ▶ Pepperoni Pinwheels

Instead of serving pizza or flatbread, whip up a tray of pinwheel appetizers. You could also make a meatless batch by using chopped bell peppers instead of pepperoni.

—**CYNTHIA BENT** NEWARK, NEW JERSEY

PREP/TOTAL TIME: 25 MIN. **MAKES:** 32 APPETIZERS

- 1 package (8 ounces) cream cheese, softened
- 1 package (3½ ounces) sliced pepperoni, finely chopped
- 1 cup (4 ounces) shredded provolone cheese
- 2 tablespoons onion soup mix
- 2 tablespoons sour cream
- 1 teaspoon grated Romano cheese
- 2 tubes (13.8 ounces each) refrigerated pizza crust

1. In a small bowl, combine the first six ingredients. Unroll each tube of pizza dough into a long rectangle; spread each rectangle evenly with 1 cup pepperoni mixture.

2. Roll up jelly-roll style, starting with a short side; pinch seam to seal. Cut each roll into 16 slices; place cut side down on ungreased baking sheets.

3. Bake at 400° for 10-14 minutes or until golden brown. Serve warm. Refrigerate leftovers.

FAST FIX ▶ Sugar 'n' Spice Nuts

My daughters, grandkids and just about everyone who visits me look forward to this mix of crunchy nuts, spices and fruit during the holidays. Tucked in colorful tins, it makes a handy last-minute gift idea for busy hostesses or drop-in visitors.

—**JOAN KLINEFELTER** UTICA, ILLINOIS

PREP/TOTAL TIME: 30 MIN. **MAKES:** 3½ CUPS

- ¼ cup packed brown sugar
- ½ teaspoon ground cinnamon
- ¼ teaspoon cayenne pepper
- 1 egg white
- 1 cup salted cashews
- 1 cup pecan halves
- 1 cup dry roasted peanuts
- ½ cup dried cranberries

1. In a small bowl, combine the brown sugar, cinnamon and cayenne; set aside. In a large bowl, whisk egg white; add nuts and cranberries. Sprinkle with sugar mixture and toss to coat. Spread in a single layer on a greased baking sheet.

2. Bake at 300° for 18-20 minutes or until golden brown, stirring once. Cool. Store in an airtight container.

Candy Cane Punch

Peppermint ice cream makes this beverage taste and look more like a dessert than a punch! I've mixed the sipper many times for ladies' lunches and buffets. It's a great way to start a gathering. For a fun garnish you can hang mini candy canes around the punch bowl and cups.

—**NEVA SCHNAUBER** FORT COLLINS, COLORADO

PREP: 10 MIN. + CHILLING **MAKES:** 3½ QUARTS

2 jars (10 ounces each) strawberry jelly
2 liters lemon-lime soda, divided
2 quarts peppermint stick ice cream
  Miniature candy canes, optional

In a large saucepan, melt jelly with 2 cups soda. Chill the jelly mixture and remaining soda. Just before serving, place 6 cups ice cream in a punch bowl. Gently stir in jelly mixture. Add remaining soda. Add remaining ice cream by scoopfuls. Garnish with candy canes if desired.

FAST FIX ▶ Sangria Wine

Give your partytime sangria a twist with this refreshing citrus blend. During the Christmas season, go for the red and green look by garnishing it with limes.

—COLLEEN STURMA MILWAUKEE, WISCONSIN

PREP/TOTAL TIME: 10 MIN. **MAKES:** 10 SERVINGS

1 bottle (750 milliliters) dry red wine
1 cup lemon-flavored rum
2 cans (12 ounces each) lemon-lime soda, chilled
2 medium lemons, sliced
2 medium limes, sliced
  Ice cubes

In a pitcher, combine the wine, rum and soda; add lemon and lime slices. Serve over ice.

Tomato-Walnut Pesto Spread

Whenever I take this awesome spread to parties, I bring along copies of the recipe. Once people taste it, they alway ask how I make it. And the color combination makes it especially festive.

—MARSHA DAWSON APPLETON, WISCONSIN

PREP: 15 MIN. + CHILLING **MAKES:** 2⅓ CUPS

3 tablespoons chopped oil-packed sun-dried tomatoes, patted dry
1 package (8 ounces) cream cheese, softened
½ cup grated Parmesan cheese
¼ cup sour cream
2 tablespoons butter, softened
½ cup finely chopped walnuts
½ cup prepared pesto
  Assorted crackers

1. Line a 4-cup mold with plastic wrap; coat with cooking spray. Place tomatoes in bottom of mold; set aside.
2. In a large bowl, beat the cheeses, sour cream and butter until blended. In another bowl, combine walnuts and pesto. Spread cheese mixture over tomatoes in prepared mold; top with walnut mixture.
3. Bring edges of plastic wrap together over pesto; press down gently to seal. Refrigerate for at least 4 hours or until firm. Open plastic wrap; invert mold onto a serving plate. Serve with crackers.

SLOW-COOKED CRAB DIP

Slow-Cooked Crab Dip

Slow-cooked dips are ideal for holiday entertaining since they free up the oven for my turkey or ham. Plus, leftovers are fantastic served over a baked potato the next day.

—**SUSAN D'AMORE** WEST CHESTER, PENNSYLVANIA

PREP: 20 MIN.   **COOK:** 2 HOURS   **MAKES:** 2⅓ CUPS

- 1 **package (8 ounces) cream cheese, softened**
- 2 **green onions, chopped**
- ¼ **cup chopped sweet red pepper**
- 2 **tablespoons minced fresh parsley**
- 2 **tablespoons mayonnaise**
- 1 **tablespoon Dijon mustard**
- 1 **teaspoon Worcestershire sauce**
- ¼ **teaspoon salt**
- ¼ **teaspoon pepper**
- 2 **cans (6 ounces each) lump crabmeat, drained**
- 2 **tablespoons capers, drained**
  Dash hot pepper sauce
  Assorted crackers

1. In a 1½-qt. slow cooker, combine the first nine ingredients; stir in crab.

2. Cover and cook on low for 1-2 hours. Stir in capers and pepper sauce; cook 30 minutes longer to allow flavors to blend. Serve with crackers.

Vanilla-Almond Coffee

Instead of buying expensive flavored coffees, I make my own using flavored extracts for baking. You can prepare this with decaffeinated coffee, too.

—**TINA CHRISTENSEN** ADDISON, ILLINOIS

PREP/TOTAL TIME: 5 MIN.   **MAKES:** 1 POUND

- 1 **pound ground coffee**
- 2 **tablespoons almond extract**
- 2 **tablespoons vanilla extract**

Place coffee in a large jar with tight-fitting lid. Add extracts. Cover and shake well. Store in an airtight container in a cool, dark and dry place or in the freezer. Prepare coffee as usual.

Party Shrimp

I love to serve these shrimp when I'm entertaining. They're easy to prepare, but what's better is that they're so flavorful, no dipping sauce is required.

—KENDRA DOSS COLORADO SPRINGS, COLORADO

PREP: 15 MIN. + MARINATING **BROIL:** 10 MIN. **MAKES:** 2½ DOZEN

- 1 tablespoon olive oil
- 1½ teaspoons brown sugar
- 1½ teaspoons lemon juice
- 1 garlic clove, thinly sliced
- ½ teaspoon paprika
- ½ teaspoon Italian seasoning
- ½ teaspoon dried basil
- ¼ teaspoon pepper
- 1 pound uncooked large shrimp, peeled and deveined

1. In a large resealable plastic bag, combine the first eight ingredients. Add shrimp; seal bag and turn to coat. Refrigerate for 2 hours. Drain and discard marinade.

2. Place shrimp on an ungreased baking sheet. Broil 4 in. from the heat for 3-4 minutes on each side or until shrimp turn pink.

Spiced Cider Punch

PREP: 15 MIN. + CHILLING **MAKES:** 13 SERVINGS (ABOUT 3 QUARTS)

- 1 cup sugar
- 2 quarts apple cider or juice, divided
- 1 teaspoon ground cinnamon
- 1 teaspoon ground allspice
- 1 can (12 ounces) frozen orange juice concentrate, thawed
- 1 quart ginger ale, chilled

1. In a Dutch oven, combine the sugar, 1 cup cider, cinnamon and allspice. Cook and stir over medium heat until sugar is dissolved. Remove from the heat; add orange juice concentrate and remaining cider. Cool. Cover and refrigerate until chilled.

2. Just before serving, transfer to a punch bowl; stir in the ginger ale.

> **❝**I've been serving up this spicy punch for so long, I could make it blindfolded. I've passed the recipe along to many friends. It never wears out its welcome!**❞**

—CHARLES PIATT LITTLE ROCK, ARKANSAS

GARLIC-ONION PIZZA WEDGES

FAST FIX Garlic-Onion Pizza Wedges

Using a prebaked crust, you can have this delicious appetizer hot and ready to serve in just 20 minutes. The wedges can even make a light main dish.

—CLYDA CONRAD YUMA, ARIZONA

PREP/TOTAL TIME: 20 MIN. **MAKES:** 8 SERVINGS

- ½ cup grated Parmesan cheese
- ½ cup chopped red onion
- ½ cup mayonnaise
- ¼ cup minced fresh basil
- 4 garlic cloves, minced
  Pepper to taste
- 1 prebaked 12-inch thin pizza crust

1. In a small bowl, combine the cheese, onion, mayonnaise, basil, garlic and pepper; spread over crust.
2. Place on an ungreased baking sheet or pizza pan. Bake at 450° for 8-10 minutes or until lightly browned. Cut into wedges.

FAST FIX Champagne Cocktail

This amber drink is a champagne twist on the traditional old-fashioned. We prefer it with extra-dry champagne.

—TASTE OF HOME TEST KITCHEN

PREP/TOTAL TIME: 5 MIN. **MAKES:** 1 SERVING

- 1 sugar cube or ½ teaspoon sugar
- 6 dashes bitters
- ½ ounce brandy
- ½ cup champagne, chilled

GARNISH
  Maraschino cherry and lemon slice

Place sugar in a champagne flute or cocktail glass; sprinkle with bitters. Pour brandy into the glass. Top with champagne. Garnish as desired.

Hot Spiced Wine

My friends, family and I enjoy a spiced wine during cold winter gatherings. This warm drink will be especially pleasing to people who enjoy dry red wines.

—NOEL LICKENFELT BOLIVAR, PENNSYLVANIA

PREP: 15 MIN. **COOK:** 4 HOURS **MAKES:** 8 SERVINGS

- 2 **cinnamon sticks (3 inches)**
- 3 **whole cloves**
- 2 **bottles (750 milliliters each) dry red wine**
- 3 **medium tart apples, peeled and sliced**
- ½ **cup sugar**
- 1 **teaspoon lemon juice**

1. Place cinnamon sticks and cloves on a double thickness of cheesecloth; bring up corners of cloth and tie with string to form a bag.
2. In a 3-qt. slow cooker, combine the wine, apples, sugar and lemon juice. Add spice bag. Cover and cook on low for 4-5 hours or until heated through. Discard spice bag. Serve warm.

Mediterranean Dip with Garlic Pita Chips

I keep trying to find new ways to use dip. My chunky, veggie-laden mixture of eggplant, onion and sweet peppers is terrific on pita chips as an appetizer, or served over pasta, chicken or fish as an entree.

—SARAH GEARY OKLAHOMA CITY, OKLAHOMA

PREP: 35 MIN. **BAKE:** 1 HOUR **MAKES:** 2½ CUPS DIP (30 CHIPS)

- 2 **medium eggplants, peeled**
- 1 **large sweet red pepper**
- 1 **large sweet yellow pepper**
- 1 **large red onion**
- ¼ **cup olive oil**
- 1 **teaspoon salt**
- ¼ **teaspoon pepper**
- 2 **garlic cloves, minced**
- 4 **teaspoons tomato paste**

PITA CHIPS
- ¼ **cup olive oil**
- 2 **tablespoons grated Parmesan cheese**
- 2 **garlic cloves, minced**
- 1 **teaspoon dried basil**
- 1 **teaspoon dried thyme**
- ½ **teaspoon salt**
- ½ **teaspoon dried tarragon**
- ¼ **teaspoon coarsely ground pepper**
- 1 **package (12 ounces) whole pita breads**

1. Cut the eggplants, peppers and onion into 1-in. pieces; place in a large bowl. Add the oil, salt and pepper; toss to coat. Transfer to two greased 15-in. x 10-in. x 1-in. baking pans.
2. Bake at 400° for 40 minutes, stirring once. Stir in garlic; bake 5-10 minutes longer or until vegetables are tender. Cool for 10 minutes. Place vegetables and tomato paste in a food processor; cover and process until desired consistency.
3. For pita chips, in a small bowl, combine the oil, cheese, garlic and seasonings. Place pita breads on baking sheets; brush with half of oil mixture. Bake at 350° for 7 minutes. Turn over; brush with remaining mixture. Bake 7-9 minutes longer or until crisp. Cut each pita into six wedges. Serve with dip.

Raspberry Chipotle Dip

FAST FIX

Commit this nifty recipe to memory for the times you need a quick and impressive appetizer. Just by keeping these four ingredients on hand during the holidays, you'll be prepared for any impromptu get-togethers.

—**PAT STEVENS** GRANBURY, TEXAS

PREP/TOTAL TIME: 5 MIN. **MAKES:** 3 CUPS

 3 cartons (8 ounces each) whipped cream cheese
 1 cup raspberry chipotle salsa
 ½ cup pecan halves, toasted
    Assorted crackers

Spread cream cheese onto a small serving platter. Top with salsa and pecans. Refrigerate until serving. Serve with crackers.
Editor's Note: *This recipe was tested with Mrs. Renfro's raspberry chipotle salsa.*

Cranberry Raspberry Punch

FAST FIX

This pretty pink punch is not too sweet but is very refreshing. My family never tires of it at special occasions throughout the year.

—**SUSAN ROGERS** WILMINGTON, MASSACHUSETTS

PREP/TOTAL TIME: 10 MIN. **MAKES:** ABOUT 5 QUARTS

 2 packages (10 ounces each) frozen sweetened sliced strawberries
 1 can (12 ounces) frozen lemonade concentrate, thawed
 1 can (11½ ounces) frozen cranberry raspberry juice concentrate, thawed
 2 liters ginger ale, chilled
 2 liters club soda, chilled
 1 quart raspberry or orange sherbet

In a blender, combine the strawberries, lemonade concentrate and cranberry raspberry concentrate; cover and process until smooth. Transfer to a punch bowl. Gently stir in ginger ale and club soda. Top with scoops of sherbet. Serve immediately.

Mini Phyllo Tacos

This is a handy recipe if you need a simple crowd-pleaser. All the savory goodness of traditional tacos is packed into crispy, bite-sized shells.

—**ROSEANN WESTON** PHILIPSBURG, PENNSYLVANIA

PREP: 30 MIN. **BAKE:** 10 MIN. **MAKES:** 2½ DOZEN

 1 pound lean ground beef (90% lean)
 ½ cup finely chopped onion
 1 envelope taco seasoning
 ¾ cup water
 1¼ cups shredded Mexican cheese blend, divided
 2 packages (1.9 ounces each) frozen miniature phyllo tart shells

1. In a small skillet, cook beef and onion over medium heat until meat is no longer pink; drain. Stir in taco seasoning and water. Bring to a boil. Reduce heat; simmer, uncovered for 5 minutes. Remove from the heat; stir in ½ cup cheese blend.
2. Place tart shells in an ungreased 15-in. x 10-in. x 1-in. baking pan. Fill with taco mixture.
3. Bake at 350° for 6 minutes. Sprinkle with remaining cheese blend; bake 2-3 minutes longer or until cheese is melted.

MAKE AHEAD ▶ Hot Artichoke Spinach Dip

This hot dip is favored by my family and friends, so it always appears on my party buffets.
—**CANDY JENSEN** MARRERO, LOUISIANA

PREP: 20 MIN. **BAKE:** 30 MIN. **MAKES:** 5 CUPS

- ½ cup chopped green onions
- 2 tablespoons butter
- 4 ounces cream cheese, softened
- 2 packages (10 ounces each) frozen creamed spinach, thawed
- 1 can (14 ounces) water-packed artichoke hearts, rinsed, drained and chopped
- 1 cup (4 ounces) shredded Monterey Jack cheese
- 1 cup (4 ounces) shredded Swiss cheese
- 1 tablespoon Worcestershire sauce
- ½ teaspoon Cajun seasoning
- ½ teaspoon minced fresh thyme
- ½ teaspoon hot pepper sauce
- 1 garlic clove, minced
- ¼ cup grated Parmesan cheese
  Toasted baguette slices or pita chips

1. In a small skillet, cook onions in butter until tender; set aside. In a large bowl, beat cream cheese until smooth. Stir in the onion mixture, spinach, artichokes, Monterey Jack and Swiss cheeses, Worcestershire sauce, Cajun seasoning, thyme, hot pepper sauce and garlic.
2. Transfer to a greased 1½-qt. baking dish. Bake, uncovered, at 350° for 25-30 minutes or until bubbly around the edges.
3. Top with Parmesan cheese. Broil 4-6 in. from the heat for 3-5 minutes or until golden brown. Serve warm with baguette slices or pita chips. Refrigerate leftovers.

Make Ahead Note: *The night before, prepare mixture as noted in step 1. Cover with plastic wrap and store in refrigerator overnight. The next day, follow baking instructions in step 2.*

FAST FIX Frothy Mexi-Mocha Coffee

Knowing that this cup of coffee is waiting for me on the other side of the alarm clock makes for a bright start to my morning!
—**MARIA REGAKIS** SOMERVILLE, MASSACHUSETTS

PREP/TOTAL TIME: 15 MIN. **MAKES:** 4 SERVINGS

- 1 cup packed brown sugar
- 4 ounces semisweet chocolate, chopped
- 2 orange peel strips (1 to 3 inches)
- ½ teaspoon ground cinnamon
- ¼ teaspoon ground allspice
- 3 cups hot strong brewed coffee
- ½ cup half-and-half cream, warmed
  Optional garnishes: cinnamon sticks, orange peel and whipped cream

1. Place the first five ingredients in a blender; cover and process until chocolate is finely chopped. Add coffee; cover and process for 1-2 minutes or until chocolate is melted. Transfer to a small saucepan; heat through.
2. Return mixture to blender; add cream. Cover and process until frothy. Strain, discarding solids; serve in mugs. Garnish with cinnamon sticks, orange peel and whipped cream if desired.

MAKE AHEAD ▶ Asiago Chicken Spread

Guests with hearty appetites will love the chunks of chicken, crunchy cashews and Asiago cheese found here!

—**JAMES KORZENOWSKI** FENNVILLE, MICHIGAN

PREP: 25 MIN. + CHILLING **MAKES:** 2 CUPS

- ¾ **pound boneless skinless chicken breasts, cut into ½-inch cubes**
- ¼ **teaspoon salt**
- ⅛ **teaspoon pepper**
- 2 **tablespoons butter**
- 2 **garlic cloves, minced**
- ⅓ **cup salted cashew halves**
- ⅓ **cup mayonnaise**
- ½ **cup chopped onion**
- ¼ **cup shredded Asiago cheese**
- ¼ **cup minced fresh basil**
- ½ **teaspoon hot pepper sauce**
  Assorted crackers or toasted baguette slices

1. Season chicken with salt and pepper. In a large skillet, saute chicken in butter for 5-6 minutes or until chicken is no longer pink. Add garlic; cook 1 minute longer. Stir in cashews. Remove from the heat; cool.

2. In a food processor, combine the mayonnaise, onion, cheese, basil, pepper sauce and chicken mixture; cover and process until blended. Press into a 2-cup bowl; cover and refrigerate for at least 2 hours.

3. If desired, unmold onto a serving platter; serve with crackers or baguette slices.

Make Ahead Note: *Spread can be prepared, covered and stored in the refrigerator up to 2 days in advance.*

FAST FIX ▶ Winter's Warmth Hot Chocolate

I discovered this recipe as a newlywed when I was looking for something to warm us up during winter. We make it every year when we get our first snow; that's why my husband gave it this name!

—**JANINE JOHNSON** MINOOKA, ILLINOIS

PREP/TOTAL TIME: 25 MIN. **MAKES:** 4-6 SERVINGS

- 4 **ounces semisweet chocolate, coarsely chopped**
- ¼ **cup light corn syrup**
- ½ **teaspoon vanilla extract**
- ¼ **teaspoon ground cinnamon**
- 4 **cups 2% milk**
- 1 **cup heavy whipping cream**
  White chocolate curls, optional

1. In a small heavy saucepan, melt chocolate with corn syrup over low heat, stirring occasionally until smooth. Remove from the heat; stir in vanilla and cinnamon. Cover and set aside until cool. In a large saucepan, heat milk until small bubbles form around edge. (Do not boil.)

2. Meanwhile, in a small bowl, beat cream and cooled chocolate mixture on medium-low speed until soft peaks form. To serve, spoon chocolate cream into mugs; add hot milk and stir gently. Garnish with chocolate curls if desired.

> I came across a similar cheese roll recipe and started trying different combinations to come up with these spirals. They're very popular during the holidays, and I just can't seem to make enough of them! —**LISA HARKE** OLD MONROE, MISSOURI

CRAB 'N' CHEESE SPIRALS

Crab 'n' Cheese Spirals

PREP: 20 MIN. **BAKE:** 15 MIN. **MAKES:** 2½ DOZEN

  2   packages (8 ounces each) cream cheese, softened
  2   cups chopped imitation crabmeat
  1   can (4¼ ounces) chopped ripe olives
  ¼   cup minced chives
  3   tubes (8 ounces each) refrigerated crescent rolls
  ¾   cup shredded part-skim mozzarella cheese
  ¾   cup shredded Parmesan cheese

1. In a small bowl, beat the cream cheese, crab, olives and chives. Unroll one tube of crescent dough into one long rectangle; seal seams and perforations.
2. Spread with 1 cup cream cheese mixture; sprinkle with ¼ cup of each cheese. Roll up jelly-roll style, starting with a long side; pinch seam to seal.
3. Using a serrated knife, cut into 10 slices; place cut side down on a greased baking sheet. Repeat with remaining crescent dough, cream cheese mixture and cheeses.
4. Bake at 375° for 14-16 minutes or until golden brown. Serve warm.

FAST FIX Coffee Punch

At the Propst family gatherings, this is a must! My mouth waters just thinking about the richness of this creamy vanilla treat.

—**DIANE PROPST** DENVER, NORTH CAROLINA

PREP/TOTAL TIME: 15 MIN.
MAKES: 13 SERVINGS (2½ QUARTS)

  4   cups brewed vanilla-flavored coffee, cooled
  1   can (12 ounces) evaporated milk
  ½   cup sugar
  ½   gallon vanilla ice cream, softened
      Ground cinnamon

In a large container, combine the coffee, milk and sugar; stir until sugar is dissolved. Spoon ice cream into a punch bowl; pour coffee mixture over the top. Sprinkle with cinnamon. Serve immediately.

5. To serve, spread each crepe with about 2 tablespoons filling. Fold the crepes into quarters; cut each folded crepe into two wedges.

Make Ahead Note: *Stack unfilled crepes between layers of waxed paper or white paper towel. Cool; place in an airtight container. Refrigerate 2 to 3 days or freeze for 4 months. (Thaw frozen crepes overnight in the refrigerator when ready to use.)*

Shrimp Wrapped in Bacon

It seems like an odd combination—goat cheese, basil and barbecue sauce—but these savory-sweet bacon-wrapped shrimp are a must-try.

—**EILEEN STEFANSKI** WALES, WISCONSIN

PREP: 25 MIN. **BAKE:** 20 MIN. **MAKES:** 20 APPETIZERS

- 10 **bacon strips**
- 20 **large fresh basil leaves**
- 20 **uncooked medium shrimp, peeled and deveined**
- ¼ **cup barbecue sauce**
- ½ **cup finely crumbled goat cheese**

1. Cut each bacon strip in half widthwise; set aside. Wrap a basil leaf around each shrimp. Wrap a piece of bacon around each; secure with wooden toothpicks.
2. Place in a foil-lined 15-in. x 10-in. x 1-in. baking pan. Bake at 375° for 14-16 minutes or until bacon is crisp.
3. Brush with barbecue sauce; sprinkle with cheese. Bake 2-4 minutes longer or until heated through.

MAKE AHEAD ▶ Smoked Salmon Appetizer Crepes

I love to serve mini crepes as appetizers—so many choices, such little crepes! Every bite is full of French flair and beaucoup flavor.

—**KAREN SUE GARBACK-PRISTERA** ALBANY, NEW YORK

PREP: 15 MIN. + CHILLING **COOK:** 5 MIN. **MAKES:** 20 APPETIZERS

- 1 **cup 2% milk**
- 2 **eggs**
- 2 **egg yolks**
- 2 **tablespoons butter, melted**
- 2 **tablespoons brandy or unsweetened apple juice**
- 1 **cup all-purpose flour**
- ½ **teaspoon salt**

FILLING

- 2 **packages (3 ounces each) cream cheese, softened**
- 3 **tablespoons heavy whipping cream**
- 4 **teaspoons minced chives**
- 1 **package (4 ounces) smoked salmon or lox**

1. In a small bowl, whisk first five ingredients. Combine flour and salt; add to egg mixture and mix well. Refrigerate 1 hour.
2. Heat a lightly greased 8-in. nonstick skillet over medium heat; pour 3 tablespoons batter into the center of skillet. Lift and tilt pan to coat bottom evenly. Cook until top appears dry; turn and cook 15-20 seconds longer.
3. Remove to a wire rack. Repeat with remaining batter, greasing skillet as needed. When cool, stack crepes with waxed paper or paper towels in between.
4. For filling, in a large bowl, beat the cream cheese, cream and chives until fluffy. Stir in salmon.

Chicken Satay

A fun, hearty appetizer even kids will enjoy, this Asian-inspired dish comes complete with an easy-to-prepare peanut dipping sauce.

—TASTE OF HOME TEST KITCHEN

PREP: 15 MIN. + MARINATING **BROIL:** 5 MIN. **MAKES:** 10-12 SERVINGS

- 2 pounds boneless skinless chicken breasts
- ⅓ cup soy sauce
- 1 green onion, sliced
- 2 tablespoons sesame oil
- 1 tablespoon brown sugar
- 1 tablespoon honey
- 2 garlic cloves, minced
- ½ teaspoon ground ginger

PEANUT SAUCE

- ½ cup salted peanuts
- ¼ cup chopped green onions
- 1 garlic clove, minced
- 3 tablespoons chicken broth
- 3 tablespoons butter, melted
- 2 tablespoons reduced-sodium soy sauce
- 1 tablespoon lemon juice
- 1 tablespoon honey
- ½ teaspoon ground ginger
- ¼ to ½ teaspoon crushed red pepper flakes

1. Flatten chicken to ¼-in. thickness; cut lengthwise into 1-in.-wide strips. In a large resealable plastic bag, combine soy sauce, onion, sesame oil, brown sugar, honey, garlic and ginger; add chicken. Seal bag and turn to coat; refrigerate for 4 hours.

2. In a food processor, combine the peanuts, onions and garlic; cover and process until mixture forms a paste. Add the broth, butter, soy sauce, lemon juice, honey, ginger and pepper flakes; cover and process until smooth. Transfer to a serving bowl. Refrigerate until serving.

3. Drain and discard marinade. Thread chicken strips onto soaked wooden skewers. Broil 6 in. from the heat for 2-4 minutes on each side or until chicken is no longer pink. Serve with peanut sauce.

FAST FIX ▶ Apple & Blue Cheese on Endive

For the filling I sometimes use pears instead of apples or use the mixture to stuff celery sticks or top crackers. The endive leaves are nice for a more formal holiday dinner or buffet.

—KATIE FLEMING EDMONDS, WASHINGTON

PREP/TOTAL TIME: 30 MIN. **MAKES:** 32 APPETIZERS

- 1 tablespoon lemon juice
- 1 tablespoon water
- 1 large red apple, finely chopped
- 2 celery ribs, finely chopped
- ¾ cup crumbled blue cheese
- 3 tablespoons mayonnaise
- 4 heads Belgian endive, separated into leaves
- ½ cup chopped hazelnuts, toasted

1. In a small bowl, combine lemon juice and water; add apple and toss to coat. Drain and pat dry.

2. Combine the apple, celery, blue cheese and mayonnaise; spoon 1 tablespoonful onto each endive leaf. Sprinkle with hazelnuts.

FAST FIX ▶ Cranberry Glogg

Winter's a perfect time to cozy up with a hot drink, and this glogg is our favorite. It's heady with spices and full of cranberry flavor.

—**JUNE LINDQUIST** HAMMOND, WISCONSIN

PREP/TOTAL TIME: 30 MIN. **MAKES:** 7 SERVINGS

- 4 **cups cranberry juice**
- 2 **cups ruby port wine or grape juice**
- 1 **cup golden raisins**
- ¼ **cup sugar**
- 2 **cinnamon sticks (3 inches)**
- 4 **cardamom pods, crushed**
- 6 **whole cloves**
  Additional cinnamon sticks, optional

1. In a large saucepan, combine the cranberry juice, wine, raisins and sugar. Place the cinnamon, cardamom and cloves on a double thickness of cheesecloth; bring up corners of cloth and tie with string to form a bag. Add to the pan.

2. Bring just to a simmer (do not boil). Reduce heat; simmer gently, uncovered, for 15 minutes or until flavors are blended. Discard spice bag. Serve warm in mugs with additional cinnamon if desired.

Spicy Pork Baguette Bites

Here's an interesting twist on mini open-faced sandwiches. Lime mayonnaise provides a cool counterpoint to spiced pork, and toasted baguette slices give a satisfying crunch.

—**VIRGINIA ANTHONY** JACKSONVILLE, FLORIDA

PREP: 20 MIN. + MARINATING **BAKE:** 20 MIN. **MAKES:** 2 DOZEN

- 1 **teaspoon paprika**
- ½ **teaspoon salt**
- ½ **teaspoon dried oregano**
- ½ **teaspoon ground cumin**
- ¼ **teaspoon garlic powder**
- ¼ **teaspoon cayenne pepper**
- ¼ **teaspoon pepper**
- 1 **pork tenderloin (1 pound)**

LIME MAYONNAISE
- ½ **cup mayonnaise**
- 1 **tablespoon lime juice**
- ½ **teaspoon grated lime peel**
- 1 **French bread baguette (1 pound), sliced and toasted**
  Additional grated lime peel, optional

1. In a small bowl, combine the first seven ingredients; rub over tenderloin. Place in a large resealable plastic bag; seal and refrigerate overnight.

2. Place tenderloin on a rack in a foil-lined shallow roasting pan. Bake, uncovered, at 425° for 20-30 minutes or until a thermometer reads 145°. Let stand for 5 minutes before slicing.

3. Meanwhile, in a small bowl, combine the mayonnaise, lime juice and peel. Thinly slice pork; serve on toasted bread with a dollop of lime mayonnaise. Sprinkle with additional lime peel if desired.

A perennial favorite, stuffed mushrooms are what most guests look forward to at a party. In fact, you might want to make a double batch. This Italian adaptation, done in less than an hour, will have company begging for more.

—**BEATRICE VETRANO** LANDENBERG, PENNSYLVANIA

Sausage-Stuffed Mushrooms

PREP: 25 MIN. **BAKE:** 20 MIN.
MAKES: 12-15 SERVINGS

- 12 **to 15 large fresh mushrooms**
- 2 **tablespoons butter, divided**
- 2 **tablespoons chopped onion**
- 1 **tablespoon lemon juice**
- ¼ **teaspoon dried basil**
  Salt and pepper to taste
- 4 **ounces bulk Italian sausage**
- 1 **tablespoon chopped fresh parsley**
- 2 **tablespoons dry bread crumbs**
- 2 **tablespoons grated Parmesan cheese**

1. Remove stems from the mushrooms. Chop stems finely; set mushroom caps aside. Place stems in paper towels and squeeze to remove any liquid.

2. In a large skillet, heat 1½ tablespoons butter. Cook stems and onion until tender. Add lemon juice, basil, salt and pepper; cook until almost all liquid has evaporated. Cool.

3. In a large bowl, combine the mushroom mixture, sausage and parsley; stuff reserved mushroom caps. Combine crumbs and cheese; sprinkle over tops. Dot each with remaining butter.

4. Place in a greased baking pan. Bake at 400° for 20 minutes or until sausage is no longer pink, basting occasionally with pan juices. Serve hot.

top tip

Bring It Along

Appetizers such as stuffed mushrooms, tartlets, mini biscuits and other bite-sized finger foods can be easily transported to a party in a deviled egg tray.

FAST FIX ▶ Cherry-Brandy Baked Brie

I sometimes substitute dried cranberries or chopped dried apricots for the cherries, and I use apple juice for the brandy.
—**KEVIN PHEBUS** KATY, TEXAS

PREP/TOTAL TIME: 20 MIN. **MAKES:** 8 SERVINGS

- 1 round (8 ounces) Brie cheese
- ½ cup dried cherries
- ½ cup chopped walnuts
- ¼ cup packed brown sugar
- ¼ cup brandy or unsweetened apple juice
   French bread baguette, sliced and toasted, or assorted crackers

1. Place cheese in a 9-in. pie plate. Combine the cherries, walnuts, brown sugar and brandy; spoon over cheese.
2. Bake at 350° for 15-20 minutes or until cheese is softened. Serve with baguette.

top tip
Mock Champagne Punch

Combine 1 quart each chilled white grape juice and ginger ale in a punch bowl and garnish with berries. It really tastes like champagne!
—**BETTY CLAYCOMB** ALVERTON, PENNSYLVANIA

Marinated Mushrooms and Cheese

I like to serve these savory mushrooms alongside sliced baguettes and crackers. It's such a simple recipe; you'll want to keep this at your fingertips for the holidays.
—**KIM MARIE VAN RHEENEN** MENDOTA, ILLINOIS

PREP: 10 MIN. + MARINATING **MAKES:** 12-14 SERVINGS

- ½ cup sun-dried tomatoes (not packed in oil), julienned
- 1 cup boiling water
- ½ cup olive oil
- ½ cup white wine vinegar
- 2 garlic cloves, minced
- ½ teaspoon salt
- ½ pound sliced fresh mushrooms
- 8 ounces Monterey Jack cheese, cubed

1. In a small bowl, combine the tomatoes and water. Let stand for 5 minutes; drain.
2. In a large resealable plastic bag, combine the oil, vinegar, garlic and salt; add the tomatoes, mushrooms and cheese. Seal bag and toss to coat. Refrigerate for at least 4 hours before serving. Drain and discard marinade.

Chicken, Pear & Gorgonzola Tarts

I was experimenting with candied bacon and came up with these little bites during the holiday season.

—KATHLEEN BOULANGER WILLISTON, VERMONT

PREP: 30 MIN. **COOK:** 5 MIN. **MAKES:** 2½ DOZEN

- 8 **bacon strips**
- 1½ **teaspoons brown sugar**
- ¼ **teaspoon ground cinnamon**
- ¾ **cup finely chopped cooked chicken breast**
- ⅓ **cup pear nectar**
- ¼ **cup finely chopped dried pears**
- 3 **tablespoons apricot preserves**
- 2 **teaspoons butter**
- ¼ **teaspoon salt**
- ¼ **teaspoon pepper**
- 2 **packages (1.9 ounces each) frozen miniature phyllo tart shells**
- ⅓ **cup crumbled Gorgonzola cheese**

1. Place bacon in a 15-in. x 10-in. x 1-in. baking pan; broil 4 in. from the heat for 4-6 minutes on each side or until crisp. Combine brown sugar and cinnamon; sprinkle over bacon. Broil 1 minute longer or until bacon is glazed and bubbly. Drain on paper towels. Cool slightly and crumble.

2. In a small skillet, combine the chicken, pear nectar, pears, preserves, butter, salt and pepper. Bring to a boil; cook, stirring occasionally, for 3-4 minutes or until thickened. Spoon about 1 teaspoonful of filling into each tart shell; place tarts on a baking sheet. Sprinkle with bacon and cheese.

3. Bake at 350° for 5-7 minutes or until heated through.

MAKE AHEAD ▶ Greek Deli Kabobs

Tangy and savory, these easy-to-eat skewers are an enjoyable addition to a holiday potluck or lunch. Also try them with different combinations of red and green veggies.

—VIKKI SPENGLER OCALA, FLORIDA

PREP: 30 MIN. + MARINATING **MAKES:** 2 DOZEN

- 2 **jars (7½ ounces each) roasted sweet red peppers, drained**
- 1 **pound part-skim mozzarella cheese, cut into ½-inch cubes**
- 24 **fresh broccoli florets**
- 24 **slices hard salami**
- ½ **cup Greek vinaigrette**

1. Cut red peppers into 24 strips; place in a large resealable plastic bag. Add the remaining ingredients. Seal bag and turn to coat; refrigerate for 4 hours or overnight.

2. Drain and discard marinade. Thread cheese, vegetables and meat onto frilled toothpicks or short skewers.

Make Ahead Note: *Kabobs can be prepared and assembled a day in advance. Cover in plastic wrap and store in refrigerator.*

STROMBOLI RING, PIZZA RUSTICANA AND TIJUANA TIDBITS, PAGE 47

Holiday Parties

39

51

45

Lunch with Friends

C'mon, friends, let's do lunch! Spend an afternoon swapping stories on the best and worst gifts you've ever received; find out what blogs everyone's reading; and get feedback on whether you should try a new look in the new year. This kicked-back menu keeps things casual yet stylish enough for entertaining half a dozen of your dearest friends.

GRILLED CHEESE SUPREME, ROASTED RED PEPPER BISQUE AND SPINACH FESTIVAL SALAD

FAST FIX ▶ Grilled Cheese Supreme

We like to use light rye with dill bread for this sandwich. It's our favorite after-church lunch on Sunday, especially if someone brings soup.

—BILLIE MOSS WALNUT CREEK, CALIFORNIA

PREP/TOTAL TIME: 20 MIN. **MAKES:** 6 SERVINGS

- 12 **slices hearty rye bread**
- 12 **teaspoons mayonnaise**
- 18 **slices cheddar cheese**
- 3 **small tomatoes, thinly sliced**
- 1½ **cups sliced fresh mushrooms**
- 6 **thin slices sweet onion**
- 1 **medium ripe avocado, peeled and cut into 12 wedges**
- 12 **teaspoons butter, softened**

1. Spread each of six slices of bread with 1 teaspoon mayonnaise; layer with a cheese slice, tomato slices, mushrooms, another cheese slice, onion, 2 avocado wedges and remaining cheese slice. Spread remaining bread with remaining mayonnaise; place on top.

2. Butter outsides of sandwiches. Toast on a heated griddle for 2-3 minutes on each side or until bread is lightly browned and cheese is melted.

Roasted Red Pepper Bisque

I put this soup together for anyone on a low-carb diet. It can be served warm or cold and makes an especially good first course or accompaniment to a meal-size salad for lunch.

—MARY ANN ZETTLEMAIER CHELSEA, MICHIGAN

PREP: 30 MIN. + STANDING **COOK:** 20 MIN.
MAKES: 6 SERVINGS (2 QUARTS)

- 8 **medium sweet red peppers**
- 1 **large onion, chopped**
- 2 **tablespoons butter**
- 3 **cups chicken broth, divided**
- 2 **cups half-and-half cream**
- ½ **teaspoon salt**
- ½ **teaspoon white pepper**
- 6 **tablespoons shredded Parmesan cheese**

1. Broil peppers 4 in. from the heat until skins blister, about 5 minutes. With tongs, rotate peppers a quarter turn. Broil and rotate until all sides are blistered and blackened. Immediately place peppers in a large bowl; cover and let stand for 15-20 minutes.

2. Peel off and discard charred skin. Remove stems and seeds; set peppers aside.

3. In a large saucepan, saute onion in butter until tender; cool slightly. In a blender, combine the onion mixture, 2 cups broth and roasted peppers; cover and process until smooth. Return to the pan.

4. Stir in cream and remaining broth; heat through (do not boil). Stir in salt and pepper. Sprinkle each serving with 1 tablespoon cheese.

Spinach Festival Salad

I first whipped up this salad for my sister before we headed out for a day of shopping. "You could sell this in a deli," she said. Now I'm asked to make it for her whenever she comes over.

—MALINDA SMITH STONE MOUNTAIN, GEORGIA

PREP: 30 MIN. + STANDING **MAKES:** 6 SERVINGS

- 1 **medium sweet yellow pepper**
- 1 **medium sweet red pepper**
- ½ **pound sliced deli turkey, cut into strips**
- 1 **package (6 ounces) fresh baby spinach**
- 2 **plum tomatoes, sliced**
- 2 **green onions, sliced**
- ½ **cup crumbled tomato and basil feta cheese**
- 3 **pepperoncini, sliced**
- 2 **tablespoons grated Romano cheese**
- 1 **to 2 garlic cloves, minced**
- 1 **teaspoon Italian seasoning**
- ½ **teaspoon crushed red pepper flakes**
- ½ **teaspoon pepper**
- ¾ **cup balsamic vinaigrette**

1. Broil peppers 4 in. from the heat until skins blister, about 5 minutes. With tongs, rotate peppers a quarter turn. Broil and rotate until all sides are blistered and blackened. Immediately place peppers in a bowl; cover and let stand for 15-20 minutes.

2. Meanwhile, in a salad bowl, combine the turkey, spinach, tomatoes, onions, feta cheese, pepperoncini, Romano cheese, garlic and seasonings.

3. Peel off and discard charred skin from peppers. Remove stems and seeds. Slice peppers; add to salad and toss to combine. Serve with vinaigrette.

Editor's Note: *Look for pepperoncini (pickled peppers) in the pickle and olive section of your grocery store.*

Winter Wonderland Coasters

Go green this year by turning old holiday greeting cards into coasters. We chose black-and-white winter scenes for a contemporary feel, but any cards will work just fine. What a fun way for hostesses to add a touch of Christmas cheer to winter get-togethers!

MATERIALS—FOR ONE

- Ceramic tile about 4¼ in. square
- Recycled cards or decorative papers
- Paper trimmer
- Sticky back stiffened felt
- Decoupage glue
- Sponge brush
- Clear acrylic sealer

DIRECTIONS

1. From recycled cards or decorative papers, cut a 4-in. square.
2. Use sponge to apply a thin coat of decoupage glue to top surface of tile and adhere paper square centered on tile. Let glue dry.
3. Apply a thin layer of decoupage glue covering paper and edges of tile. Let glue dry.
4. Following manufacturer's instructions, apply a coat of clear acrylic sealer to make the tile water-resistant. Let sealer dry.
5. Cut a 4-in. square piece of sticky back stiffened felt. Adhere centered on back of tile coaster.
6. Repeat steps 1-5 for desired number of tile coasters to create a complete set.

1. Line the bottom and sides of a 9-in. x 5-in. loaf pan with plastic wrap. Combine vanilla ice cream and pecans; spread into prepared pan. Freeze for 30 minutes.
2. Spread raspberry sherbet over ice cream. Freeze for 30 minutes. Spread chocolate ice cream over the top. Cover and freeze for 8 hours or until firm.
3. Mash and strain raspberries, reserving ¼ cup juice (discard seeds and save remaining raspberry juice for another use). In a microwave-safe bowl, melt chocolate chips and butter; stir until smooth. Whisk in the corn syrup, water and reserved raspberry juice; cool.
4. Remove dessert from the freezer 10 minutes before serving. Using plastic wrap, remove loaf from pan; discard plastic wrap. Using a serrated knife, cut ice cream into 12 slices. Spoon chocolate sauce onto dessert plates; top with ice cream. Garnish with fresh raspberries if desired.

Mushroom Tartlets

I first helped my mom make these appetizers when I was just 11 years old. Now, as a military wife, I serve these tarts to friends all over the world!

—**JENNIE MCCOMSEY** HANSCOM AFB, MASSACHUSETTS

PREP: 20 MIN. + CHILLING **BAKE:** 15 MIN. **MAKES:** ABOUT 3 DOZEN

  1 **package (8 ounces) cream cheese, softened**
  ½ **cup butter, softened**
  1½ **cups all-purpose flour**
FILLING
  1 **pound fresh mushrooms, finely chopped**
  2 **tablespoons butter**
  1 **package (3 ounces) cream cheese, cubed**
  ½ **teaspoon salt**
  ¼ **teaspoon dried thyme**

1. In a small bowl, beat cream cheese and butter until light and fluffy. Add flour; beat until mixture forms a ball. Cover and refrigerate for 1 hour.
2. For filling, in a large skillet, saute mushrooms in butter. Drain and pat dry. Return to the pan; stir in cream cheese until melted. Stir in salt and thyme; set aside.
3. On a lightly floured surface, roll dough to ¹⁄₁₆-in. thickness; cut into 2½-in. circles. Press onto the bottoms and up the sides of greased miniature muffin cups. Place a rounded teaspoonful of filling in each cup.
4. Bake at 350° for 12-17 minutes or until edges are lightly browned. Remove from pans to wire racks. Serve warm.

MAKE AHEAD **Raspberry-Fudge Frozen Dessert**

I'm not sure where I got this recipe, but I just love trying new things. This has turned out to be my favorite ice cream dessert, and I serve it for company and for friends from church. I also made it for my daughter's birthday and everyone loved it! Try it with different flavors of sorbets and ice creams.

—**SUE KROENING** MATTOON, ILLINOIS

PREP: 15 MIN. + FREEZING **MAKES:** 12 SERVINGS

  2 **cups vanilla ice cream, partially softened**
  ½ **cup chopped pecans, toasted**
  2 **cups raspberry sherbet or sorbet, partially softened**
  2 **cups chocolate fudge ice cream, partially softened**
  1 **package (10 ounces) frozen sweetened raspberries, thawed**
  2 **cups (12 ounces) semisweet chocolate chips**
  ¼ **cup butter, cubed**
  ½ **cup light corn syrup**
  ½ **cup water**
     Fresh raspberries, optional

BAKED CRAB RANGOON, ROAST BEEF AND PEAR CROSTINI AND GRAPE JUICE SPARKLER

FAST FIX ▸ Baked Crab Rangoon

Baking the rangoon instead of deep frying them not only saves time but reduces the mess.
—**SUE BENNETT** SHELBURN, INDIANA

PREP/TOTAL TIME: 30 MIN.   **MAKES:** 1 DOZEN

- 12 wonton wrappers
- 4 ounces cream cheese, softened
- ¼ cup mayonnaise
- 1 can (6 ounces) crabmeat, drained, flaked and cartilage removed
- ¼ cup thinly sliced green onions

1. Press wonton wrappers into greased miniature muffin cups. Bake at 350° for 6-7 minutes or until lightly browned.
2. Meanwhile, in a small bowl, beat cream cheese and mayonnaise until smooth. Stir in crab and onions; spoon into wonton cups. Bake for 10-12 minutes or until heated through. Serve warm.

FAST FIX ▸ Grape Juice Sparkler

Every friendly gathering should have a seasonal punch on the menu. We like the predominating grape flavors in this bubbly beverage—a must at holiday parties.
—**TASTE OF HOME TEST KITCHEN**

PREP/TOTAL TIME: 15 MIN.
MAKES: 10 SERVINGS (2 QUARTS)

- 1 can (11½ ounces) frozen cranberry-raspberry juice concentrate, thawed
- 1 bottle (1 liter) club soda, chilled
- 1 bottle (750 ml) sparkling white grape juice, chilled
- 20 to 30 fresh raspberries

Just before serving, combine juice concentrate with club soda in a large pitcher. Stir in sparkling grape juice. Place two to three raspberries in the bottom of each glass; add juice.
Editor's Note: *Use 2 cans of cranberry-raspberry juice concentrate and 2 teaspoons lemon juice for a sweeter, fruitier beverage.*

FAST FIX Roast Beef and Pear Crostini

Friends ask me to bring this whenever we get together. It has an unexpected flavor combination that seems to delight everyone.
—**MARIE RIZZIO** INTERLOCHEN, MICHIGAN

PREP/TOTAL TIME: 30 MIN. **MAKES:** 40 APPETIZERS

- 1 **French bread baguette (1 pound)**
- 3 **tablespoons olive oil**
- 1 **garlic clove, minced**
- 1 **cup blue cheese salad dressing**
- 1 **medium pear, diced**
- ¼ **cup thinly sliced green onions**
- 2 **cups cubed cooked roast beef**
- 1 **cup diced seeded tomatoes**
- ½ **teaspoon salt**
- ¼ **teaspoon pepper**
- ½ **cup fresh basil leaves, thinly sliced**

1. Cut the baguette into 40 slices. Combine oil and garlic; brush over one side of each slice of bread. Place on an ungreased baking sheet. Bake at 350° for 6-9 minutes or until lightly toasted.

2. Combine the salad dressing, pear and onions. Combine the roast beef, tomatoes, salt and pepper. Spread dressing mixture over toasted bread; top with beef mixture and basil.

FAST FIX Layered Blue Cheese Spread

I actually have fun preparing this dish, even though it's so easy. I like to surround the finished spread with assorted crackers and party-sized pumpernickel and rye breads.
—**LILY JULOW** GAINESVILLE, FLORIDA

PREP/TOTAL TIME: 25 MIN. **MAKES:** 4 CUPS

- 3 **packages (8 ounces each) cream cheese, softened, divided**
- 1 **cup (4 ounces) crumbled blue cheese**
- ¼ **cup plus 1 tablespoon sour cream, divided**
- 2 **tablespoons minced fresh parsley**
- 1 **tablespoon minced fresh cilantro**
- 1 **tablespoon minced chives**
- ½ **teaspoon coarsely ground pepper**
- ½ **cup chopped walnuts**
  Assorted breads or crackers

1. On a serving plate, spread two packages of cream cheese into an 8-in. circle. In a small bowl, combine the blue cheese, ¼ cup sour cream, parsley, cilantro, chives and pepper until blended. Spread over cream cheese layer to within ½ in. of the edges.

2. In a small bowl, beat remaining cream cheese and sour cream until smooth. Spread over blue cheese layer to within 1 in. of the edges. Sprinkle with walnuts just before serving. Serve with breads or crackers.

Apricot Chicken Wings

I'm a fan of simple-to-make appetizers that are a hit at parties. A five-ingredient marinade flavors these juicy and tender chicken wings.
—**ROBIN SPIRES** TAMPA, FLORIDA

PREP: 15 MIN. + MARINATING **BAKE:** 30 MIN. **MAKES:** 2 DOZEN

- 2 **pounds chicken wings**
- 1 **cup apricot preserves**
- 2 **tablespoons cider vinegar**
- 2 **teaspoons hot pepper sauce**
- 1 **teaspoon chili powder**
- 1 **garlic clove, minced**

1. Cut chicken wings into three sections; discard wing tips. In a small bowl, combine the remaining ingredients; pour ½ cup into a large resealable plastic bag. Add chicken; seal bag and turn to coat. Refrigerate for 4 hours or overnight. Cover and refrigerate remaining marinade.

2. Drain wings and discard marinade. Place wings in a greased foil-lined 15-in. x 10-in. x 1-in. baking pan. Bake at 400° for 30-35 minutes or until juices run clear, turning and basting occasionally with remaining marinade.

Editor's Note: *Uncooked chicken wing sections (wingettes) may be substituted for whole chicken wings.*

Holiday Tea Party

Remember entertaining your favorite stuffed animals with a pretend tea set? It's time to bring those enchanting imaginations to life. So dust off the real tea cups and saucers and invite the ladies over for an afternoon of seasonal teas, finger sandwiches and petite desserts almost too adorable to eat. Pinkies up or down, this menu's all about having a little holiday fun.

PETITE APRICOT PASTRIES AND PETITE CHOCOLATE-HAZELNUT CAKES

Petite Apricot Pastries

These fancifully fruity bites will leave guests speechless...and reaching for more.

—**MELISSA ROSE LUNDIN** KERSEY, PENNSYLVANIA

PREP: 45 MIN. **BAKE:** 45 MIN. + COOLING
MAKES: 12½ DOZEN

- 1 package (¼ ounce) active dry yeast
- ½ cup warm 2% milk (110° to 115°)
- 4 cups all-purpose flour
- 1 teaspoon plus ⅔ cup sugar, divided
- ½ teaspoon salt
- 1½ cups cold butter, cubed
- 4 egg yolks, lightly beaten
- 2 cups ground walnuts
- 2 cans (12 ounces each) apricot cake and pastry filling

FROSTING
- 4 cups confectioners' sugar
- ⅔ cup butter, softened
- 1 teaspoon vanilla extract
- 2 to 4 tablespoons 2% milk

1. In a small bowl, dissolve yeast in warm milk. In a large bowl, combine 3 cups flour, 1 teaspoon sugar and salt. Cut in butter until crumbly. Add yeast mixture and egg yolks; mix well. Stir in enough remaining flour to form a soft dough. Combine walnuts and remaining sugar; set aside.

2. Divide dough into thirds. Between waxed paper, roll one portion into a 15-in. x 10-in. rectangle. Transfer to a greased 15-in. x 10-in. baking pan. Sprinkle with 1½ cups walnut mixture. Roll out second portion of dough; place over walnut layer. Spread apricot filling to within 1 in. of edges. Roll out remaining portion; place over filling.

3. Bake at 325° for 45-50 minutes or until golden brown. Cool completely on a wire rack. In a large bowl, beat the confectioners' sugar, butter, vanilla and enough milk to achieve desired consistency. Spread over top; sprinkle with remaining walnut mixture. Cut into 1-in. squares. Refrigerate leftovers.

Make Ahead Note: *Dough can be made a day in advance; cover and refrigerate each portion.*

MAKE AHEAD ▶ Petite Chocolate-Hazelnut Cakes

If you like Nutella, these petite party cakes will make you swoon. We started by making a rich torte topped with a chocolate-hazelnut ganache and cut it into 1-inch squares for a dessert tray.

—TASTE OF HOME TEST KITCHEN

PREP: 50 MIN. **BAKE:** 20 MIN. + COOLING **MAKES:** 8 DOZEN

- ½ cup butter, softened
- ⅔ cup sugar
- 2 eggs
- 1½ teaspoons vanilla extract
- 1⅓ cups all-purpose flour
- ½ cup baking cocoa
- 1½ teaspoons baking soda
- ¼ teaspoon baking powder
- ¼ teaspoon salt
- ¾ cup plus 2 tablespoons buttermilk

FILLING
- 1 teaspoon unflavored gelatin
- 1¼ cups heavy whipping cream, divided
- ¼ cup Nutella

GANACHE
- 6 ounces semisweet chocolate, chopped
- ⅔ cup heavy whipping cream
- 1 teaspoon instant espresso granules
- 1¼ cups hazelnuts, toasted

1. In a large bowl, cream butter and sugar until light and fluffy. Add eggs, one at a time, beating well after each addition. Beat in vanilla. Combine the flour, cocoa, baking soda, baking powder and salt; gradually add to the creamed mixture alternately with buttermilk, beating well after each addition.

2. Pour into a greased and floured 13-in. x 9-in. baking pan. Bake at 350° for 18-22 minutes or until a toothpick inserted near the center comes out clean.

3. Cool for 10 minutes before inverting onto a wire rack to cool completely. Trim ½ in. from edges of cake. Cut cake horizontally into two layers; set aside.

4. In a small saucepan, sprinkle gelatin over ¼ cup cream; let stand for 1 minute. Heat over low heat, stirring until gelatin is completely dissolved. Remove from the heat; cool to room temperature.

5. In a bowl, beat gelatin mixture and remaining cream until it begins to thicken. Add Nutella; beat until stiff peaks form.

6. Place bottom cake layer on a cutting board; spread with whipped cream mixture. Top with remaining cake layer.

7. Place chocolate in a small bowl. In a small saucepan, bring cream and espresso granules just to a boil. Pour over chocolate; whisk until smooth.

8. Cool, stirring occasionally, to room temperature or until ganache reaches a spreading consistency, about 30 minutes. Spread over top of cake. Cut cake into 1-in. squares; top each with a hazelnut.

Make Ahead Note: *Cakes can be made a day in advance. Place each cake square in a miniature muffin cup liner and place in an airtight container in the refrigerator.*

Cranberry Tea

On cold winter afternoons, my friends and I like to sip this tangy cranberry tea while sitting next to a glowing fire and enjoying good conversation. It's a great alternative to mulled cider.

—POLLY HOLBROOK GREELEY, COLORADO

PREP/TOTAL TIME: 30 MIN. **MAKES:** 3 QUARTS

- 3 cinnamon sticks (3 inches)
- 6 whole cloves
- 6 cups water
- 3 cups fresh or frozen cranberries
- 9 slices peeled fresh gingerroot
- 6 individual tea bags
- 6 cups unsweetened apple juice
- ⅓ cup honey

1. Place cinnamon and cloves on a double thickness of cheesecloth. Bring up corners of cloth; tie with a string to form a bag.

2. In a large saucepan, combine the water, cranberries and ginger; add spice bag. Bring to a boil. Reduce heat; cover and simmer for 15-20 minutes or until berries have popped, stirring occasionally. Remove from the heat. Add tea bags; cover and steep for 5 minutes.

3. Discard tea bags and spice bag. Strain cranberry mixture through a cheesecloth-lined colander. Return to saucepan. Stir in juice and honey; heat through. Serve warm.

top tip

Keep Gingerroot Frozen

Fresh gingerroot is easy to peel and slice or grate if it's frozen.

—GENEVIEVE DOLLAR EVERETT, WASHINGTON

FAST FIX Lobster-Shrimp Salad Croissants

Lightly dressed with a crisp, clean flavor, this simple lobster salad is an ideal buffet food for showers and tea parties. Plus, the filling can be made a day in advance.
—**ATHENA RUSSELL** FLORENCE, SOUTH CAROLINA

PREP/TOTAL TIME: 25 MIN. **MAKES:** 10 SERVINGS

- ½ cup mayonnaise
- 1 tablespoon snipped fresh dill
- 1 tablespoon minced chives
- 1 tablespoon lemon juice
- ½ teaspoon salt
- ¼ teaspoon pepper
- ½ pound imitation lobster
- ½ pound cooked small shrimp, peeled and deveined and coarsely chopped
- 10 miniature croissants, split

In a large bowl, combine the mayonnaise, dill, chives, lemon juice, salt and pepper. Stir in lobster and shrimp. Cover and refrigerate until serving. Serve on croissants.

FAST FIX Turkey, Gouda & Apple Tea Sandwiches

Cut into triangles or quarters, these fun mini sandwiches are a tasty addition to an afternoon tea gathering. The cranberry mayo lends an original flavor twist, and the apples give them a sweet-tart crunch.
—**TASTE OF HOME TEST KITCHEN**

PREP/TOTAL TIME: 25 MIN. **MAKES:** 4 DOZEN

- ⅔ cup reduced-fat mayonnaise
- 2 tablespoons whole-berry cranberry sauce
- 24 very thin slices white bread, crusts removed
- 12 slices deli turkey
- 2 medium apples, thinly sliced
- 12 thin slices smoked Gouda cheese
- 4 cups fresh baby spinach

1. Place mayonnaise and cranberry sauce in a small food processor. Cover and process until blended. Spread over each bread slice.
2. Layer the turkey, apples, cheese and spinach over each of 12 bread slices; top with remaining bread. Cut each sandwich into quarters.
Make Ahead Note: *Cranberry spread can be prepared a day in advance; cover and store in the refrigerator.*

FAST FIX ▶ Vanilla Chai Tea

An aromatic chai is comfort in a cup. It's extra special with a dollop of fresh whipped cream and a sprinkling of ground allspice on top.
—**TASTE OF HOME TEST KITCHEN**

PREP/TOTAL TIME: 25 MIN. **MAKES:** 6 SERVINGS

- 8   **whole peppercorns**
- ½   **teaspoon whole allspice**
- 2   **cardamom pods**
- 1   **cinnamon stick (3 inches)**
- 4   **whole cloves**
- 8   **individual tea bags**
- 1   **tablespoon honey**
- 4   **cups boiling water**
- 2   **cups 2% milk**
- 1   **tablespoon vanilla extract**
- ½   **cup heavy whipping cream**
- 1½ **teaspoons confectioners' sugar**
      Ground allspice

1. In a large bowl, crush peppercorns, allspice, cardamom, cinnamon stick and cloves with the end of a wooden spoon until aroma is released. Add tea bags, honey and boiling water. Cover and steep for 6 minutes.

2. Meanwhile, in a small saucepan, heat milk. Strain tea into a heatproof pitcher; stir in milk and vanilla.

3. In a small bowl, beat whipping cream and confectioners' sugar until soft peaks form. Serve individual servings of tea with whipped cream; garnish with ground allspice.

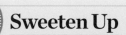

top tip ▶ Sweeten Up

Sweetening whipped cream with confectioners' sugar instead of granulated sugar helps it hold up longer and stay fluffier.

CRANBERRY TEA (RECIPE ON PAGE 43) AND VIENNA TRIANGLES

Vienna Triangles

I took a cooking class many years ago, and the instructor gave us the recipe for these delicate pastry triangles. I asked if I could share this recipe with *Taste of Home*, and she couldn't have been happier that more people would be able to enjoy her almondy treats.
—**JOANNE WRIGHT** NILES, MICHIGAN

PREP: 1 HOUR **BAKE:** 15 MIN. + COOLING **MAKES:** 9 DOZEN

- 3   **cups all-purpose flour**
- ¾   **cup confectioners' sugar**
- ½   **teaspoon salt**
- 1½ **cups cold butter, cubed**

FILLING

- 3   **cups sliced almonds**
- 1½ **cups sugar**
- 5   **egg whites**
- 3   **tablespoons all-purpose flour**
- 1   **tablespoon corn syrup**
- 1   **teaspoon ground cinnamon**
- ½   **teaspoon almond extract**
- ¼   **teaspoon baking powder**
- ⅔   **cup seedless raspberry jam**

COATING

- 8   **ounces semisweet chocolate, chopped**
- 1   **tablespoon shortening**

1. In a large bowl, combine the flour, confectioners' sugar and salt; cut in butter until crumbly. Pat into a greased 15-in. x 10-in. x 1-in. baking pan. Bake at 350° for 15-18 minutes or until lightly browned. Cool on a wire rack.

2. Meanwhile, in a large saucepan, combine the almonds, sugar, egg whites, flour, corn syrup and cinnamon; cook over low heat until a thermometer reads 200°, stirring constantly. Remove from the heat; stir in extract and baking powder. Spread jam over crust; spread almond mixture over top.

3. Bake at 350° for 15-20 minutes or until golden brown. Cool completely on a wire rack. Cut into 54 squares; cut each diagonally into two triangles.

4. In a microwave, melt chocolate and shortening; stir until smooth. Dip half of each triangle in chocolate; allow excess to drip off. Place on waxed paper; let stand until set.

Make Ahead Note: *Can be made 2 days in advance. Store in an airtight container at room temperature.*

Holiday Movie Night

Coming to a living room near you, *Miracle on 34th Street*, *A Christmas Story* and *White Christmas*, not to mention delicious snacks. Gather the gang, pass the pizza and cuddle up with a batch of chocolaty fudge cups for screenings of your favorite Christmas classics. Now that sounds like a wonderful life.

STROMBOLI RING, PIZZA RUSTICANA AND TIJUANA TIDBITS

Stromboli Ring

A friend of mine gave me this fun recipe years ago, and it's so incredibly good! I like to serve it warm with marinara sauce.
—**BARRIE PEAGLER** SCOTTSDALE, ARIZONA

PREP: 20 MIN. + RISING **BAKE:** 30 MIN. **MAKES:** 12 SERVINGS

- 1 **pound bulk Italian sausage**
- 1½ **cups (6 ounces) shredded Monterey Jack or part-skim mozzarella cheese**
- 2 **eggs**
- ½ **teaspoon Italian seasoning**
- 1 **loaf (1 pound) frozen bread dough, thawed**
- 1 **tablespoon grated Parmesan cheese**
  Marinara sauce, warmed, optional

1. In a large skillet, cook sausage over medium heat until no longer pink; drain. Stir in the Monterey Jack cheese, one egg and Italian seasoning.
2. On a lightly floured surface, roll dough into an 18-in. x 6-in. rectangle. Spoon sausage mixture over dough to within ½ in. of edges. Roll up jelly-roll style, starting with a long side; pinch seam to seal.
3. Place seam side down on a greased baking sheet; pinch ends together to form a ring. With scissors, cut from outside edge to two-thirds of the way toward center of ring at 1-in. intervals.
4. Beat remaining egg; brush over dough. Sprinkle with Parmesan cheese. Cover and let rise in a warm place until doubled, about 30 minutes.
5. Bake at 350° for 28-32 minutes or until golden brown. Serve with marinara sauce if desired.

Pizza Rusticana

Broiling the veggies before topping this pizza is what gives it all the flavor. I think it's wonderful with a wheat crust, too. For a cozy night in, this is the perfect dish.
—**SALLY SIERAK** SHORELINE, WASHINGTON

PREP: 30 MIN. **BAKE:** 15 MIN. **MAKES:** 35 APPETIZER SERVINGS

- 1 **tube (13.8 ounces) refrigerated pizza crust**
- 4 **tablespoons olive oil, divided**
- 2 **large tomatoes, thinly sliced**
- 1 **tablespoon Italian seasoning**
- 2 **medium red onions, cut into thin wedges**
- 2 **medium sweet red peppers, cut into ¼-inch strips**
- 1 **large portobello mushroom, cut into ⅛-inch strips**
- 2 **cups (8 ounces) shredded Parmesan cheese**

1. Unroll crust into a lightly greased 15-in. x 10-in. x 1-in. baking pan; flatten dough and build up edges slightly. Brush crust with 1 tablespoon oil. Bake at 425° for 7 minutes.
2. Meanwhile, in a small bowl, combine the tomatoes, 1 tablespoon oil and Italian seasoning; set aside.
3. In a large resealable plastic bag, combine the onions, red peppers, mushroom and remaining oil; seal bag and toss to coat. Place vegetables in a single layer on a greased broiler pan. Broil 4 in. from the heat until skins blister, about 15 minutes.
4. Arrange tomatoes over crust; top with roasted vegetables. Sprinkle with cheese.
5. Bake at 425° for 12-15 minutes or until golden brown.

Tijuana Tidbits

PREP: 20 MIN. **BAKE:** 1 HOUR + COOLING **MAKES:** 4¾ QUARTS

- 12 **cups popped popcorn**
- 4 **cups bite-size tortilla chips**
- 3 **cups Crispix**
- 1 **can (11½ ounces) mixed nuts**
- ½ **cup butter, cubed**
- ½ **cup light corn syrup**
- ½ **cup packed brown sugar**
- 3 **teaspoons chili powder**
- ¼ **teaspoon salt**
- ⅛ **to ¼ teaspoon cayenne pepper**
- ⅛ **teaspoon ground cinnamon**

1. In a large greased roasting pan, combine the popcorn, tortilla chips, cereal and nuts.
2. In a small saucepan, combine the remaining ingredients. Bring to a boil, stirring constantly. Pour over popcorn mixture and toss to coat.
3. Bake, uncovered, at 250° for 1 hour, stirring every 20 minutes. Cool on waxed paper. Store in an airtight container.

❝I love how Tex-Mex salty-sweet flavors come together in this mix, and a kick of heat sneaks up on you at the end. Served in a holiday tin, it's the ultimate movie snack.❞
—**BEVERLY PHILLIPS** DUNCANVILLE, TEXAS

Coconut-Almond Fudge Cups

What movie night would be complete without candy? With a coconut filling, the flavor of these fudgy bites is reminiscent of an Almond Joy candy bar.

—MAYBRIE, TASTE OF HOME ONLINE COMMUNITY

PREP: 30 MIN. **BAKE:** 10 MIN./BATCH + COOLING **MAKES:** 4 DOZEN

- 1 package chocolate fudge cake mix (regular size)
- ½ cup butter, melted
- 1 egg

FILLING
- ¼ cup sugar
- ¼ cup evaporated milk
- 7 large marshmallows
- 1 cup flaked coconut

TOPPING
- ¾ cup semisweet chocolate chips
- ¼ cup evaporated milk
- 2 tablespoons butter
- ½ cup sliced almonds

1. In a bowl, beat the cake mix, butter and egg until well blended. Shape into 1-in. balls; place in foil-lined miniature muffin cups. Bake at 350° for 8 minutes.

2. Using the end of a wooden spoon handle, make a ½-in.-deep indentation in the center of each cup. Bake 2-3 minutes longer or until cake springs back when lightly touched. Remove from pans to wire racks to cool.

3. For filling, in a microwave-safe bowl, heat sugar and milk on high for 2 minutes, stirring frequently. Add marshmallows; stir until melted. Stir in coconut. Spoon into cooled cups.

4. For topping, in another microwave-safe bowl, combine the chocolate chips, milk and butter. Microwave in 10- to 20-second intervals until melted; stir until smooth. Stir in almonds. Spread over filling. Store in the refrigerator.

Editor's Note: *This recipe was tested in a 1,100-watt microwave.*

FAST FIX Greek Pasta

This is my go-to easy vegetarian dish. Sweet sun-dried tomatoes, olives and basil are tossed with hot pasta. But you can also make it in advance to let the flavors blend. Simply reheat and serve.

—JENNIFER MENTO BOSTON, MASSACHUSETTS

PREP/TOTAL TIME: 25 MIN. **MAKES:** 15 SERVINGS

- 1 jar (6 ounces) pitted Greek olives, drained
- ¾ cup oil-packed sun-dried tomatoes
- ½ cup grated Romano cheese
- ¼ cup olive oil
- 1 tablespoon capers, drained
- 1 teaspoon lime juice
- ¼ teaspoon pepper
- ¼ teaspoon crushed red pepper flakes
- 3 to 4 drops hot pepper sauce, optional
- 1 package (16 ounces) spiral pasta
- ¾ cup minced fresh basil
  Additional grated Romano cheese, optional

1. In a small bowl, combine the olives, tomatoes, cheese, oil, capers, lime juice, pepper, pepper flakes and, if desired, pepper sauce; let stand for 10-15 minutes. Meanwhile, cook pasta according to package directions.

2. Drain pasta; place in a large bowl. Add olive mixture and basil; toss to coat. Serve with additional cheese if desired.

top tip

For the Little Whos in Whoville

Keep restless movie watchers busy with fun Christmas crafts or engaging games, such as movie bingo. Fill homemade bingo cards with holiday words or props that appear in the movie. Then use candy or marshmallows to mark the words as you go.

Countdown-to-Christmas Blocks

Little ones will enjoy counting down the days to Christmas with these colorful numbered blocks. Change them daily and watch how quickly the time passes until the big day finally arrives!

MATERIALS

- Medium flat paintbrush
- Red acrylic paint
- 5-in. x 3-in. wooden base
- Glitter varnish
- Paper trimmer
- Patterned scrapbook paper
- Red card stock
- Decorative corner punch
- Decoupage or tacky glue
- Small sponge brush
- Two 2-in. wooden blocks
- 1-in. white sticker numbers

DIRECTIONS

1. With medium flat brush and red acrylic paint, apply base coat to wooden base. Let dry and repeat as needed for complete coverage. Apply a coat of glitter varnish as a sealer.

2. Use paper trimmer to cut twelve 2-in. squares from patterned paper and twelve 1½-in. squares from the red card stock.

3. Use decorative corner punch on each corner of the 1½-in. squares of red card stock.

4. With sponge brush and decoupage or tacky glue, adhere a patterned square to each side of the blocks; let dry. Glue a red square centered on each patterned square. Let dry.

5. On one block, center and adhere one of the number stickers on each red square: 0, 1, 2, 3, 4 and 5. On the other block adhere these numbers: 0, 1, 2, 6, 7 and 8.

6. Set blocks side by side on wooden base. Position blocks to count the days until Christmas, from 25 to 1.

Elegant Cocktail Party

Although cocktail parties had their heyday in the 1950s, they truly never went out of style. An upscale cocktail party featuring sensational appetizers and beverages can be a fun-filled way to gather with friends over the holiday season.

Roasted Rosemary Beet Skewers

Red and green never tasted so good together. Using fresh rosemary sprigs to skewer roasted beets is a simple way to serve a gourmet appetizer. Plus, the pomegranate-ginger dipping sauce can be used on a variety of vegetables, seafood and chicken skewers.

—CHERYL PERRY HERTFORD, NORTH CAROLINA

PREP: 45 MIN. **BAKE:** 20 MIN.
MAKES: 4 DOZEN (⅔ CUP SAUCE)

- 3 medium fresh beets (about 1 pound)
- 24 fresh rosemary sprigs (3 inches)
- ¼ cup olive oil
- 1 tablespoon grated orange peel
- 2 teaspoons minced fresh gingerroot
- 1 teaspoon pepper
- ½ teaspoon salt

POMEGRANATE SAUCE

- 1 cup pomegranate juice
- ⅔ cup sugar
- 1½ teaspoons lemon juice
- 1 tablespoon brown sugar
- 1 tablespoon water

1. Scrub beets; cut each into 16 wedges. Poke a hole through each wedge with a wooden skewer. Thread two wedges onto each rosemary sprig. Place in a greased shallow baking pan.

2. In a small bowl, combine the oil, orange peel, ginger, pepper and salt. Drizzle over beets; gently toss to coat. Bake at 350° for 20-30 minutes or until beets are tender, turning once.

3. Meanwhile, in a small saucepan, combine the pomegranate juice, sugar and lemon juice. Bring to a boil. Reduce heat; simmer, uncovered, until mixture is syrupy and reduced by half. Stir in brown sugar and water. Serve with beets.

Fast Coconut Shrimp

We love this as an appetizer, but it's equally good served as a meal. The rum and marmalade dipping sauce is a fun recipe to keep on hand for drizzling over pineapple fried rice or sauteed pea pods.

—**ELAINE BONICA** BETHEL, MAINE

PREP: 20 MIN. **COOK:** 25 MIN. **MAKES:** 2 DOZEN (1⅓ CUPS SAUCE)

- 1 **egg**
- 1 **tablespoon water**
- 1 **cup panko (Japanese) bread crumbs**
- 1 **cup flaked coconut**
- 1 **pound uncooked large shrimp, peeled and deveined**
  Oil for deep-fat frying
- 1 **jar (12 ounces) orange marmalade**
- ¼ **cup rum**

1. In a shallow bowl, whisk egg and water. In another shallow bowl, combine bread crumbs and coconut. Dip shrimp into egg mixture, then roll in crumb mixture.

2. In an electric skillet or deep fryer, heat ¼ in. of oil to 375°. Fry shrimp, a few at a time, for 1-2 minutes on each side or until golden brown. Drain on paper towels.

3. Meanwhile, in a small saucepan, bring orange marmalade and rum to a boil. Reduce heat; simmer, uncovered, for 5 minutes. Serve with shrimp.

FAST FIX▶ Goat Cheese-Pesto Crostini

Guests would be surprised to learn that I can make about two dozen of these elegant appetizers in less than half an hour. Goat cheese, pesto and bacon give these crunchy bites a distinct personality.

—**CINDIE HARAS** BOCA RATON, FLORIDA

PREP/TOTAL TIME: 25 MIN. **MAKES:** 2 DOZEN

- 6 **tablespoons olive oil**
- 6 **tablespoons prepared pesto**
- 3 **tablespoons grated Parmesan cheese**
- 1 **French bread baguette (10½ ounces), cut into 24 slices**
- 8 **bacon strips, diced**
- 1 **package (4 ounces) herbed goat cheese**
- ½ **cup fresh arugula or baby spinach, finely chopped**
- 3 **tablespoons pine nuts, toasted**

In a small bowl, combine the oil, pesto and Parmesan cheese. Place bread slices on an ungreased baking sheet; brush with pesto mixture. Broil 3-4 in. from the heat for 3-4 minutes or until edges are lightly browned.

4. Meanwhile, in a large skillet, cook bacon over medium heat until crisp. Remove to paper towels to drain.

5. Combine goat cheese and arugula; spread over bread. Sprinkle with bacon and pine nuts.

Prosciutto Bundles

All wrapped up and secured with a chive, these Prosciutto Bundles are a rewarding way to satisfy a craving for a salty snack—without which no holiday cocktail party would be complete.

—**GINA QUARTERMAINE** ALEXANDRIA, VIRGINIA

PREP: 40 MIN. **MAKES:** 32 APPETIZERS

- 1 **package (8 ounces) cream cheese, softened**
- ½ **cup minced fresh parsley**
- 1 **can (4¼ ounces) chopped ripe olives, drained**
- 2 **green onions, chopped**
- 2 **tablespoons finely chopped red onion**
- 2 **garlic cloves, minced**
- ¼ **teaspoon pepper**
- 16 **thin slices prosciutto (about 10 inches x 3½ inches)**
- 32 **whole chives**

1. In a small bowl, beat the cream cheese, parsley, olives, onions, garlic and pepper until blended.

2. Cut each prosciutto slice in half widthwise; place about 2 teaspoons of filling on the center of each piece. Bring up corners of prosciutto and tie with a chive, forming a bundle. Refrigerate until serving.

FAST FIX▶ Orange Razzletini

Raspberry-flavored rum and orange juice? We gave it a try and loved it! Try this spirited combination at your next holiday event.

—**TASTE OF HOME TEST KITCHEN**

PREP/TOTAL TIME: 5 MIN. **MAKES:** 2 SERVINGS

- **Ice cubes**
- ½ **cup orange juice**
- 2 **ounces raspberry-flavored rum**
- ½ **ounce Triple Sec**
  Orange slices and fresh raspberries, optional

1. Fill a mixing glass or tumbler three-fourths full with ice. Add the orange juice, rum and Triple Sec; stir until condensation forms on outside of glass.

2. Strain into two chilled cocktail glasses. Garnish with orange slices and raspberries if desired. Serve immediately.

MAKE AHEAD ▶ Shredded Pork Sandwiches

I like to share this dish at potlucks because it can be made ahead, which I especially appreciate during the busy holiday season. The sweet-and-spicy sauce is always a crowd favorite.

—**MARTHA ANNE CARPENTER** MESA, ARIZONA

PREP: 20 MIN.   **COOK:** 8½ HOURS
MAKES: 10 SERVINGS

- 1 **boneless pork loin roast (4 pounds)**
- 1 **can (14½ ounces) beef broth**
- ⅓ **cup plus ½ cup Worcestershire sauce, divided**
- ⅓ **cup plus ¼ cup Louisiana-style hot sauce, divided**
- 1 **cup ketchup**
- 1 **cup molasses**
- ½ **cup prepared mustard**
- 10 **kaiser rolls, split**

1. Cut roast in half; place in a 5-qt. slow cooker. In a small bowl, combine the broth, ⅓ cup Worcestershire sauce and ⅓ cup hot sauce; pour over roast. Cover and cook on low for 8-10 hours or until tender.

2. Remove pork; shred with two forks. Drain and discard cooking liquid. Return shredded pork to the slow cooker. For sauce, combine the ketchup, molasses, mustard and the remaining Worcestershire sauce and hot sauce. Pour over pork. Cover and cook on high for 30 minutes or until heated through. Serve on rolls.

top tip 6 Ways to Eat Pulled Pork

Having extra shredded pork is never a bad thing. Use it to top a baked potato, fill a quesadilla or add extra flavor to baked beans, or simply stir it into hash browns, macaroni or cole slaw to turn side dishes into entrees.

Let It Snow

When your dreams of a white Christmas come true, call up your friends for an afternoon of skiing, sledding, snowshoeing and ice skating. Afterward, offer the gang a chance to warm frozen toes and noses with some hot soup, sandwiches and the most adorable—and delicious—indoor snowmen on the block.

SHREDDED PORK SANDWICHES
AND TORTELLINI MEATBALL STEW

Tortellini Meatball Stew

Loaded with meatballs, tortellini, tomatoes and kidney beans, this hearty stew is sure to warm you up on cold winter days. Sprinkle servings with shredded Parmesan for even more flavor.

—LORI MARTIN MARYSVILLE, MICHIGAN

PREP: 40 MIN. **COOK:** 45 MIN. **MAKES:** 6 SERVINGS (2½ QUARTS)

- 1 egg, lightly beaten
- 1 package (10 ounces) frozen chopped spinach, thawed and squeezed dry
- ¼ cup seasoned bread crumbs
- ½ teaspoon salt
- ¼ teaspoon pepper
- 1 pound lean ground beef
- 2 tablespoons canola oil, divided
- 1 large onion, chopped
- 1 cup chopped celery
- 1 cup chopped carrots
- 4 cups beef broth
- 1 can (16 ounces) kidney beans, rinsed and drained
- 1 can (14-½ ounces) Italian diced tomatoes, undrained
- ½ teaspoon dried basil
- ½ teaspoon dried oregano
- 1 package (9 ounces) refrigerated cheese tortellini
- ¼ cup shredded Parmesan cheese

1. In a large bowl, combine the egg, spinach, bread crumbs, salt and pepper. Crumble beef over mixture and mix well. Shape into ¾-in. balls.

2. In a large saucepan, brown meatballs in batches in 1 tablespoon oil; drain. Remove meatballs and keep warm.

3. In the same pan, saute onion in remaining oil for 2 minutes. Add celery and carrots; saute 2 minutes longer. Stir in the broth, beans, tomatoes, basil and oregano. Add meatballs; bring to a boil. Reduce heat; cover and simmer for 10 minutes.

4. Return to a boil. Add the tortellini; cook for 7-9 minutes or until tender, stirring several times. Garnish with the Parmesan cheese.

Joyful Snowman Cookies

While my family loves the subtle cheesecake flavor of these cookies, I like the fact that I don't need to use a cookie cutter to shape them. Plus, the scrumptious snowmen look so cute on a cookie tray.

—CATHY MEDLEY CLYDE, OHIO

PREP: 45 MIN. + CHILLING **BAKE:** 15 MIN./BATCH **MAKES:** ABOUT 4 DOZEN

- 1 cup butter, softened
- 1 package (8 ounces) cream cheese, softened
- 2¼ cups sugar, divided
- 1 egg
- 1 teaspoon vanilla extract
- ¼ teaspoon almond extract
- 3¾ cups all-purpose flour
- 1 teaspoon baking powder
- 1 teaspoon salt
- 50 pretzel sticks
  Frosting of your choice
  Orange gumdrops

1. In a large bowl, cream the butter, cream cheese and 2 cups sugar until light and fluffy. Beat in egg and extracts. Combine the flour, baking powder and salt; gradually add to creamed mixture and mix well. Cover and refrigerate dough for at least 30 minutes or until easy to handle.

2. Shape dough into 1-in., ¾-in. and ½-in. balls. For each snowman, gently press one of each size ball together; gently roll in remaining sugar. Place 2 in. apart on ungreased baking sheets. Break pretzel sticks in half; press into the sides of each cookie, forming arms.

3. Bake at 325° for 15-18 minutes or until bottoms are lightly browned. Cool 1 minute before removing to wire racks. Decorate as desired using frosting and orange gumdrop noses.

After singing your way around the block, invite the carolers in to warm up their vocal cords with a cup of hot soup and fresh warm bread. Did we mention there's hot chocolate, too?

CALIFORNIA TOSSED SALAD, ROSEMARY GARLIC FOCACCIA AND ROUNDUP CHILI

California Tossed Salad

Even though I'm retired, I'm busier than ever! My tossed salad is a quick and healthy dish to serve alongside soup and bread. Plus, it's easy to make ahead if you're expecting company.

—**PATRICIA NIEH** PORTOLA VALLEY, CALIFORNIA

PREP: 15 MIN. + CHILLING **MAKES:** 12 SERVINGS

- 2 jars (7½ ounces each) marinated quartered artichoke hearts, undrained
- 2 jars (4½ ounces each) whole mushrooms, drained
- 1½ cups cherry tomatoes
- 1½ cups cubed Monterey Jack cheese
- 2 large ripe avocados, peeled and cubed
- 1 can (6 ounces) pitted ripe olives, drained
- 2 tablespoons lemon juice
- 4 cups torn romaine

1. In a large bowl, combine the first seven ingredients. Cover and refrigerate for at least 1 hour.

2. Just before serving, add romaine and toss to coat.

Rosemary Garlic Focaccia

Don't let your bread machine go unused. This fragrant focaccia bread has been fine-tuned to yield a soft and airy texture with a golden brown top. Serve it as a rustic appetizer with garlic-infused olive oil or couple it with a warming bowl of stew.

—**TAMMY BOLLMAN** MINATARE, NEBRASKA

PREP: 45 MIN. + RISING **BAKE:** 15 MIN.
MAKES: 2 LOAVES (10 WEDGES EACH)

- 1 cup warm 2% milk (70° to 80°)
- 1 egg
- ¼ cup water (70° to 80°)
- ¼ cup butter, softened
- 2¾ cups bread flour
- 2 tablespoons sugar
- 1 teaspoon salt
- 2 teaspoons active dry yeast
- 4 teaspoons olive oil
- 4 teaspoons minced fresh rosemary
- 3 garlic cloves, minced
- 1 teaspoon kosher salt

In bread machine pan, place the first eight ingredients in order suggested by manufacturer. Select dough setting (check dough after 5 minutes of mixing; add 1 to 2 tablespoons of water or flour if needed).

3. When cycle is completed, turn dough onto a lightly floured surface (dough will be sticky). Divide into two portions; place on greased baking sheets. Cover and let rest for 10 minutes. Shape each portion into an 8-in. circle. Cover and let rise until doubled, about 30 minutes.

4. Using the end of a wooden spoon handle, make ¼-in. indentations in dough. Brush with oil; sprinkle with rosemary, garlic and salt. Bake at 400° for 12-15 minutes or until golden brown. Remove to wire racks.

Roundup Chili

I like to serve this two-meat chili with diced onions, shredded cheese and bread for dipping. Because it's made in the slow cooker, it's a great choice for casual Christmas gatherings.

—**LINDA STEMEN** MONROEVILLE, INDIANA

PREP: 35 MIN. **COOK:** 6 HOURS **MAKES:** 12 SERVINGS (3 QUARTS)

- 2 pounds lean ground beef (90% lean)
- 1 beef flank steak (1½ pounds), cubed
- 1 medium onion, chopped
- 1 celery rib, chopped
- 1 can (29 ounces) tomato sauce
- 2 cans (14½ ounces each) diced tomatoes, undrained
- 1 can (16 ounces) kidney beans, rinsed and drained
- 1 can (15 ounces) pinto beans, rinsed and drained
- 1 can (4 ounces) chopped green chilies
- 2 to 3 tablespoons chili powder
- 3 teaspoons ground cumin
- 2 teaspoons salt
- 2 teaspoons pepper
- ½ teaspoon ground mustard
- ½ teaspoon paprika
- ½ teaspoon cayenne pepper
- ¼ teaspoon garlic powder
  Hot pepper sauce, shredded cheddar cheese and additional chopped onion, optional

1. In a skillet, cook the ground beef, flank steak, onion and celery over medium heat until meat is no longer pink; drain.

2. Transfer to a 6-qt. slow cooker. Stir in the tomato sauce, tomatoes, beans, chilies and seasonings. Cover and cook on low for 6-8 hours or until steak is tender.

3. Serve with the hot pepper sauce, shredded cheese and onion if desired.

1. In a large skillet, brown pork in oil; drain. Transfer to a 5-qt. slow cooker.
2. Stir in the tomatoes, broth, vegetable blend, wine, marmalade, garlic, oregano, fennel seed, pepper and, if desired, pepper flakes. Cover and cook on low for 8-10 hours or until meat is tender.
3. Combine cornstarch and water until smooth; gradually stir into stew. Cover and cook on high for 30 minutes or until thickened. Serve with fettuccine if desired.

FAST FIX Chocolate-Covered Coffee Beans

You know you love them, but how do you make them? It's so easy. Enjoy them as a snack or use them to top mocha desserts.
—**TASTE OF HOME TEST KITCHEN**

PREP/TOTAL TIME: 30 MIN. **MAKES:** 1 CUP

- ⅔ **cup semisweet chocolate chips**
- 1½ **teaspoons shortening**
- ½ **cup coffee beans**
  Baking cocoa, optional

1. In a microwave, melt chocolate chips and shortening; stir until smooth. Dip coffee beans in chocolate; allow excess to drip off. Place on waxed paper; let stand for 10-15 minutes.
2. Roll in cocoa if desired; let stand until set. Store in an airtight container.

MAKE AHEAD Tuscan Pork Stew

Tender chunks of pork are slowly cooked in a wine-infused sauce. I like to add crushed red pepper flakes for a little added kick.
—**PENNY HAWKINS** MEBANE, NORTH CAROLINA

PREP: 15 MIN. **COOK:** 8½ HOURS **MAKES:** 8 SERVINGS

- 1½ **pounds boneless pork loin roast, cut into 1-inch cubes**
- 2 **tablespoons olive oil**
- 2 **cans (14½ ounces each) Italian diced tomatoes, undrained**
- 2 **cups reduced-sodium chicken broth**
- 2 **cups frozen pepper stir-fry vegetable blend, thawed**
- ½ **cup dry red wine or additional reduced-sodium chicken broth**
- ¼ **cup orange marmalade**
- 2 **garlic cloves, minced**
- 1 **teaspoon dried oregano**
- ½ **teaspoon fennel seed**
- ½ **teaspoon pepper**
- ⅛ **teaspoon crushed red pepper flakes, optional**
- 2 **tablespoons cornstarch**
- 2 **tablespoons cold water**
  Hot cooked fettuccine, optional

Truffle Hot Chocolate

PREP/TOTAL TIME: 25 MIN. **MAKES:** 6 SERVINGS

- 4 **cups 2% milk**
- 6 **ounces 70% cacao dark baking chocolate, chopped**
- 3 **tablespoons brown sugar**
- 1 **teaspoon instant espresso powder**
- 1 **teaspoon vanilla extract**
  Dash salt

ADDITIONAL INGREDIENTS

FOR DULCE DE LECHE WHIPPED CREAM

- 3 **tablespoons sugar**
- ½ **cup heavy whipping cream**

FOR CHOCOLATE WHIPPED CREAM

- ½ **cup heavy whipping cream**
- 2 **tablespoons chocolate syrup**

FOR PEPPERMINT WHIPPED CREAM

- ½ **cup heavy whipping cream**
- 1 **tablespoon sugar**
- ⅛ **teaspoon peppermint extract**
- 1 **tablespoon crushed peppermint candies**

FOR COFFEE WHIPPED CREAM

- ½ **cup heavy whipping cream**
- 1 **teaspoon instant espresso powder**
- 1 **tablespoon sugar**
  Chocolate-covered coffee beans, optional

FOR IRISH WHIPPED CREAM

- ½ **cup heavy whipping cream**
- 1 **tablespoon Irish cream liqueur**

In a large saucepan, heat milk over medium heat until bubbles form around sides of pan (do not boil). Remove from the heat; whisk in the chocolate, brown sugar, espresso powder, vanilla and salt until smooth. Return to the heat; cook and stir until heated through. Pour into mugs; top with desired flavor of whipped cream.

To prepare dulce de leche whipped cream: *In a heavy skillet, melt sugar until golden. Gradually stir in cream; cook and stir until sugar is dissolved. Transfer to a small bowl; cover and refrigerate for 4 hours. Beat until stiff peaks form.*

Chocolate whipped cream: *In a small bowl, beat cream until it begins to thicken. Add chocolate syrup; beat until stiff peaks form.*

Peppermint whipped cream: *In a small bowl, beat cream until it begins to thicken. Add sugar and extract; beat until stiff peaks form. Garnish with candies.*

Coffee whipped cream: *In a small bowl, beat cream and espresso powder until it begins to thicken. Add sugar; beat until stiff peaks form. Garnish with coffee beans if desired.*

Irish whipped cream: *In a small bowl, beat cream and liqueur until stiff peaks form.*

> ❝When company comes calling during winter, set up a hot-chocolate bar. Hand the guests a mug of cocoa each. Then let them garnish it with whipped cream toppings and sweet add-ins.❞
> —**TASTE OF HOME TEST KITCHEN**

COLORFUL BRUNCH FRITTATA, PAGE 64

Joyful Brunches

63

72

60

FAST FIX Southwestern Omelet

Avocado, bacon and tomato fold up into a smoky, creamy omelet for four. Top with red or green salsa—or both—for a festive Christmastime brunch.

—PATRICIA COLLINS IMBLER, OREGON

PREP/TOTAL TIME: 20 MIN. **MAKES:** 4 SERVINGS

- ½ cup chopped onion
- 1 jalapeno pepper, minced
- 1 tablespoon canola oil
- 6 egg, lightly beaten
- 6 bacon strips, cooked and crumbled
- 1 small tomato, chopped
- 1 ripe avocado, cut into 1-inch slices
- 1 cup (4 ounces) shredded Monterey Jack cheese, divided
  Salt and pepper to taste
  Salsa, optional

1. In a large skillet, saute onion and jalapeno in oil until tender; remove with a slotted spoon and set aside. Pour eggs into the same skillet; cover and cook over low heat for 3-4 minutes.
2. Sprinkle with the onion mixture, bacon, tomato, avocado and ½ cup cheese. Season with salt and pepper.
3. Fold omelet in half over filling. Cover and cook for 3-4 minutes or until eggs are set. Sprinkle with remaining cheese. Serve with salsa if desired.
Editor's Note: *Wear disposable gloves when cutting hot peppers; the oils can burn skin. Avoid touching your face.*

MAKE AHEAD Overnight Raisin French Toast

A colleague gave this recipe to me years ago and it's become a brunch favorite! I like to sprinkle it with cinnamon and sugar when removing it from the oven.

—STEPHANIE WEAVER SLIGO, PENNSYLVANIA

PREP: 15 MIN. + CHILLING **BAKE:** 45 MIN. **MAKES:** 12 SERVINGS

- 1 loaf (1 pound) cinnamon-raisin bread, cubed
- 1 package (8 ounces) cream cheese, cubed
- 8 eggs, lightly beaten
- 1½ cups half-and-half cream
- ½ cup sugar
- ½ cup maple syrup
- 2 tablespoons vanilla extract
- 1 tablespoon ground cinnamon
- ⅛ teaspoon ground nutmeg

1. Place half of the bread cubes in a greased 13-in. x 9-in. baking dish. Top with cream cheese and remaining bread.
2. In a large bowl, whisk the remaining ingredients. Pour over top. Cover and refrigerate overnight.
3. Remove from the refrigerator 30 minutes before baking. Cover and bake at 350° for 30 minutes. Uncover; bake 15-20 minutes longer or until a knife inserted near the center comes out clean.

MAKE AHEAD ► # Orange-Cranberry Coffee Cakes

Baking is my favorite thing to do. So during the holiday season, I can often be found in my kitchen preparing festive baked goods, such as these coffee cakes.

—LORAINE MEYER BEND, OREGON

PREP: 40 MIN. + RISING **BAKE:** 20 MIN. + COOLING
MAKES: 2 COFFEE CAKES (12 SERVINGS EACH)

- ½ cup sugar
- 1 package (¼ ounce) active dry yeast
- 1¼ teaspoons salt
- 4 to 4½ cups all-purpose flour
- 1 cup 2% milk
- ½ cup butter, cubed
- ¼ cup water
- 1 egg

FILLING

- 1 cup fresh or frozen cranberries, thawed
- ¼ cup sugar
- ¼ cup chopped walnuts
- ¼ cup dark corn syrup
- 1 tablespoon grated orange peel
- ¼ teaspoon ground ginger

ICING

- 2½ cups confectioners' sugar
- 3 tablespoons plus 1 teaspoon orange juice
- ¼ cup toasted chopped walnuts

1. In a large bowl, combine the sugar, yeast, salt and 2½ cups flour. In a small saucepan, heat the milk, butter and water to 120°-130°. Add to dry ingredients; beat just until moistened. Add egg; beat until smooth. Stir in enough remaining flour to form a stiff dough.

2. Turn onto a floured surface; knead until smooth and elastic, about 6-8 minutes. Place in a greased bowl, turning once to grease the top. Cover and let rise in a warm place until doubled, about 1 hour.

3. Place cranberries in a blender; cover and process until chopped. Drain well; discard liquid from cranberries. In a small bowl, combine cranberries with remaining filling ingredients. Set aside.

4. Punch down dough; turn onto a lightly floured surface. Divide in half. Roll each half into a 16-in. x 10-in. rectangle; spread with filling to within 1 in. of edges. Roll up each jelly-roll style, starting with a long side; seal seams. Place in greased 15-in. x 10-in. x 1-in. baking pans; shape ends to form crescent shapes.

5. With kitchen scissors or a small sharp knife, cut a lengthwise slit down the center of each loaf, ½ in. deep and stopping 2 in. from the ends.

6. Cover loaves and let rise in a warm place until doubled, about 30 minutes. Bake at 350° for 20-25 minutes or until golden brown. Remove from pans to wire racks to cool.

7. Combine confectioners' sugar and orange juice; drizzle over coffee cakes. Top with walnuts; press onto icing to secure.

Make Ahead Note: *Prepare cakes as directed. Allow to cool completely. Store unfrosted cakes in an airtight container on the counter overnight. To reheat, place in a 350° oven until warm to the touch. Drizzle with icing and top with walnuts.*

FAST FIX ► # Citrus Cooler

Brunch for two? Mix up a refreshing ginger-infused punch for a special guest. Served in stemware and garnished with a wedge of citrus, it's ready to toast to a wonderful day.

—CAROL HEMKER PHENIX CITY, ALABAMA

PREP/TOTAL TIME: 5 MIN. **MAKES:** 2 SERVINGS

- ½ cup grapefruit juice
- ½ cup orange juice
- 1 to 2 teaspoons lime juice
- 1 cup ginger ale, chilled
- 8 ice cubes
  Lime and orange slices, optional

In a large bowl, combine the grapefruit juice, orange juice, lime juice and ginger ale. Serve in two chilled glasses over ice. Garnish with lime and orange slices if desired.

Chocolate Chip Caramel Rolls

PREP: 40 MIN. + RISING **BAKE:** 30 MIN. **MAKES:** 1 DOZEN

- 1 package (¼ ounce) active dry yeast
- ¾ cup warm water (110° to 115°)
- ¾ cup warm 2% milk (110° to 115°)
- 3 tablespoons canola oil
- ¼ cup sugar
- 1½ teaspoons salt
- 3¾ to 4½ cups all-purpose flour
- ¾ cup miniature semisweet chocolate chips

FILLING

- ¼ cup butter, softened
- ⅓ cup sugar
- 2 tablespoons ground cinnamon
- 1 cup miniature semisweet chocolate chips

SYRUP

- 1 cup packed brown sugar
- ¾ cup heavy whipping cream

1. In a large bowl, dissolve yeast in warm water. Add the milk, oil, sugar, salt and 3 cups flour; beat on medium speed for 3 minutes. Stir in enough remaining flour to form a firm dough.

2. Turn onto a floured surface; knead in chocolate chips until dough is smooth and elastic, about 6-8 minutes. Place in a greased bowl, turning once to grease top. Cover and let rise in a warm place until doubled, about 1 hour.

3. Punch dough down. Turn onto a lightly floured surface. Roll into an 18-in. x 12-in. rectangle. Spread butter over dough to within ½ in. of edges. Combine sugar and cinnamon; sprinkle over butter. Sprinkle with chocolate chips; gently press into dough. Roll up jelly-roll style, starting with a long side; pinch seam to seal. Cut into 12 slices.

4. In a small bowl, combine brown sugar and cream; pour into a greased 13-in. x 9-in. baking dish. Arrange rolls cut side up over syrup. Cover and let rise until doubled, about 50 minutes.

5. Bake at 375° for 30-35 minutes or until golden brown. Cool for 10 minutes before removing to a serving platter. Serve warm.

As a teenager, I keep active with sports and friends. But baking is my favorite hobby. My five older brothers eat these delicious breakfast rolls right out of the oven! —JULIA HOLM NORTHFIELD, MINNESOTA

Egg Scramble

Easy does it. When you need a satisfying egg dish to feed a crowd, this scramble is a simple go-to. Diced potatoes, ham and veggies mixed with sour cream and cheese make this scramble an all-in-one favorite.

—VICKI HOLLOWAY JOELTON, TENNESSEE

PREP: 15 MIN. **COOK:** 20 MIN. **MAKES:** 10 SERVINGS

  1½ cups diced peeled potatoes
  ½ cup chopped sweet red pepper
  ½ cup chopped green pepper
  ½ cup chopped onion
  2   teaspoons canola oil, divided
  2   cups cubed fully cooked ham
 16   eggs
  ⅔ cup sour cream
  ½ cup 2% milk
  1   teaspoon onion salt
  ½ teaspoon garlic salt
  ¼ teaspoon pepper
  2   cups (8 ounces) shredded cheddar cheese, divided

1. Place potatoes in a small saucepan and cover with water. Bring to a boil. Reduce heat; cover and simmer for 10-15 minutes or until tender. Drain.

2. In a large skillet, saute half of the peppers and onion in 1 teaspoon oil until tender. Add half of the ham and potatoes; saute 2-3 minutes longer.

3. Meanwhile, in a blender, combine eggs, sour cream, milk, onion salt, garlic salt and pepper. Cover and process until smooth.

4. Pour half over vegetable mixture; cook and stir over medium heat until eggs are completely set. Sprinkle with 1 cup cheese. Repeat with remaining ingredients.

FAST FIX Vanilla Fruit Salad

Seldom can my guests figure out the secret ingredient in this fruit salad, but it's the peach pie filling. It pulls it all together and makes everyone want seconds.

—NANCY DODSON SPRINGFIELD, ILLINOIS

PREP/TOTAL TIME: 20 MIN. **MAKES:** 10 SERVINGS

  1   pound fresh strawberries, quartered
  1½ cups seedless red and/or green grapes, halved
  2   medium bananas, sliced
  2   kiwifruit, peeled, sliced and quartered
  1   cup cubed fresh pineapple
  1   can (21 ounces) peach pie filling
  3   teaspoons vanilla extract

In a large bowl, combine the strawberries, grapes, bananas, kiwi and pineapple. Fold in pie filling and vanilla. Chill until serving.

Colorful Brunch Frittata

A friend called and asked me for a special recipe that could be served at his daughter's wedding brunch. I created this recipe for the occasion. It's loaded with colorful veggies and looks beautiful on a buffet.

—KRISTIN ARNETT ELKHORN, WISCONSIN

PREP: 15 MIN. **BAKE:** 55 MIN. + STANDING **MAKES:** 12-15 SERVINGS

- 1 **pound fresh asparagus, trimmed and cut into 1-inch pieces**
- ½ **pound sliced fresh mushrooms**
- 1 **medium sweet red pepper, diced**
- 1 **medium sweet yellow pepper, diced**
- 1 **small onion, chopped**
- 3 **green onions, chopped**
- 3 **tablespoons olive oil**
- 2 **garlic cloves, minced**
- 3 **plum tomatoes, seeded and chopped**
- 14 **eggs, lightly beaten**
- 2 **cups half-and-half cream**
- 2 **cups (8 ounces) shredded Colby-Monterey Jack cheese**
- 3 **tablespoons minced fresh parsley**
- 3 **tablespoons minced fresh basil**
- ½ **teaspoon salt**
- ¼ **teaspoon pepper**
- ½ **cup shredded Parmesan cheese**

1. In a large skillet, saute the asparagus, mushrooms, peppers and onions in oil until tender. Add garlic; cook 1 minute longer. Add tomatoes; set aside.

2. In a large bowl, whisk the eggs, cream, Colby-Monterey Jack cheese, parsley, basil, salt and pepper; stir into vegetable mixture.

3. Pour into a greased 13-in. x 9-in. baking dish. Bake, uncovered, at 350° for 45 minutes.

4. Sprinkle with Parmesan cheese. Bake 10-15 minutes longer or until a knife inserted near the center comes out clean. Let stand for 10 minutes before cutting.

Hot Fruit Compote

Not your ordinary fruit salad, this sweet compote is served warm, and it can bake right alongside most egg dishes, so everything is conveniently done at the same time.

—JOYCE MOYNIHAN LAKEVILLE, MINNESOTA

PREP: 15 MIN. **BAKE:** 40 MIN. **MAKES:** 20 SERVINGS

- 2 **cans (15¼ ounces each) sliced pears, drained**
- 1 **can (29 ounces) sliced peaches, drained**
- 1 **can (20 ounces) unsweetened pineapple chunks, drained**
- 1 **package (20 ounces) pitted dried plums**
- 1 **jar (16 ounces) unsweetened applesauce**
- 1 **can (21 ounces) cherry pie filling**
- ¼ **cup packed brown sugar**

1. In a large bowl, combine the first five ingredients. Pour into a 13-in. x 9-in. baking dish coated with cooking spray. Spread pie filling over fruit mixture; sprinkle with brown sugar.

2. Cover and bake at 350° for 40-45 minutes or until bubbly. Serve warm.

MAKE AHEAD ▶ Crepe Quiche Cups

When it comes to trying out new recipes, I'm always up for the challenge, and crepe cups have turned out to be one of my favorite things to serve while entertaining.

—SHERYL RILEY UNIONVILLE, MISSOURI

PREP: 40 MIN. + CHILLING **BAKE:** 25 MIN. **MAKES:** 16 CREPE CUPS

- 2 eggs
- 1 cup plus 2 tablespoons 2% milk
- 2 tablespoons butter, melted
- 1 cup all-purpose flour
- ⅛ teaspoon salt

FILLING

- ½ pound bulk pork sausage
- ¼ cup chopped onion
- 3 eggs
- ½ cup 2% milk
- ½ cup mayonnaise
- 2 cups (8 ounces) shredded cheddar cheese

1. For crepe batter, in a small bowl, beat the eggs, milk and butter. Combine flour and salt; add to egg mixture and mix well. Cover and refrigerate for 1 hour.

2. In a small skillet, cook sausage and onion over medium heat until meat is no longer pink; drain. In a large bowl, whisk eggs, milk and mayonnaise. Stir in sausage mixture and cheese; set aside.

3. Heat a lightly greased 8-in. nonstick skillet. Stir crepe batter; pour 2 tablespoons into center of skillet. Lift and tilt pan to coat bottom evenly. Cook until top appears dry; turn and cook 15-20 seconds longer.

4. Remove to a wire rack. Repeat with remaining batter, greasing skillet as needed. When cool, stack crepes with waxed paper or paper towels in between.

5. Line greased muffin cups with crepes; fill two-thirds full with sausage mixture. Bake at 350° for 15 minutes. Cover loosely with foil; bake 10-15 minutes longer or until a knife inserted near the center comes out clean.

Make Ahead Note: *Crepes can be stacked with waxed paper in between and stored in an airtight container in the fridge for 2 days or in the freezer up to 4 months.*

FAST FIX ▶ Sage Breakfast Patties

You'll want to skip store-bought breakfast patties when you try this simple recipe. It combines ground turkey and pork with plenty of sage and other seasonings for down-home flavor.

—LAURA MCDOWELL LAKE VILLA, ILLINOIS

PREP/TOTAL TIME: 30 MIN. **MAKES:** 1½ DOZEN

- 2 teaspoons rubbed sage
- 2 teaspoons minced chives
- ¾ teaspoon salt
- ¾ teaspoon white pepper
- ¼ teaspoon onion powder
- ¼ teaspoon chili powder
- ⅛ teaspoon dried thyme
- 1 pound ground turkey
- ½ pound ground pork

1. In a large bowl, combine the first seven ingredients. Crumble turkey and pork over mixture and mix well.

2. Shape into eighteen 2-in. patties. In a large skillet, cook patties over medium heat for 3-4 minutes on each side or until thermometer reads 165°. Drain on paper towels.

MAKE AHEAD ▶ Apple Raisin Crepes

I've been making and eating these breakfast crepes for as long as I can remember. Heating the filled crepes a second time adds a golden crispness.

—**DARLENE BRENDEN** SALEM, OREGON

PREP: 20 MIN. + CHILLING **COOK:** 30 MIN. **MAKES:** 1 DOZEN

1½ **cups all-purpose flour**	**FILLING**
¼ **cup sugar**	5 **cups thinly sliced peeled tart**
1 **cup 2% milk**	**apples**
6 **tablespoons water**	1 **cup sugar**
¼ **cup canola oil**	½ **cup raisins**
1 **egg**	2 **teaspoons ground cinnamon**
	1 **tablespoon confectioners' sugar**

1. For batter, in small bowl, whisk the egg, milk water and oil. Combine flour and sugar; add to egg mixture and mix well. Cover and refrigerate for 1 hour.
2. In large saucepan, combine apples, sugar, raisins and cinnamon. Cook and stir over medium heat for 8-10 minutes or until apples are tender; set aside.
3. Heat a lightly greased 8-in. nonstick skillet; pour 3 tablespoons of batter into the center of skillet. Lift and tilt pan to evenly coat bottom. Cook until top appears dry; turn and cook 15-20 seconds longer. Remove to a wire rack. Repeat with remaining batter, greasing skillet as needed. When cool, stack crepes with waxed paper or paper towels in between.
4. With a slotted spoon, fill each crepe with ¼ cup of apples; roll up. On a lightly greased griddle or in a large skillet, cook crepes over medium heat for 3-4 minutes on each side or until golden brown. Sprinkle with confectioners' sugar. Serve immediately with remaining sauce from apples.
Make Ahead Note: *For instructions on storing and freezing crepes, see Make Ahead Note on p. 65.*

FAST FIX ▶ Gingerbread Pancakes

The cinnamon-ginger aroma of these puffy pancakes is how I wake up my gang on Christmas.

—**MICHELLE SMITH** SYKESVILLE, MARYLAND

PREP/TOTAL TIME: 20 MIN. **MAKES:** 3 SERVINGS

- 1 **cup all-purpose flour**
- 2 **tablespoons sugar**
- 1 **teaspoon baking powder**
- ½ **teaspoon ground cinnamon**
- ¼ **teaspoon ground ginger**
- ¼ **teaspoon ground allspice**
- 1 **egg**
- ¾ **cup 2% milk**
- 2 **tablespoons molasses**
- 1 **tablespoon canola oil**
- 6 **tablespoons maple pancake syrup**
- ¾ **cup apple pie filling, warmed**
- 3 **tablespoons dried cranberries**

1. Combine the first six ingredients in large bowl. Combine egg, milk, molasses and oil; stir into dry ingredients just until moistened.
2. Pour batter by ¼ cupfuls onto a greased hot griddle; turn when bubbles form on top. Cook until the second side is golden brown.
3. To serve, place two pancakes on each plate; drizzle with 2 tablespoons syrup. Top with ¼ cup apple pie filling; sprinkle with cranberries.

I've been making this cake for gatherings or on cold winter mornings for years, and the platter is always empty. I think it's doubly delicious because of the cream cheese and vanilla chip filling. One piece just leads to another! —**MARY SHIVERS** ADA, OKLAHOMA

MAKE AHEAD ▶ Almond Coffee Cake

PREP: 35 MIN. + RISING **BAKE:** 20 MIN. + COOLING
MAKES: 8-10 SERVINGS

- 1 loaf (1 pound) frozen bread dough, thawed
- 1 package (8 ounces) cream cheese, softened
- ¼ cup sugar
- 1 egg
- ½ teaspoon almond extract
- ¾ cup vanilla or white chips
- 1 tablespoon 2% milk

GLAZE
- 1 cup confectioners' sugar
- ¼ teaspoon almond extract
- 1 to 2 tablespoons 2% milk
- ½ cup slivered almonds, toasted

1. On a lightly floured surface, roll dough into a 15-in. x 9-in. rectangle. Transfer to a lightly greased baking sheet.

2. In small bowl, beat cream cheese and sugar until smooth. Beat in egg and extract (filling will be soft). Spread down center of rectangle; sprinkle with chips. On each long side, cut 1-in.-wide strips, about ½ in. from filling.

3. Starting at one end, fold alternating strips at angle across filling. Seal ends. Cover and let rise in warm place until doubled, about 1 hour.

4. Brush with the milk. Bake at 350° for 20-30 minutes or until golden brown. Cool on a wire rack.

5. For glaze, in a small bowl, combine confectioners' sugar and extract. Stir in enough milk to achieve desired consistency. Drizzle over warm coffee cake. Sprinkle with almonds.

Make Ahead Note: *Prepare coffee cake as directed. Allow to cool completely. Cover in plastic wrap and store in refrigerator overnight. To reheat, place in a 350° oven until warm to the touch. Drizzle with icing and top with nuts.*

Glazed Cinnamon Braids

My mother-in-law tried a recipe that was similar to this. We made it with cinnamon candies and now it's a Christmas tradition.

—GEORGIA STULL HARRISONVILLE, MISSOURI

PREP: 40 MIN. + RISING **BAKE:** 25 MIN.
MAKES: 2 LOAVES (12 SLICES EACH)

- 2 **packages (¼ ounce each) active dry yeast**
- ¼ **cup warm water (110° to 115°)**
- 1 **cup warm 2% milk (110° to 115°)**
- 2 **eggs**
- ½ **cup sugar**
- ¼ **cup shortening**
- 2 **teaspoons salt**
- 5 **to 5½ cups all-purpose flour**

FILLING
- 1 **cup chopped pecans**
- ½ **cup red-hot candies**
- ¼ **cup sugar**
- 2 **teaspoons ground cinnamon**
- 2 **tablespoons butter, softened**

GLAZE
- 1 **cup confectioners' sugar**
- ½ **teaspoon vanilla extract**
- 1 **to 2 tablespoons 2% milk**

1. In a large bowl, dissolve yeast in warm water. Add the milk, eggs, sugar, shortening, salt and 3 cups flour. Beat until smooth. Stir in enough remaining flour to form a soft dough (dough will be sticky).

2. Turn onto a floured surface; knead until smooth and elastic, about 6-8 minutes. Place in a greased bowl, turning once to grease the top. Cover and let rise in a warm place until doubled, about 1 hour. Meanwhile, in a small bowl, combine the pecans, red-hots, sugar and cinnamon; set aside.

3. Punch dough down. Divide in half. On a greased baking sheet, roll out one portion into a 12-in. x 10-in. rectangle. Spread 1 tablespoon butter down the center; sprinkle with half of the pecan mixture.

4. On each long side, cut 1-in.-wide strips about 2½ in. into center. Starting at one end, fold alternating strips at angle across filling. Pinch ends to seal. Repeat with remaining dough, butter and pecan mixture. Cover; let rise until doubled, about 45 min.

5. Bake at 350° for 25-30 minutes or until golden brown. Remove from pans to wire racks. In a small bowl, combine the confectioners' sugar, vanilla and enough milk to achieve desired consistency; drizzle over loaves. Serve warm.

Cinnamon Peach Kuchen

With its flaky, buttery crust and sweet peach topping, this is one of my favorite desserts. It's a tried-and-true recipe from my mother.

—RACHEL GARCIA FORT KNOX, KENTUCKY

PREP: 25 MIN. **BAKE:** 45 MIN. + COOLING **MAKES:** 10 SERVINGS

- 2 **cups all-purpose flour**
- 2 **tablespoons sugar**
- ½ **teaspoon salt**
- ¼ **teaspoon baking powder**
- ½ **cup cold butter, cubed**
- 2 **cans (15¼ ounces each) peach halves, drained and patted dry**
- 1 **cup packed brown sugar**
- 1 **teaspoon ground cinnamon**
- 2 **egg yolks, lightly beaten**
- 1 **cup heavy whipping cream**

1. In a small bowl, combine the flour, sugar, salt and baking powder; cut in butter until crumbly. Press onto the bottom and 1½ in. up the sides of a greased 9-in. springform pan.

2. Place pan on baking sheet. Lay peach halves, cut side up, in crust. Combine brown sugar and cinnamon; sprinkle on top.

3. Bake at 350° for 20 minutes. Combine egg yolks and cream; pour over peaches. Bake 25-30 minutes longer or until top is set. Cool on a wire rack. Refrigerate leftovers.

Candy Cane Coffee Cake

Dotted with dried apricots and maraschino cherries, this tender coffee cake has a festive flavor and look. I love to serve it at Christmastime for my family, fellow teachers and students. It makes a fun holiday gift, too.

—LINDA HOLLINGSWORTH QUITMAN, MISSISSIPPI

PREP: 35 MIN. + RISING **BAKE:** 20 MIN.
MAKES: 3 LOAVES (12 SLICES EACH)

    2 packages (¼ ounce each) active dry yeast
    ½ cup warm water (110° to 115°)
    2 cups warm sour cream (110° to 115°)
    6 tablespoons butter, divided
    ⅓ cup sugar
    2 eggs
    2 teaspoons salt
  5¾ to 6¼ cups all-purpose flour
  1½ cups finely chopped dried apricots
  1½ cups finely chopped maraschino cherries
    2 cups confectioners' sugar
    2 tablespoons cold water
       Additional cherries, halved

1. In a large bowl, dissolve yeast in warm water. Beat in the sour cream, 4 tablespoons butter, sugar, eggs, salt and 2 cups flour; beat until smooth. Stir in enough remaining flour to form a soft dough.

2. Turn onto a floured surface; knead until smooth and elastic, about 6-8 minutes. Place in a greased bowl, turning once to grease top. Cover and let rise in a warm place until doubled, about 1 hour.

3. Punch dough down. Turn onto a lightly floured surface; divide into thirds. Roll each portion into a 14-in. x 7-in. rectangle on a greased baking sheet.

4. Combine apricots and cherries; spoon down the center of each rectangle. On each long side, cut ¾-in.-wide strips about 2 in. into center. Starting at one end, fold alternating strips at an angle across filling. Pinch ends to seal. Curve top.

5. Bake at 375° for 18-20 minutes or until golden brown. Melt remaining butter; brush over warm coffee cakes. Combine confectioners' sugar and cold water until smooth; drizzle over the tops. Garnish with additional cherries.

Almond Pastry Puffs

I call this my nut puff pastry. You'll be surprised how easy it is, and the frosting...*mmm*, what an excellent treat!

—**BETTY CLAYCOMB** ALVERTON, PENNSYLVANIA

PREP: 40 MIN. **BAKE:** 20 MIN. + COOLING
MAKES: 2 PASTRIES (11 SERVINGS EACH)

  2 **cups all-purpose flour, divided**
  ¼ **teaspoon salt**
  1 **cup cold butter, divided**
  2 **tablespoons plus 1 cup cold water, divided**
  ¼ **teaspoon almond extract**
  3 **eggs**
FROSTING
  1½ **cups confectioners' sugar**
  2 **tablespoons butter, softened**
  4 **teaspoons water**
  ¼ **teaspoon almond extract**
  ⅔ **cup chopped almonds, toasted**

1. In a large bowl, combine 1 cup flour and salt; cut in ½ cup butter until mixture resembles coarse crumbs. Add 2 tablespoons cold water; stir with a fork until blended. Shape dough into a ball; divide in half. Place dough 3 in. apart on an ungreased baking sheet; pat each into a 12-in. x 3-in. rectangle.
2. In a large saucepan, bring remaining butter and water to a boil. Remove from the heat; stir in extract and remaining flour until a smooth ball forms. Remove from the heat; let stand for 5 minutes. Add eggs, one at a time, beating well after each addition. Continue beating until mixture is smooth and shiny.
3. Spread over rectangles. Bake at 400° for 18-20 minutes or until topping is lightly browned. Cool for 5 minutes before removing from pan to wire racks.
4. For frosting, in a small bowl, combine the confectioners' sugar, butter, water and extract; beat until smooth. Spread over pastries; sprinkle with almonds.

Canadian Bacon Onion Quiche

For over 20 years, we sold homegrown specialty onions at the farmers market. I handed out this classic quiche recipe to all our customers.

—JANICE REDFORD CAMBRIDGE, WISCONSIN

PREP: 30 MIN. **BAKE:** 40 MIN. **MAKES:** 6-8 SERVINGS

- 1 **cup all-purpose flour**
- ¾ **teaspoon salt, divided**
- ½ **cup plus 3 tablespoons cold butter, divided**
- ½ **cup 4% small-curd cottage cheese**
- 3 **large sweet onions, sliced (about 6 cups)**
- 4 **ounces Canadian bacon, diced**
- ¼ **teaspoon pepper**
- 3 **eggs, lightly beaten**
- 1 **cup (4 ounces) shredded cheddar cheese**

1. In a small bowl, combine flour and ¼ teaspoon salt; cut in ½ cup butter until crumbly. Gradually add cottage cheese, tossing with a fork until dough forms a ball.

2. Roll out pastry dough to fit a 9-in. pie plate. Transfer pastry to pie plate. Trim pastry to ½ in. beyond edge of plate; flute edges.

3. In a large skillet, saute onions in remaining butter until golden brown. Stir in the Canadian bacon, pepper and remaining salt. Remove from the heat; add eggs and cheddar cheese. Pour into pastry shell.

4. Bake at 350° for 40-45 minutes or until a knife inserted near the center comes out clean.

Majestic Cinnamon Rolls

I got this dough recipe many years ago while visiting a friend's home where we were served the most delicious dinner rolls. I use it for crescent rolls, bread and these jumbo cinnamon rolls. And let me tell you, these buns are no wimps when it comes to packing in big cinnamon flavor.

—BETTE LU LERWICK ALBIN, WYOMING

PREP: 40 MIN. + RISING **BAKE:** 35 MIN. **MAKES:** 1 DOZEN

- 1 **tablespoon active dry yeast**
- ⅓ **cup sugar**
- ¾ **cup warm water (110° to 115°)**
- ¾ **cup warm 2% milk (110° to 115°)**
- 2 **eggs**
- 3 **tablespoons butter, melted**
- 1½ **teaspoons salt**
- 4½ **to 5 cups all-purpose flour**

FILLING
- 1½ **cups packed brown sugar**
- ½ **cup butter, melted**
- 2 **tablespoons ground cinnamon**

TOPPING
- 1½ **cups packed brown sugar**
- ¾ **cup butter, melted**
- 3 **tablespoons half-and-half cream**

1. In a large bowl, dissolve yeast and 1 tablespoon sugar in warm water. Add the milk, eggs, butter, salt, remaining sugar and 2 cups flour. Beat until smooth. Stir in enough remaining flour to form a soft dough (dough will be sticky).

2. Turn onto a floured surface; knead until smooth and elastic, about 6-8 minutes. Place in a greased bowl, turning once to grease the top. Cover and let rise in a warm place until doubled, about 1 hour.

3. Punch dough down. On a lightly floured surface, roll into an 18-in. x 12-in. rectangle. In a small bowl, combine the brown sugar, butter and cinnamon; spread over rectangle to within ½ in. of edges. Roll up jelly-roll style, starting with a long side; pinch seam to seal. Cut into 1½-in. slices.

4. In a small bowl, combine brown sugar, butter and cream; pour into a greased 13-in. x 9-in. baking dish. Place rolls, cut side down, in brown sugar mixture.

5. Cover and let rise in a warm place until doubled, about 30 minutes. Bake at 350° for 35-40 minutes or until golden brown. Cool in dish for 5 minutes; invert onto a serving platter. Serve warm.

Pear Mushroom Strudels

Brunch guests may raise their eyebrows when you tell them the ingredients in this unconventional strudel, but after one taste, they're raising their hands for the recipe.

—CAROLE RESNICK CLEVELAND, OHIO

PREP: 45 MIN. **BAKE:** 20 MIN. **MAKES:** 2 STRUDELS (12 SLICES EACH)

- 1 cup finely chopped mushrooms
- 1 small onion, finely chopped
- ½ cup butter, divided
- 2 small pears, peeled and thinly sliced
- ¾ cup shredded Gruyere or Swiss cheese
- ⅓ cup sliced almonds
- 1 tablespoon stone-ground mustard
- ½ teaspoon salt
- ¼ teaspoon pepper
- 10 sheets phyllo dough (14 inches x 9 inches)
- ⅓ cup grated Parmesan cheese

1. In a large skillet, cook mushrooms and onion in 2 tablespoons butter until tender. Stir in pears; cook 3 minutes longer. Remove from the heat; stir in the Gruyere, almonds, mustard, salt and pepper. Cool to room temperature.

2. Melt remaining butter. Place one sheet of phyllo dough on a work surface; brush evenly with butter. Sprinkle with 1½ teaspoons Parmesan cheese. Layer with four more sheets of phyllo, brushing each sheet with butter and sprinkling with cheese. (Keep remaining phyllo dough covered with plastic wrap and a damp towel to prevent it from drying out.)

3. Spread half of the pear mixture in a 2-in.-wide strip along a short side of dough. Roll up jelly-roll style, starting with the pear side; pinch seams to seal. Brush with butter. Transfer to a parchment paper-lined 15-in. x 10-in. x 1-in. baking pan.

4. Repeat with remaining phyllo, butter, Parmesan cheese and pear mixture.

5. Bake at 375° for 16-20 minutes or until golden brown. Cool for 5 minutes. Cut each strudel into 12 slices.

Jack Cheese Oven Omelet

A bacon and cheese omelet that bakes in the oven saves you from hovering over the stovetop while brunch guests arrive. Plus, there's no flipping involved. For a meatless option, try using mushrooms instead of bacon.

—LAUREL ROBERTS VANCOUVER, WASHINGTON

PREP: 20 MIN. **BAKE:** 35 MIN. **MAKES:** 6 SERVINGS

- 8 bacon strips, diced
- 4 green onions, sliced
- 8 eggs
- 1 cup 2% milk
- ½ teaspoon seasoned salt
- 2½ cups (10 ounces) shredded Monterey Jack cheese, divided

1. In a large skillet, cook bacon until crisp. Drain, reserving 1 tablespoon drippings. Set bacon aside. Saute onion in drippings until tender; set aside.

2. In a large bowl, beat eggs. Add the milk, seasoned salt, 2 cups cheese, bacon and sauteed onions. Transfer to a greased shallow 2-qt. baking dish.

3. Bake, uncovered, at 350° for 35-40 minutes. Sprinkle with remaining cheese.

FAST FIX Maple-Glazed Sausages

I love to coat a skillet full of breakfast sausages with this cinnamony syrup. They're my first choice when I want to round out a morning menu of French toast and fruit compote.

—TRUDIE HAGEN ROGGEN, COLORADO

PREP/TOTAL TIME: 20 MIN. **MAKES:** 10 SERVINGS

- 2 packages (6.4 ounces each) brown-and-serve sausage links
- 1 cup maple syrup
- ½ cup packed brown sugar
- 1 teaspoon ground cinnamon

In a large skillet, brown sausage links. In a small bowl, combine the syrup, brown sugar and cinnamon; pour over sausages. Bring to a boil. Reduce heat; simmer, uncovered, until sausages are glazed.

FAST FIX ## Mini Spinach Frittatas

PREP/TOTAL TIME: 30 MIN. **MAKES:** 2 DOZEN

- 1 cup ricotta cheese
- ¾ cup grated Parmesan cheese
- ⅔ cup chopped fresh mushrooms
- 1 package (10 ounces) frozen chopped spinach, thawed and squeezed dry
- 1 egg
- ½ teaspoon dried oregano
- ¼ teaspoon salt
- ¼ teaspoon pepper
- 24 slices pepperoni

1. In a small bowl, combine the first eight ingredients. Place a slice of pepperoni in each of 24 greased miniature muffin cups. Fill muffin cups three-fourths full with cheese mixture.
2. Bake at 375° for 20-25 minutes or until completely set. Carefully run a knife around edges of muffin cups to loosen. Serve warm.

❝I make these pepperoni appetizers when I'm tired of the 'same old.' It's easy to double the recipe for a larger breakfast or brunch crowd.❞
—**NANCY STATKEVICUS** TUCSON, ARIZONA

MAKE AHEAD ## Pecan French Toast

The orange-pecan flavors are reminiscent of the South, but I call this Wisconsin French Toast. Thick bread slices are key for soaking up the zesty orange flavors overnight.
—**ALLAN WHYTOCK** LEBANON, OREGON

PREP: 10 MIN. + CHILLING **BAKE:** 20 MIN. **MAKES:** 6 SERVINGS

- 4 eggs
- ⅔ cup orange juice
- ⅓ cup 2% milk
- ¼ cup sugar
- 1 tablespoon grated orange peel
- ½ teaspoon vanilla extract
- ¼ teaspoon ground nutmeg
- 6 slices Italian bread (1 inch thick)
- ⅓ cup butter, melted
- ¾ cup chopped pecans
  Maple syrup

1. In a small bowl, whisk the first seven ingredients. Place bread in a 13-in. x 9-in. dish; pour egg mixture over the top. Cover and refrigerate overnight, turning slices once.
2. Pour butter into a 15-in. x 10-in. x 1-in. baking pan; top with bread. Sprinkle with pecans. Bake at 400° for 20-25 minutes or until golden brown. Serve with syrup.

MAKE AHEAD Eggs Benedict Casserole

Eggs Benedict for a bunch? Everything you love about this classic brunch dish is baked into an easy-to-serve casserole.

—**SANDIE HEINDEL** LIBERTY, MISSOURI

PREP: 25 MIN. + CHILLING **BAKE:** 45 MIN. **MAKES:** 12 SERVINGS (1⅔ CUPS SAUCE)

¾ **pound Canadian bacon, chopped**
6 **English muffins, split and cut into 1-inch pieces**
8 **eggs**
2 **cups 2% milk**
1 **teaspoon onion powder**
¼ **teaspoon paprika**

SAUCE
4 **egg yolks**
½ **cup heavy whipping cream**
2 **tablespoons lemon juice**
1 **teaspoon Dijon mustard**
½ **cup butter, melted**

1. Place half of the bacon in a greased 13-in. x 9-in. baking dish; top with English muffins and remaining bacon. In a large bowl, whisk the eggs, milk and onion powder; pour over the top. Cover and refrigerate overnight.
2. Remove from the refrigerator 30 minutes before baking. Sprinkle with paprika. Cover and bake at 375° for 35 minutes. Uncover; bake 10-15 minutes longer or until a knife inserted near the center comes out clean.
3. In a double boiler or metal bowl over simmering water, constantly whisk the egg yolks, cream, lemon juice and mustard until mixture reaches 160° or is thick enough to coat the back of a spoon. Reduce heat to low. Slowly drizzle in warm melted butter, whisking constantly. Serve immediately with casserole.

FAST FIX Lemon Pull-Apart Coffee Cake

I found this recipe in a newspaper and make it often. I keep a tube of biscuit dough on hand so I can bake it when unexpected company stops in.

—**MARY TALLMAN** ARBOR VITAE, WISCONSIN

PREP/TOTAL TIME: 30 MIN. **MAKES:** 10 SERVINGS

¼ **cup sugar**
¼ **cup chopped walnuts**
¼ **cup golden raisins**
2 **tablespoons butter, melted**
2 **teaspoons grated lemon peel**
1 **tube (12 ounces) refrigerated buttermilk biscuits**

GLAZE
½ **cup confectioners' sugar**
1 **tablespoon lemon juice**

1. In a large bowl, combine the first five ingredients. Separate biscuits and cut each into quarters; toss with sugar mixture. Place in a greased 9-in. round baking pan.
2. Bake at 400° for 20-25 minutes or until golden brown. Immediately invert onto a wire rack. Combine glaze ingredients until smooth; drizzle over warm coffee cake.

Mocha-Cinnamon Coffee Cake

Everyone calls this Bette's Fabulous Coffee Cake. It's my signature cake at luncheons and club meetings, and it's so easy to make.
—**BETTE MINTZ** GLENDALE, CALIFORNIA

PREP: 15 MIN. **BAKE:** 40 MIN. + COOLING
MAKES: 12-16 SERVINGS

- ¾ cup chopped walnuts
- ⅓ cup sugar
- 1 tablespoon baking cocoa
- 1 teaspoon instant coffee granules
- 1 teaspoon ground cinnamon

BATTER

- ¾ cup butter, softened
- 1½ cups sugar
- 4 eggs
- 1 teaspoon vanilla extract
- 2¼ cups all-purpose flour
- 2 teaspoons baking powder
- 1 teaspoon baking soda
- 1½ cups (12 ounces) sour cream
- ½ cup semisweet chocolate chips
  Confectioners' sugar, optional

1. In a small bowl, combine the first five ingredients; set aside. In a large bowl, cream butter and sugar until light and fluffy. Add eggs, one at a time, beating well after each addition. Beat in vanilla. Combine the flour, baking powder and baking soda; add to creamed mixture alternately with sour cream just until combined. Stir in chocolate chips.
2. Pour a third of the batter into a greased 10-in. fluted tube pan. Sprinkle with half of the walnut mixture; repeat layers. Top with remaining batter.
3. Bake at 350° for 40-45 minutes or until a toothpick inserted near the center comes out clean. Cool for 10 minutes before removing to a wire rack. Dust with confectioners' sugar if desired.

Chocolate Braids

I'm a big fan of recipes that use common ingredients yet turn out spectacular. This bread is fantastic and gets smiles every time I serve it. The recipe is a little more complicated than some but is worth the extra effort.

—ERIKA AYLWARD CLINTON, MICHIGAN

PREP: 40 MIN. + RISING **BAKE:** 30 MIN. + COOLING
MAKES: 2 LOAVES (8 SLICES EACH)

- 2 packages (¼ ounce each) active dry yeast
- ½ cup warm water (110° to 115°)
- ⅓ cup honey, divided
- 6 tablespoons butter, softened
- 1 egg
- ½ cup baking cocoa
- ½ teaspoon salt
- 2½ to 3 cups bread flour

CREAM CHEESE FILLING

- 4 ounces cream cheese, softened
- ¼ cup sugar
- ¼ cup all-purpose flour
- 1 teaspoon vanilla extract
- ¼ teaspoon ground nutmeg

TOPPING

- ¼ cup all-purpose flour
- ¼ cup sugar
- ½ teaspoon ground cinnamon
- 2 tablespoons cold butter
- ¼ cup chopped macadamia nuts

ICING

- 1½ cups confectioners' sugar
- 1 tablespoon baking cocoa
- ¼ teaspoon vanilla extract
- 3 to 4 tablespoons 2% milk

1. In a large bowl, dissolve yeast in warm water. Add 2 teaspoons honey; let stand for 5 minutes. Add the butter, egg, cocoa, salt, 1½ cups bread flour and remaining honey. Beat for 2 minutes or until smooth. Stir in enough remaining bread flour to form a soft dough.

2. Turn onto a floured surface; knead until smooth and elastic, about 6-8 minutes. Place in a greased bowl, turning once to grease top. Cover and let rise in a warm place until doubled, about 1 hour.

3. Punch dough down; divide in half. On a lightly floured surface, roll one portion into a 12-in. x 7-in. rectangle.

4. In a small bowl, beat filling ingredients until smooth. Spread half of the filling over dough to within 1 in. of edges. Roll up jelly-roll style, starting with a long side; pinch seams to seal.

5. Place seam side down on a large greased baking sheet. With a sharp knife, cut roll in half lengthwise, leaving one end intact. Carefully turn cut sides up. Loosely twist strips around each other, keeping cut side up. Pinch ends to seal. Repeat with remaining dough and filling. Cover and let rise in a warm place for 30 minutes.

6. For topping, combine the flour, sugar and cinnamon in a small bowl; cut in butter until crumbly. Add nuts. Sprinkle over loaves.

7. Bake at 350° for 30-35 minutes or until golden brown. Remove from pans to wire racks to cool. In a small bowl, combine the confectioner's sugar, cocoa, vanilla and enough milk to achieve desired consistency; drizzle over warm loaves.

FAST FIX Fluffy Hot Chocolate

This is our daughter's favorite hot chocolate recipe. It may look like ordinary cocoa, but a touch of vanilla sets it apart from the rest. And the melted marshmallows give it a frothy body you won't get from a cocoa packet.

—JO ANN SCHIMCEK WEIMAR, TEXAS

PREP/TOTAL TIME: 15 MIN. **MAKES:** 4 SERVINGS

- 8 teaspoons sugar
- 4 teaspoons baking cocoa
- 4 cups 2% milk
- 1½ cups miniature marshmallows
- 1 teaspoon vanilla extract

In a small saucepan, combine the first four ingredients. Cook and stir over medium heat until marshmallows are melted, about 8 minutes. Remove from the heat; stir in vanilla. Ladle into mugs.

Breakfast Rice Pudding

My husband makes this rice pudding quite often for breakfast. It's equally good with fresh blueberries instead of cherries.

—**SUE DRAHEIM** WATERFORD, WISCONSIN

PREP: 15 MIN. **BAKE:** 25 MIN. **MAKES:** 8 SERVINGS

- 1⅓ cups uncooked long grain or basmati rice
- 1 can (15¼ ounces) peach halves, drained
- 1 cup canned or frozen pitted tart cherries, drained
- 1 cup heavy whipping cream
- ½ cup packed brown sugar, divided
- ¼ cup old-fashioned oats
- ¼ cup flaked coconut
- ¼ cup chopped pecans
- ¼ cup butter, melted

1. Cook rice according to package directions. In a large bowl, combine the rice, peaches, cherries, cream and ¼ cup brown sugar. Transfer to a greased 1½ quart baking dish.

2. Combine the oats, coconut, pecans, butter and remaining brown sugar; sprinkle over rice. Bake, uncovered, at 375° for 25-30 minutes or until golden brown.

Mashed Potato Kolachkes

My husband's Bohemian mother brought a kolachke recipe with her when she came to America. I was not able to meet her but have heard so many wonderful stories. I like to make them when my husband's daughters visit; kolachkes are an important part of their heritage.

—**JAN WAGNER-CUDA** DEER PARK, WASHINGTON

PREP: 45 MIN. + RISING **BAKE:** 10 MIN. **MAKES:** ABOUT 2 DOZEN

- 1 medium potato, peeled and cubed
- 1¼ teaspoons active dry yeast
- 2 tablespoons warm water (110° to 115°)
- ¾ cup sugar
- ½ cup warm 2% milk (110° to 115°)
- ¼ cup shortening
- 6 tablespoons butter, softened, divided
- 1 egg, lightly beaten
- ¾ teaspoon salt
- 3 to 4 cups all-purpose flour
- ⅓ cup apricot cake and pastry filling
- ⅓ cup raspberry cake and pastry filling
- ⅔ cup confectioners' sugar
- 4 teaspoons 2% milk

1. Place potato in a small saucepan and cover with water. Bring to a boil. Reduce heat; cover and cook for 10-15 minutes or until tender. Drain, reserving ½ cup cooking liquid. Mash potato; set aside ½ cup (discard or save remaining potato for another use).

2. In a large bowl, dissolve yeast in warm water. Add the sugar, milk, shortening, 4 tablespoons butter, egg, salt, reserved cooking liquid and mashed potato. Beat in 2 cups flour until smooth. Stir in enough of the remaining flour to form a soft dough.

3. Turn onto a floured surface; knead until smooth and elastic, about 6-8 minutes. Place in a greased bowl, turning once to grease top. Cover and let rise in a warm place until doubled, about 45 minutes.

4. Turn onto a well-floured surface. Shape into 1½-in. balls; place 2 in. apart on greased baking sheets. Flatten to ½-in. thickness. Cover and let rise for 15 minutes or until almost doubled. Melt the remaining butter.

5. Using the end of a wooden spoon handle, make an indentation in the center of each ball; brush with butter and fill with a rounded teaspoon of filling.

6. Bake at 400° for 10-15 minutes or until lightly browned. Remove from pans to wire racks. Combine confectioners' sugar and milk; drizzle over warm rolls.

MAKE AHEAD ▶ Granola Yogurt Parfaits

PREP: 30 MIN. + CHILLING **BAKE:** 25 MIN. + COOLING
MAKES: 6 SERVINGS

- 4 cups (32 ounces) plain yogurt
- ½ cup orange juice
- ¼ cup honey
- 1½ teaspoons vanilla extract
- 4 teaspoons grated orange peel

GRANOLA

- 1½ cups old-fashioned oats
- ¾ cup chopped walnuts
- 3 tablespoons dark brown sugar
- 3 tablespoons honey
- 2 tablespoons canola oil
- 1 teaspoon vanilla extract
- ¼ teaspoon salt
- ¾ cup dried cranberries

1. Line a strainer with four layers of cheesecloth or one coffee filter and place over a large bowl. Place yogurt in prepared strainer; cover yogurt with edges of cheesecloth. Refrigerate for 8 hours or overnight.

2. Remove yogurt from cheesecloth and discard liquid from bowl. In another bowl, combine the yogurt, orange juice, honey, vanilla and orange peel. Cover and refrigerate until serving.

3. For granola, in a large bowl, combine oats and walnuts. Combine the brown sugar, honey, oil, vanilla and salt; pour over oat mixture and toss to coat. Transfer to a greased 15-in. x 10-in. x 1-in. baking pan.

4. Bake at 300° for 25-30 minutes or until golden brown, stirring twice. Cool on a wire rack. Transfer to a large bowl; stir in cranberries. Store in an airtight container.

5. To serve, alternate layers of yogurt and granola in six parfait glasses.

Make Ahead Note: *Once cooled, granola can be stored in an airtight container for 2 weeks at room temperature, for 2 months in the refrigerator, and up to 6 months in the freezer.*

"I love this recipe because the granola and vanilla-orange yogurt can be made the day before. The next morning, just roll out of bed and assemble the parfaits in pretty glasses."

—**LAUREEN PITTMAN** RIVERSIDE, CALIFORNIA

FAST FIX Smoked Salmon and Egg Wraps

Served hot from the oven, these smoked salmon wraps are ideal for serving a brunch bunch of 10. Plus, start to finish, they're ready in less than 30 minutes.

—**MARY LOU WAYMAN** SALT LAKE CITY, UTAH

PREP/TOTAL TIME: 25 MIN. **MAKES:** 10 SERVINGS

- 12 **eggs, lightly beaten**
- ¼ **cup snipped fresh dill or 4 teaspoons dill weed**
- 2 **tablespoons 2% milk**
- ½ **teaspoon seasoned salt**
- 10 **flour tortillas (8 inches)**
- 1 **package (4 ounces) smoked salmon or lox**
- ½ **cup finely chopped red onion**
- 6 **ounces Havarti cheese, thinly sliced**

1. In a large bowl, whisk the eggs, dill, milk and seasoned salt. Coat a large nonstick skillet with cooking spray and place over medium heat. Add egg mixture. Cook and stir over medium heat until eggs are completely set.

2. Spoon a scant ⅓ cup egg mixture down the center of each tortilla. Top with salmon, onion and cheese. Fold opposite sides of tortilla over filling (sides will not meet in center). Roll up tortilla, beginning at one of the open ends. Place wraps, seam side down, in 15-in. x 10-in. x 1-in. baking pan coated with cooking spray.

3. Cover and bake at 350° for 10 minutes or until cheese is melted.

FAST FIX Silver Dollar Oat Pancakes

I combined two of my grandson Joshua's favorite foods—applesauce and oatmeal—into these wholesome little pancakes. He likes the smaller serving size.

—**MARGARET WILSON** SUN CITY, CALIFORNIA

PREP/TOTAL TIME: 25 MIN. **MAKES:** 4 SERVINGS

- ½ **cup all-purpose flour**
- ½ **cup quick-cooking oats**
- 1½ **teaspoons sugar**
- 1 **teaspoon baking powder**
- ½ **teaspoon baking soda**
- ½ **teaspoon salt**
- 1 **egg**
- ¾ **cup buttermilk**
- ½ **cup cinnamon applesauce**
- 2 **tablespoons butter, melted**
  Maple syrup or topping of your choice

1. In a large bowl, combine the dry ingredients. In a small bowl, beat the egg, buttermilk, applesauce and butter; stir into dry ingredients just until moistened.

2. Pour batter by 2 tablespoonfuls onto a hot griddle coated with cooking spray; turn when bubbles form on top. Cook until second side is golden brown. Serve with syrup.

3. Cool remaining pancakes; arrange in a single layer on baking sheets. Freeze overnight or until frozen. Transfer to a resealable plastic freezer bag. May be frozen for up to 2 months.

To use frozen pancakes: *Place on a lightly greased baking sheet. Bake at 400° for 4-6 minutes or until heated through. Serve with syrup if desired.*

TURKEY WITH APPLE STUFFING, PAGE 95

Christmas Dinner Menus

100

93

96

Down-Home Dinner

Peppercorn Beef Top Loin Roast
PAGE 83

Garlic Baby Potatoes
PAGE 84

Jarlsberg Popovers
PAGE 84

Zesty Broccolini
PAGE 84

Coconut Cranberry Shortcakes
PAGE 85

PEPPERCORN BEEF TOP LOIN ROAST,
GARLIC BABY POTATOES,
JARLSBERG POPOVERS & ZESTY BROCCOLINI

Peppercorn Beef Top Loin Roast

A red wine sauce complements the caramelized brown sugar coating on the crust of this special-occasion roast. The down-home flavor makes it the ultimate Christmas entree.

—TASTE OF HOME TEST KITCHEN

PREP: 30 MIN. **BAKE:** 1 HOUR + STANDING
MAKES: 10 SERVINGS (1½ CUPS SAUCE)

- 1 **beef top round roast (4 pounds)**
- ⅓ **cup packed brown sugar**
- 3 **tablespoons whole peppercorns, crushed**
- 4 **garlic cloves, minced**
- ¾ **teaspoon salt**
- 1 **large onion, finely chopped**
- 1 **tablespoon olive oil**
- 2 **tablespoons tomato paste**
- 2 **teaspoons Worcestershire sauce**
- 1½ **cups port wine**
- 1½ **cups dry red wine**

1. Trim fat from roast. In a small bowl, combine the brown sugar, peppercorns, garlic and salt. Rub over meat. Place in a shallow roasting pan.

2. Bake at 325° for 1 to 1½ hours or until meat reaches desired doneness (for medium-rare, a meat thermometer should read 145°; medium, 160°; well-done, 170°). Let stand for 15 minutes before slicing.

3. Meanwhile, in a large saucepan, saute onion in oil until tender. Stir in tomato paste and Worcestershire sauce until blended. Add wines. Bring to a boil; cook until liquid is reduced to about 1½ cups. Serve with roast.

TRY THIS CRAFT

Luminous Lantern Centerpiece

Let it glow! Purchase lanterns in two sizes in a color that coordinates with your dishes. Remember that an odd number will create more interest and look more appealing.

Place pillar candles in the large lanterns and votive candles in the small ones. If desired, put a candle wreath inside each lantern or simply add small beads as shown. Set a runner down the length of your table. For added color, you can place some Christmas greens in the center. Arrange the lanterns on top of the greens.

For an even more glorious glow, put a small, votive-filled clear glass container at each place setting. Wrap each candle holder with a ribbon and a coordinating strand of tiny beads.

Garlic Baby Potatoes

We suggest this recipe when you need a classic potato dish that pairs well with a variety of meaty entrees. It's assembled in a flash, then it roasts in the oven for an aromatic side dish.
—TASTE OF HOME TEST KITCHEN

PREP: 20 MIN. **BAKE:** 50 MIN. **MAKES:** 8 SERVINGS

- 6 tablespoons olive oil
- 12 garlic cloves, minced
- ¼ cup minced fresh oregano
- 4½ teaspoons balsamic vinegar
- 3 teaspoons kosher salt
- 1½ teaspoons paprika
- ¾ teaspoon lemon-pepper seasoning
- 24 small red or fingerling potatoes, halved

1. In a large bowl, combine the first seven ingredients. Add potatoes; toss to coat. Transfer potatoes to a greased 9-in. square baking pan; drizzle with garlic mixture.
2. Cover and bake at 350° for 40 minutes, stirring every 10 minutes. Uncover; bake 10-20 minutes longer or until potatoes are tender.

MAKE AHEAD ▶ Jarlsberg Popovers

When you're hosting holiday dinners, these cheesy popovers are a must-try instead of ordinary dinner rolls.
—TASTE OF HOME TEST KITCHEN

PREP: 15 MIN. **BAKE:** 30 MIN. **MAKES:** 9 SERVINGS

- 4½ teaspoons shortening
- 3 egg whites
- 2 eggs
- 1½ cups 2% milk
- ½ cup heavy whipping cream
- 2 cups all-purpose flour
- 1 tablespoon sugar
- ¾ teaspoon salt
- ¼ teaspoon white pepper
- 4 ounces Jarlsberg cheese, shredded

1. Using ½ teaspoon shortening for each cup, grease the bottoms and sides of nine popover cups; set aside.
2. In a small bowl, beat egg whites and eggs; beat in milk and cream. Add the flour, sugar, salt and pepper; beat until smooth (do not overbeat). Fold in cheese. Fill prepared cups two-thirds full with batter. Fill empty cups two-thirds full with water.
3. Bake at 450° for 15 minutes. Reduce heat to 350° (do not open door). Bake 15 minutes longer or until deep golden brown (do not underbake). Immediately cut a slit in the top of each popover to allow steam to escape.

Make Ahead Note: *Make popovers up to a day in advance. Cool completely before storing in an airtight container. Reheat just before serving.*

FAST FIX ▶ Zesty Broccolini

We use garlic, gingerroot and red pepper flakes to give this side dish a little kick. These green spears with delicate florets are especially fitting to round out any Christmas entree.
—TASTE OF HOME TEST KITCHEN

PREP/TOTAL TIME: 20 MIN. **MAKES:** 6 SERVINGS

- 1 pound Broccolini or broccoli spears
- ½ teaspoon salt
- 2 garlic cloves, minced
- ½ teaspoon grated fresh gingerroot
- 3 tablespoons olive oil
- ⅛ teaspoon crushed red pepper flakes

1. Place Broccolini and salt in a large skillet; cover with water. Bring to a boil. Reduce heat; cover and simmer for 5-7 minutes or until tender. Drain well. Remove and keep warm.
2. In the same skillet, saute the garlic and ginger in oil for 1 minute. Add Broccolini and the pepper flakes; saute for 1-2 minutes or until heated through.

top tip | Broccolini Basics

Broccolini is the trademarked name of the hybrid vegetable that's a cross between broccoli and Chinese kale. It's also called baby broccoli. The long, slender stalks are topped with small buds that resemble a miniature broccoli head. The flavor is slightly sweet with a subtle peppery taste. Broccolini is rich in vitamins A and C, iron, fiber and potassium.

"We turned our favorite summertime treat into an elegant Christmas-season dessert with a touch of tender coconut cake and a sauce that will make you pucker up for more."

—TASTE OF HOME TEST KITCHEN

FAST FIX Coconut Cranberry
Shortcakes

PREP/TOTAL TIME: 30 MIN. **MAKES:** 9 SERVINGS

 3 **cups all-purpose flour**
 ⅓ **cup sugar**
 4 **teaspoons baking powder**
 1 **teaspoon salt**
 2 **cups coconut milk**

TOPPING

 1 **package (12 ounces) fresh or frozen**
    cranberries
 1 **cup sugar**
 ½ **cup coconut milk**
 ½ **cup cranberry juice**
    Whipped cream, flaked coconut and fresh
    mint leaves, optional

1. In a large bowl, combine the flour, sugar, baking powder and salt. Stir in coconut milk just until moistened.
2. Drop by ⅓ cupfuls 1 in. apart onto a greased baking sheet. Bake at 400° for 15-20 minutes or until lightly browned.
3. For topping, in a large saucepan, combine the cranberries, sugar, coconut milk and cranberry juice. Cook over medium heat until the berries pop, about 15 minutes.
4. Just before serving, cut shortcakes in half horizontally. Place bottoms on dessert plates; top with half of cranberry mixture. Add tops and remaining cranberry mixture. Garnish with whipped cream, coconut and mint if desired.

Holiday Ham Menu

Apple Cider-Glazed Ham
PAGE 87

Merry Berry Salad
PAGE 87

Dijon Green Beans
PAGE 88

Overnight Honey-Wheat Rolls
PAGE 88

Gingered Strawberry Tart
PAGE 89

APPLE CIDER–GLAZED HAM

Apple Cider-Glazed Ham

When I wanted to try something new with our holiday ham, I created this cider glaze. Slightly sweet, it still has a kick.
—**REBECCA LAWARE** HILTON, NEW YORK

PREP: 15 MIN. **BAKE:** 2½ HOURS **MAKES:** 10 SERVINGS (1 CUP SAUCE)

- ½ fully cooked bone-in ham (6 to 7 pounds)
- 2 cups apple cider
- 1 cup honey
- ½ cup cider vinegar
- ¼ cup Dijon mustard
- 1 tablespoon butter
- 2 teaspoons chili powder
- ½ teaspoon apple pie spice

1. Place ham on a rack in a shallow roasting pan. Score the surface of the ham, making diamond shapes ½ in. deep. Cover and bake at 325° for 2 hours.

2. Meanwhile, in a saucepan, combine the cider, honey, vinegar and mustard; bring to a boil. Reduce heat; simmer, uncovered, for 15 minutes, stirring frequently. Stir in the butter, chili powder and apple pie spice. Set aside 1 cup for serving.

3. Cook the remaining sauce until thickened; spoon over ham. Bake, uncovered, 30-35 minutes longer or until a thermometer reads 140°. Warm reserved sauce; serve with ham.

FAST FIX Merry Berry Salad

Every fall and winter we go through a cranberry craze, and we love developing recipes that celebrate the season with a subtle twist.
—**TASTE OF HOME TEST KITCHEN**

PREP/TOTAL TIME: 20 MIN. **MAKES:** 10 SERVINGS

- 1 package (10 ounces) mixed salad greens
- 1 medium red apple, diced
- 1 medium green apple, diced
- 1 cup (4 ounces) shredded Parmesan cheese
- ½ cup dried cranberries
- ½ cup slivered almonds, toasted

DRESSING

- 1 cup fresh cranberries
- ½ cup sugar
- ½ cup cider vinegar
- ¼ cup thawed apple juice concentrate
- 1 teaspoon salt
- 1 teaspoon ground mustard
- 1 teaspoon grated onion
- 1 cup canola oil

1. In a large salad bowl, toss the first six ingredients.

2. In a blender, combine the cranberries, sugar, vinegar, apple juice concentrate, salt, mustard and onion; cover and process until blended. While processing, gradually add oil in a steady stream.

3. Drizzle desired amount of dressing over salad and toss to coat. Refrigerate any leftover dressing.

TRY THIS CRAFT

Holiday Ornament Centerpiece

This centerpiece can be easily assembled using simple holiday items you may already have in your home. Start with a shallow dish with a low lip. Arrange round ornaments of various sizes in the dish. Add little wrapped ornaments and a snowflake or two. For an elegant, monochromatic look, use all one color or add a pop of color with some small balls (like the red ones we used).

FAST FIX ▶ Dijon Green Beans

I love this recipe because it combines the freshness of green beans with a warm and tangy dressing, and it's ready in 20 minutes. I call them my warm-and-snappy beans.

—JANNINE FISK MALDEN, MASSACHUSETTS

PREP/TOTAL TIME: 20 MIN. **MAKES:** 10 SERVINGS

- 1½ pounds fresh green beans, trimmed
- 2 tablespoons red wine vinegar
- 2 tablespoons olive oil
- 2 teaspoons Dijon mustard
- ½ teaspoon salt
- ¼ teaspoon pepper
- 1 cup grape tomatoes, halved
- ½ small red onion, sliced
- 2 tablespoons grated Parmesan cheese

1. Place beans in a saucepan and cover with water. Bring to a boil. Cook, covered, for 10-15 minutes or until crisp-tender.
2. Meanwhile, whisk the vinegar, oil, mustard, salt and pepper in a small bowl. Drain beans; place in a large bowl. Add tomatoes and onion. Drizzle with dressing and toss to coat. Sprinkle with cheese.

MAKE AHEAD ▶ Overnight Honey-Wheat Rolls

This no-knead dough can be made the night before to save you time on the day of your holiday meal. But the best part is the hint of honey flavor.

—LISA VARNER EL PASO, TEXAS

PREP: 30 MIN. + CHILLING **BAKE:** 10 MIN.
MAKES: 1½ DOZEN

- 1 package (¼ ounce) active dry yeast
- 1¼ cups warm water (110° to 115°), divided
- 2 egg whites
- ⅓ cup honey
- ¼ cup canola oil
- 1 teaspoon salt
- 1½ cups whole wheat flour
- 2½ cups all-purpose flour
  Melted butter, optional

1. In a small bowl, dissolve yeast in ¼ cup warm water. In a large bowl, beat egg whites until foamy. Add the yeast mixture, honey, oil, salt, whole wheat flour and remaining water. Beat on medium speed for 3 minutes. Beat until smooth. Stir in enough all-purpose flour to form a soft dough (dough will be sticky). Cover and refrigerate overnight.
2. Punch dough down. Turn onto a floured surface; divide in half. Shape each portion into nine balls. To form knots, roll each ball into a 10-in. rope; tie into a knot. Tuck ends under.
3. Place rolls 2 in. apart on greased baking sheets. Cover and let rise until doubled, about 50 minutes.
4. Bake at 375° for 10-12 minutes or until golden brown. Brush with melted butter if desired.

> **When I came across this strawberry dessert recipe years ago, I knew I had to try it. I love trying and baking new things, and I especially like the elegance of this tart.**

—**MARIE RIZZIO** INTERLOCHEN, MICHIGAN

MAKE AHEAD ▸ Gingered Strawberry Tart

PREP: 35 MIN. + CHILLING **MAKES:** 8 SERVINGS

- 24 **gingersnap cookies (about 1 cup)**
- 2 **tablespoons plus ⅓ cup sugar, divided**
- ¼ **cup butter, melted**
- 2 **tablespoons cornstarch**
- 1 **teaspoon finely chopped crystallized ginger, optional**
- 3 **cups chopped fresh strawberries**
- ¼ **cup water**

TOPPING
- 2 **cups sliced fresh strawberries**
- 5 **tablespoons seedless strawberry jam**

1. In a food processor, combine the gingersnaps, 2 tablespoons sugar and butter. Cover and process until blended. Press onto the bottom and up the sides of a 9-in. fluted tart pan with a removable bottom; set aside.

2. In a large saucepan, combine the cornstarch, ginger if desired and remaining sugar. Stir in chopped strawberries and water. Bring to a boil; cook and stir for 2 minutes. Reduce heat; simmer, uncovered, for 4-6 minutes or until thickened. Cool for 30 minutes. Pour into crust. Cover and refrigerate 2 hours or until set.

3. Arrange sliced berries over filling. In a small microwave-safe bowl, heat jam on high for 15-20 seconds or until pourable; brush over berries.

Make Ahead: *Prepare steps 1 and 2 of tart up to 2 days in advance. Store in refrigerator. Just before serving, proceed with step 3.*

top tip ▸ Prevent Soggy Tart Crusts

Brush tart crusts with melted jelly before layering with fruit. This seals the crusts and keeps juices from absorbing.

Stellar Tenderloin Menu

GOAT CHEESE & PEAR STUFFED TENDERLOIN

Goat Cheese & Pear Stuffed Tenderloin

I think this recipe is awesome because the flavors don't compete, they complement. Pears provide a bit of sweetness to the stuffing for beef tenderloin and balance the arugula and goat cheese.

—CINDIE HARAS BOCA RATON, FLORIDA

PREP: 40 MIN. **BAKE:** 40 MIN. + STANDING
MAKES: 8 SERVINGS (¾ CUP SAUCE)

- 2 medium pears, peeled and sliced
- 1 tablespoon butter
- 1 beef tenderloin roast (2½ pounds)
- 1 cup fresh arugula or baby spinach
- ½ cup crumbled goat cheese
- 1 tablespoon plus 1 teaspoon each minced fresh parsley, basil and tarragon
- 1 tablespoon olive oil
- ⅛ teaspoon salt
- ⅛ teaspoon pepper

SAUCE

- 4 shallots, finely chopped
- 2 teaspoons butter
- ½ cup sherry
- ½ cup reduced-sodium beef broth
- 2 tablespoons minced fresh tarragon
- 2 teaspoons cornstarch
- 2 teaspoons cold water

1. In a large skillet, saute pears in butter until tender.
2. Cut a lengthwise slit down the center of the tenderloin to within ½ in. of bottom. Open tenderloin so it lies flat. On each half, make another lengthwise slit down the center to within ½ in. of bottom; open roast and cover with plastic wrap. Flatten to ½-in. thickness. Remove plastic.
3. Spread the pears, arugula, cheese and herbs over meat to within 1 in. of edge. Roll up jelly-roll style, starting with a long side. Tie the roast at 1½-inch intervals with kitchen string.
4. Place on a rack in a shallow roasting pan. Combine the oil, salt and pepper; rub over roast. Bake at 425° for 40-50 minutes or until meat reaches desired doneness (for medium-rare, a thermometer should read 145°; medium, 160°; well-done, 170°). Let stand for 15 minutes before slicing.
5. In a small saucepan, saute shallots in butter until tender. Add sherry; cook over low heat for 4 minutes. Add broth and tarragon. Combine cornstarch and water until smooth; gradually stir into the pan. Bring to a boil; cook and stir for 1 minute or until thickened. Serve with beef.

MAKE AHEAD ▶ Bacon Caesar Salad

Family and friends always say my Caesar salad rivals any restaurant version. The addition of bacon is a little untraditional, but it lends a slightly smoky flavor and makes it unique.

—SHARON TIPTON WINTER GARDEN, FLORIDA

PREP/TOTAL TIME: 20 MIN. **MAKES:** 12 SERVINGS (¾ CUP EACH)

- 2 cups cubed day-old bread
- 2 tablespoons olive oil
- 3 garlic cloves, sliced

DRESSING

- ½ cup olive oil
- ¼ cup lemon juice
- 1 tablespoon Dijon mustard
- 3 garlic cloves, minced
- 1½ teaspoons anchovy paste
-   Dash pepper

SALAD

- 1 large bunch romaine, torn
- 4 bacon strips, cooked and crumbled
- ½ cup shredded Parmesan cheese

1. In a large skillet, cook bread cubes in oil over medium heat for 4-5 minutes or until golden brown, stirring frequently. Add garlic; cook 1 minute longer. Remove to paper towels; cool.
2. For dressing, in a small bowl, whisk the oil, lemon juice, mustard, garlic, anchovy paste and pepper. In a serving bowl, combine romaine and bacon. Drizzle with dressing; toss to coat. Sprinkle with croutons and cheese.

Make Ahead Note: *Prepare the croutons 1 to 2 days in advance and store in an airtight container.*

Baked Sweet Onions

Baking enhances the natural sweetness of my family's favorite Vidalia onions. Perfect alongside beef entrees, this side dish has a taste that's similar to French onion soup.
—**ANN BAKER** TEXARKANA, TEXAS

PREP: 25 MIN. **BAKE:** 40 MIN. **MAKES:** 8 SERVINGS

- 8 **large sweet onions, peeled**
- ½ **cup butter, melted**
- ½ **cup Burgundy wine or beef broth**
- 8 **teaspoons beef bouillon granules**
- 1 **teaspoon dried thyme**
- 1 **teaspoon pepper**
- 1½ **cups shredded Swiss cheese**

1. Cut each onion into six wedges to within ½ in. of the bottom. Place each onion on a piece of heavy-duty foil (about 12 in. square).
2. In a small bowl, combine the butter, wine, bouillon, thyme and pepper. Spoon over onions; sprinkle with cheese. Fold foil around each onion and seal tightly. Place on a baking sheet. Bake at 425° for 40-45 minutes or until onions are tender. Open foil carefully to allow steam to escape.

FAST FIX Garlic Roasted Broccoli

Balsamic vinegar's sweet-tart flavor enhances roasted broccoli spears seasoned with garlic. You can conveniently pop this dish into the oven while a beef roast or turkey is resting.
—**NELLA PARKER** HERSEY, MICHIGAN

PREP/TOTAL TIME: 30 MIN. **MAKES:** 8 SERVINGS

- 2 **bunches broccoli, cut into spears**
- ⅓ **cup olive oil**
- 4 **garlic cloves, minced**
- ½ **teaspoon salt**
- ¼ **teaspoon pepper**
- 2 **tablespoons balsamic vinegar**

1. Place broccoli in a greased 15-in. x 10-in. x 1-in. baking pan. Combine the oil, garlic, salt and pepper; drizzle over broccoli and toss to coat.
2. Bake, uncovered, at 425° for 15-20 minutes or until tender, stirring occasionally. Drizzle with vinegar.

Dressed-Up Candle

Add a little flair to a plain pillar candle by embellishing it with costume jewelry.

Raid your jewelry box for long chain or beaded necklaces. Using T-pins or U-pins to hold them in place, wrap several necklaces around a large pillar candle. (The pins are available at craft stores.) Mix and match colors and textures as desired to create a unique focal point.

MAKE AHEAD ▶ Cranberry-Champagne Granita

After serving a heavy holiday meal, I like to offer a light, refreshing dessert, such as this gorgeous granita. Because it can be made ahead, there's no last-minute fuss.
—**JOYCE GEMPERLEIN** ROCKVILLE, MARYLAND

PREP: 20 MIN. + FREEZING **MAKES:** 4 CUPS

- 3½ teaspoons grated lime peel
- 1¾ cups unsweetened cranberry juice
- 1½ cups sugar
- 1¾ cups champagne

1. Place the lime peel in a small saucepan and cover with water. Bring to a boil. Cook and stir for 1 minute. Drain and discard liquid; set the peel aside.
2. In a small saucepan, bring cranberry juice and sugar to a boil. Cook and stir until sugar is dissolved. Remove from the heat; stir in champagne and lime peel. Transfer to a 13-in. x 9-in. x 2-in. dish; cool to room temperature. Freeze for 1 hour; stir with a fork. Freeze 2-3 hours longer or until completely frozen, stirring every 30 minutes.
3. Stir granita with a fork just before serving; spoon into dessert dishes.
Make Ahead Note: *While best served the same day, the granita can be made 1 to 2 days in advance and stored in the freezer.*

Tasty Turkey Meal

TURKEY WITH APPLE STUFFING

Turkey with Apple Stuffing

Complementing this golden bird is a well-seasoned bread stuffing that gets sweetness from apples and raisins. It can easily become a staple on anyone's holiday menu.

—NANCY ZIMMERMAN CAPE MAY COURT HOUSE, NEW JERSEY

PREP: 20 MIN. **BAKE:** 3¾ HOURS + STANDING **MAKES:** 10-12 SERVINGS

- 1½ cups chopped celery
- ¾ cup chopped onion
- ¾ cup butter, cubed
- 9 cups day-old cubed whole wheat bread
- 3 cups finely chopped apples
- ¾ cup raisins
- 1½ teaspoons salt
- 1½ teaspoons dried thyme
- ½ teaspoon rubbed sage
- ¼ teaspoon pepper
- 1 turkey (14 to 16 pounds)
  Additional butter, melted

1. In a Dutch oven, saute celery and onion in butter until tender. Remove from the heat; stir in the bread cubes, apples, raisins, salt, thyme, sage and pepper.

2. Just before baking, loosely stuff turkey with 4 cups stuffing. Place remaining stuffing in a greased 2-qt. baking dish; refrigerate until ready to bake. Skewer turkey openings; tie drumsticks together. Place breast side up on a rack in a roasting pan. Brush with melted butter.

3. Bake, uncovered, at 325° for 3¾ to 4 hours or until a thermometer reads 180° for the turkey and 165° for the stuffing, basting occasionally with pan drippings. (Cover loosely with foil if turkey browns too quickly.)

4. Bake additional stuffing, covered, for 20-30 minutes. Uncover; bake 10 minutes longer or until browned. Cover turkey and let stand for 20 minutes before removing stuffing and carving turkey. If desired, thicken pan drippings for gravy.

Editor's Note: *Stuffing may be prepared as directed and baked separately in a greased 3-qt. baking dish. Cover and bake at 325° for 30 minutes. Uncover and bake 10 minutes longer or until a thermometer reads 165°.*

Gorgonzola Pear Salad

Roasted pears served warm on top of spring greens make this salad a memorable first course.

—MELINDA SINGER TARZANA, CALIFORNIA

PREP: 15 MIN. **BAKE:** 25 MIN. **MAKES:** 12 SERVINGS

- 6 medium pears, quartered and cored
- ⅓ cup olive oil
- 1 teaspoon salt
- 12 cups spring mix salad greens
- 4 plum tomatoes, seeded and chopped
- 2 cups crumbled Gorgonzola cheese
- 1 cup pecan halves, toasted
- 1½ cups balsamic vinaigrette

1. Place pears in ungreased 13-in. x 9-in. baking dish. Drizzle with oil and sprinkle with salt. Bake, uncovered, at 400° for 25-30 minutes, basting occasionally with cooking juices.

2. In a large salad bowl, combine the greens, tomatoes, cheese and pecans. Drizzle with dressing and toss to coat. Divide among 12 serving plates; top each with two pear pieces.

Almond Cranberry Squash Bake

We love sharing this dish so much that when my husband and I visit family in North Dakota, I bring along the ingredients to make it. It gets compliments every time.

—RONICA BROWNSON MADISON, WISCONSIN

PREP: 20 MIN. **BAKE:** 50 MIN. **MAKES:** 8 SERVINGS

4 cups mashed cooked butternut squash
4 tablespoons butter, softened, divided
½ teaspoon salt
½ teaspoon ground cinnamon
¼ teaspoon ground allspice
¼ teaspoon ground nutmeg
1 can (14 ounces) whole-berry cranberry sauce
½ cup sliced almonds
¼ cup packed brown sugar

1. In a large bowl, combine the squash, 2 tablespoons butter, salt, cinnamon, allspice and nutmeg. Transfer to a greased 2-qt. baking dish. Stir cranberry sauce until softened; spoon over squash.
2. Combine the almonds, brown sugar and remaining butter; sprinkle over cranberry sauce.
3. Bake, uncovered, at 350° for 50-60 minutes or until golden and bubbly.

FAST FIX ◗ Broccoli Saute

I came up with this recipe while looking for a different way to cook broccoli that was lower in fat and sodium.

—JIM MACNEAL WATERLOO, NEW YORK

PREP/TOTAL TIME: 15 MIN. **MAKES:** 10 SERVINGS

1 cup chopped onion
1 cup julienned sweet red pepper
¼ cup olive oil
12 cups fresh broccoli florets
1⅓ cups water
3 teaspoons minced garlic
½ teaspoon salt
½ teaspoon pepper

In a Dutch oven, saute onion and red pepper in oil for 2-3 minutes or until crisp-tender. Stir in the broccoli, water, garlic, salt and pepper. Cover and cook over medium heat for 5-6 minutes or until broccoli is crisp-tender.

Truffle Torte

A small slice of this rich and fudgelike torte will go a long way to satisfy sweet tooths. Chocolate lovers will thank you.

—MARY CHOATE SPRING HILL, FLORIDA

PREP: 35 MIN. **BAKE:** 30 MIN. + CHILLING **MAKES:** 18 SERVINGS

¾ **cup butter, cubed**	**GANACHE**
8 **ounces semisweet chocolate, chopped**	4 **ounces semisweet chocolate, chopped**
6 **eggs**	½ **cup heavy whipping cream**
¾ **cup sugar**	2 **tablespoons butter**
1 **teaspoon vanilla extract**	**GARNISH**
¾ **cup ground pecans**	2 **ounces white baking chocolate**
¼ **cup all-purpose flour**	¾ **cup finely chopped pecans**

1. Line the bottom of a greased 9-in. springform pan with waxed paper; grease the paper and set aside.

2. In a microwave, melt butter and chocolate; stir until smooth. Cool. In a large bowl, beat eggs until frothy; gradually add sugar, beating for 4-5 minutes or until mixture triples in volume. Gradually beat in chocolate mixture and vanilla. Combine pecans and flour; fold into batter. Pour into prepared pan.

3. Bake at 350° for 30-35 minutes or until cake springs back when lightly touched. Cool on a wire rack for 15 minutes. Run a knife around edge of pan; remove sides of pan. Invert cake onto wire rack; carefully remove pan bottom and waxed paper. Cool completely.

4. For ganache, place chocolate in a small bowl. In a small saucepan, bring cream just to a boil. Pour over chocolate; whisk until smooth. Stir in butter.

5. Transfer to a small bowl; cover and refrigerate until mixture reaches spreading consistency, stirring occasionally. Place cake on a serving plate. Pour ganache over cake and quickly spread to edges.

6. In a microwave, melt white chocolate; stir until smooth. Transfer to a heavy-duty resealable plastic bag; cut a small hole in a corner of bag.

7. Pipe thin horizontal lines 1 in. apart over ganache. Use a sharp knife to draw right angles across the piped lines. Press pecans onto side of torte. Cover and refrigerate for 30 minutes or until set.

TRY THIS CRAFT

Custom Place Cards

A cute, bow-topped name card is a thoughtful accent for dinner guests. Fold a 3½-in. x 4-in. piece of card stock in half to form a 3½-in. x 2-in. rectangle. Open the card; use a craft knife to cut a ½-in.-long slit through the center of the fold.

With an embossing pen, write dinner guest's name on the card. Sprinkle with embossing powder; melt powder with a heat gun.

Wrap a 22-in. length of organza (sheer) ribbon around a 1-in.-wide piece of cardboard once. Tie in a bow. Slip the bow off the cardboard piece. Thread the bottom loop of the ribbon through the slit in the card to hold the bow in place.

Scrumptious Pork Loin Spread

SAVORY PORK LOIN ROAST, TENDER CRESCENT ROLLS & APPLE RYE DRESSING

Savory Pork Loin Roast

I like to give this tender roast a double boost of flavor. First it's seasoned with an herb rub, then it's paired with a creamy horseradish gravy.

—DEETTA RASMUSSEN FORT MADISON, IOWA

PREP: 15 MIN. **BAKE:** 1 HOUR 15 MIN. + STANDING
MAKES: 8 SERVINGS (2 CUPS SAUCE)

- ¼ **cup reduced-sodium soy sauce**
- 6 **garlic cloves, minced**
- 1 **tablespoon each minced fresh basil, rosemary and sage**
- 1 **tablespoon ground mustard**
- 1 **whole pork loin roast (3½ pounds), trimmed**
- 1 **cup water**
- 8 **green onions, chopped**
- 2 **tablespoons butter**
- ¼ **cup brown gravy mix**
- 2½ **cups beef broth**
- 1¼ **cups sour cream**
- 2 **tablespoons prepared horseradish**

1. In a small bowl, combine the soy sauce, garlic, herbs and mustard; rub over roast. Place on a rack in a shallow roasting pan. Pour water into the pan.

2. Bake, uncovered, at 350° for 1¼ to 1½ hours or until a thermometer reads 145°. Let stand for 15 minutes before slicing.

3. Meanwhile, in a large saucepan, saute onions in butter until tender. Combine gravy mix and broth until smooth; stir into the pan. Bring to a boil. Reduce heat; cook and stir until thickened. Stir in sour cream and horseradish; heat through (do not boil). Serve with pork.

Tender Crescent Rolls

We have a large holiday meal with several soups and breads, but these rolls are a favorite. Nothing compares to the aroma and from-scratch flair of the crescents.

—BONNIE MYERS CALLAWAY, NEBRASKA

PREP: 45 MIN. + RISING **BAKE:** 10 MIN./BATCH **MAKES:** 4 DOZEN

- 2 **envelopes (¼ ounce each) active dry yeast**
- 1 **cup warm water (110° to 115°)**
- 1 **cup warm 2% milk (110° to 115°)**
- 3 **eggs**
- ½ **cup sugar**
- 6 **tablespoons shortening**
- 1 **teaspoon salt**
- 6½ **to 7 cups all-purpose flour**

1. In a large bowl, dissolve yeast in warm water. Add the milk, eggs, sugar, shortening, salt and 3 cups flour. Beat on medium speed for 3 minutes or until smooth. Stir in enough remaining flour to form a soft dough (dough will be sticky).

2. Turn onto a floured surface; knead until smooth and elastic, about 6-8 minutes. Place in a greased bowl, turning once to grease top. Cover and let rise in a warm place until doubled, about 1 hour.

3. Punch dough down. Turn onto a lightly floured surface; divide into four portions. Roll each portion into a 12-in. circle; cut each circle into 12 wedges. Roll up wedges from the wide end and place point side down 2 in. apart on greased baking sheets. Curve ends to form a crescent shape.

4. Cover and let rise until doubled, about 30 minutes. Bake at 350° for 8-10 minutes or until golden brown. Remove to wire racks.

TRY THIS CRAFT

No-Fuss Napkin Rings

Instead of napkin rings, try these sparkling ideas.

- Use a wreath made of miniature sleigh bells strung on a wire.
- Tuck a favorite holiday photo or wish inside a plastic key chain and tie a napkin on with a bow. Have the key chains double as place cards by writing your guests' names inside of them.
- Wrap beaded ribbon around a napkin then stuff the ends into a small seasonal cookie cutter.

Apple Rye Dressing

I've been a professional cook for years, and this is one of my favorite dressing recipes. I think the apple juice and rye bread are the key ingredients.

—**JUDY BEEN** WAUKESHA, WISCONSIN

PREP: 30 MIN. **BAKE:** 50 MIN. **MAKES:** 12 SERVINGS

- 1   **pound bulk pork sausage**
- 4   **celery ribs, finely chopped**
- 2   **large onions, finely chopped**
- 1   **loaf (1 pound) rye bread, cubed**
- ½   **cup butter, melted**
- 2   **teaspoons seasoned salt**
- 3   **cups chopped tart apples**
- 1   **cup chopped walnuts**
- 1   **cup raisins**
- 1   **cup unsweetened apple juice**
- ½   **cup water**

1. In a large skillet, cook the sausage, celery and onions over medium heat until meat is no longer pink; drain and set aside.

2. In a large bowl, toss the bread cubes with butter and the seasoned salt. Transfer to a 15-in. x 10-in. x 1-in. baking pan. Bake, uncovered, at 300° for 10-15 minutes or until lightly toasted.

3. In a large bowl, combine the sausage mixture, apples, walnuts, raisins, apple juice and water. Add toasted bread cubes; stir to combine.

4. Transfer to a greased 13-in. x 9-in. baking dish. Cover and bake at 350° for 50-60 minutes or until browned.

MAKE AHEAD Colorful Gazpacho Salad

I was first introduced to this salad by a friend more than 10 years ago. The combination of tomatoes, jicama and cilantro is a refreshing way to kick off a holiday meal.

—**BRENDA HOFFMAN** STANTON, MICHIGAN

PREP: 20 MIN. + CHILLING **MAKES:** 8 SERVINGS

- 5   **medium tomatoes, seeded and chopped**
- 1   **cup chopped peeled cucumber**
- ¾   **cup chopped red onion**
- 1   **small sweet red pepper, chopped**
- ½   **cup fresh or frozen corn**
- 1   **tablespoon lime juice**
- 1   **tablespoon red wine vinegar**
- 2   **teaspoons water**
- 2   **garlic cloves, minced**
- 1   **teaspoon olive oil**
- ¼   **teaspoon salt**
- ¼   **teaspoon pepper**
- ⅛   **teaspoon crushed red pepper flakes**
- 8   **cups torn romaine**
- 1   **cup diced peeled jicama**
- ½   **cup minced fresh cilantro**

1. In a large bowl, combine tomatoes, cucumber, onion, red pepper and corn. In a small bowl, whisk the lime juice, vinegar, water, garlic, oil, salt, pepper and pepper flakes. Drizzle over tomato mixture; toss to coat. Refrigerate until chilled.

2. Just before serving, combine the romaine, jicama and cilantro. Place 1 cup on each of eight salad plates; top each with ⅓ cup tomato mixture.

Cheese-Topped Roasted Vegetables

Looking for a crowd-pleasing way to serve veggies? Try this colorful medley. It features three kinds of cheese and fresh herbs.
—**MEREDITH HOLMAN** SILVER SPRING, MARYLAND

PREP: 15 MIN. **BAKE:** 45 MIN. **MAKES:** 8 SERVINGS

- 3 **small red potatoes, quartered**
- 2 **medium carrots, cut into ½-inch slices**
- 1 **small onion, cut into wedges**
- 3 **teaspoons olive oil, divided**
- ¼ **teaspoon salt, divided**
- ¼ **teaspoon pepper, divided**
- 1 **large zucchini, cut into ½-inch pieces**
- 1 **large sweet red pepper, cut into 1-inch pieces**
- 6 **large fresh mushrooms, quartered**
- 2 **garlic cloves, minced**
- ½ **cup shredded cheddar cheese**
- ½ **cup shredded part-skim mozzarella cheese**
- 1 **tablespoon grated Parmesan cheese**
- 1 **teaspoon minced fresh basil**
- 1 **teaspoon minced fresh oregano**

1. Place the potatoes, carrots and onion in a large resealable plastic bag. Add 1½ teaspoons oil, ⅛ teaspoon salt and ⅛ teaspoon pepper; turn to coat.

2. Place mixture in single layer in greased 15-in. x 10-in. x 1-in. baking pan (set bag aside). Bake at 425° for 20 minutes.

3. Add the zucchini, red pepper, mushrooms and garlic to the reserved bag. Add the remaining oil, salt and pepper; turn to coat. Stir into potato mixture.

4. Bake 25-30 minutes longer or until vegetables are tender. Transfer to serving bowl. Sprinkle with cheeses and herbs.

MAKE AHEAD ▸ Chocolate Mousse with Cranberry Sauce

I call this chocolate paté and like to serve it with a side of whipped cream. Its firm, fudgy texture cuts well, and the sweet-tart sauce makes a festive presentation.
—**BARBARA NOWAKOWSKI** NORTH TONAWANDA, NEW YORK

PREP: 45 MIN. + CHILLING **MAKES:** 10 SERVINGS (ABOUT 1 CUP SAUCE)

- 2 **cups (12 ounces) semisweet chocolate chips**
- ¼ **cup butter, cubed**
- 1 **egg yolk, lightly beaten**
- 1½ **cups heavy whipping cream, divided**
- ⅓ **cup light corn syrup**
- 1 **teaspoon vanilla extract**

CRANBERRY SAUCE

- ⅓ **cup cranberry juice**
- 1 **teaspoon lime juice**
- 1 **cup jellied cranberry sauce**

1. In a large microwave-safe bowl, melt chocolate chips and butter; stir until smooth. In a small heavy saucepan, combine the egg yolk, ¼ cup cream and corn syrup. Cook and stir over low heat until mixture reaches 160°, about 2 minutes.

2. Remove from the heat; stir into chocolate mixture. Refrigerate for 20 minutes or until cooled and slightly thickened, stirring occasionally. Line a 1-qt. bowl with plastic wrap; set aside.

3. In a large bowl, beat remaining cream until it begins to thicken. Add vanilla; beat until soft peaks form. Fold into chocolate mixture. Spoon into prepared bowl. Cover and refrigerate overnight.

4. Place the sauce ingredients in a blender; cover and process until smooth. Transfer to a small bowl; cover and refrigerate until serving.

5. Just before serving, invert mousse onto a platter; remove plastic wrap. Cut into wedges; serve with cranberry sauce.

CRAB MACARONI & CHEESE, PARMESAN POTATO BREADSTICK AND MUSHROOM SPINACH SALAD WITH CHEESE CROUTONS

Crab Macaroni & Cheese

Crab and mushrooms put a deliciously different spin on classic macaroni and cheese. It's an upscale casserole for special occasions...but my family could eat it every day!
—ANGELA OCHOA LAKE ELSINORE, CALIFORNIA

PREP: 45 MIN. **BAKE:** 15 MIN. **MAKES:** 10 SERVINGS

- 1 **package (16 ounces) elbow macaroni**
- 6 **baby portobello mushrooms**
- 2 **green onions, sliced**
- 1 **tablespoon plus ¼ cup butter, divided**
- ¼ **cup all-purpose flour**
- 1 **teaspoon ground mustard**
- 1 **teaspoon pepper**
- ½ **teaspoon salt**
- ¼ **teaspoon paprika**
- 2½ **cups half-and-half cream**
- 1½ **cups (6 ounces) shredded part-skim mozzarella cheese, divided**
- 1½ **cups (6 ounces) shredded medium cheddar cheese, divided**

TOPPING
- ½ **cup panko (Japanese) bread crumbs**
- 3 **tablespoons butter, melted**
- 1 **tablespoon dried basil**
- 1½ **pounds cooked snow crab legs, meat removed**
- 4 **thin slices Swiss cheese**
- ¼ **cup grated Parmesan cheese**

1. Cook macaroni according to package directions. Drain pasta and rinse in cold water.
2. Meanwhile, in a large skillet, saute mushrooms and onions in 1 tablespoon butter until tender; set aside.
3. In a large saucepan, melt remaining butter. Stir in the flour, mustard, pepper, salt and paprika until smooth; gradually add cream. Bring to a boil; cook and stir for 2 minutes or until thickened. Stir in ¾ cup each mozzarella and cheddar cheeses until blended. Remove from the heat; fold in macaroni.
4. In a small bowl, combine the bread crumbs, butter and basil. Transfer half of the macaroni mixture into a greased 13-in. x 9-in. baking dish. Layer with reserved mushroom mixture, remaining macaroni mixture, mozzarella and cheddar cheeses. Top with crab and Swiss cheese. Sprinkle with crumb mixture and Parmesan cheese.
5. Bake at 350° for 15-20 minutes or until golden brown. Let stand for 5 minutes before serving.

Parmesan Potato Breadsticks

More than 20 years ago, our son was looking through an old county fair cookbook and came across this recipe. I've made a few adjustments over time to get these soft and tender breadsticks.
—KATIE KOZIOLEK HARTLAND, MINNESOTA

PREP: 50 MIN. + RISING **BAKE:** 10 MIN. **MAKES:** 2 DOZEN

- 1 **tablespoon active dry yeast**
- 1½ **cups warm water (110° to 115°)**
- 6 **tablespoons mashed potato flakes**
- 6 **tablespoons butter, cubed**
- ¼ **cup sugar**
- 3 **tablespoons nonfat dry milk powder**
- ¾ **teaspoon salt**
- 4 **to 4½ cups all-purpose flour**
- 2 **tablespoons butter, melted**
- 1 **tablespoon grated Parmesan cheese**
- 2 **teaspoons sesame seeds**
- 1 **teaspoon poppy seeds**
- 1 **teaspoon kosher salt**

1. In a large bowl, dissolve yeast in warm water. Add potato flakes, butter, sugar, milk powder, salt and 2 cups flour. Beat until smooth. Stir in enough remaining flour to form stiff dough.
2. Turn onto a floured surface; knead until smooth and elastic, about 6-8 minutes. Place in a greased bowl, turning once to grease the top. Cover and let rise in a warm place until doubled, about 1 hour.
3. Punch dough down. Turn onto a lightly floured surface; divide into 24 pieces. Roll each into a 5-in. rope. Place 2 in. apart on greased baking sheets. Cover and let rise until doubled, about 30 minutes.
4. Brush with melted butter. Sprinkle with cheese, seeds and kosher salt. Bake at 375° for 10-12 minutes or until golden brown. Remove from pans to wire racks to cool.

top tip

Get a Quick Rise

Quick-rise yeast can be used instead, but remember, it does not need to be dissolved in water before mixing, and it requires only one rise. In place of the first rise, let dough rest, covered, for 10 minutes before shaping. Once shaped, the dough's rise should take about half the time listed in a recipe that calls for active dry yeast.

FAST FIX Mushroom Spinach Salad

PREP/TOTAL TIME: 20 MIN. **MAKES:** 12 SERVINGS

- 8 bacon strips, diced
- 1½ cups thinly sliced fresh mushrooms
- 1 medium red onion, thinly sliced
- ¼ cup balsamic vinegar
- 1 package (10 ounces) fresh spinach, torn
- ¼ cup chopped walnuts, toasted
- ¼ cup crumbled blue cheese
- 2 hard-cooked eggs, sliced

1. In a large skillet, cook bacon over medium heat until crisp. Using a slotted spoon, remove to paper towels to drain. Saute mushrooms and onion in drippings. Stir in vinegar.

2. In a large bowl, combine the spinach, walnuts, cheese and bacon; toss with mushroom mixture. Top with egg slices.

MAKE AHEAD Cheese Croutons

Hands down, these are the ultimate salad topper. Make a big batch and store leftovers in the freezer.
—**ANITA DELSIGNORE** YOUNGSTOWN, OHIO

PREP: 15 MIN. **BAKE:** 35 MIN. + COOLING **MAKES:** 4 CUPS

- 3 eggs
- 2 cups (8 ounces) shredded Swiss cheese
- ¼ cup all-purpose flour
- 2 tablespoons grated Romano cheese
- 1½ teaspoons Italian seasoning
- ¼ teaspoon baking powder

1. In a large bowl, beat eggs. In another bowl, combine the remaining ingredients; gradually add to eggs. Spread evenly into a parchment paper-lined 9-in. square baking pan.

2. Bake at 350° for 25-30 minutes or until lightly browned. Cool for 10 minutes before removing from pan; cut into 1-in. cubes. Increase temperature to 450°. Place cubes on an ungreased baking sheet. Bake 10 minutes longer, turning once. Transfer to a wire rack to cool completely.

Make Ahead Note: *Cooled croutons can be frozen and reheated in a 450° oven for 5 min.*

I had this salad at a restaurant one night and couldn't stop telling people about it. I love its richness and think it works as either a before-dinner salad or an entree.
—**DOLORES BRIGHAM** INGLEWOOD, CALIFORNIA

MAKE AHEAD ▶ Ginger Chocolate Temptation

Chocolate-covered candied ginger is one of my favorite treats, so this recipe has my name all over it! Every bite of this creamy custard is rich, smooth and decadent.

—ELISE LALOR ISSAQUAH, WASHINGTON

PREP: 10 MIN. **COOK:** 15 MIN. + CHILLING **MAKES:** 12 SERVINGS

- 2 **cups heavy whipping cream**
- 1 **vanilla bean**
- 8 **ounces bittersweet chocolate, chopped**
- 6 **egg yolks, lightly beaten**
- ¼ **cup minced crystallized ginger, divided**
  Heavy whipping cream, whipped, optional

1. Place cream in a small heavy saucepan. Split vanilla bean and scrape seeds into cream. Add bean. Bring cream mixture to a boil. Reduce heat; simmer, uncovered, for 5 minutes. Discard vanilla bean.

2. Stir in chocolate until melted. Stir ½ cup chocolate mixture into egg yolks; return all to the pan. Cook and stir until mixture reaches 160° and coats the back of a metal spoon. Remove from the heat. Stir in 2 tablespoons ginger.

3. Pour into 12 demitasse or espresso cups. Refrigerate for at least 1 hour. Just before serving, garnish with remaining ginger and, if desired, whipped cream.

TRY THIS CRAFT

Birch Bark Centerpiece

We found 8-in.-high birch bark cylinders online and cut them in half crosswise to make two 4-in.-high cylinders. Insert an 8-in. Styrofoam circle inside each cylinder.

(You could also glue a sheet of birch bark around the Styrofoam circles. If you can't find birch bark cylinders or sheets, use birch bark-patterned scrapbook paper.)

Place a 9-in.-tall pillar candle in the center of each Styrofoam circle. Add green reindeer moss, pinecones and bunches of small artificial green berries around each candle.

If desired, lay a sheet of birch bark or birch bark scrapbook paper on the table. Set the candle-filled birch bark cylinders on top. Place a third pillar candle on the sheet; add berries and pinecones around base of the candle.

GARLIC PORK ROAST, PAGE 113

Merry Entrees

108

115

110

"Beef sweetened by onions makes this a recipe you'll repeat. Fix a double batch—serving half tonight and freezing the rest. It's great with mashed potatoes."

—**LINDA STEMEN** MONROEVILLE, INDIANA

Beef Tips & Caramelized Onion Casserole

PREP: 40 MIN. **BAKE:** 1½ HOURS **MAKES:** 8 SERVINGS

- 4 **pounds beef sirloin tip roast, cut into 1-inch cubes**
- ½ **teaspoon salt**
- ½ **teaspoon pepper**
- 2 **tablespoons olive oil**
- 4 **large sweet onions, halved and thinly sliced**
- 3 **tablespoons butter**
- 4 **garlic cloves, minced**
- ⅔ **cup all-purpose flour**
- 2 **cans (10½ ounces each) condensed beef consomme, undiluted**
- 1 **can (14½ ounces) reduced-sodium beef broth**
- 2 **tablespoons Worcestershire sauce**
- 2 **bay leaves**
- ½ **cup heavy whipping cream**
- 8 **slices French bread (½ inch thick), toasted**
- 1 **cup (4 ounces) shredded part-skim mozzarella cheese**

1. Sprinkle beef with salt and pepper. In a large skillet, brown meat in oil in batches; drain. Transfer to a greased 13-in. x 9-in. baking dish.

2. In the same skillet, cook onions in butter over medium-low heat for 25-30 minutes or until golden brown, stirring occasionally. Add garlic; cook 1 minute longer.

3. Stir in flour until blended; gradually add consomme and broth. Stir in Worcestershire sauce and bay leaves. Bring to boil; cook and stir for 1 minute or until thickened. Pour over beef.

4. Cover and bake at 325° for 1 hour. Carefully stir in cream; discard bay leaves. Bake, uncovered, 25-35 minutes longer or until meat is tender. Place toast over beef mixture; sprinkle with cheese. Bake for 5 minutes or until cheese is melted.

Cherry-Stuffed Pork Chops

Grilled pork chops have a lovely stuffing of couscous, cherries and seasonings in this quick and elegant main dish. Served with a salad, it's perfect for special occasions, but speedy enough for everyday family suppers.

—TASTE OF HOME TEST KITCHEN

PREP: 20 MIN. **GRILL:** 20 MIN. **MAKES:** 6 SERVINGS

- 1 **package (5.6 ounces) couscous with toasted pine nuts**
- 6 **boneless pork loin chops (1 inch thick and 6 ounces each)**
- ½ **cup dried cherries**
- 1 **tablespoon brown sugar**
- 1 **tablespoon butter, melted**
- ½ **teaspoon minced fresh gingerroot**
- ½ **teaspoon garlic powder**
- ½ **teaspoon pepper**

1. Prepare couscous according to package directions. Meanwhile, cut a deep slit in each pork chop, forming a pocket. Stir the cherries, brown sugar, butter and ginger into prepared couscous. Stuff ⅓ cup into each chop; secure with toothpicks. Sprinkle with garlic powder and pepper.

2. Grill pork chops, covered, over medium heat for 10-12 minutes on each side or until a thermometer reads 160°. Discard toothpicks.

Individual Beef Wellingtons

This recipe has been tweaked to perfection with truly stunning results. A savory mushroom-wine sauce is draped over a golden pastry in this specialty.

—TASTE OF HOME TEST KITCHEN

PREP: 30 MIN. **BAKE:** 25 MIN. **MAKES:** 6 SERVINGS

- 6 **beef tenderloin steaks (1½ to 2 inches thick and 8 ounces each)**
- 4 **tablespoons butter, divided**
- 3 **sheets frozen puff pastry, thawed**
- 1 **egg, lightly beaten**
- ½ **pound sliced fresh mushrooms**
- ¼ **cup chopped shallots**
- 2 **tablespoons all-purpose flour**
- 1 **can (10½ ounces) condensed beef consomme, undiluted**
- 3 **tablespoons port wine**
- 2 **teaspoons minced fresh thyme**

1. In a large skillet, brown steaks in 2 tablespoons butter for 2-3 minutes on each side. Remove and keep warm.

2. On a lightly floured surface, roll each puff pastry sheet into a 14-in. x 9½-in. rectangle. Cut each into two 7-in. squares (discard scraps). Place a steak in the center of each square. Lightly brush pastry edges with water. Bring opposite corners of pastry over steak; pinch seams to seal tightly. Cut four small slits in top of pastry.

3. Place in a greased 15-in. x 10-in. x 1-in. baking pan. Brush with egg. Bake at 400° for 25-30 minutes or until pastry is golden brown and meat reaches desired doneness (for medium-rare, a thermometer should read 145°; medium, 160°; well-done, 170°).

4. Meanwhile, in the same skillet, saute the mushrooms and shallots in remaining butter for 3-5 minutes or until tender. Combine flour and consomme until smooth; stir into mushroom mixture. Bring to a boil; cook and stir for 2 minutes or until thickened. Stir in wine and thyme. Cook and stir 2 minutes longer. Serve with beef.

Turkey Roulades

The filling in this recipe goes so well with turkey. I love the hint of lemon and the savory combo of apples, mushrooms and spinach—and the bread-crumb coating adds a nice crunch.

—KARI WHEATON SOUTH BELOIT, ILLINOIS

PREP: 40 MIN. **BAKE:** 40 MIN. **MAKES:** 8 SERVINGS

- 1 cup diced peeled tart apple
- 1 cup chopped fresh mushrooms
- ½ cup finely chopped onion
- 2 teaspoons olive oil
- 5 ounces frozen chopped spinach, thawed and squeezed dry
- 2 tablespoons lemon juice
- 2 teaspoons grated lemon peel
- ¾ teaspoon salt, divided
- Pinch ground nutmeg
- 4 turkey breast tenderloins (8 ounces each)
- ¼ teaspoon pepper
- 1 egg, lightly beaten
- ½ cup seasoned bread crumbs

1. In a large nonstick skillet coated with cooking spray, saute the apple, mushrooms and onion in oil until tender. Remove from the heat; stir in the spinach, lemon juice, lemon peel, ¼ teaspoon salt and nutmeg.

2. Make a lengthwise slit down the center of each tenderloin to within ½ in. of bottom. Open tenderloins so they lie flat; cover with plastic wrap. Flatten to ¼-in. thickness. Remove plastic; sprinkle turkey with pepper and remaining salt.

3. Spread spinach mixture over tenderloins to within 1 in. of edges. Roll up jelly-roll style, starting with a short side; tie with kitchen string. Place egg and bread crumbs in separate shallow bowls. Dip roulades in egg, then roll in crumbs.

4. Place roulades in an 11-in. x 7-in. baking pan coated with cooking spray. Bake, uncovered, at 375° for 40-45 minutes or until a thermometer reads 170°. Let stand for 5 minutes before slicing.

Seafood en Croute

When I got married, this recipe was handed down to me from family overseas. It looks difficult, but it's really quite easy. Now that I have children, I don't have time to spend all day in the kitchen, so I choose my "recipes to impress" carefully.

—ALEXANDRA ARMITAGE NOTTINGHAM, NEW HAMPSHIRE

PREP: 25 MIN. **BAKE:** 20 MIN. **MAKES:** 4 SERVINGS

- 1 package (17.3 ounces) frozen puff pastry, thawed
- 4 salmon fillets (6 ounces each)
- ½ pound fresh sea or bay scallops, finely chopped
- ⅓ cup heavy whipping cream
- 2 green onions, chopped
- 1 tablespoon minced fresh parsley
- ½ teaspoon minced fresh dill
- ¼ teaspoon salt
- ⅛ teaspoon pepper
- 1 egg white
- 1 egg, lightly beaten

1. On a lightly floured surface, roll each pastry sheet into a 12-in. x 10-in. rectangle. Cut each sheet into four 6-in. x 5-in. rectangles. Place a salmon fillet in the center of four rectangles.

2. In a large bowl, combine the scallops, cream, onions, parsley, dill, salt and pepper. In a small bowl, beat egg white on medium speed until soft peaks form; fold into scallop mixture. Spoon about ½ cup over each salmon fillet.

3. Top each with a pastry rectangle and crimp to seal. With a small sharp knife, cut several slits in the top. Place in a greased 15-in. x 10-in. x 1-in. baking pan; brush with egg.

4. Bake at 400° for 20-25 minutes or until a thermometer reads 160°.

Baked Lobster Tails

In this recipe, three lobster tails are cut in half to feed six people. It's exceptional served alongside steak.
—**TASTE OF HOME TEST KITCHEN**

PREP: 15 MIN. **BAKE:** 20 MIN. **MAKES:** 6 SERVINGS

- 3 **lobster tails (8 to 10 ounces each)**
- 1 **cup water**
- 1 **tablespoon minced fresh parsley**
- ⅛ **teaspoon salt**
  Dash pepper
- 1 **tablespoon butter, melted**
- 2 **tablespoons lemon juice**
  Lemon wedges and additional melted butter, optional

1. Split lobster tails in half lengthwise. With cut side up and using scissors, cut along the edge of shell to loosen the cartilage covering the tail meat from the shell; remove and discard cartilage.

2. Pour water into a 13-in. x 9-in. baking dish; place lobster tails in dish. Combine the parsley, salt and pepper; sprinkle over lobster. Drizzle with butter and lemon juice.

3. Bake, uncovered, at 375° for 20-25 minutes or until meat is firm and opaque. Serve with lemon and melted butter if desired.

Italian Baked Chicken

I've been cooking for more than 20 years, and I work in an Italian restaurant in Florida. This is my recipe for chicken colombo—and one that would be a nice dinner entree for a holiday gathering.
—**MARCELLO BASCO** DEERFIELD BEACH, FLORIDA

PREP: 25 MIN. **BAKE:** 35 MIN. **MAKES:** 4 SERVINGS

- ½ **cup all-purpose flour**
- ½ **teaspoon salt**
- ⅛ **teaspoon pepper**
- 4 **boneless skinless chicken breast halves (6 ounces each)**
- 3 **tablespoons olive oil, divided**
- 5 **garlic cloves, minced**
- 1 **teaspoon dried oregano**
- 1 **teaspoon dried basil**
- 2 **cups chicken broth**
- 1 **cup tomato puree**
- 4 **slices mozzarella cheese**
- 4 **tomato slices**
- 4 **teaspoons grated Parmesan cheese**
  Hot cooked angel hair pasta
  Minced fresh parsley

1. In a large resealable plastic bag, combine the flour, salt and pepper; add chicken, one piece at a time, and shake to coat. In a large skillet over medium heat, brown chicken in 2 tablespoons oil on each side. Transfer to a greased 11-in. x 7-in. baking dish.

2. In the same skillet, saute the garlic, oregano and basil in remaining oil for 1 minute. Stir in broth and tomato puree. Bring to a boil. Pour mixture over chicken.

3. Cover and bake at 400° for 25-30 minutes or until a thermometer reads 170°.

4. Remove chicken and set aside. Pour sauce into a small bowl and keep warm. Return chicken to the pan; top with mozzarella and tomato. Sprinkle with Parmesan cheese.

5. Bake, uncovered, for 6-8 minutes or until cheese is melted. Arrange pasta on a large serving platter; top with chicken. Pour sauce over chicken and sprinkle with parsley.

Spiral Ham with Cranberry Glaze

Baked ham with cranberry glaze has been a tradition in my family for as long as I can remember. We love to dice up the leftovers to put in dips for an appetizer the next night.

—PATTIE PRESCOTT MANCHESTER, NEW HAMPSHIRE

PREP: 15 MIN. **BAKE:** 3 HOURS
MAKES: 12-16 SERVINGS

- 1 bone-in fully cooked spiral-sliced ham (8 pounds)
- 1 can (14 ounces) whole-berry cranberry sauce
- 1 package (12 ounces) fresh or frozen cranberries
- 1 jar (12 ounces) red currant jelly
- 1 cup light corn syrup
- ½ teaspoon ground ginger

1. Place ham on a rack in a shallow roasting pan. Cover and bake at 325° for 2½ hours.
2. Meanwhile, for glaze, combine the remaining ingredients in a saucepan. Bring to a boil. Reduce heat; simmer, uncovered, until cranberries pop, stirring occasionally. Remove from the heat; set aside.
3. Uncover ham; bake 30 minutes longer or until a thermometer reads 140°, basting twice with 1½ cups glaze. Serve remaining glaze with ham.

FAST FIX ## Spinach Steak Pinwheels

With just four ingredients, I can wow family and friends. Even those who dislike spinach gobble it up. My mom has made this dish with veal, but I prefer to make it with beef flank steak.

—MARY ANN MARINO WEST PITTSBURGH, PENNSYLVANIA

PREP/TOTAL TIME: 30 MIN. **MAKES:** 4 SERVINGS

- 1 beef flank steak (1½ pounds)
- 1 package (10 ounces) frozen chopped spinach, thawed and squeezed dry
- ¼ cup grated Parmesan cheese
- ¼ cup sour cream
  Dash each salt and pepper

1. Cut steak horizontally from a long side to within ½ in. of opposite side. Open meat so it lies flat; cover with plastic wrap. Flatten to ¼-in. thickness. Remove plastic.
2. In a small bowl, combine the spinach, cheese and sour cream; spread over steak to within ½ in. of edges. With the grain of the meat going from left to right, roll up jelly-roll style. Slice beef across the grain into eight slices.
3. Transfer to an ungreased baking sheet. Sprinkle with salt and pepper. Broil 4-6 in. from the heat for 5-7 minutes on each side or until meat reaches desired doneness (for medium-rare, a thermometer should read 145°; medium, 160°; well-done, 170°).

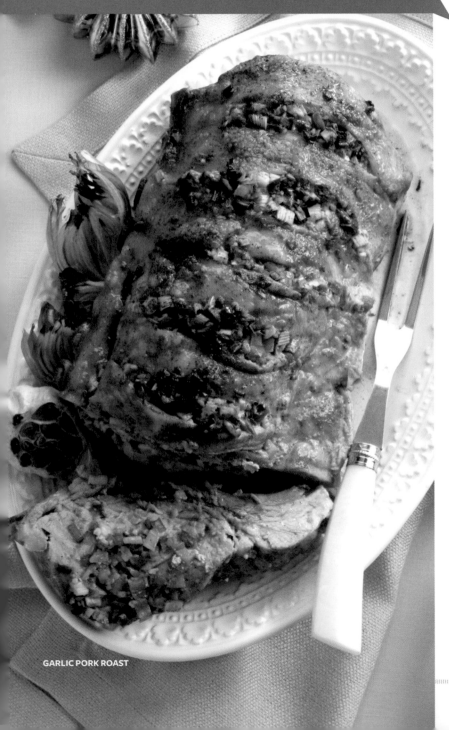

GARLIC PORK ROAST

> Mom cooked for 11 children, so her menus usually featured basic, simple foods. But on New Year's Day, she always treated us to this special pork roast.
>
> —**RUBY WILLIAMS** BOGALUSA, LOUISIANA

Garlic Pork Roast

PREP: 10 MIN. **BAKE:** 1 HOUR 30 MIN. + STANDING
MAKES: 8 SERVINGS

- 1 **bone-in pork loin roast (5 pounds)**
- ½ **medium green pepper, finely chopped**
- ½ **cup thinly sliced green onions**
- ½ **cup chopped celery**
- 8 **garlic cloves, minced**
- 1 **teaspoon salt**
- ¼ **teaspoon cayenne pepper**

1. With a sharp knife, cut a deep pocket between each rib on meaty side of roast. In a small bowl, mix the green pepper, green onions, celery and garlic; stuff into pockets. Sprinkle salt and cayenne pepper over roast.

2. Place roast in a shallow roasting pan, stuffing side up. Roast at 350° for 1½ to 1¾ hours or until a thermometer inserted in pork reads 145°. Remove roast from oven; tent with foil. Let stand for 15 minutes before carving.

Duck with Cherry Sauce

My mom prepared this golden tender roast duck often for dinner when I was growing up. The cherry sauce stirs up easily and makes this main dish delightful.

—**SANDY JENKINS** ELKHORN, WISCONSIN

PREP: 15 MIN. **BAKE:** 2 HOURS + STANDING
MAKES: 4-5 SERVINGS

- 1 **domestic duckling (4 to 5 pounds)**
- 1 **jar (12 ounces) cherry preserves**
- 1 **to 2 tablespoons red wine vinegar**

1. Prick skin of duckling well and place breast side up on a rack in a shallow roasting pan. Tie drumsticks together. Bake, uncovered, at 350° for 2 to 2½ hours or until juices run clear and a thermometer reads 180°. (Drain fat from pan as it accumulates.) Cover and let stand 20 minutes before carving.

2. Meanwhile, for sauce, combine preserves and vinegar in a small saucepan. Cook and stir over medium heat until heated through. Serve with duck.

Cherry-Stuffed Pork Loin

Imagine slicing through a beautifully cooked pork roast to reveal a sweet and savory cherry stuffing waiting inside.

—JAMES KORZENOWSKI FENNVILLE, MICHIGAN

PREP: 55 MIN. **BAKE:** 1 HOUR + STANDING **MAKES:** 10-12 SERVINGS

- 1 cup dried cherries
- ½ cup water
- ⅔ cup chopped onion
- ½ cup chopped celery
- ½ cup minced fresh parsley
- ¼ cup shredded carrot
- 1 tablespoon rubbed sage
- 1 teaspoon minced fresh rosemary
- 3 tablespoons butter
- ½ teaspoon minced garlic
- 2½ cups salad croutons
- 1 cup chicken broth
- ½ teaspoon pepper, divided
- ¼ teaspoon ground nutmeg
- ¼ teaspoon almond extract
- 1 boneless whole pork loin roast (about 3 pounds)

GRAVY
- 1¾ cups chicken broth
- ½ cup water
- ½ cup heavy whipping cream
- ½ teaspoon minced fresh rosemary

1. In a small saucepan, bring cherries and water to a boil, Remove from the heat; set aside (do not drain).

2. In a large skillet, saute the onion, celery, parsley, carrot, sage and rosemary in butter until tender. Add garlic; cook 1 minute longer. Remove from the heat. Stir in the croutons, broth, ¼ teaspoon pepper, nutmeg, extract and cherries. Let stand until liquid is absorbed.

3. Cut a lengthwise slit down the center of the roast to within ½ in. of bottom. Open roast so it lies flat; cover with plastic wrap. Flatten to ¾-in. thickness. Remove plastic; spread stuffing over meat to within 1 in. of edges. Close roast; tie several times with kitchen string and secure ends with toothpicks. Place fat side up on a rack in a shallow roasting pan. Sprinkle with remaining pepper.

4. Bake, uncovered, at 350° for 1 to 1¼ hours or until a thermometer reads 145°. Let meat stand for 10 minutes before slicing.

5. Meanwhile, add broth and water to roasting pan; stir to loosen browned bits. Pour into a small saucepan. Bring to a boil over medium-high heat; cook until reduced by half. Stir in cream and rosemary. Bring to a boil. Reduce heat; simmer, uncovered, until thickened. Serve with roast.

Cranberry-Stuffed Pork Loin: *Substitute dried cranberries for the cherries.*

Baked Ham with Orange Glaze

Baked in apple cider and orange juice, this tender ham is brushed with a sweet-tangy mustard and marmalade glaze.

—TASTE OF HOME TEST KITCHEN

PREP: 5 MIN. **BAKE:** 1 HOUR 50 MIN. + STANDING **MAKES:** 10 SERVINGS

- 1 fully cooked bone-in ham (6 to 7 pounds)
- 2 cups apple cider or unsweetened juice
- 2 cups orange juice
- ⅓ cup orange marmalade
- ¼ cup packed brown sugar
- ¼ cup Dijon mustard
- ¼ teaspoon ground ginger

1. Place ham on a rack in a shallow roasting pan. Score the surface of the ham, making diamond shapes ¼ in. deep. Add cider and orange juice to pan. Loosely cover ham with foil; bake at 325° for 1 hour. Combine remaining ingredients; brush some over ham.

2. Bake, uncovered, 50-60 minutes longer or until a thermometer reads 140°, brushing occasionally with glaze. Serve with remaining glaze.

Creamy Seafood-Stuffed Shells

Inspired by my love of lasagna, pasta shells and seafood, I made these crab- and shrimp-stuffed shells. My family loves them!
—**KATIE SLOAN** CHARLOTTE, NORTH CAROLINA

PREP: 40 MIN. **BAKE:** 30 MIN. **MAKES:** 8 SERVINGS

- 24 uncooked jumbo pasta shells
- 1 tablespoon finely chopped green pepper
- 1 tablespoon chopped red onion
- 1 teaspoon plus ¼ cup butter, divided
- 2 cans (6 ounces each) lump crabmeat, drained
- 1 package (5 ounces) frozen cooked salad shrimp, thawed
- 1 egg, lightly beaten
- ½ cup shredded part-skim mozzarella cheese
- ¼ cup mayonnaise
- 2 tablespoons plus 4 cups 2% milk, divided
- 1½ teaspoons seafood seasoning, divided
- ¼ teaspoon pepper
- ¼ cup all-purpose flour
- ¼ teaspoon coarsely ground pepper
- 1½ cups grated Parmesan cheese

1. Cook pasta according to package directions. Meanwhile, in a small skillet, saute green pepper and onion in 1 teaspoon butter until tender; set aside.
2. In a large bowl, combine the crab, shrimp, egg, mozzarella cheese, mayonnaise, 2 tablespoons milk, 1 teaspoon seafood seasoning, pepper and green pepper mixture.
3. Drain and rinse pasta; stuff each shell with 1 tablespoon of seafood mixture. Place in a greased 13-in. x 9-in. baking dish.
4. In a small saucepan, melt remaining butter over medium heat. Whisk in flour and coarsely ground pepper; gradually whisk in remaining milk. Bring to a boil; cook and stir for 2 minutes or until thickened. Stir in Parmesan cheese.
5. Pour over stuffed shells. Sprinkle with remaining seafood seasoning. Bake, uncovered, at 350° for 30-35 minutes.

TRY THIS CRAFT

Snowy Candle Centerpiece

Bring a bit of nature's winter wonderland indoors! Place two sheets of copy paper inside a clear glass vase so that each piece is against the inside of the vase. The papers will overlap and extend from the top. Slip natural or artificial flat greens between the paper and the vase. Pour Epsom salt, canning salt or sugar into the vase until it's about two-thirds full. Carefully remove each piece of paper so that the greens remain pressed against the side of the vase. Set small red berries on top of the Epsom salt. Insert a white taper candle in the center, pushing it down to the bottom of the vase.

Rack of Lamb with Figs

I've been making rack of lamb for years. My grandma gave me this recipe because she knew how much I love figs. And the toasted walnuts sprinkled on top give it just the right touch.

—**SYLVIA CASTANON** LONG BEACH, CALIFORNIA

PREP: 30 MIN. **BAKE:** 45 MIN. **MAKES:** 6-8 SERVINGS

- 2 **racks of lamb (2 pounds each)**
- 1 **teaspoon salt, divided**
- 1 **cup water**
- 1 **small onion, finely chopped**
- 1 **tablespoon canola oil**
- 1 **garlic clove, minced**
- 2 **tablespoons cornstarch**
- 1 **cup port wine or ½ cup grape juice plus ½ cup reduced-sodium beef broth**
- 10 **dried figs, halved**
- ¼ **teaspoon pepper**
- ½ **cup coarsely chopped walnuts, toasted**

1. Rub lamb with ½ teaspoon salt. Place meat side up on a rack in a greased roasting pan. Bake, uncovered, at 375° for 45-60 minutes or until meat reaches desired doneness (for medium-rare, a thermometer should read 145°; medium, 160°; well-done, 170°).

2. Remove to a serving platter; cover loosely with foil. Add 1 cup water to roasting pan; stir to loosen browned bits from pan. Using a fine sieve, strain mixture; set drippings aside.

3. In a small saucepan, saute onion in oil until tender. Add garlic; cook 1 minute longer. Stir in cornstarch until blended; gradually add the wine, drippings, figs, pepper and remaining salt. Bring to a boil. Reduce heat to medium-low; cook, uncovered, until figs are tender and sauce is thickened, about 10 minutes, stirring occasionally.

4. Sprinkle walnuts over lamb; serve with fig sauce.

Pesto Pepper Tortellini

This is a shortcut version of a rich, creamy pasta dish I sampled years ago. I've served this tortellini as both a special side dish and a meatless entree.

—MICKIE TAFT MILWAUKEE, WISCONSIN

PREP/TOTAL TIME: 20 MIN. **MAKES:** 4 SERVINGS

- 1 **package (19 ounces) frozen cheese tortellini**
- ½ **cup julienned sweet red pepper**
- ½ **cup butter**
- 3 **garlic cloves, minced**
- 2 **cups heavy whipping cream**
- ¼ **cup ground walnuts**
- 2 **tablespoons minced fresh basil or 2 teaspoons dried basil**
- 1 **tablespoon chopped green onion or chives**

1. Prepare tortellini according to package directions.

2. Meanwhile, in a large skillet, saute red pepper in butter until pepper is crisp-tender. Add garlic; cook 1 minute longer. Stir in the cream; cook for 8-10 minutes or until slightly thickened.

3. Add the walnuts, basil and onion; heat through. Drain tortellini; add to sauce and toss to coat.

Tuscan Pork Medallions

I love experimenting with new recipes and finding ones this satisfying. The Italian herbs come through and the whole dish comes together in a creamy tomato sauce.

—LORRAINE CALAND SHUNIAH, ONTARIO

PREP/TOTAL TIME: 30 MIN. **MAKES:** 2 SERVINGS

- ¾ **pound pork tenderloin, cut into 1-inch slices**
- ¼ **teaspoon salt**
- ⅛ **teaspoon pepper**
- 1 **tablespoon butter**
- 2 **thin slices prosciutto or deli ham, chopped**
- 2 **garlic cloves, minced**
- 1½ **teaspoons minced fresh sage or ½ teaspoon dried sage leaves**
- 2 **tablespoons balsamic vinegar**
- ½ **cup heavy whipping cream**
- ¾ **cup chopped plum tomatoes**
- 4 **fresh basil leaves, thinly sliced**
- 1 **teaspoon grated Parmesan cheese**

1. Sprinkle pork with salt and pepper. In a large skillet over medium heat, cook pork in butter until a thermometer reads 145°. Remove; let meat stand for 5 minutes.

2. Meanwhile, in the same skillet, saute prosciutto in the drippings until browned. Add garlic and sage; cook 1 minute longer. Add vinegar, stirring to loosen browned bits from pan.

3. Stir in cream; bring to a boil. Reduce heat; cook and stir for 1-2 minutes or until slightly thickened. Add tomatoes and pork; heat through. Sprinkle each serving with basil and cheese.

FAST FIX ▶ Gorgonzola Chicken Penne

I actually made this recipe up when I tried to re-create a meal I was served in an Italian restaurant in Stockholm, Sweden. Every year, I entertain about 50 family and friends on my Pennsylvania farm, and this pasta dish is on the menu; it's easy to double or triple.

—C.W. STEVE STEVENSON NEWFOUNDLAND, PENNSYLVANIA

PREP/TOTAL TIME: 30 MIN. **MAKES:** 6 SERVINGS

- 2 cups uncooked penne pasta
- 2 cups fresh broccoli florets
- 1 tablespoon water
- 1 pound boneless skinless chicken breasts, cut into 1-inch cubes
- 9 tablespoons butter, divided
- 1 large onion, chopped
- 6 tablespoons all-purpose flour
- 2 cups chicken broth
- ¾ cup white wine or additional chicken broth
- 1½ cups (6 ounces) crumbled Gorgonzola cheese
  Pepper to taste

1. Cook pasta according to package directions. Meanwhile, place broccoli and water in a small microwave-safe bowl. Cover and microwave on high for 2 to 2½ minutes or until crisp-tender. Set aside.

2. In a large skillet, saute chicken in 3 tablespoons butter until no longer pink. Remove and keep warm. In the same skillet, saute onion in remaining butter until tender.

3. Stir in flour until blended. Gradually add broth and wine. Bring to a boil; cook and stir for 2 minutes or until thickened. Reduce heat to low; stir in cheese until blended.

4. Drain pasta and broccoli; add to onion mixture. Add chicken; heat through. Season with pepper.

Champagne Baked Ham

Champagne, brown sugar and honey combine to make a beautiful glossy glaze. The ham slices turn out tender and juicy every time.

—LINDA FOREMAN LOCUST GROVE, OKLAHOMA

PREP: 10 MIN. **BAKE:** 2 HOURS **MAKES:** 18 SERVINGS

- 1 boneless fully cooked ham (9 pounds)
- 1½ cups champagne
- ¾ cup packed brown sugar
- 4½ teaspoons honey
- ¾ teaspoon ground ginger
- ¾ teaspoon ground mustard

1. Place ham on a rack in a shallow roasting pan. Score the surface of the ham, making diamond shapes ½ in. deep. Bake, uncovered, at 325° for 1½ hours.

2. Meanwhile, in a small saucepan, combine the remaining ingredients. Bring to a boil; cook until glaze is reduced by half. Remove from the heat.

3. Baste ham with glaze; bake 30 minutes longer or until a thermometer reads 140°, basting twice with glaze. Serve with the remaining glaze.

> **"**I created this entree years ago when a friend gave me some fresh-caught mahi mahi. Shortly after, I entered the recipe in a contest and won! I think it's a keeper.**"**
> —**VIRGINIA ANTHONY** JACKSONVILLE, FLORIDA

Mediterranean Mahi Mahi

PREP: 30 MIN. **BAKE:** 10 MIN. **MAKES:** 4 SERVINGS

- 1 **medium onion, chopped**
- 1 **medium green pepper, chopped**
- 4½ **teaspoons olive oil, divided**
- 1 **garlic clove, minced**
- ¾ **cup salsa**
- ½ **cup white wine or chicken broth**
- ¼ **cup halved Greek olives**
- ½ **teaspoon Greek seasoning**
- 4 **mahi mahi fillets (6 ounces each)**
- ¼ **teaspoon salt**
- ¼ **teaspoon pepper**
- ¼ **cup crumbled tomato and basil feta cheese**

1. In a large ovenproof skillet, saute onion and green pepper in 1½ teaspoons oil until tender. Add garlic; saute 1 minute longer.

2. Stir in the salsa, wine, olives and Greek seasoning. Bring to a boil. Reduce heat; simmer, uncovered, for 5 minutes or until slightly thickened. Transfer to a bowl; set aside.

3. Sprinkle mahi mahi with salt and pepper. In the same skillet, lightly brown fillets in remaining oil for 2 minutes on each side. Spoon salsa mixture over fillets.

4. Bake, uncovered, at 425° for 6 minutes. Sprinkle with cheese; bake 2-3 minutes longer or until fish just turns opaque.

top tip

Go Fish

If you can't find the fish you're looking for, it's best to substitute based on how lean or fatty the fish is. Mahi mahi is a lean fish with a sweet flavor and firm meat. Good substitutions include halibut, haddock, grouper, flounder, red snapper, sole, cod and tilapia.

Artichoke Spinach Lasagna

We were served this meatless entree while visiting friends in Maryland. We took the recipe with us when we left and have since added a few more ingredients to give it our own touch.

—CAROLE RAGO ALTOONA, PENNSYLVANIA

PREP: 25 MIN. **BAKE:** 55 MIN. + STANDING **MAKES:** 12 SERVINGS

- ½ cup chopped onion
- 1 tablespoon olive oil
- 4 garlic cloves, minced
- 1 can (14½ ounces) vegetable or chicken broth
- 1 teaspoon dried rosemary, crushed
- ¼ teaspoon ground nutmeg
- ¼ teaspoon pepper
- 1 can (14 ounces) water-packed artichoke hearts, rinsed, drained and quartered
- 1 package (10 ounces) frozen chopped spinach, thawed and squeezed dry
- ½ cup sliced fresh mushrooms
- 1 jar (15 ounces) roasted garlic Alfredo sauce
- 12 no-cook lasagna noodles
- 3 cups (12 ounces) shredded part-skim mozzarella cheese, divided
- 1 cup crumbled tomato and basil feta cheese or feta cheese
- ⅛ teaspoon garlic powder
- ⅛ teaspoon each dried oregano, parsley flakes and basil

1. In a large saucepan, saute onion in oil for 2-3 minutes or until tender. Add garlic; cook 1 minute longer. Stir in the broth, rosemary, nutmeg and pepper. Bring to a boil. Add the artichokes, spinach and mushrooms. Reduce heat; cover and simmer for 5 minutes. Stir in Alfredo sauce.

2. Spread 1 cup sauce mixture into a greased 13-in. x 9-in. baking dish. Top with three noodles and ⅔ cup mozzarella cheese. Repeat layers three times. Top with remaining sauce mixture and mozzarella cheese. Sprinkle with feta cheese, garlic powder, oregano, parsley and basil.

3. Cover and bake at 350° for 40 minutes. Uncover; bake 15 minutes longer or until noodles are tender. Let stand for 10 minutes before cutting.

Herbed Standing Rib Roast

We're a meat-and-potatoes family, so this roast is right up our alley. It really is the highlight of an elegant dinner for special guests. Leftovers are great for sandwiches, too.

—CAROL STEVENS BASYE, VIRGINIA

PREP: 10 MIN. **BAKE:** 2¼ HOURS + STANDING **MAKES:** 12 SERVINGS

- 3 tablespoons grated onion
- 2 tablespoons olive oil
- 4 garlic cloves, minced
- 2 teaspoons celery seed
- 1 teaspoon coarsely ground pepper
- 1 teaspoon paprika
- ¼ teaspoon dried thyme
- 1 bone-in beef rib roast (6 to 7 pounds)
- 2 large onions, cut into wedges
- 2 large carrots, cut into 2-inch pieces
- 2 celery ribs, cut into 2-inch pieces
- ¼ cup red wine or beef broth
  Assorted herbs and fruit, optional

1. In a small bowl, combine the first seven ingredients; rub over roast. Place the onions, carrots and celery in a large roasting pan; place roast over vegetables.

2. Bake, uncovered, at 350° for 2¼ to 3 hours or until meat reaches desired doneness (for medium-rare, a thermometer should read 145°; medium, 160°; well-done, 170°).

3. Remove roast to a serving platter and keep warm; let stand for 15 minutes before slicing.

4. Meanwhile, for au jus, strain and discard vegetables. Pour drippings into a measuring cup; skim fat. Add wine to roasting pan, stirring to remove any browned bits. Stir in drippings; heat through. Serve with roast. Garnish platter with herbs and fruit if desired.

Filet Mignon with Red Wine Sauce

In this filet mignon recipe, it's all about the sauce. A buttery red wine reduction with fresh garlic is what takes this steak to the next level.

—TARAH PESSEL CLARKSTON, MICHIGAN

PREP: 30 MIN. **GRILL:** 15 MIN. **MAKES:** 6 SERVINGS

- 1 **medium onion, thinly sliced**
- 3 **tablespoons butter, divided**
- 2 **garlic cloves, minced**
- ¾ **teaspoon salt, divided**
- ½ **teaspoon dried oregano**
- 2 **tablespoons tomato paste**
- 1¼ **cups dry red wine or beef broth**
- ½ **teaspoon pepper, divided**
- 6 **beef tenderloin steaks (4 to 6 ounces each)**
- 3 **tablespoons olive oil**

1. In a saucepan, saute onion in 1 tablespoon butter until tender. Add garlic, ¼ teaspoon salt and oregano; cook and stir 1 minute. Add tomato paste; cook and stir 2 minutes longer.

2. Gradually whisk in wine. Bring to a boil. Reduce heat; simmer until reduced by half. Strain sauce and return to pan. Gradually stir in remaining butter until melted. Add ¼ teaspoon pepper. Remove from the heat; keep warm.

3. Sprinkle steaks with remaining salt and pepper. Drizzle with oil. Grill, covered, over medium heat or broil 4 in. from the heat for 6-8 minutes on each side or until meat reaches desired doneness (for medium-rare, a thermometer should read 145°; medium, 160°; well-done, 170°). Cover and let stand for 3-5 minutes. Serve with wine sauce.

Tomato-Cream Stuffed Chicken

For a pretty presentation at your holiday gathering, whip up a sun-dried tomato sauce to serve alongside chicken or veggies.

—JAQUI HUMPHREY KIRKLAND, WASHINGTON

PREP: 30 MIN. **BAKE:** 20 MIN. **MAKES:** 4 SERVINGS

- ½ **cup cream cheese, softened**
- ½ **cup shredded part-skim mozzarella cheese**
- ½ **cup chopped fresh spinach**
- ½ **cup oil-packed sun-dried tomatoes, chopped**
- 2 **garlic cloves, minced**
- 4 **bone-in chicken breast halves (8 ounces each)**
- ¼ **teaspoon salt**
- ¼ **teaspoon pepper**
- 3 **tablespoons butter**
- 1 **tablespoon olive oil**

SAUCE
- ¾ **cup white wine or chicken broth**
- ¼ **cup oil-packed sun-dried tomatoes, chopped**
- 3 **teaspoons chopped shallot**
- 3 **garlic cloves, minced**
- 6 **fresh basil leaves, thinly sliced**
- ¾ **cup heavy whipping cream**
- ¼ **cup butter, cubed**

1. In a small bowl, combine the first five ingredients. Carefully loosen the skin on one side of each chicken breast to form a pocket; spread cheese mixture under the skin. Sprinkle with salt and pepper. In a large skillet, brown chicken on both sides in butter and oil.

2. Transfer to an ungreased 13-in. x 9-in. baking dish. Bake, uncovered, at 400° for 20-25 minutes or until a thermometer reads 170°.

3. Meanwhile, in a small saucepan, combine the wine, tomatoes, shallot, garlic and basil. Bring to a boil over medium-high heat; cook until reduced by half. Add cream and butter. Bring to a boil. Reduce heat; simmer, uncovered, until thickened, stirring occasionally. Serve with chicken.

"This seafood casserole is our traditional Christmas Eve dinner. It's easy to make it larger or smaller depending on how many guests we have.**"**

—**MARILYN BISHOP** REDBRIDGE, ONTARIO

Seafood Medley

PREP: 25 MIN. **COOK:** 10 MIN. **MAKES:** 6 SERVINGS

- 5 **cups water**
- 2 **tablespoons lemon juice**
- ½ **teaspoon salt**
- 2 **pounds orange roughy fillets**
- 1 **pound uncooked medium shrimp, peeled and deveined**
- ½ **pound bay scallops**
- 2 **tablespoons butter**
- 3 **tablespoons all-purpose flour**
- 1 **teaspoon chicken bouillon granules**
- 1 **teaspoon Dijon mustard**
  Dash pepper
- 1 **cup heavy whipping cream**
- 1 **cup (4 ounces) shredded Gruyere or Swiss cheese**
  Hot cooked pasta

1. In a Dutch oven, bring the water, lemon juice and salt to a boil. Reduce heat; carefully add fillets and cook, uncovered, for 4 minutes. Add shrimp; cook for 3 minutes. Add scallops; cook 3-4 minutes longer or until fish flakes easily with a fork, shrimp turn pink and scallops are firm and opaque. Strain, reserving 1½ cups cooking liquid.

2. In a saucepan, melt butter. Stir in the flour, bouillon, mustard and pepper until smooth. Gradually add cream and reserved liquid. Bring to a boil; cook and stir for 1-2 minutes or until thickened. Stir in the cheese and seafood mixture; heat through. Serve with pasta.

Frozen Fish

Try thawing fish fillets in milk; the milk absorbs any off flavors.

Chicken with Cranberry-Balsamic Sauce

I use cranberry juice and cranberry sauce to transform ordinary chicken into something special and elegant. Sometimes I'll serve this dish with a side of polenta or brown or wild rice.

—SUSAN CORTESI NORTHBROOK, ILLINOIS

PREP: 20 MIN. **BAKE:** 15 MIN. **MAKES:** 4 SERVINGS

- 4 boneless skinless chicken breast halves (6 ounces each)
- 1¼ teaspoons salt, divided
- ½ teaspoon pepper
- 1 tablespoon olive oil
- 1 cup cranberry juice
- ⅓ cup balsamic vinegar
- ¼ cup whole-berry cranberry sauce
- 2 tablespoons finely chopped shallot
- 3 tablespoons butter

1. Sprinkle chicken with 1 teaspoon salt and the pepper. In a large skillet, brown chicken in oil on both sides. Transfer to a greased 13-in. x 9-in. baking pan. Bake at 425° for 12-15 minutes or until a thermometer reads 170°.
2. Add the cranberry juice, vinegar, cranberry sauce and shallot to the skillet, stirring to loosen browned bits from pan. Bring to a boil; cook until liquid is reduced to about ½ cup. Stir in butter and remaining salt until butter is melted. Serve with chicken.

Pork Tenderloin with Glazed Onions

My husband and I love pork, especially when it's dressed up like this. Sweet apricots and glazed onions go beautifully with the juicy meat.

—JANICE CHRISTOFFERSON EAGLE RIVER, WISCONSIN

PREP: 20 MIN. **BAKE:** 20 MIN. **MAKES:** 8 SERVINGS

- 4 large sweet onions, sliced (about 8 cups)
- ¼ cup butter, cubed
- 1 cup chopped dried apricots or golden raisins
- ¼ cup packed brown sugar
- ¼ cup balsamic vinegar
- ½ teaspoon salt
- ½ teaspoon pepper
- 2 pork tenderloins (1 pound each)

1. In a large skillet, saute onions in butter for 2 minutes. Stir in the apricots, brown sugar, vinegar, salt and pepper; cook until onions are tender.
2. Place pork tenderloins on a rack coated with cooking spray in a shallow roasting pan; top with onion mixture.
3. Bake, uncovered, at 425° for 20-27 minutes or until a thermometer reads 145°. Let stand for 5 minutes before slicing. Serve with onion mixture.

SWEET-AND-SOUR RED CABBAGE, PAGE 135

Jolly Sides

139

130

142

FAST FIX Company's Coming Salad

Sugared almonds give my delicious salad an over-the-top kick that will have guests coming back for seconds.

—DOLORES LUCKEN FERDINAND, INDIANA

PREP/TOTAL TIME: 30 MIN. **MAKES:** 8 SERVINGS

- 2 **tablespoons sugar**
- ½ **cup sliced almonds**
- 1 **package (5 ounces) spring mix salad greens**
- 6 **cups torn romaine**
- 1 **can (11 ounces) mandarin oranges, drained**
- 2 **celery ribs, thinly sliced**
- 1 **small red onion, chopped**
- 2 **green onions, thinly sliced**

DRESSING
- 3 **tablespoons canola oil**
- 2 **tablespoons cider vinegar**
- 5 **teaspoons sugar**
- 1 **tablespoon minced fresh parsley**
- ¼ **teaspoon salt**

1. In a small heavy skillet, cook and stir the sugar over medium-low heat until melted. Stir in almonds; cook for 1 minute or until lightly browned. Spread onto foil coated with cooking spray; set aside.

2. In a large salad bowl, combine the mixed greens, romaine, oranges, celery and onions. In a small bowl, whisk the dressing ingredients. Drizzle over salad; add almonds and toss to coat.

FAST FIX Beans with Parsley Sauce

PREP/TOTAL TIME: 30 MIN. **MAKES:** 8 SERVINGS

- 2 **pounds fresh green beans, trimmed**
- 2 **tablespoons butter**
- 2 **tablespoons all-purpose flour**
- 1 **teaspoon salt**
- ⅛ **teaspoon pepper**
- 1½ **cups chicken broth**
- 2 **egg yolks**
- ½ **cup 2% milk**
- 1 **cup minced fresh parsley**

1. Place beans in a large saucepan and cover with water; bring to a boil. Cook, uncovered, for 8-10 minutes or until crisp-tender. Meanwhile, in a large skillet, melt butter over medium heat. Stir in the flour, salt and pepper until smooth. Gradually whisk in broth. Bring to a boil; cook and stir for 1-2 minutes or until thickened. Remove from the heat.

2. In a small bowl, combine egg yolks and milk. Stir a small amount of hot broth mixture into egg mixture. Return all to the pan, stirring constantly. Bring to a gentle boil; cook and stir for 2 minutes or until thickened and coats the back of a metal spoon. Stir in parsley. Drain beans; serve with sauce.

"For a fresh, natural-tasting take on green bean casserole, try these crisp green beans gently coated in a buttery homemade white sauce. It's wonderful served with a slice of lemon.**"**

—VERONICA TEIPEL MANCHESTER, MISSOURI

Gingered Orange Beets

My husband was pleasantly surprised when he tried my new twist on beets. The orange and ginger are a great pair, making this particular vegetable a welcome addition to our holiday menu.

—**MARION TIPTON** PHOENIX, ARIZONA

PREP: 10 MIN. **BAKE:** 70 MIN. **MAKES:** 4 SERVINGS

- 1½ **pounds whole fresh beets (about 4 medium), trimmed and cleaned**
- 6 **tablespoons olive oil, divided**
- ¼ **teaspoon salt**
- ¼ **teaspoon white pepper**
- 1 **tablespoon rice vinegar**
- 1 **tablespoon thawed orange juice concentrate**
- 1½ **teaspoons grated orange peel, divided**
- ½ **teaspoon minced fresh gingerroot**
- 1 **medium navel orange, peeled, sectioned and chopped**
- ⅓ **cup pecan halves, toasted**

1. Brush beets with 4 tablespoons oil; sprinkle with salt and pepper. Wrap loosely in foil; place on a baking sheet. Bake at 425° for 70-75 minutes or until fork-tender. Cool slightly.

2. In a small bowl, whisk the vinegar, orange juice concentrate, 1 teaspoon orange peel, ginger and remaining oil; set aside.

3. Peel beets and cut into wedges; place in a serving bowl. Add the orange sections and pecans. Drizzle with orange sauce and toss to coat. Sprinkle with remaining orange peel.

top tip — Beet Basics

Look for beets with smooth, unblemished skin. The greens, if attached, should be brightly colored and not wilted. Before storing, remove the greens. Place the beets in a plastic bag and refrigerate for up to 3 weeks.

FAST FIX ▸ Spinach Almond Salad

For Christmas, I love the combination of dark green spinach and dried cranberries. Every year I serve this, people ask for the dressing recipe.
—**JENNIE RICHARDS** RIVERTON, UTAH

PREP/TOTAL TIME: 15 MIN. **MAKES:** 8 SERVINGS

- 1 **package (6 ounces) fresh baby spinach**
- 2 **large tart apples, thinly sliced**
- 10 **bacon strips, cooked and crumbled**
- 1 **cup dried cranberries**
- ¾ **cup slivered almonds, toasted**

VINAIGRETTE

- ¼ **cup sugar**
- 3 **tablespoons cider vinegar**
- 2 **teaspoons finely chopped onion**
- ¼ **teaspoon salt**
- ⅓ **cup olive oil**

In a large bowl, combine the first five ingredients. In a blender, combine the sugar, vinegar, onion and salt; cover and process until blended. While processing, gradually add oil in a steady stream. Pour over salad; toss to coat.

Black-Eyed Peas with Bacon

A real Southern favorite, black-eyed peas are traditionally served on New Year's Day to bring good luck. My mother's recipe with bacon, garlic and thyme makes them extra special for us.
—**RUBY WILLIAMS** BOGALUSA, LOUISIANA

PREP: 10 MIN. + SOAKING **COOK:** 35 MIN. **MAKES:** 8 SERVINGS

- 1 **pound dried black-eyed peas, rinsed and sorted**
- ½ **pound bacon, cooked and crumbled**
- 1 **tablespoon butter**
- 1 **large onion, chopped**
- 1 **garlic clove, minced**
- ½ **teaspoon dried thyme**
   Salt to taste
   Additional cooked and crumbled bacon, optional

1. Place peas and bacon in a large Dutch oven; add water to cover. Bring to a boil; boil for 2 minutes. Remove from the heat; let soak, covered, for 1 hour. Do not drain.

2. In a skillet, heat butter over medium-high heat. Add onion; cook and stir until tender. Add garlic; cook 1 minute longer. Stir in thyme and salt.

3. Add to pea mixture; return to the heat. Cook, covered, over medium heat for 30 minutes or until peas are tender, stirring occasionally. If desired, top with additional crumbled bacon.

MAKE AHEAD › Cranberry Gelatin Mold

Tangy and fruity, this classic gelatin mold is surprisingly easy to prepare. Once you get a taste of the sweet-tart combination of cranberries and pineapple, you'll be going back for more.

—JUNE BLOMQUIST EUGENE, OREGON

PREP: 15 MIN. + CHILLING **MAKES:** 8 SERVINGS

- 2 packages (3 ounces each) raspberry gelatin
- 3 cups boiling water
- 1 can (14 ounces) whole-berry cranberry sauce
- 2 tablespoons lemon juice
- 1 can (8 ounces) unsweetened crushed pineapple, drained
- ½ cup finely chopped celery

1. In a large bowl, dissolve gelatin in boiling water. Stir in cranberry sauce and lemon juice until blended. Chill until partially set.

2. Stir in pineapple and celery. Pour into a 6-cup ring mold coated with cooking spray. Refrigerate until firm. Unmold onto a serving platter.

Au Gratin Potatoes 'n' Leeks

I don't have a lot of time to cook, but when I do, I love to make casseroles. This is my favorite one to make for holiday potlucks; it made me a fan of Gruyere cheese.

—ROSALIE HUGHES BOISE, IDAHO

PREP: 45 MIN. **BAKE:** 55 MIN. **MAKES:** 12 SERVINGS

- 8 cups sliced peeled potatoes (¼-inch slices)
- 3 medium leeks (white portion only), cut into ½-inch slices
- 2 tablespoons butter
- 3 tablespoons all-purpose flour
- ½ teaspoon salt
- ⅛ teaspoon pepper
- 1⅓ cups 2% milk
- 1 block (4 ounces) Gruyere or Swiss cheese, shredded
- ⅛ teaspoon ground nutmeg
  - **CRUMB TOPPING**
- ⅓ cup dry bread crumbs
- 2 tablespoons butter, melted
- ¼ cup shredded cheddar cheese

1. Place potatoes in a Dutch oven and cover with water. Bring to a boil. Add leeks; return to a boil. Cover and cook for 5 minutes. Drain and pat dry. Place in a greased 13-in. x 9-in. baking dish.

2. In a large saucepan, melt butter. Stir in the flour, salt and pepper until smooth; gradually add milk. Bring to a boil; cook and stir for 2 minutes or until thickened. Stir in cheese and nutmeg until cheese is melted. Pour over potato mixture. Toss bread crumbs and butter; sprinkle over the top.

3. Cover and bake at 325° for 40 minutes. Uncover; sprinkle with cheddar cheese. Bake 15-20 minutes longer or until potatoes are tender.

Au Gratin Potatoes: *Omit the leeks. Increase potatoes to 9 cups sliced. Prepared as directed.*

White Cheddar Scalloped Potatoes

I've been tweaking my scalloped potatoes for more than eight years. After I added thyme, ham and sour cream, my husband said, "This is it!"

—**HOPE TOOLE** MUSCLE SHOALS, ALABAMA

PREP: 40 MIN. **BAKE:** 70 MIN. **MAKES:** 8 SERVINGS

- 1 **medium onion, finely chopped**
- ¼ **cup butter, cubed**
- ¼ **cup all-purpose flour**
- 1 **teaspoon dried parsley flakes**
- 1 **teaspoon salt**
- ½ **teaspoon pepper**
- ½ **teaspoon dried thyme**
- 3 **cups 2% milk**
- 1 **can (10¾ ounces) condensed cream of mushroom soup, undiluted**
- 1 **cup (8 ounces) sour cream**
- 8 **cups thinly sliced peeled potatoes**
- 3½ **cups cubed fully cooked ham**
- 2 **cups (8 ounces) shredded white cheddar cheese**

1. In a large saucepan, saute onion in butter until tender. Stir in the flour, parsley, salt, pepper and thyme until blended. Gradually add milk. Bring to a boil; cook and stir for 2 minutes or until thickened. Stir in soup. Remove from the heat; stir in sour cream until blended.

2. In a large bowl, combine potatoes and ham. In a greased 13-in. x 9-in. baking dish, layer with half of the potato mixture, cheese and white sauce. Repeat layers.

3. Cover and bake at 375° for 30 minutes. Uncover; bake 40-50 minutes longer or until potatoes are tender.

top tip

The Next Day

When I have leftover scalloped potatoes, I add them to corn chowder for a rich and filling soup.

—**JEAN CHULA** VISTA, CALIFORNIA

MAKE AHEAD ▶ Marinated Italian Salad

Marinated salad is a busy cook's best friend, especially when preparing for a potluck or dinner guests. Keep this recipe around for summer, too. It's always handy to have a mayo-free side for outdoor cookouts.

—**MUGGS NASH** BLOOMINGTON, MINNESOTA

PREP: 30 MIN. + MARINATING **MAKES:** 12 SERVINGS

- 4 **cups fresh broccoli florets**
- 3 **cups fresh cauliflowerets**
- ½ **pound sliced fresh mushrooms**
- 2 **celery ribs, chopped**
- 4 **green onions, thinly sliced**
- 1 **can (8 ounces) sliced water chestnuts, drained**
- 1 **bottle (16 ounces) Italian salad dressing**
- 1 **envelope Italian salad dressing mix**
- 1 **pint cherry tomatoes, halved**
- 1 **can (2¼ ounces) sliced ripe olives, drained**

1. In a large serving bowl, combine the broccoli, cauliflower, mushrooms, celery, onions and water chestnuts. In a small bowl, whisk salad dressing and dressing mix; drizzle over vegetables and toss to coat.

2. Cover and refrigerate overnight. Just before serving, add tomatoes and olives; toss to coat.

FAST FIX ▶ Peas in Cheese Sauce

PREP/TOTAL TIME: 20 MIN. **MAKES:** 8 SERVINGS

- 4½ **teaspoons butter**
- 4½ **teaspoons all-purpose flour**
- ¼ **teaspoon salt**
- ⅛ **teaspoon white pepper**
- 1½ **cups 2% milk**
- ¾ **cup cubed process cheese (Velveeta)**
- 2 **packages (10 ounces each) frozen peas, thawed**

In a large saucepan, melt butter over low heat. Stir in the flour, salt and pepper until smooth. Gradually add milk. Bring to a boil; cook and stir for 2 minutes or until thickened. Add the cheese; stir until melted. Stir in peas; cook 1-2 minutes longer or until heated through.

> **66** My mom started cooking when she was just 12 years old. Her creamed peas are part of a special meal she used to serve, and one that my family has fond memories of. **99**

—**JUNE BLOMQUIST** EUGENE, OREGON

Sausage Corn Bread Dressing

You wouldn't know it from tasting it, but my holiday corn bread dressing only has 3 grams of fat per serving. Made with turkey sausage, herbs, fruit and veggies, it's a healthy alternative to traditional dressing recipes.

—REBECCA BAIRD SALT LAKE CITY, UTAH

PREP: 30 MIN. **BAKE:** 50 MIN. **MAKES:** 16 SERVINGS

- 1   cup all-purpose flour
- 1   cup cornmeal
- ¼   cup sugar
- 3   teaspoons baking powder
- 1   teaspoon salt
- 1   cup buttermilk
- ¼   cup unsweetened applesauce
- 2   egg whites

DRESSING
- 1   pound turkey Italian sausage links, casings removed
- 4   celery ribs, chopped
- 1   medium onion, chopped
- 1   medium sweet red pepper, chopped
- 2   medium tart apples, chopped
- 1   cup chopped roasted chestnuts
- 3   tablespoons minced fresh parsley
- 2   garlic cloves, minced
- ½   teaspoon dried thyme
- ½   teaspoon pepper
- 1   cup reduced-sodium chicken broth
- 1   egg white

1. For corn bread, combine the first five ingredients in a large bowl. Combine the buttermilk, applesauce and egg whites; stir into dry ingredients just until moistened.

2. Pour into an 9-in. square baking dish coated with cooking spray. Bake at 400° for 20-25 minutes or until a toothpick inserted near the center comes out clean. Cool on a wire rack.

3. In a large nonstick skillet, cook the sausage, celery, onion and red pepper over medium heat until meat is no longer pink; drain. Transfer to a large bowl. Crumble corn bread over mixture. Add the apples, chestnuts, parsley, garlic, thyme and pepper. Stir in broth and egg white.

4. Transfer to a 13-in. x 9-in. baking dish coated with cooking spray. Cover and bake at 325° for 40 minutes. Uncover; bake 10 minutes longer or until lightly browned.

Editor's Note: *Dressing can be prepared as directed and used to stuff a 10- to 12-pound turkey.*

Baked Rice Pilaf

PREP: 10 MIN. **BAKE:** 40 MIN. **MAKES:** 4 SERVINGS

- 1¾ cups water
- 1   cup shredded carrot
- 1   cup chopped celery
- ¾   cup uncooked long grain rice
- 3   tablespoons minced fresh parsley
- 2   tablespoons finely chopped onion
- 2   tablespoons butter, melted
- 1   tablespoon chicken bouillon granules

In an ungreased 8-in. square baking dish, combine all the ingredients. Cover and bake at 375° for 40-45 minutes or until rice is tender, stirring after 25 minutes.

> **❝**I'm always in search of inexpensive yet delicious recipes like this one to serve at potlucks. I particularly like that you just mix everything in one dish and pop it in the oven.**❞**
>
> **—SHEREE FEERO** GOLDEN, COLORADO

FAST FIX ▶ Balsamic-Glazed Brussels Sprouts

My relatives claim to hate Brussels sprouts, which I took as a challenge to come up with a recipe they'd love. When I served this at my Christmas buffet, there wasn't a sprout left in the bowl!

—CAROLE BESS WHITE PORTLAND, OREGON

PREP/TOTAL TIME: 30 MIN. **MAKES:** 8 SERVINGS

- 2 **pounds fresh Brussels sprouts**
- ½ **pound bacon strips, cut into ½-inch pieces**
- 1 **medium onion, sliced**
- ¼ **cup white balsamic vinegar**
- 2 **tablespoons stone-ground mustard**
- ½ **teaspoon garlic powder**
- ⅛ **teaspoon salt**
- ½ **cup soft bread crumbs**

1. Cut an "X" in the core of each Brussels sprout. Place in a large saucepan; add 1 in. of water. Bring to a boil. Reduce heat; cover and simmer for 8-10 minutes or until crisp-tender.

2. Meanwhile, in a large ovenproof skillet, cook bacon over medium heat until crisp. Using a slotted spoon, remove to paper towels; drain, reserving 2 tablespoons drippings.

3. Saute onion in drippings until tender. Stir in the vinegar, mustard, garlic powder, salt, Brussels sprouts and bacon; cook 2-3 minutes longer.

4. Sprinkle with bread crumbs; broil 4-6 in. from the heat for 2-3 minutes or until golden brown.

FAST FIX ▶ Asparagus Nut Stir-Fry

This pretty side dish is an excellent way to perk up a party table with some colorful vegetables. I never have leftovers since everyone goes for the fresh taste of the asparagus, the crunch of the walnuts and the zippy seasoning.

—MARGARET SOUDER ELIZABETHTOWN, PENNSYLVANIA

PREP/TOTAL TIME: 20 MIN. **MAKES:** 6 SERVINGS

- 1½ **pounds fresh asparagus spears, trimmed**
- 2 **tablespoons canola oil**
- ¼ **cup thinly sliced sweet red pepper**
- ¼ **cup coarsely chopped walnuts**
- ¼ **teaspoon ground ginger**
- 1 **garlic clove, minced**
- ⅛ **teaspoon crushed red pepper flakes**
- 2 **tablespoons chicken broth**
- 2 **tablespoons reduced-sodium soy sauce**
- ½ **teaspoon sugar**
- ½ **teaspoon salt**

1. In a large skillet or wok, stir-fry asparagus in oil until crisp-tender, about 10 minutes. Remove and keep warm.

2. In the same pan, stir-fry the red pepper, walnuts, ginger, garlic and pepper flakes for 2 minutes or until red pepper is crisp-tender. Stir in the broth, soy sauce, sugar and salt; heat through. Add asparagus; toss to coat.

Green Beans with Pecans

I collect cookbooks from all over the world and love to try new recipes for my husband or for entertaining. When I find a recipe like this, I make a copy and put it in a protective sleeve so we can make it again and again.

—SHARON DELANEY-CHRONIS SOUTH MILWAUKEE, WISCONSIN

PREP: 20 MIN. **COOK:** 15 MIN. **MAKES:** 8 SERVINGS

1 tablespoon butter
1 cup chopped pecans
2 tablespoons maple syrup
⅛ teaspoon salt
BEANS
¼ cup finely chopped shallots
2 tablespoons butter
2 teaspoons all-purpose flour
½ teaspoon grated orange peel
Dash cayenne pepper

1½ pounds fresh green beans, trimmed
⅔ cup reduced-sodium chicken broth
⅓ cup orange juice
1 teaspoon fresh sage or
¼ teaspoon dried sage leaves
¼ teaspoon salt
⅛ teaspoon pepper

1. In a small heavy skillet, melt butter. Add pecans; cook over medium heat until toasted, about 4 minutes. Stir in syrup and salt. Cook and stir for 2-3 minutes or until pecans are glossy. Spread on foil to cool.
2. Meanwhile, in a large skillet, saute shallots in butter until tender; stir in the flour, orange peel and cayenne. Add the remaining ingredients; cover and cook for 5 minutes. Uncover; cook and stir 4-5 minutes longer or until beans are crisp-tender. Transfer to a serving bowl. Sprinkle with pecans.

FAST FIX Peas a la Francaise

I love peas, and this recipe is a favorite. It features tiny pearl onions touched with thyme and chervil, and its presentation is lovely.

—CHRISTINE FRAZIER AUBURNDALE, FLORIDA

PREP/TOTAL TIME: 30 MIN.
MAKES: 12 SERVINGS (½ CUP EACH)

1½ cups pearl onions, trimmed
¼ cup butter, cubed
¼ cup water
1 tablespoon sugar
1 teaspoon salt
¼ teaspoon dried thyme
¼ teaspoon dried chervil
¼ teaspoon pepper
2 packages (16 ounces each) frozen peas, thawed
2 cups shredded lettuce

1. In a Dutch oven, bring 6 cups water to boil. Add pearl onions; boil for 3 minutes. Drain and rinse in cold water; peel and set aside.
2. In the same saucepan, melt butter over medium heat. Stir in the onions, water, sugar and seasonings. Add peas and lettuce; stir until blended. Cover and cook for 6-8 minutes or until tender. Serve with a slotted spoon.

My grandfather was German, so my grandmother prepared many German dishes for him. This is the one I like best. And it adds such a lovely color to the tablescape. —**LEONIE KENYON** NARRAGANSETT, RHODE ISLAND

SWEET-AND-SOUR RED CABBAGE

Sweet-and-Sour Red Cabbage

PREP: 20 MIN. **COOK:** 1¼ HOURS **MAKES:** 8 SERVINGS

- 1 **medium onion, chopped**
- ¼ **cup butter, cubed**
- 1 **medium head red cabbage, chopped (about 8 cups)**
- 1 **teaspoon salt**
- ¼ **teaspoon pepper**
- 2 **medium tart apples, peeled and chopped**
- ¼ **cup water**
- ½ **cup white vinegar**
- ⅓ **cup packed brown sugar**

1. In a large saucepan, saute onion in butter until tender. Stir in the cabbage, salt and pepper. Reduce heat; cover and simmer for 10 minutes. Stir in apples and water; cover and simmer 45 minutes longer or until cabbage and apples are tender.

2. Combine vinegar and brown sugar; stir into cabbage mixture. Bring to a boil. Reduce heat; simmer, uncovered, for 15 minutes or until cabbage and apples are glazed.

FAST FIX Lemon Almond Asparagus

Here's my time-easing way to dress up fresh asparagus: Just drizzle butter and lemon juice over cooked asparagus spears before topping them with almonds and lemon peel.
—**LINDA BARRY** YAKIMA, WASHINGTON

PREP/TOTAL TIME: 15 MIN. **MAKES:** 8-10 SERVINGS

- 2 **pounds fresh asparagus, trimmed**
- ¼ **cup butter, cubed**
- 5 **teaspoons lemon juice**
- ⅓ **cup slivered almonds, toasted**
   Lemon peel strips, optional

In a large skillet, bring asparagus and ½ in. of water to a boil. Reduce heat; cover and simmer for 3-5 minutes or until crisp-tender. Meanwhile, melt butter; stir in lemon juice. Drain asparagus; top with butter mixture, almonds and, if desired, lemon peel.

Sweet Potato Casserole

We have so many sweet potatoes, and I'm always looking for ways to use them. This is a favorite dish of mine for taking to potlucks.
—**KATHY RAIRIGH** MILFORD, INDIANA

PREP: 30 MIN. **BAKE:** 35 MIN. **MAKES:** 8 SERVINGS

- 2¼ **pounds sweet potatoes (about 3 large), peeled and cubed**
- 3 **egg whites, lightly beaten**
- 3 **tablespoons maple syrup**
- 1 **teaspoon vanilla extract**

TOPPING
- ¼ **cup chopped pecans**
- 1 **tablespoon brown sugar**
- 1 **tablespoon butter, melted**
- ⅛ **teaspoon ground cinnamon**
- ⅓ **cup dried apricots, chopped**
- ⅓ **cup dried cherries, chopped**

1. Place sweet potatoes in a Dutch oven and cover with water. Bring to a boil. Reduce heat; cover and simmer for 15-20 minutes or until tender. Drain and place in a large bowl; mash. Cool slightly. Stir in the egg whites, syrup and vanilla.
2. Transfer to an 8-in. square baking dish coated with cooking spray. Combine the pecans, brown sugar, butter and cinnamon; sprinkle over the top.
3. Bake, uncovered, at 350º for 30 minutes. Sprinkle with apricots and cherries. Bake 5-7 minutes longer or until a thermometer reads 160º and the fruits are heated through.

FAST FIX▶ Corn and Berry Couscous

My husband, Doug, wowed me with what we call "Confetti Couscous" the first time he cooked for me while we were dating.
—**LAUREL PORTERFIELD** BRISTOW, VIRGINIA

PREP/TOTAL TIME: 20 MIN. **MAKES:** 4-6 SERVINGS

- 2¼ **cups chicken broth**
- 1 **tablespoon butter**
- ½ **teaspoon salt**
- 1½ **cups frozen corn**
- ¾ **cup dried cranberries**
- ¼ to ½ **teaspoon ground cinnamon**
- 1 **package (10 ounces) couscous**

1. In a large saucepan, bring the broth, butter and salt to a boil. Stir in the corn, cranberries and cinnamon. Cover and return to a boil; cook for 2 minutes. Stir in couscous.
2. Remove from the heat; cover and let stand for 5 minutes or until broth is absorbed. Fluff with a fork.

Savory Mediterranean Orzo

For something other than rice, I make a savory feta-topped orzo medley. To make it vegetarian, use reduced-sodium vegetable broth instead of chicken broth.

—**KRISTI SILK** FERNDALE, WASHINGTON

PREP: 25 MIN. **BAKE:** 20 MIN. **MAKES:** 12 SERVINGS (⅔ CUP EACH)

- 4 **cups reduced-sodium chicken broth**
- 1 **package (16 ounces) orzo pasta**
- 1 **medium onion, finely chopped**
- 2 **tablespoons olive oil**
- 4 **garlic cloves, minced**
- 2 **cups (8 ounces) crumbled feta cheese, divided**
- 1 **package (10 ounces) frozen chopped spinach, thawed and squeezed dry**
- 1 **jar (7½ ounces) roasted sweet red peppers, drained and chopped**
- 1 **small yellow summer squash, finely chopped**
- ½ **teaspoon salt**
- ½ **teaspoon pepper**

1. In a large saucepan, bring broth to a boil. Stir in orzo; cook over medium heat for 6-8 minutes. Remove from the heat.

2. In a small skillet, saute onion in oil until tender. Add garlic; cook 1 minute longer. Stir into orzo mixture. Stir in 1 cup cheese, spinach, red peppers, squash, salt and pepper.

3. Transfer to a greased 13-in. x 9-in. baking dish; sprinkle with remaining cheese. Bake at 350° for 20-25 minutes or until heated through.

Vegetable Noodle Casserole

This is the favorite side dish of my husband, Rory. I found the recipe in an old magazine I bought at a yard sale right after we got married. A wonderful side dish for meat, it has stood the test of time.

—**TARA BRICCO** COVINGTON, TENNESSEE

PREP: 15 MIN. **BAKE:** 30 MIN. **MAKES:** 6-8 SERVINGS

- 1 **can (10¾ ounces) condensed cream of mushroom soup, undiluted**
- 1 **cup (8 ounces) sour cream**
- ¾ **cup chopped onion**
- 1 **teaspoon salt**
- ¼ **teaspoon pepper**
- 3 **cups frozen chopped broccoli, thawed**
- 1¾ **cups frozen cauliflower, thawed and cut into bite-size pieces**
- 8 **ounces wide egg noodles, cooked and drained**
- 1½ **cups (6 ounces) shredded Swiss cheese, divided**

1. In a large bowl, combine the soup, sour cream, onion, salt and pepper. Add the broccoli, cauliflower, noodles and ¼ cup of cheese; mix gently.

2. Pour into a greased 13-in. x 9-in. baking dish. Top with remaining cheese. Bake, uncovered, at 350° for 30 minutes or until heated through.

Warm Roasted Beet Salad

Blue cheese and orange juice add a flavor like no other. I prefer to use hazelnut oil, but any other nut oil or plain olive oil will work.

—**JILL ANDERSON** SLEEPY EYE, MINNESOTA

PREP: 30 MIN. **BAKE:** 40 MIN. **MAKES:** 6 SERVINGS

- 8   whole fresh beets
-     Cooking spray
- 1½   cups orange juice
- 1   shallot, chopped
- 2   tablespoons olive oil
- 2   tablespoons balsamic vinegar
- 1   teaspoon minced fresh thyme or ¼ teaspoon dried thyme
- ½   teaspoon grated orange peel
- ⅛   teaspoon salt
- ⅛   teaspoon pepper
- 6   cups fresh arugula or baby spinach
- 3   tablespoons crumbled blue cheese
- 3   tablespoons chopped hazelnuts, toasted

1. Scrub beets and cut into wedges; place on baking sheet coated with cooking spray. Lightly coat beets with additional cooking spray. Bake at 350° for 40-50 minutes or until tender, turning occasionally.

2. Meanwhile, for dressing, place orange juice in a small saucepan. Bring to a boil. Reduce heat; simmer, uncovered, until liquid is syrupy and reduced to about ⅓ cup. Remove from the heat. Whisk in the shallot, oil, vinegar, thyme, orange peel, salt and pepper. Set aside to cool.

3. Just before serving, place arugula in a large bowl. Drizzle with ¼ cup dressing and toss. Divide mixture among six salad plates. Place beets in the same bowl; add remaining dressing and toss. Arrange on plates. Top salads with cheese and nuts.

Spiced Squash Rings

Fanned out on a platter and dusted in cinnamon, these squash rings could practically be the centerpiece of the holiday table. I serve them as an alternative to sweet potatoes.

—**KATHY BIESHEUVEL** BROADUS, MONTANA

PREP: 15 MIN. **BAKE:** 35 MIN. **MAKES:** 6-8 SERVINGS

- 2   medium acorn squash
- 2   eggs
- ¼   cup 2% milk
- ½   cup cornmeal
- ¼   cup packed brown sugar
- ¾   teaspoon ground cinnamon
- ¼   teaspoon salt
- ¼   teaspoon ground nutmeg
- ⅓   cup butter, melted

1. Wash squash. Cut into ½-in. rings; remove and discard seeds and membranes. In a shallow dish, beat eggs and milk. In another shallow dish, combine the cornmeal, brown sugar, cinnamon, salt and nutmeg. Dip squash rings into egg mixture, then into cornmeal mixture; turn to coat.

2. Place in a greased 15-in. x 10-in. x 1-in. baking pan; drizzle with butter. Cover and bake at 400° for 25 minutes. Uncover; bake 10 minutes longer or until the squash is tender.

FAST FIX ▶ Zesty Broccoli

I've been a vegetarian for more than 20 years and often experiment with flavors that work with vegetables. My nephew, who lived with me while going to graduate school, thought this was one of my best creations. A dash of red pepper flakes works wonders on broccoli.

—**LOUISA KEMYAN** PALM SPRINGS, CALIFORNIA

PREP/TOTAL TIME: 15 MIN. **MAKES:** 4 SERVINGS

- 4   cups fresh broccoli florets
- ¼   cup water
- 2   teaspoons olive oil
- 1   to 2 garlic cloves, minced
- ½   teaspoon salt
-     Dash crushed red pepper flakes

In a large saucepan, combine the first five ingredients. Bring to a boil. Reduce heat; cover and simmer for 5 minutes or until broccoli is crisp-tender. Drain. Add pepper flakes; toss to combine.

This is my mother-in-law's recipe, but I've made it so often I feel as though it's my own! Squash and apples remind me of fall in New England, and they taste fabulous when baked together.

—JUDITH HAWES CHELMSFORD, MASSACHUSETTS

SQUASH-APPLE BAKE

Squash-Apple Bake

PREP: 15 MIN. **BAKE:** 50 MIN. **MAKES:** 4-6 SERVINGS

- 1 medium buttercup or butternut squash (about 1¼ pounds), peeled and cut into ¾-inch slices
- 2 medium apples, peeled and cut into wedges
- ½ cup packed brown sugar
- 1 tablespoon all-purpose flour
- ¼ cup butter, melted
- ½ teaspoon salt
- ½ teaspoon ground mace

1. Arrange squash in a 2-qt. baking dish. Top with apple wedges. Combine the remaining ingredients; spoon over apples.
2. Bake, uncovered, at 350° for 50-60 minutes or until tender.

MAKE AHEAD ▶ Cranberry Chutney

You can serve this chunky chutney over cream cheese or Brie with crackers, or as a condiment with roast pork or poultry. It's a smart and tasty way to take advantage of cranberry season.

—KARYN GORDON ROCKLEDGE, FLORIDA

PREP: 40 MIN. + CHILLING **MAKES:** 3 CUPS

- 4 cups (1 pound) fresh or frozen cranberries
- 1 cup sugar
- 1 cup water
- ½ cup packed brown sugar
- 2 teaspoons ground cinnamon
- 1½ teaspoons ground ginger
- ½ teaspoon ground cloves
- ¼ teaspoon ground allspice
- 1 cup chopped tart apple
- ½ cup golden raisins
- ½ cup diced celery

In a large saucepan, combine the first eight ingredients. Cook over medium heat until berries pop, about 15 minutes. Add the apple, raisins and celery. Simmer, uncovered, until thickened, about 15 minutes. Transfer to a small bowl; refrigerate until chilled.

Maple-Ginger Root Vegetables

My family loves the drizzling of maple syrup on these roasted vegetables. I prefer to use dark maple syrup and fresh grated ginger. Either way, it's an easy way to get kids (and adults) to eat their veggies.

—KELLI RITZ INNISFAIL, ALBERTA

PREP: 35 MIN. **BAKE:** 45 MIN. **MAKES:** 24 SERVINGS

- 5   medium parsnips, peeled and sliced
- 5   small carrots, sliced
- 3   medium turnips, peeled and cubed
- 1   large sweet potato, peeled and cubed
- 1   small rutabaga, peeled and cubed
- 1   large sweet onion, cut into wedges
- 1   small red onion, cut into wedges
- 2   tablespoons olive oil
- 1   tablespoon minced fresh gingerroot
- 1   teaspoon salt
- ½   teaspoon pepper
- 1   cup maple syrup

1. Place the first seven ingredients in a large resealable plastic bag; add the oil, ginger, salt and pepper. Seal bag and shake to coat. Arrange vegetables in a single layer in two 15-in. x 10-in. x 1-in. baking pans coated with cooking spray.
2. Bake, uncovered, at 425° for 25 minutes, stirring once. Drizzle with syrup. Bake 20-25 minutes longer or until vegetables are tender, stirring once.

Christmas Cauliflower

A Swiss cheese sauce gives this vegetable casserole an extra-special taste. It's a tradition for us, as I have served it every Christmas for more than 20 years.

—BETTY CLAYCOMB ALVERTON, PENNSYLVANIA

PREP: 25 MIN. **BAKE:** 25 MIN. **MAKES:** 8-10 SERVINGS

- 1   large head cauliflower, broken into florets
- ¼   cup chopped green pepper
- 1   jar (7.3 ounces) sliced mushrooms, drained
- ¼   cup butter, cubed
- ⅓   cup all-purpose flour
- 2   cups 2% milk
- 1   cup (4 ounces) shredded Swiss cheese
- 2   tablespoons diced pimientos
- 1   teaspoon salt
     Paprika, optional

1. Place 1 in. of water in a large saucepan; add cauliflower. Bring to a boil. Reduce heat; cover and cook for 6-8 minutes or until crisp-tender. Drain and pat dry.
2. Meanwhile, in a large saucepan, saute green pepper and mushrooms in butter for 2 minutes or until crisp-tender. Add flour; gradually stir in milk. Bring to a boil; cook and stir for 2 minutes or until thickened. Remove from the heat; stir in cheese until melted. Add pimientos and salt.
3. Place half of the cauliflower in a greased 2-qt. baking dish; top with half of the sauce. Repeat layers. Bake, uncovered, at 325° for 25 minutes or until bubbly. Sprinkle with paprika if desired.

Bacon & Oyster Stuffing

Smoky bacon leads the way in this East Coast-inspired stuffing. If you really like oysters, add an extra can.
—**SHERRY THOMPSON** SENECA, SOUTH CAROLINA

PREP: 25 MIN. **BAKE:** 30 MIN. **MAKES:** 12 SERVINGS

- 2 **celery ribs, chopped**
- 1 **bunch green onions, chopped**
- ½ **cup butter, cubed**
- 3 **garlic cloves, minced**
- ¼ **cup minced fresh parsley**
- 1½ **teaspoons minced fresh sage or ½ teaspoon rubbed sage**
- 1½ **teaspoons minced fresh thyme or ½ teaspoon dried thyme**
- ½ **teaspoon poultry seasoning**
- ⅛ **teaspoon pepper**
- 12 **cups cubed day-old French bread**
- ½ **pound bacon strips, cooked and crumbled**
- 2 **eggs**
- 1 **cup chicken broth**
- 1 **can (8 ounces) whole oysters, drained and chopped**
- ¼ **cup white wine or additional chicken broth**

1. In a large skillet, saute celery and onions in butter until tender. Add the garlic; cook 1 minute longer. Add the parsley, sage, thyme, poultry seasoning and pepper.

2. Place bread cubes in a large bowl; add celery mixture and bacon. In another bowl, whisk the eggs, broth, oysters and wine. Add to bread mixture; stir just until moistened.

3. Transfer to a greased 3-qt. baking dish. Cover and bake at 350° for 20 minutes. Uncover; bake 10-15 minutes longer or until lightly browned and a thermometer reads 160°.

FAST FIX New England Butternut Squash

Even the little picky eaters in my house eat this dish. They love the hint of sweetness, and I love that it's healthy. If you don't have maple syrup, try it with a bit of brown sugar.
—**LINDA MASSICOTTE-BLACK** COVENTRY, CONNECTICUT

PREP/TOTAL TIME: 30 MIN. **MAKES:** 5 SERVINGS

- 1 **medium butternut squash**
- ¼ **cup butter, melted**
- ¼ **cup maple syrup**
- ¾ **teaspoon ground cinnamon**
- ¼ **teaspoon ground nutmeg**

1. Cut squash in half lengthwise; discard seeds. Place cut side down in a microwave-safe dish; add ½ in. of water. Cover and microwave on high for 15-20 minutes or until very tender; drain.

2. When cool enough to handle, scoop out pulp and mash. Stir in the butter, syrup, cinnamon and nutmeg.

Editor's Note: *This recipe was tested in a 1,100-watt microwave.*

top tip — Move Over, Carrots

Do you have an abundance of squash at the end of the season? I substituted grated squash for carrots in our favorite carrot cake recipe. My family loved it and could not tell the difference.
—**PATSY D.** PFAFFTOWN, NORTH CAROLINA

CRUNCHY POMEGRANATE SALAD

FAST FIX ## Crunchy Pomegranate Salad

Thanksgivings here in Utah wouldn't be the same without this traditional, tasty salad. You can even stir in sliced bananas, mandarin oranges or pineapple tidbits.

—JAN OLPIN SALT LAKE CITY, UTAH

PREP/TOTAL TIME: 15 MIN.
MAKES: 16 SERVINGS (½ CUP EACH)

- 2 **cups heavy whipping cream**
- ¼ **cup sugar**
- 2 **teaspoons vanilla extract**
- 2½ **cups pomegranate seeds (about 2 pomegranates)**
- 2 **medium apples, peeled and cubed**
- 1 **cup chopped pecans, toasted**

In a large bowl, beat cream until it begins to thicken. Add sugar and vanilla; beat until stiff peaks form. Fold in pomegranate seeds and apples. Sprinkle with pecans.

Scalloped Corn

My mom got this creamy old-style casserole recipe from her mother. By the time it's passed around the dinner table, the dish is scraped clean.

—SANDY JENKINS ELKHORN, WISCONSIN

PREP: 10 MIN. **BAKE:** 1 HOUR **MAKES:** 6 SERVINGS

- 4 **cups fresh or frozen corn**
- 3 **eggs, lightly beaten**
- 1 **cup 2% milk**
- 1 **cup crushed saltines (about 30 crackers), divided**
- 3 **tablespoons butter, melted**
- 1 **tablespoon sugar**
- 1 **tablespoon finely chopped onion**
  Salt and pepper to taste

1. In a large bowl, combine the corn, eggs, milk, ¾ cup cracker crumbs, butter, sugar, onion, salt and pepper. Transfer to a greased 1½-qt. baking dish. Sprinkle with remaining cracker crumbs.

2. Bake, uncovered, at 325° for 1 hour or until a thermometer reads 160°.

Winter Vegetables

For me this is an easy and simple way to prepare a colorful array of rustic veggies. With a hint of thyme and pepper, they make a nice side to beef, pork or chicken dishes.

—CHARLENE AUGUSTYN
GRAND RAPIDS, MICHIGAN

PREP: 25 MIN. **COOK:** 20 MIN. **MAKES:** 12 SERVINGS

- 3 **medium turnips, peeled and cut into 2-inch julienne strips**
- 1 **large rutabaga, peeled and cut into 2-inch julienne strips**
- 4 **medium carrots, cut into 2-inch julienne strips**
- 3 **fresh broccoli spears**
- 1 **tablespoon butter**
- 1 **tablespoon minced fresh parsley**
- ½ **teaspoon salt**
- ½ **teaspoon dried thyme**
  Pepper to taste

1. Place the turnips, rutabaga and carrots in a large saucepan and cover with water. Bring to a boil. Reduce heat; cover and cook for 10 minutes.

2. Meanwhile, cut florets from broccoli and save for another use. Cut broccoli stalks into 2-in. julienne strips; add to saucepan. Cover and cook 5 minutes longer or until vegetables are crisp-tender; drain well.

3. In a large skillet, saute vegetables in butter. Stir in the parsley, salt, thyme and pepper.

FAST FIX Herbed Garlic Potatoes

My mom cooks from scratch and rarely uses a recipe. That's how I learned, too, using a pinch of this, a dash of that. But it was actually my dad who prepared this recipe. It's one of those dishes that can go with a holiday entree or a casual burger.

—SHERRY DESJARDIN FAIRBANKS, ALASKA

PREP/TOTAL TIME: 30 MIN. **MAKES:** 8 SERVINGS

- 15 **small red potatoes (about 2 pounds), cut in half**
- ⅓ **cup butter**
- ¼ **cup minced fresh parsley**
- 2 **tablespoons minced chives**
- 1½ **teaspoons minced fresh tarragon or ½ teaspoon dried tarragon**
- 2 **to 3 garlic cloves, minced**
- 3 **bacon strips, cooked and crumbled**
- ½ **teaspoon salt**
- ¼ **teaspoon pepper**

1. Place potatoes in a large saucepan and cover with water. Bring to a boil. Reduce heat; cover and cook for 15-20 minutes or until tender. Drain well.

2. In a large skillet, melt butter. Add the parsley, chives, tarragon and garlic; cook and stir over low heat for 1-2 minutes. Add the potatoes, bacon, salt and pepper; toss to coat. Cook until heated through, about 5 minutes.

Wholesome Apple-Hazelnut Stuffing

Tart apples and toasted nuts add a delicious new spin on holiday stuffing. Herbs and hazelnuts balance the sweetness of the apples and give this dish a warm, nutty flavor.

—**DONNA NOEL** GRAY, MAINE

PREP: 20 MIN. **BAKE:** 30 MIN. **MAKES:** 6 CUPS

- 2 **celery ribs, chopped**
- 1 **large onion, chopped**
- 1 **tablespoon olive oil**
- 1 **small carrot, shredded**
- 3 **tablespoons minced fresh parsley or 1 tablespoon dried parsley flakes**
- 1 **tablespoon minced fresh rosemary or 1 teaspoon dried rosemary, crushed**
- 2 **garlic cloves, minced**
- 4 **cups cubed day-old whole wheat bread**
- 1½ **cups shredded peeled tart apples (about 2 medium)**
- ½ **cup chopped hazelnuts, toasted**
- 1 **egg, lightly beaten**
- ¾ **cup apple cider or unsweetened apple juice**
- ½ **teaspoon coarsely ground pepper**
- ¼ **teaspoon salt**

1. In a large nonstick skillet, saute celery and onion in oil for 4 minutes. Add the carrot, parsley and rosemary; saute 2-4 minutes longer or until vegetables are tender. Add garlic; cook 1 minute longer.

2. In a large bowl, combine the vegetable mixture, bread cubes, apples and hazelnuts. In a small bowl, combine the egg,

cider, pepper and salt. Add to stuffing mixture and mix well.

3. Transfer to an 8-in. square baking dish coated with cooking spray. Cover and bake at 350° for 20 minutes. Uncover; bake 10-15 minutes longer or until a thermometer reads 165°.

Candied-Ginger Sweet Potatoes

I don't like sweet potatoes, so when my cousin served these last Thanksgiving, I took some just to be polite. The combination of maple, apricot and ginger flavors made me go back for seconds!

—**INGRID HAMM** CHATHAM, ONTARIO

PREP: 20 MIN. **BAKE:** 40 MIN. **MAKES:** 10 SERVINGS

- 4 **pounds sweet potatoes, peeled and cubed**
- 2 **tablespoons olive oil**
- ½ **cup maple syrup**
- ⅓ **cup chopped crystallized ginger**
- ⅓ **cup apricot preserves**
- 2 **tablespoons butter**
- ½ **teaspoon salt**

1. Place the sweet potatoes in a 15-in. x 10-in. x 1-in. baking pan. Drizzle with oil; toss to coat. Bake, uncovered, at 450° for 30 minutes, stirring twice.

2. In a microwave-safe bowl, combine the remaining ingredients. Cover and microwave on high for 1-2 minutes or until heated through. Pour over sweet potatoes; toss to coat. Bake 10-15 minutes longer or until tender.

Cheese & Parsnip Mashed Potatoes

I roasted the vegetables with bacon first to get a deeper flavor in this mashed veggie dish. It adds a nice smoky flavor that goes well with the cheeses. I prefer not to blend them too much, as I like the chunks of potato.

—**JIM RUDE** JANESVILLE, WISCONSIN

PREP: 20 MIN. **BAKE:** 40 MIN. **MAKES:** 6 SERVINGS

- 2 **medium Yukon Gold potatoes**
- 4 **small red potatoes**
- 3 **medium parsnips, peeled and cut into 1-inch pieces**
- 2 **bacon strips, cut into 1-inch pieces**
- 2 **tablespoons butter, melted**
- ¼ **teaspoon salt**
- ¼ **teaspoon seasoned salt**
- ¼ **teaspoon coarsely ground pepper**
- ½ **cup shredded Havarti cheese**
- ½ **cup shredded Parmesan cheese**
- ½ **cup heavy whipping cream, warmed**
- 1 **tablespoon minced chives**
- 2 **tablespoons crumbled blue cheese**

1. Scrub potatoes and cut into 1-in. pieces; place in a large bowl. Add the parsnips, bacon, butter, salt, seasoned salt and pepper; toss to coat.

2. Transfer to a greased 15-in. x 10-in. x 1-in. baking pan. Bake at 425° for 40-45 minutes or until parsnips are tender, stirring once.

3. In a large bowl, mash the potato mixture with Havarti cheese, Parmesan cheese, cream and chives. Stir in the blue cheese.

MAKE AHEAD ▶ Creamy Succotash

This is a creation from my sister, Jenny. When I saw her make it, I didn't think the combination would be very tasty, but I changed my mind as soon as I sampled it.

—**SHANNON KOENE** BLACKSBURG, VIRGINIA

PREP: 10 MIN. **COOK:** 20 MIN. + COOLING **MAKES:** 10 SERVINGS

- 4 **cups frozen lima beans**
- 1 **cup water**
- 4 **cups frozen corn**
- ⅔ **cup reduced-fat mayonnaise**
- 2 **teaspoons Dijon mustard**
- ½ **teaspoon onion powder**
- ½ **teaspoon garlic powder**
- ¼ **teaspoon salt**
- ¼ **teaspoon pepper**
- 2 **medium tomatoes, finely chopped**
- 1 **small onion, finely chopped**

1. In a large saucepan, bring lima beans and water to a boil. Reduce heat; cover and simmer for 10 minutes. Add corn; return to a boil. Reduce heat; cover and simmer 5-6 minutes longer or until vegetables are tender. Drain; cool for 15 minutes.

2. Meanwhile, in large bowl, combine mayonnaise, mustard, onion powder, garlic powder, salt and pepper. Stir in bean mixture, tomatoes and onion. Serve immediately or refrigerate.

Make Ahead Note: *Succotash can be prepared the night before, covered, and stored in the refrigerator. Serve chilled or at room temperature.*

GRANDMA'S HONEY MUFFINS, PAGE 151

Glorious Breads

164

156

162

Merry Christmas Scones

I keep a supply of scones in my freezer to pull out and glaze for drop-in holiday guests. They taste great alongside coffee or hot chocolate.

—JOAN PECSEK CHESAPEAKE, VIRGINIA

PREP: 25 MIN. **BAKE:** 15 MIN. **MAKES:** 1 DOZEN

2 **cups all-purpose flour**	½ **cup green candied cherries, quartered**
3 **teaspoons baking powder**	
½ **teaspoon salt**	**GLAZE**
2 **tablespoons cold butter**	½ **cup confectioners' sugar**
1 **cup eggnog**	1 **teaspoon rum extract**
1 **cup chopped pecans**	4 **to 5 teaspoons heavy whipping cream**
½ **cup red candied cherries, quartered**	

1. In a large bowl, combine the flour, baking powder and salt; cut in butter until mixture resembles coarse crumbs. Stir in eggnog just until moistened. Stir in pecans and candied cherries.

2. Turn onto a floured surface; knead 10 times. Transfer dough to a greased baking sheet. Pat into a 9-in. circle. Cut into 12 wedges, but do not separate.

3. Bake at 425° for 12-14 minutes or until golden brown. Combine glaze ingredients; drizzle over scones. Serve warm.

Multigrain Bread

It's hard to get a good whole grain bread where I live, so my bread machine comes in handy. I adapted this recipe from an old one, and I've been enjoying it ever since. Cornmeal and wheat germ give it a wonderful texture and the nutty flavor I love.

—MICHELE MACKINLAY MADOC, ONTARIO

PREP: 10 MIN. **BAKE:** 3-4 HOURS
MAKES: 1 LOAF (2 POUNDS)

 1 **cup water (70° to 80°)**
 2 **tablespoons canola oil**
 2 **egg yolks**
 ¼ **cup molasses**
 1 **teaspoon salt**
 1½ **cups bread flour**
 1 **cup whole wheat flour**
 ½ **cup rye flour**
 ½ **cup nonfat dry milk powder**
 ¼ **cup quick-cooking oats**
 ¼ **cup toasted wheat germ**
 ¼ **cup cornmeal**
 2¼ **teaspoons active dry yeast**

1. In bread machine pan, place all ingredients in order suggested by manufacturer. Select basic bread setting. Choose crust color and loaf size if available.

2. Bake according to bread machine directions (check dough after 5 minutes of mixing; add 1 to 2 tablespoons water or flour if needed).

Editor's Note: *We recommend you do not use a bread machine's time-delay feature for this recipe.*

I got this recipe from my husband's aunt. Everyone likes it, even me, and I was never crazy about fruitcake before. It's very colorful, like a stained-glass window. —JOANN HUHN CLEVELAND, WISCONSIN

Fruitcake Loaves

PREP: 25 MIN. **BAKE:** 1 HOUR + COOLING
MAKES: 2 LOAVES (12 SLICES EACH)

- 2 **packages (8 ounces each) pitted dates, chopped**
- 1 **pound chopped candied pineapple**
- 1 **pound red candied cherries**
- ½ **pound walnut halves**
- ½ **pound Brazil nuts**
- 1 **cup all-purpose flour**
- 1 **cup sugar**
- 2 **teaspoons baking powder**
   Dash salt
- 4 **eggs, separated**
- 1 **teaspoon vanilla extract**

1. In a large bowl, combine the dates, pineapple, cherries and nuts. Combine the flour, sugar, baking powder and salt; stir into fruit mixture until well coated.

2. In a small bowl, whisk egg yolks until slightly thickened. In another bowl, beat egg whites and vanilla until stiff peaks form. With a spatula, stir a fourth of the egg whites into egg yolk mixture until no white streaks remain.

3. Fold in remaining egg whites until combined. Add to fruit mixture; gently fold until blended. Pour into two well-greased and floured 8-in. x 4-in. loaf pans.

4. Bake at 300° for 1 to 1½ hours or until a toothpick inserted near the center comes out clean. Cool for 20 minutes before removing from pans to wire racks. Cool completely. Wrap tightly and store in a cool dry place. Using a serrated knife, cut into slices.

top tip

No Bad Nuts

To keep nuts from going rancid, store them in an airtight container or sealed plastic bag in the freezer. This will also prevent the nuts from absorbing odors from surrounding items.

Cracked Pepper Cheddar Muffins

Served warm, these golden muffins make a great accompaniment to soup, stew or holiday meals. My family loves the cheese and pepper flavor.

—SUSAN KELM MINERAL POINT, WISCONSIN

PREP: 15 MIN. **BAKE:** 25 MIN. **MAKES:** 1 DOZEN

- 2 cups all-purpose flour
- 1 tablespoon sugar
- 3 teaspoons baking powder
- ½ teaspoon coarsely ground pepper
- 1 egg
- 1¼ cups 2% milk
- 2 tablespoons canola oil
- 1 cup (4 ounces) shredded cheddar cheese

1. In a large bowl, combine the flour, sugar, baking powder and pepper. In another bowl, whisk the egg, milk and oil. Stir into dry ingredients just until moistened. Fold in cheese.
2. Fill muffins cups coated with cooking spray two-thirds full. Bake at 375° for 25-30 minutes or until a toothpick inserted near the center comes out clean. Cool for 5 minutes before removing from pan to a wire rack. Serve warm.

Garlic Parmesan Breadsticks

I found this recipe in a farm newspaper many years ago. Fresh from the oven, these buttery breadsticks are great with Italian meals.

—LORETTA FISHER ABBOTTSTOWN, PENNSYLVANIA

PREP: 25 MIN. + STANDING **BAKE:** 20 MIN. **MAKES:** 2½ DOZEN

- 3 teaspoons active dry yeast
- 1½ cups warm water (110° to 115°)
- 4 tablespoons canola oil, divided
- 1 tablespoon sugar
- ¼ teaspoon salt
- 4 cups all-purpose flour
- ½ cup butter, melted
- 3 tablespoons grated Parmesan cheese
- 2 tablespoons dried parsley flakes
- 1½ teaspoons garlic powder

1. In a large bowl, dissolve yeast in warm water. Add 1 tablespoon oil, sugar, salt and 3 cups flour. Beat until smooth. Stir in enough remaining flour to form a soft dough (dough will be sticky). Cover and let rest for 10 minutes.
2. On a lightly floured surface, roll dough into a 15-in. square. Cut in half lengthwise; cut each half widthwise into 1-in. strips.
3. In a shallow bowl, combine the butter, cheese, parsley, garlic powder and remaining oil. Dip each strip into butter mixture, then twist two or three times.
4. Place 1 in. apart on greased baking sheets. Bake at 350° for 18-21 minutes or until golden brown. Serve warm.

Onion Dill Bread

This savory bread is crisp and golden brown on the outside but soft and tender on the inside. The dill and onion give it great flavor without overwhelming your taste buds.

—CHARLOTTE ELLIOTT NEENAH, WISCONSIN

PREP: 25 MIN. + RISING **BAKE:** 15 MIN. + COOLING
MAKES: 2 LOAVES (9 SLICES EACH)

- 1½ cups water (70° to 80°)
- 2 tablespoons olive oil, divided
- ¼ cup dried minced onion
- 2 teaspoons sugar
- 1¼ teaspoons salt
- 1 teaspoon dill weed
- ½ teaspoon onion powder
- 3½ cups all-purpose flour
- ¾ cup whole wheat flour
- 1 package (¼ ounce) active dry yeast

1. In bread machine pan, place the water, 1 tablespoon oil, minced onion, sugar, salt, dill, onion powder, flours and yeast in the order suggested by manufacturer. Select dough setting (check dough after 5 minutes of mixing; add 1 to 2 tablespoons of water or flour if needed).

2. When cycle is completed, turn dough onto a lightly floured surface. Divide dough in half; shape each portion into a 7-in. round loaf. Place on greased baking sheets. Cover and let rise until doubled, about 40 minutes.

3. Bake at 400° for 15-20 minutes or until golden brown. Brush with remaining oil. Remove from pans to wire racks.

FAST FIX Grandma's Honey Muffins

I can remember Grandma Wheeler making these delicious muffins. We'd eat them nice and warm, right out of the oven! She was a "pinch of this" and "handful of that" kind of cook, so getting the ingredient amounts correct for the recipe was a challenge, but now it's a family treasure!

—DARLIS WILFER WEST BEND, WISCONSIN

PREP/TOTAL TIME: 30 MIN. **MAKES:** 1 DOZEN

- 2 cups all-purpose flour
- ½ cup sugar
- 3 teaspoons baking powder
- ½ teaspoon salt
- 1 egg
- 1 cup 2% milk
- ¼ cup butter, melted
- ¼ cup honey

1. In a large bowl, combine the flour, sugar, baking powder and salt. In a small bowl, combine the egg, milk, butter and honey. Stir into dry ingredients just until moistened.

2. Fill greased or paper-lined muffin cups three-fourths full. Bake at 400° for 15-18 minutes or until a toothpick inserted near the center comes out clean. Remove from pan to a wire rack. Serve warm.

Mini Toffee Rolls

I found this delicious recipe in a magazine a long time ago and adapted it to make it my own. The rich bite-sized treats are full of cinnamon. I call them mini-cinnis.

—CAROL GILLESPIE
CHAMBERSBURG, PENNSYLVANIA

PREP: 20 MIN. **BAKE:** 15 MIN. **MAKES:** 4 DOZEN

- 6 tablespoons butter, softened
- ½ cup packed brown sugar
- 1 teaspoon ground cinnamon
- ⅓ cup milk chocolate English toffee bits
- 2 tubes (8 ounces each) refrigerated crescent rolls
- 1 cup confectioners' sugar
- 4½ teaspoons 2% milk
- ¼ teaspoon vanilla extract

1. In a small bowl, cream the butter, brown sugar and cinnamon until light and fluffy. Stir in toffee bits.

2. Separate each tube of crescent dough into four rectangles; seal perforations. Spread evenly with butter mixture. Roll up each rectangle jelly-roll style, starting with a long side.

3. Cut each into six 1-in. slices; place cut side down into two greased 8-in. square baking dishes. Bake at 375° for 14-16 minutes or until golden brown.

4. In a small bowl, combine the confectioners' sugar, milk and vanilla until smooth. Drizzle over warm rolls.

top tip

All About the Icing

Change up the drizzle by using maple flavoring instead of vanilla extract, or try the glaze from the Raspberry-Pecan Mini Loaves on page 153.

Apple Spice Muffins

When I ran out of muffin mix, I came up with this recipe by improvising with ingredients I had on hand. I was so happy with the results!

—BECKIE LAPOINTE
ABBOTSFORD, BRITISH COLUMBIA

PREP: 15 MIN. **BAKE:** 20 MIN. **MAKES:** 1 DOZEN

- 2 **cups all-purpose flour**
- 1 **cup granola without raisins**
- ⅔ **cup sugar**
- 3 **teaspoons baking powder**
- 1 **teaspoon salt**
- ½ **teaspoon ground cinnamon**
- ¼ **teaspoon ground nutmeg**
- 2 **eggs**
- ⅔ **cup unsweetened apple juice**
- ¼ **cup canola oil**
- 1½ **cups grated peeled apples**

1. In a large bowl, combine the first seven ingredients. In another bowl, whisk the eggs, apple juice and oil. Stir into dry ingredients just until moistened. Fold in apples.

2. Fill greased or paper-lined muffin cups three-fourths full. Bake at 400° for 18-20 minutes or until a toothpick inserted near the center comes out clean. Cool for 5 minutes before removing from pan to a wire rack. Serve warm.

Raspberry-Pecan Mini Loaves

Dotted with raspberries and pecans, these mini loaves make lovely Christmas treats. The recipe yields six, so you'll have plenty to share.

—KATHLEEN SHOWALTER SHORELINE, WASHINGTON

PREP: 20 MIN. **BAKE:** 25 MIN. + COOLING **MAKES:** 6 MINI LOAVES (6 SLICES EACH)

- 2 **cups all-purpose flour**
- ½ **cup sugar**
- 2 **teaspoons baking powder**
- ½ **teaspoon salt**
- ¼ **teaspoon baking soda**
- 2 **eggs**
- ½ **cup vanilla yogurt**
- ⅓ **cup orange juice**
- ¼ **cup unsweetened applesauce**
- ¼ **cup canola oil**
- ½ **teaspoon orange extract**
- 1 **cup chopped pecans, toasted**
- 1 **cup fresh or frozen raspberries**

GLAZE
- 1 **cup confectioners' sugar**
- 4 **to 5 teaspoons orange juice**

1. In a large bowl, combine the flour, sugar, baking powder, salt and baking soda. In a small bowl, whisk the eggs, yogurt, orange juice, applesauce, oil and extract. Stir into dry ingredients just until moistened. Fold in pecans and raspberries.

2. Transfer to six greased 4½-in. x 2½-in. x 1½-in. loaf pans. Bake at 350° for 25-28 minutes or until a toothpick inserted near the center comes out clean. Cool for 10 minutes before removing from pans to wire racks.

3. For glaze, combine confectioners' sugar and enough orange juice to achieve desired consistency. Drizzle over warm loaves.

Editor's Note: *If using frozen raspberries, use without thawing to avoid discoloring the batter.*

Buttery Croissants

I've been making these rolls for more than 30 years—not only for holidays, but year-round. I have been asked to sell them, but it's more fun to give them away.

—LORAINE MEYER BEND, OREGON

PREP: 1 HOUR + CHILLING **BAKE:** 15 MIN./BATCH **MAKES:** ABOUT 3 DOZEN

- 1½ **cups butter, softened**
- ⅓ **cup all-purpose flour**

DOUGH

- 1 **package (¼ ounce) active dry yeast**
- ¼ **cup warm water (110° to 115°)**
- 1 **cup warm 2% milk (110° to 115°)**
- ¼ **cup sugar**
- 1 **egg**
- 1 **teaspoon salt**
- 3½ to 3¾ **cups all-purpose flour**

1. In a small bowl, beat butter and flour until combined; spread into a 12-in. x 6-in. rectangle on a piece of waxed paper. Cover with another piece of waxed paper; refrigerate for at least 1 hour.

2. In a large bowl, dissolve yeast in warm water. Add the milk, sugar, egg, salt and 2 cups flour; beat until smooth. Stir in enough remaining flour to form a soft dough. Turn onto a floured surface; knead until smooth and elastic, about 6-8 minutes.

3. Roll dough into a 14-in. square. Remove top sheet of waxed paper from butter; invert onto half of dough. Remove waxed paper. Fold dough over butter; seal edges.

4. Roll into a 20-in. x 12-in. rectangle. Fold into thirds. Repeat rolling and folding twice. (If butter softens, chill after folding.) Wrap in plastic wrap; refrigerate overnight.

5. Unwrap dough. On a lightly floured surface, roll into a 25-in. x 20-in. rectangle. Cut into 5-in. squares. Cut each square diagonally in half, forming two triangles.

6. Roll up triangles from the wide end; place 2 in. apart with point down on ungreased baking sheets. Curve ends down to form crescent shape. Cover and let rise until doubled, about 45 minutes.

7. Bake at 375° for 12-14 minutes or until golden brown. Remove to wire racks. Serve warm.

Cheddar Garlic Biscuits

Like many of my favorite recipes, this one came from a friend. It's a quick and savory way to customize biscuit mix for cheese and garlic lovers.

—FRANCES POSTE WALL, SOUTH DAKOTA

PREP/TOTAL TIME: 25 MIN. **MAKES:** 15 BISCUITS

- 2 **cups biscuit/baking mix**
- ½ **cup shredded cheddar cheese**
- ½ **teaspoon dried minced onion**
- ⅔ **cup 2% milk**
- ¼ **cup butter, melted**
- ½ **teaspoon garlic powder**

1. Combine the biscuit mix, cheese and onion in a large bowl. Stir in milk until a soft dough forms; stir 30 seconds longer.

2. Drop by rounded tablespoonfuls 2 in. apart onto ungreased baking sheets. Bake at 450° for 8-10 minutes or until golden brown. Combine butter and garlic powder; brush over biscuits. Serve warm.

Christmas Tree Savory Rolls

I came up with this crab- and cream cheese-filled recipe for a baking contest many years ago—and won first prize! I like to decorate it for many different holidays; this one uses red and green bell peppers for the stars.

—MARYALICE WOOD LANGLEY, BRITISH COLUMBIA

PREP: 1 HOUR + RISING **BAKE:** 25 MIN. + COOLING
MAKES: 1 TREE (22 ROLLS)

- 4 to 4½ cups all-purpose flour
- ⅔ cup sugar
- 1 tablespoon active dry yeast
- 2 teaspoons grated lemon peel
- 1 teaspoon salt
- ¾ cup 2% milk
- ⅔ cup water
- ⅓ cup canola oil
- 1 tablespoon lemon juice

FILLING

- 1 package (8 ounces) cream cheese, softened, divided
- 2 tablespoons mayonnaise
- 2 teaspoons lemon juice, divided
- 1 teaspoon lemon-pepper seasoning
- 1 teaspoon dried parsley flakes
- 1 can (6 ounces) crabmeat, drained, flaked and cartilage removed, optional
- 1 each small green and sweet red pepper
- 1 medium lemon

1. In a large bowl, combine 3 cups flour, sugar, yeast, lemon peel and salt. In a small saucepan, heat milk and water to 120°-130°. Stir in oil and lemon juice. Add to dry ingredients; beat until smooth. Stir in enough remaining flour to form a soft dough.

2. Turn onto a floured surface; knead until smooth and elastic, about 6-8 minutes. Place in a greased bowl, turning once to grease the top. Cover and let rise in a warm place until doubled, about 1 hour.

3. Meanwhile, in a small bowl, beat 4 ounces cream cheese until smooth. Add the mayonnaise, 1 teaspoon lemon juice, lemon-pepper and parsley; mix well. Stir in crabmeat if desired; set aside.

4. Turn dough onto a lightly floured surface; roll out into a 22-in. x 14-in. rectangle. Spread prepared filling to within ½ in. of edges. Roll up jelly-roll style, starting with a long side; pinch seams to seal. Cut into 22 slices.

5. Cover a baking sheet with foil and grease well. Place one slice near the top center of prepared baking sheet. Place two slices in the second row with sides touching. Repeat, adding one slice per row, until tree has five rows. Repeat last row. Center remaining two slices below last row for the trunk. Cover and let rise until doubled, about 30 minutes.

6. Bake at 325° for 25-30 minutes or until golden brown. Carefully transfer rolls with foil onto a wire rack to cool completely.

7. Meanwhile, in a small bowl, beat remaining cream cheese and lemon juice until smooth. Cut a small hole in the corner of pastry or plastic bag; fill with cream cheese mixture. Pipe onto rolls for garland.

8. Cut peppers in half vertically; remove stems and seeds. Using a 1½-in. star-shaped cookie cutter, cut out stars from peppers; place on tree. Carefully remove a 2-in. piece of peel from lemon (save lemon for another use). With a 2-in. star-shaped cookie cutter, cut out a star from peel; place on top of tree. Remove foil before serving. Refrigerate leftovers.

top tip Measuring Yeast

Envelopes of yeast generally measure approximately 2¼ teaspoons. Three teaspoons equal 1 tablespoon, so if you open another packet, store the leftovers in the packet in the fridge.

Braid Dough

Place three ropes almost touching on a baking sheet. Starting in the middle, loosely bring left rope under center rope. Bring the right rope under the new center rope and repeat until you reach the end.

Turn the pan and repeat braiding, bringing the ropes over instead of under.

Press each end to seal; tuck ends under.

Golden Sesame Braid

Our daughter won a blue ribbon at the state fair when she submitted this delicious bread. People always comment on the crisp crust and tender inside.

—BARBARA SUNBERG CAMDEN, OHIO

PREP: 25 MIN. + RISING **BAKE:** 30 MIN. **MAKES:** 1 LOAF (32 SLICES)

2 packages (¼ ounce each) active dry yeast	1 tablespoon salt
½ cup warm water (110° to 115°)	4 eggs
1-½ cups warm milk (110° to 115°)	7 to 8 cups all-purpose flour
¼ cup shortening	1 tablespoon cold water
¼ cup sugar	2 tablespoons sesame seeds

1. In a large bowl, dissolve yeast in warm water. Add the milk, shortening, sugar, salt, 3 eggs and 4 cups flour. Beat until smooth. Stir in enough remaining flour to form a soft dough.

2. Turn onto a floured surface; knead until smooth and elastic, about 6-8 minutes. Place in a greased bowl, turning once to grease top. Cover and let rise in a warm place until doubled, about 1 hour.

3. Punch dough down. Turn onto a lightly floured surface; divide in half. Divide each portion into thirds. Shape each piece into a 12-in. rope. Place three ropes on a greased baking pan; braid. Pinch ends to seal and tuck under. Repeat with remaining dough. Cover and let rise until doubled, about 45 minutes.

4. Beat remaining egg and cold water; brush over braids. Sprinkle with sesame seeds. Bake at 350° for 30-35 minutes or until golden brown. Remove from pans to wire racks to cool.

> **❝**I call this my hostess gift pumpkin bread, but it's fantastic for any occasion at all. Swirls of cinnamon-sugar make every slice irresistible.**❞**
>
> —**SHIRLEY RUNKLE** ST. PARIS, OHIO

Swirled Pumpkin Yeast Bread

PREP: 45 MIN. + RISING **BAKE:** 55 MIN. + COOLING
MAKES: 2 LOAVES (16 SLICES EACH)

- 4½ to 5 cups all-purpose flour
- 3 cups whole wheat flour
- 2 cups quick-cooking oats
- ⅔ cup packed brown sugar
- 2½ teaspoons pumpkin pie spice
- 1½ teaspoons salt
- 1 teaspoon sugar
- 2 packages (¼ ounce each) active dry yeast
- 1½ cups warm water (120° to 130°)
- 1 cup canned pumpkin
- ⅓ cup unsweetened applesauce
- ⅓ cup canola oil
- 2 eggs, lightly beaten
- ½ cup raisins

FILLING

- ¼ cup butter, softened
- ½ cup packed brown sugar
- 1 teaspoon ground cinnamon

1. In a large bowl, combine 2 cups all-purpose flour, whole wheat flour, oats, brown sugar, pumpkin pie spice, salt, sugar and yeast. Beat in the warm water, pumpkin, applesauce and oil just until moistened. Add eggs; beat until smooth. Stir in enough remaining all-purpose flour to form a firm dough. Add raisins.

2. Turn onto a lightly floured surface; knead until smooth and elastic, about 6-8 minutes. Place in a greased bowl, turning once to grease top. Cover and let rise in a warm place until doubled, about 1 hour.

3. Punch dough down. Turn onto a lightly floured surface; divide in half. Roll each portion into an 18-in. x 9-in. rectangle; brush with butter to within ½ in. of edges. Combine brown sugar and cinnamon; sprinkle over dough. Roll up jelly-roll style, starting with a short side; pinch seam to seal.

4. Place seam side down in two greased 9-in. x 5-in. loaf pans. Cover and let rise until doubled, about 30 minutes.

5. Bake at 350° for 55-65 minutes or until golden brown. Cool for 10 minutes before removing from pans to wire racks.

Holiday Braids

Once you slice into these braids, you'll be so happy you have two. The sweet, creamy inside layer gets a burst of flavor from grated orange peel and dried fruit. My guests are always trying to pinpoint what makes the filling so good.

—SALLY HOOK MONTGOMERY, TEXAS

PREP: 40 MIN. + RISING **BAKE:** 15 MIN.
MAKES: 2 LOAVES (12 SLICES EACH)

- 2 tablespoons active dry yeast
- 1 cup warm 2% milk (110° to 115°)
- 4 eggs
- ½ cup butter, softened
- ⅓ cup sugar
- 2 tablespoons grated orange peel
- 1½ teaspoons vanilla extract
- 1 teaspoon salt
- 4 to 5 cups all-purpose flour

FILLING

- 1 package (8 ounces) cream cheese, softened
- 1 cup packed brown sugar
- 1 egg
- 2 tablespoons grated orange peel
- 1 teaspoon ground cinnamon
- 1 cup chopped pecans
- 1 cup dried cranberries

GLAZE

- 1 cup confectioners' sugar
- 1 to 2 tablespoons 2% milk

1. In a large bowl, dissolve yeast in warm milk. Add the eggs, butter, sugar, orange peel, vanilla, salt and 2 cups flour. Beat on medium speed for 3 minutes. Stir in enough remaining flour to form a soft dough (dough will be sticky).

2. Turn onto a floured surface; knead until smooth and elastic, about 6-8 minutes. Place in a greased bowl, turning once to grease top. Cover and let rise in a warm place until doubled, about 1 hour.

3. In a small bowl, beat the cream cheese and brown sugar until smooth. Beat in the egg, orange peel and cinnamon; set aside.

4. Turn dough onto a lightly floured surface; divide in half. On greased baking sheets, roll each portion into a 15-in. x 9-in. rectangle. Spread filling down the center of each; sprinkle with pecans and cranberries.

5. On each long side, cut ¾-in.-wide strips about 2 in. into center. Starting at one end, fold alternating strips at an angle across filling. Pinch ends to seal. Cover and let rise until doubled, about 45 minutes.

6. Bake at 375° for 15-20 minutes or until golden brown. Remove from pans to wire racks. Combine glaze ingredients; drizzle over braids. Serve warm.

Apple Coffee Cake Braids: *Omit filling. Combine 4 cups thinly sliced peeled tart apples, ⅔ cup each raisins and packed brown sugar, 4 teaspoons all-purpose flour and 2½ teaspoons apple pie spice. Spread each portion of rolled-out dough with 2 tablespoons softened butter. Spoon apple mixture down the center of each.*

Sweet Potato Biscuits

This was one of my great-grandmother's favorite recipes. I'm 87, so you can bet this recipe has stood the test of time!

—VALLIE WILLIAMS SMYRNA, GEORGIA

PREP/TOTAL TIME: 30 MIN. **MAKES:** 1½ DOZEN

- 2 cups self-rising flour
- ⅛ teaspoon salt
- ½ cup shortening
- 1 cup mashed sweet potatoes
- 4 to 5 tablespoons 2% milk

1. In a large bowl, combine flour and salt. Cut in shortening and sweet potatoes until mixture resembles coarse crumbs. Stir in enough milk just until dough clings together. Knead lightly on a floured surface.

2. Roll dough to ½-in. thickness. Cut with a 2-in. biscuit cutter and place on a lightly greased baking sheet. Bake at 450° for 12 minutes or until golden brown. Serve warm.

Editor's Note: *As a substitute for each cup of self-rising flour, place 1½ teaspoons baking powder and ½ teaspoon salt in a measuring cup. Add all-purpose flour to measure 1 cup.*

Herb Potato Rolls

My grandma always made these rolls. She herself enjoyed them as a child in Germany. I practiced for years before I finally perfected the recipe!

—LONNA SMITH WOODRUFF, WISCONSIN

PREP: 30 MIN. + RISING **BAKE:** 30 MIN. **MAKES:** 2 DOZEN

- 5 **to 5½ cups all-purpose flour**
- 1 **cup mashed potato flakes**
- 2 **packages (¼ ounce each) active dry yeast**
- 1 **tablespoon sugar**
- 1 **tablespoon minced chives**
- 2 **teaspoons salt**
- 2 **teaspoons minced fresh parsley**
- 2 **cups 2% milk**
- ½ **cup sour cream**
- 2 **eggs**

1. In a large bowl, combine 3 cups flour, potato flakes, yeast, sugar, chives, salt and parsley. In a small saucepan, heat milk and sour cream to 120°-130°; add to dry ingredients. Beat on medium speed for 2 minutes. Add eggs and ½ cup flour; beat 2 minutes longer. Stir in enough remaining flour to form a soft dough.

2. Turn onto a floured surface; knead until smooth and elastic, about 6-8 minutes. Place in a greased bowl, turning once to grease top. Cover and let rise in a warm place until doubled, about 45 minutes.

3. Punch dough down. Turn onto a lightly floured surface; divide into 24 pieces. Shape each into a roll. Place in a greased 13-in. x 9-in. baking pan. Cover and let rise until doubled, about 35 minutes.

4. Bake at 375° for 30-35 minutes or until golden brown. Remove to wire racks.

Lemony Poppy Seed Muffins

I love the strong lemon flavor in these muffins, especially paired with blueberry jam. They're a favorite of mine at holiday brunches.

—KIMBERLY BAXTER EXETER, RHODE ISLAND

PREP: 25 MIN. **BAKE:** 20 MIN. **MAKES:** 6 JUMBO MUFFINS

- ½ **cup butter, softened**
- ¾ **cup sugar**
- 2 **eggs**
- ¾ **cup sour cream**
- ¼ **cup lemon juice**
- 3 **teaspoons lemon extract**
- 1 **teaspoon vanilla extract**
- 1 **teaspoon grated lemon peel**
- 2 **cups all-purpose flour**
- 1 **teaspoon baking powder**
- 1 **teaspoon baking soda**
- ¼ **teaspoon salt**
- 2 **tablespoons poppy seeds**

1. In a large bowl, cream butter and sugar until light and fluffy. Add eggs, one at a time, beating well after each addition. Beat in the sour cream, lemon juice, extracts and lemon peel.

2. Combine the flour, baking powder, baking soda and salt; gradually add to creamed mixture just until moistened. Fold in poppy seeds.

3. Fill six greased jumbo muffin pans. Bake at 375° for 20-23 minutes or until a toothpick inserted near the center comes out clean. Remove to a wire rack. Serve warm.

Sweet Potato Rolls

This recipe was handed down from my grandmother and has been adapted for a bread machine, which is especially convenient during the holidays. At gatherings, I like to serve them with honey and butter.

—**PEGGY BURDICK** BURLINGTON, MICHIGAN

PREP: 15 MIN. + RISING **BAKE:** 10 MIN./BATCH **MAKES:** 2½ DOZEN

½ cup water (70° to 80°)	4 to 4½ cups all-purpose flour
1 egg	3 tablespoons sugar
3 tablespoons butter, softened	1½ teaspoons salt
¾ cup mashed sweet potatoes (without added milk and butter)	2 packages (¼ ounce each) active dry yeast

1. In bread machine pan, place all ingredients in order suggested by manufacturer. Select dough setting (check dough after 5 minutes of mixing; add 1 to 2 tablespoons of water or flour if needed).
2. When cycle is completed, turn dough onto a lightly floured surface. Punch down. Divide into 30 portions; roll each into a ball. Place on greased baking sheets. Cover and let rise in a warm place until doubled, about 30 minutes.
3. Bake at 400° for 8-10 minutes or until golden brown. Serve warm.
Editor's Note: *We recommend you do not use a bread machine's time-delay feature for this recipe.*

Lemon Tea Biscuits

With subtle lemon flavor, these flaky biscuits make a nice addition to a small buffet or light lunch. Try them the next time you host a holiday tea party for friends, family or co-workers.

—**JANE ROSSEN** BINGHAMTON, NEW YORK

PREP: 25 MIN. **BAKE:** 10 MIN.
MAKES: 16 BISCUITS (½ CUP BUTTER)

   4 **cups all-purpose flour**
   ¼ **cup sugar**
   1½ **teaspoons baking soda**
   1 **teaspoon salt**
   ⅔ **cup shortening**
   1 **cup 2% milk**
   6 **tablespoons lemon juice**
LEMON BUTTER
   ½ **cup butter, softened**
   4½ **teaspoons lemon juice**
   2 **teaspoons grated lemon peel**
   1 **tablespoon finely chopped onion, optional**

1. In a large bowl, combine the flour, sugar, baking soda and salt. Cut in shortening until mixture resembles fine crumbs. Stir in milk and lemon juice just until moistened. Turn onto a lightly floured surface; knead 8-10 times.
2. Roll out to ½-in. thickness; cut with a floured 2½-in. biscuit cutter. Place 2 in. apart on ungreased baking sheets. Bake at 450° for 8-10 minutes or until golden brown.
3. Meanwhile, in a small bowl, combine lemon butter ingredients until blended. Serve with warm biscuits.

The spiral filling in this savory bread makes it an impressive addition to menus. When serving it with spaghetti or lasagna, try sprinkling a little Parmesan cheese on top. —**KARI BONCHER** GREEN BAY, WISCONSIN

Swirled Herb Bread

PREP: 30 MIN. + RISING **BAKE:** 35 MIN. + COOLING
MAKES: 2 LOAVES (12 SLICES EACH)

- 5 **to 6 cups all-purpose flour**
- 2 **packages (¼ ounce each) active dry yeast**
- 1½ **teaspoons salt**
- 1 **teaspoon sugar**
- 1 **cup 2% milk**
- ¾ **cup water**
- ½ **cup butter, cubed**

FILLING

- ½ **cup butter, softened**
- 2 **teaspoons dried basil**
- 2 **teaspoons dill weed**
- 1 **teaspoon dried minced onion**
- 1 **teaspoon garlic powder**

1. In a large bowl, combine 3 cups flour, yeast, salt and sugar. In a small saucepan, heat the milk, water and butter to 120°-130°. Add to dry ingredients; beat until smooth. Stir in enough remaining flour to form a soft dough (dough will be sticky).

2. Turn onto a floured surface; knead until smooth and elastic, about 6-8 minutes. Place in a greased bowl, turning once to grease the top. Cover and let rise in a warm place until doubled, about 1 hour. Meanwhile, in a small bowl, combine filling ingredients; set aside.

3. Punch down dough; divide in half. Turn onto a lightly floured surface. Roll each portion into a 12-in. x 8-in. rectangle. Spread filling over each to within ½ in. of edges. Roll up jelly-roll style, starting with a short side; pinch seams to seal and tuck ends under.

4. Place seam side down in two greased 8-in. x 4-in. loaf pans. Cover and let rise in a warm place until doubled, about 30 minutes.

5. Bake at 375° for 35-40 minutes or until browned. Cool loaves for 10 minutes before removing from pans to wire racks.

1. In a large bowl, combine the first six ingredients. Cut in butter until mixture resembles coarse crumbs. Add raisins. In a small bowl, combine milk and syrup; stir into crumb mixture just until moistened.

2. Turn onto floured surface; knead 8-10 times. Pat or roll out to ½-in. thickness; cut with floured 2½-in. biscuit cutter.

3. Place 1 in. apart on an ungreased baking sheet. Bake at 450° for 12-15 minutes or until golden brown.

4. Meanwhile, combine the confectioners' sugar, extract and enough milk to achieve desired consistency. Drizzle over warm biscuits. Serve warm.

5. To freeze, cool biscuits. Wrap, unfrosted, in foil and freeze for up to 3 months.

To use frozen biscuits: *Thaw at room temperature; warm if desired. Follow directions for icing.*

FAST FIX Butter-Dipped Biscuit Squares

PREP/TOTAL TIME: 20 MIN.   **MAKES:** 15 BISCUITS

- 2 **cups self-rising flour**
- 2 **tablespoons sugar**
- 1 **cup 2% milk**
- ½ **cup butter, melted**
- **All-purpose flour**

1. In a large bowl, combine the self-rising flour, sugar and milk. Turn onto a floured surface; sprinkle with all-purpose flour. Pat dough to ½-in. thickness. Cut into 3-in. x 2-in. pieces.

2. Pour butter into an ungreased 13-in. x 9-in. baking pan. Dip one side of each piece into melted butter. Carefully turn to coat. Bake, uncovered, at 450° for 10 minutes or until golden brown.

Editor's Note: *As a substitute for each cup of self-rising flour, place 1½ teaspoons baking powder and ½ teaspoon salt in a measuring cup. Add all-purpose flour to measure 1 cup.*

Iced Raisin Biscuits

Biscuits have to be both tender and flaky before we'll call them biscuits. And these have the added bonus of tasting like an oatmeal raisin cookie.
—TASTE OF HOME TEST KITCHEN

PREP: 20 MIN.   **BAKE:** 15 MIN.   **MAKES:** 10 BISCUITS

- 2 **cups all-purpose flour**
- 1 **tablespoon sugar**
- 3 **teaspoons baking powder**
- 1 **teaspoon ground cinnamon**
- ½ **teaspoon salt**
- ⅛ **teaspoon ground nutmeg**
- ½ **cup cold butter, cubed**
- ⅓ **cup raisins**
- ½ **cup 2% milk**
- 3 **tablespoons maple syrup**

ICING
- ½ **cup confectioners' sugar**
- ⅛ **teaspoon rum extract**
- 2¼ **teaspoons 2% milk**

66 These are the easiest and best biscuits I've ever made. They're light and buttery and go well with virtually any meal. 99

—REBEKAH DEWITT STAR CITY, ARKANSAS

Cheddar Loaves

Swirls of cheddar cheese give these loaves a pronounced flavor—perfect for making grilled sandwiches, dipping in creamy tomato soup or toasting for breakfast.

—AGNES WARD STRATFORD, ONTARIO

PREP: 25 MIN. + RISING **BAKE:** 35 MIN. + COOLING
MAKES: 2 LOAVES (12 SLICES EACH)

- 3 **teaspoons active dry yeast**
- ½ **cup warm water (110° to 115°)**
- 2 **cups warm 2% milk (110° to 115°)**
- 2 **tablespoons butter, melted**
- 2 **eggs**
- 3 **teaspoons sugar**
- 2 **teaspoons salt**
- 6 **to 6½ cups all-purpose flour**
- 2 **cups (8 ounces) shredded sharp cheddar cheese**

1. In a large bowl, dissolve yeast in warm water. Add the milk, butter, eggs, sugar, salt and 6 cups flour. Beat on medium speed for 3 minutes. Stir in enough remaining flour to form a soft dough.

2. Turn onto a lightly floured surface; knead until smooth and elastic, about 6-8 minutes. Place in a greased bowl, turning once to grease top. Cover and let rise in a warm place until doubled, about 1 hour.

3. Punch dough down. Turn onto a lightly floured surface; knead cheese into the dough. Divide in half; shape each portion into a 6-in. round loaf. Place on greased baking sheets. Cover and let rise until doubled, about 45 minutes.

4. Bake at 350° for 35-40 minutes or until golden brown. Remove from pans to wire racks to cool. Refrigerate leftovers.

Braided Wreath Bread

I make this attractive bread to celebrate Santa Lucia Day on Dec. 13. This Swedish custom is the symbolic start of Christmas in Scandinavia.

—JANET URAM WILLOWICK, OHIO

PREP: 30 MIN. + RISING **BAKE:** 30 MIN. + COOLING **MAKES:** 12 SERVINGS

- 1 **package (¼ ounce) active dry yeast**
- ¼ **cup warm water (110° to 115°)**
- ⅓ **cup warm 2% milk (110° to 115°)**
- ¼ **cup sugar**
- ¼ **cup butter, cubed**
- 1 **egg**
- 1 **teaspoon grated orange peel**
- ½ **teaspoon salt**
- ½ **teaspoon orange extract**
- 2½ **to 3 cups all-purpose flour**

GLAZE
- 1 **egg**

1. In large bowl, dissolve yeast in warm water. Add milk, sugar, butter, 1 egg, orange peel, salt, extract and 1 cup flour; beat until smooth. Stir in enough remaining flour to form a soft dough.

2. Turn onto a floured surface; knead until smooth and elastic, about 6-8 minutes. Place in a greased bowl, turning once to grease top. Cover and let rise in a warm place until doubled, about 1 hour.

3. Punch dough down; divide into thirds. Roll each portion into a 20-in. rope. Braid the ropes; shape into a wreath and pinch ends to seal. Place on a greased baking sheet. Cover and let rise in a warm place until doubled, about 45 minutes.

4. For glaze, beat egg; lightly brush over dough. Bake at 350° for 30-35 minutes or until golden brown. Cool for 10 minutes before removing from pan to a wire rack to cool.

Orange Cranberry Bread

The beauty of this festive quick bread is that it makes a delicious post-dinner snack as well as breakfast the next day. I like to toast leftover slices and spread them with cream cheese.

—RON GARDNER GRAND HAVEN, MICHIGAN

PREP: 20 MIN. **BAKE:** 50 MIN. + COOLING
MAKES: 2 LOAVES (16 SLICES EACH)

- 2¾ cups all-purpose flour
- ⅔ cup sugar
- ⅔ cup packed brown sugar
- 3½ teaspoons baking powder
- 1 teaspoon salt
- ½ teaspoon ground cinnamon
- ¼ teaspoon ground nutmeg
- 1 egg
- 1 cup 2% milk
- ½ cup orange juice
- 3 tablespoons canola oil
- 2 to 3 teaspoons grated orange peel
- 2 cups coarsely chopped fresh or frozen cranberries
- 1 large apple, peeled and chopped

1. In a large bowl, combine the flour, sugars, baking powder, salt, cinnamon and nutmeg. Whisk the egg, milk, orange juice, oil and orange peel; stir into dry ingredients just until blended. Fold in the cranberries and apple.

2. Pour into two greased 8-in. x 4-in. loaf pans. Bake at 350° for 50-55 minutes or until a toothpick inserted near the center comes out clean. Cool for 10 minutes before removing from pans to wire racks.

Spicy Ginger Scones

This recipe was created for Thanksgiving weekend with family members who were trying to be more health-conscious. The candied ginger gives these scones a special zing!

—REBECCA GUFFEY APEX, NORTH CAROLINA

PREP/TOTAL TIME: 30 MIN. **MAKES:** 8 SCONES

- 2 cups biscuit/baking mix
- 2 tablespoons sugar
- 1 teaspoon ground cinnamon
- ¼ teaspoon ground ginger
- ¼ teaspoon ground nutmeg
- ⅔ cup half-and-half cream
- ½ cup golden raisins
- 2 tablespoons chopped crystallized ginger
  Additional half-and-half cream and sugar

1. In a large bowl, combine the biscuit mix, sugar, cinnamon, ginger and nutmeg. Stir in cream just until moistened. Stir in raisins and ginger.

2. Turn onto a floured surface; knead 10 times. Transfer dough to a greased baking sheet. Pat into a 9-in. circle. Cut into eight wedges, but do not separate. Brush tops lightly with additional cream; sprinkle with additional sugar.

3. Bake at 425° for 12-15 minutes or until golden brown. Serve warm.

Fruit 'n' Nut Stollen

Making this stollen has become a tradition for our clan. We like it because it does not contain the usual candied fruits and citron.

—REBEKAH RADEWAHN WAUWATOSA, WISCONSIN

PREP: 40 MIN. + RISING **BAKE:** 15 MIN.
MAKES: 3 LOAVES (12 SLICES EACH)

- 4 to 4½ cups all-purpose flour
- ¼ cup sugar
- 3 teaspoons active dry yeast
- 1 teaspoon ground cardamom
- ½ teaspoon salt
- 1¼ cups 2% milk
- ½ cup plus 3 tablespoons butter, softened, divided
- 1 egg
- ¼ cup each raisins and dried cranberries
- ¼ cup each chopped dried pineapple and apricots
- ¼ cup each chopped pecans, almonds, Brazil nuts and walnuts
- ½ teaspoon lemon extract

LEMON GLAZE
- 1 cup confectioners' sugar
- 4½ teaspoons lemon juice

1. In a large bowl, combine 2 cups flour, sugar, yeast, cardamom and salt. In a small saucepan, heat milk and ½ cup butter to 120°-130°. Add to dry ingredients; beat just until moistened. Add egg; beat until smooth. Stir in enough remaining flour to form a soft dough (dough will be sticky).

2. Turn onto a floured surface; knead until smooth and elastic, about 6-8 minutes. Place in a bowl coated with cooking spray, turning once to coat top. Cover and let rise in a warm place until doubled, about 1 hour. In a small bowl, combine the dried fruits, nuts and extract; set aside.

3. Punch dough down. Turn onto a lightly floured surface; knead fruit mixture into dough. Divide into thirds. Roll each portion into a 10-in. x 8-in. oval. Melt remaining butter; brush over dough. Fold a long side over to within 1 in. of opposite side; press edges lightly to seal. Place on baking sheets coated with cooking spray. Cover and let rise until doubled, about 45 minutes.

4. Bake at 375° for 14-16 minutes or until golden brown. Remove to wire racks. Combine glaze ingredients; drizzle over warm loaves.

Rustic Pumpkin Bread

PREP: 25 MIN. **BAKE:** 1 HOUR + COOLING
MAKES: 2 LOAVES (16 SLICES EACH)

- 3 **cups sugar**
- 1 **can (15 ounces) solid-pack pumpkin**
- 1 **cup canola oil**
- 4 **eggs**
- ⅔ **cup water**
- 3½ **cups all-purpose flour**
- 2 **teaspoons baking soda**
- 1 **teaspoon salt**
- 1 **teaspoon ground cinnamon**
- 1 **teaspoon ground nutmeg**
- ½ **teaspoon ground cloves**
- ½ **cup chopped pecans**

TOPPING

- ⅓ **cup all-purpose flour**
- ¼ **cup packed brown sugar**
- ½ **teaspoon ground cinnamon**
- 2 **tablespoons cold butter**
- ¼ **cup chopped pecans**

1. In a large bowl, beat the sugar, pumpkin, oil, eggs and water until blended. In a large bowl, combine the flour, baking soda, salt, cinnamon, nutmeg and cloves; gradually beat into pumpkin mixture until blended. Stir in pecans.

2. Pour into two greased 9-in. x 5-in. loaf pans. For topping, in a small bowl, combine the flour, brown sugar and cinnamon; cut in butter until mixture resembles coarse crumbs. Stir in pecans. Sprinkle over batter.

3. Bake at 350° for 60-65 minutes or until a toothpick inserted near the center comes out clean. Cool for 10 minutes before removing from pans to wire racks.

Cranberry Pumpkin Bread: *Fold in 1½ cups fresh or thawed frozen cranberries with the pecans.*

Pistachio Pumpkin Bread: *Substitute pistachios for pecans in the batter and topping.*

Pumpkin Chip Bread: *Fold in 1 cup miniature semisweet chocolate chips with the pecans.*

I received this recipe from a co-worker who made it for an office party. It is so yummy and tender that I now make it every year at the holidays to give as a special treat. **—SANDY SANDAVAL** SANDY VALLEY, NEVADA

Strawberries 'n' Cream Scones

If you are like me, you won't be able to eat just one of these warm scones rich with cream and packed with berry goodness.

—AGNES WARD STRATFORD, ONTARIO

PREP/TOTAL TIME: 30 MIN. **MAKES:** 8 SCONES

- 2 **cups all-purpose flour**
- ⅓ **cup plus 2 teaspoons sugar, divided**
- 2¼ **teaspoons baking powder**
- 1 **teaspoon grated lemon peel**
- ¾ **teaspoon salt**
- ¼ **teaspoon ground cinnamon**
- ¼ **cup cold butter, cubed**
- ⅔ **cup half-and-half cream**
- ½ **cup coarsely chopped fresh strawberries**
- 1 **egg, lightly beaten**

1. In a large bowl, combine flour, ⅓ cup sugar, baking powder, lemon peel, salt and cinnamon. Cut in butter until the mixture resembles coarse crumbs. Stir in cream just until moistened.

2. Turn onto a lightly floured surface; knead five times. Gently knead in strawberries, about five times. Pat into an 8-in. circle; brush with egg and sprinkle with remaining sugar. Cut into eight wedges.

3. Separate wedges and place 2 in. apart on a greased baking sheet. Bake at 425° for 9-12 minutes or until golden brown. Serve warm.

Rum Raisin Muffins

Fans of rum raisin ice cream will love this recipe, which I sometimes call my butter tart muffins. I keep the recipe handy for sharing because many of my Canadian friends are familiar with butter tart squares, but not these.

—LORRAINE CALAND SHUNIAH, ONTARIO

PREP: 20 MIN. **BAKE:** 15 MIN. **MAKES:** 1 DOZEN

- ½ **cup butter, softened**
- ¾ **cup sugar**
- 2 **eggs**
- 1 **teaspoon rum extract**
- 1½ **cups plus 1 tablespoon all-purpose flour, divided**
- 2 **teaspoons baking powder**
- ½ **teaspoon baking soda**
- ⅓ **cup 2% milk**
- 1 **cup raisins**
- ½ **cup chopped pecans**
- ¼ **cup maple syrup**

1. In a large bowl, cream butter and sugar until light and fluffy. Add eggs, one at a time, beating well after each addition. Beat in extract. Combine 1½ cups flour, baking powder and baking soda; add to creamed mixture alternately with milk, beating just until combined. Toss raisins with remaining flour. Fold raisins and pecans into batter.

2. Fill paper-lined muffin cups two-thirds full. Bake at 375° for 15-20 minutes or until a toothpick inserted near the center comes out clean. Immediately brush muffins with syrup. Cool for 5 minutes before removing from pans to wire racks. Serve warm.

CHIPS GALORE COOKIES, PAGE 177

Yuletide Cookies & Bars

178

176

198

Chocolate-Mint Sandwich Cookies

PREP: 25 MIN. + CHILLING **BAKE:** 10 MIN./BATCH
MAKES: 7 DOZEN

- ¾ cup butter, softened
- 1 cup sugar
- 1 egg
- ½ teaspoon vanilla extract
- 2 cups all-purpose flour
- ¾ cup baking cocoa
- 1 teaspoon baking powder
- ½ teaspoon baking soda
- ½ teaspoon salt
- ¼ cup 2% milk

FILLING

- 3 tablespoons butter, softened
- 1½ cups confectioners' sugar
- 1 tablespoon 2% milk
- ¼ teaspoon peppermint extract
- 2 to 3 drops green food coloring, optional

1. In a large bowl, cream butter and sugar until light and fluffy. Beat in egg and vanilla. Combine the flour, cocoa, baking powder, baking soda and salt; gradually add to creamed mixture alternately with milk, beating well after each addition. Shape into two 10½-in. rolls; wrap each in plastic wrap. Refrigerate overnight.

2. Unwrap dough and cut into ⅛-in. slices. Place 2 in. apart on lightly greased baking sheets. Bake at 325° for 9-11 minutes or until edges are set. Remove to wire racks to cool.

3. In a small bowl, combine confectioners' sugar, butter, milk extract and, if desired, food coloring; beat until smooth. Spread on the bottoms of half of the cookies; top with remaining cookies.

top tip

Dough Now, Cookies Later

Generally, cookie dough can be refrigerated up to 1 week or frozen up to 6 months.

Can't decide between a Thin Mint and an Oreo? Good thing you don't have to. A batch of cocoa cookies with a creamy peppermint filling gives you the best of both. —**MONICA KNEUER** PECONIC, NEW YORK

Orange-Cinnamon Chocolate Chip Cookies

I developed this recipe after years of searching for a chocolate chip cookie that would stand out from all others.

—DANIEL KAEPP COLDWATER, MICHIGAN

PREP: 15 MIN. + CHILLING **BAKE:** 15 MIN./BATCH
MAKES: ABOUT 3 DOZEN

- 1 **cup butter, softened**
- ¾ **cup sugar**
- ¾ **cup packed brown sugar**
- 2 **eggs**
- 1 **tablespoon grated orange peel**
- 1 **teaspoon vanilla extract**
- 3½ **cups all-purpose flour**
- 1½ **teaspoons baking soda**
- 1¼ **teaspoons ground cinnamon**
- ¾ **teaspoon salt**
- 2 **cups (12 ounces) semisweet chocolate chips**
- 1 **cup chopped walnuts**

1. In a large bowl, cream butter and sugars until light and fluffy. Beat in the eggs, orange peel and vanilla. Combine the flour, baking soda, cinnamon and salt; gradually add to the creamed mixture and mix well. Stir in the chips and walnuts. Cover and chill for 2 hours or until easy to handle.

2. On lightly floured surface, roll out dough to ½-in. thickness. Cut with a lightly floured 3-in. round cookie cutter. Place 1 in. apart on greased baking sheets.

3. Bake at 375° for 12-14 minutes or until lightly browned. Remove to wire racks to cool.

Coconut Crunch Cookies

Some prefer crispy cookies; others prefer soft. In my opinion, the crisp edges and soft centers in these coconut chocolate chip treats add up to the perfect cookies.

—MARIA REGAKIS SOMERVILLE, MASSACHUSETTS

PREP: 30 MIN. **BAKE:** 10 MIN./BATCH **MAKES:** ABOUT 4½ DOZEN

- 1 **cup butter, softened**
- ¾ **cup sugar**
- ¾ **cup packed brown sugar**
- 2 **eggs**
- 2 **teaspoons vanilla extract**
- 1 **teaspoon almond extract**
- 2 **cups all-purpose flour**
- 1 **teaspoon baking soda**
- ¾ **teaspoon salt**
- 2 **cups flaked coconut**
- 1 **package (11½ ounces) milk chocolate chips**
- 1½ **cups finely chopped almonds**

1. In a large bowl, cream butter and sugars until light and fluffy. Beat in eggs and extracts. Combine the flour, baking soda and salt; gradually add to creamed mixture and mix well. Stir in the coconut, chocolate chips and almonds.

2. Drop by rounded teaspoonfuls 2 in. apart onto ungreased baking sheets. Bake at 375° for 9-11 minutes or until lightly browned. Cool for 1 minute before removing from pans to wire racks.

Raspberry Chocolate Rugalach

Since we celebrate both Hanukkah and Christmas, these cookies have always been on the menu. The unbaked cookies can be covered and refrigerated overnight or frozen for up to two months.
—**GP BUSAROW** WHITEHALL, MONTANA

PREP: 40 MIN. + CHILLING **BAKE:** 20 MIN./BATCH + COOLING
MAKES: 32 COOKIES

- ½ **cup butter, softened**
- 4 **ounces cream cheese, softened**
- 1 **cup all-purpose flour**
- ¼ **teaspoon salt**
- **FILLING**
- ¼ **cup dried currants**
- 2 **tablespoons sugar**
- ½ **teaspoon ground cinnamon**
- ¼ **cup seedless raspberry jam**
- ⅔ **cup finely chopped pecans**
- ¼ **cup miniature semisweet chocolate chips**

1. In a large bowl, beat butter and cream cheese until smooth. Combine flour and salt; gradually add to creamed mixture and mix well.

2. Divide dough in half; form into two balls. Flatten to 5-in. circles; wrap in plastic wrap. Refrigerate for 8 hours or overnight.

3. Place currants in a small bowl. Cover with boiling water; let stand for 5 minutes. Drain well and set aside. Combine sugar and cinnamon; set aside.

4. On a lightly floured surface or pastry mat, roll one portion of dough into an 11-in. circle. Brush with half of the jam. Sprinkle with half of the cinnamon-sugar, pecans, chocolate chips and currants; press down gently.

5. Cut into 16 wedges. Roll up wedges from the wide end and place point side down 2 in. apart on a parchment paper-lined baking sheet. Curve ends to form a crescent. Cover and refrigerate for 30 minutes before baking. Repeat with remaining dough and filling.

6. Bake at 350° for 18-22 minutes or until golden brown. Remove to wire racks to cool.

Snickerdoodles

The history of this whimsically named treat is widely disputed, but the popularity of these classic cinnamon-sugar-coated cookies is undeniable!
—**TASTE OF HOME TEST KITCHEN**

PREP/TOTAL TIME: 25 MIN. **MAKES:** 2½ DOZEN

- ½ **cup butter, softened**
- 1 **cup plus 2 tablespoons sugar, divided**
- 1 **egg**
- ½ **teaspoon vanilla extract**
- 1½ **cups all-purpose flour**
- ¼ **teaspoon baking soda**
- ¼ **teaspoon cream of tartar**
- 1 **teaspoon ground cinnamon**

1. In a large bowl, cream butter and 1 cup sugar until light and fluffy. Beat in egg and vanilla. Combine the flour, baking soda and cream of tartar; gradually add to the creamed mixture and mix well. In a small bowl, combine cinnamon and remaining sugar.

2. Shape dough into 1-in. balls; roll in cinnamon-sugar. Place 2 in. apart on ungreased baking sheets. Bake at 375° for 10-12 minutes or until lightly browned. Remove to wire racks to cool.

Cherry Icebox Cookies

As a home economics teacher, I often supplied treats for school functions. These lemon-cherry cookies were always popular.

—PATTY COURTNEY JONESBORO, TEXAS

PREP: 20 MIN. + CHILLING **BAKE:** 10 MIN./BATCH **MAKES:** ABOUT 16 DOZEN

- 1 **cup butter, softened**
- 1 **cup sugar**
- ¼ **cup packed brown sugar**
- 1 **egg**
- ¼ **cup maraschino cherry juice**
- 4½ **teaspoons lemon juice**
- 1 **teaspoon vanilla extract**
- 3¼ **cups all-purpose flour**
- ½ **teaspoon baking soda**
- ½ **teaspoon ground cinnamon**
- ¼ **teaspoon cream of tartar**
- ½ **cup chopped walnuts**
- ½ **cup chopped maraschino cherries**

1. In a large bowl, cream butter and sugars until light and fluffy. Beat in the egg, cherry and lemon juices and vanilla. Combine dry ingredients; gradually add to creamed mixture and mix well. Stir in nuts and cherries.

2. Shape into four 12-in. rolls; wrap each in plastic wrap. Refrigerate for 4 hours or until firm.

3. Unwrap and cut into ¼-in. slices. Place 2 in. apart on ungreased baking sheets. Bake at 375° for 8-10 minutes or until the edges begin to brown. Remove to wire racks to cool.

Decorated Christmas Cutout Cookies

Everyone should have a reliable cutout cookie recipe in the box. This one yields about six dozen sugar cookies with a delicate buttery flavor—perfect edible canvases for decorating.

—LYNN BURGESS ROLLA, MISSOURI

PREP: 15 MIN. + CHILLING **BAKE:** 10 MIN./BATCH + COOLING
MAKES: 6-7 DOZEN (2½-IN. COOKIES)

- ¾ **cup butter, softened**
- 1 **cup sugar**
- 2 **eggs**
- 1 **teaspoon vanilla extract**
- 2¾ **cups all-purpose flour**
- 1 **teaspoon baking powder**
- ½ **teaspoon salt**
  Tinted frostings, colored sugars, edible glitter and nonpareils

1. In a large bowl, cream butter and sugar until light and fluffy. Beat in eggs and vanilla. Combine the flour, baking powder and salt; gradually add to creamed mixture and mix well. Refrigerate for 1 hour or until firm.

2. On a lightly floured surface, roll out dough to ¼-in. thickness. Cut out with Christmas cookie cutters of your choice. Using a floured spatula, transfer cookies to greased baking sheets.

3. Bake at 375° for 8-10 minutes or until lightly browned. Cool completely on wire racks.

4. Decorate cookies with frosting, sugars and candies.

Rainbow Cookies

I always bake my Rainbow Cookies two weeks ahead to allow them to mellow. That leaves them soft and full of almond flavor.
—**MARY ANN LEE** CLIFTON PARK, NEW YORK

PREP: 50 MIN. + CHILLING **BAKE:** 10 MIN. + COOLING
MAKES: ABOUT 8 DOZEN

- 1 **can (8 ounces) almond paste**
- 1 **cup butter, softened**
- 1 **cup sugar**
- 4 **eggs, separated**
- 2 **cups all-purpose flour**
- 6 **to 8 drops red food coloring**
- 6 **to 8 drops green food coloring**
- ¼ **cup seedless red raspberry jam**
- ¼ **cup apricot preserves**
- 1 **cup (6 ounces) semisweet chocolate chips**

1. Grease the bottoms of three matching 13-in. x 9-in. baking pans (or reuse one pan). Line the pans with waxed paper; grease the paper.

2. Place almond paste in a large bowl; break up with a fork. Cream with butter, sugar and egg yolks until light and fluffy. Stir in flour. In another bowl, beat egg whites until soft peaks form. Fold into dough, mixing until thoroughly blended.

3. Divide dough into three portions (about 1⅓ cups each). Color one portion with red food coloring and one with green; leave the remaining portion uncolored. Spread each portion into the prepared pans. Bake at 350° for 10-12 minutes or until edges are light golden brown.

4. Invert onto wire racks; remove waxed paper. Place another wire rack on top and turn over. Cool completely.

5. Place green layer on a large piece of plastic wrap. Spread evenly with raspberry jam. Top with uncolored layer and spread with apricot jam. Top with pink layer. Bring plastic wrap over layers. Slide onto a baking sheet and set a cutting board or heavy, flat pan on top to compress layers. Refrigerate overnight.

6. The next day, melt chocolate in a microwave; stir until smooth. Spread over top layer; allow to harden. With a sharp knife, trim edges. Cut into ½-in. strips across the width; then cut each strip into 4-5 pieces. Store in airtight containers.

Cream Wafers

My sons used to help me make these cookies, and now my oldest granddaughter helps. When the smaller grandchildren are home, they help, too. It wouldn't be Christmas without my little helpers.
—**LINDA CLINKENBEARD** VINCENNES, INDIANA

PREP: 25 MIN. + CHILLING **BAKE:** 10 MIN./BATCH + COOLING
MAKES: 2 DOZEN

- ½ **cup butter, softened**
- 1 **cup all-purpose flour**
- 3 **tablespoons heavy whipping cream**
    Sugar

FILLING

¼ cup butter, softened
¾ cup confectioners' sugar
½ teaspoon vanilla extract
1½ to 2 teaspoons heavy whipping cream
1 drop each red and green food coloring

1. In a small bowl, beat the butter, flour and cream. Cover and refrigerate for 1 hour or until easy to handle.
2. On a lightly floured surface, roll out dough to ⅛-in. thickness. Cut with a floured 1¼-in. round cookie cutter. Place 1 in. apart on ungreased baking sheets. Sprinkle with sugar. Prick each cookie 3-4 times with a fork.
3. Bake at 375° for 7-9 minutes or until set. Remove to wire racks to cool.
4. In a small bowl, combine the butter, confectioners' sugar, vanilla and enough cream to achieve desired consistency. Remove half to another bowl; tint one portion of filling with red food coloring and the other half with green. Carefully spread the filling on bottoms of half of cookies; top with remaining cookies.

Slice 'n' Bake Fruitcake Cookies

A cross between classic fruitcake and buttery cookies, these treats are perfect for Christmas. Each one is chock-full of raisins and candied cherries.

—MARLENE ROBINSON SEXSMITH, ALBERTA

PREP: 20 MIN. + CHILLING **BAKE:** 15 MIN./BATCH **MAKES:** 5 DOZEN

1 cup butter, softened
1 cup confectioners' sugar
½ cup sugar
1 egg
2 teaspoons vanilla extract
2¼ cups all-purpose flour
½ teaspoon baking soda
½ cup raisins
½ cup each red and green candied cherries, chopped

1. In a large bowl, cream butter and sugars until light and fluffy. Beat in egg and vanilla. Combine flour and baking soda; gradually add to creamed mixture and mix well. Fold in raisins and cherries.
2. Shape dough into two 2-in.-thick logs; wrap each in plastic wrap. Refrigerate for 2 hours or until firm.
3. Cut logs into ¼-in. slices. Place 2 in. apart on ungreased baking sheets. Bake at 350° for 12-15 minutes or until lightly browned. Remove to wire racks to cool.

Polka-Dot Macaroons

PREP: 15 MIN. **BAKE:** 10 MIN./BATCH **MAKES:** ABOUT 4½ DOZEN

5 cups flaked coconut
1 can (14 ounces) sweetened condensed milk
½ cup all-purpose flour
1½ cups M&M's minis

1. In a large bowl, combine the coconut, milk and flour. Stir in M&M's.
2. Drop by rounded tablespoonfuls 2 in. apart onto baking sheets coated with cooking spray. Bake at 350° for 8-10 minutes or until edges are lightly browned. Remove to wire racks.

❝I love how easy these M&M macaroons are to mix up in a hurry, especially since they only have four ingredients. And they're always a favorite with kids.**❞**

—JANICE LASS DORR, MICHIGAN

Frosted Pumpkin Cookies

These caramel frosted cookies are our favorite! Plus, they freeze and travel well, especially if you let the icing dry completely, then layer the cookies between sheets of waxed paper.

—LEONA LUTTRELL SARASOTA, FLORIDA

PREP: 25 MIN. **BAKE:** 15 MIN./BATCH **MAKES:** 6½ DOZEN

1 cup shortening	1 cup chopped pecans
2 cups packed brown sugar	1 cup chopped dates
1 can (15 ounces) solid-pack pumpkin	**CARAMEL FROSTING**
4 cups all-purpose flour	½ cup butter, cubed
2 teaspoons baking powder	1½ cups packed brown sugar
2 teaspoons baking soda	¼ cup 2% milk
2 teaspoons ground cinnamon	1 teaspoon maple flavoring
⅛ teaspoon salt	½ teaspoon vanilla extract
	2 to 2½ cups confectioners' sugar

1. In a large bowl, cream shortening and brown sugar until light and fluffy. Beat in pumpkin. Combine the flour, baking powder, baking soda, cinnamon and salt; gradually add to pumpkin mixture and mix well. Stir in pecans and dates.

2. Drop by rounded teaspoonfuls 2 in. apart onto ungreased baking sheets. Bake at 375° for 13-15 minutes or until firm.

3. Meanwhile, for frosting, combine the butter, brown sugar and milk in a small saucepan. Bring to a boil over medium heat, stirring constantly; boil for 3 minutes. Remove from the heat; stir in maple flavoring and vanilla.

4. Cool slightly; beat in enough confectioners' sugar to achieve spreading consistency. Remove cookies to wire racks; frost while warm.

Cherry Kisses

My friends and family love these melt-in-your-mouth cherry morsels. They seem to disappear as fast as I can bake them.

—JO ANN BLOMQUEST FREEPORT, ILLINOIS

PREP: 10 MIN. **BAKE:** 20 MIN./BATCH
MAKES: 6 DOZEN

  4 egg whites
1¼ cups sugar
  ⅓ cup chopped walnuts
  ⅓ cup chopped pitted dates
  ⅓ cup chopped candied cherries

1. Place egg whites in a large bowl; let stand at room temperature for 30 minutes. Beat on medium speed until soft peaks form. Gradually beat in sugar, 1 tablespoon at a time, on high until stiff glossy peaks form and the sugar is dissolved. Fold in the walnuts, dates and cherries.

2. Drop by teaspoonfuls 2 in. apart onto lightly greased baking sheets. Bake at 300° for 20-30 minutes or until firm to the touch. Cool for 1 minute before removing to a wire rack. Store in an airtight container.

> We call these our "Anything Goes" cookies because they're the result of a variation on a traditional family recipe. When my daughters' friends come over, they're always asking if I have some of those "delicious cookies with all that stuff in them."
>
> —**BENNET BARLEAN** NOOKSACK, WASHINGTON

Chips Galore Cookies

PREP: 20 MIN. **BAKE:** 15 MIN./BATCH
MAKES: 2 DOZEN

- 1 **cup butter-flavored shortening**
- 1 **cup sugar**
- ½ **cup packed brown sugar**
- 2 **eggs**
- 2 **teaspoons vanilla extract**
- 2½ **cups all-purpose flour**
- 1 **teaspoon baking soda**
- ½ **teaspoon salt**
- 1 **cup chopped pecans**
- 1 **cup milk chocolate chips**
- ¾ **cup peanut butter chips**
- ¾ **cup English toffee bits or almond brickle chips**
- ¾ **cup flaked coconut**
- ⅔ **cup white baking chips**

1. In a large bowl, cream shortening and sugars. Add eggs, one at a time, beating well after each addition. Beat in vanilla. Combine the flour, baking soda and salt; gradually add to the creamed mixture and mix well. Stir in the remaining ingredients.

2. Drop by ¼ cupfuls 2 in. apart onto ungreased baking sheets. Bake at 350° for 12-14 minutes or until golden brown. Remove to wire racks.

top tip

Baking Sheets

Use heavy-gauge dull aluminum baking sheets with one or two low sides. When a recipe calls for greased baking sheets, use shortening or nonstick cooking spray. Dark finishes may cause the cookies to become overly browned.

Cran-Orange Icebox Cookies

One of our favorite Christmas cookies is this cranberry-orange cookie with chopped pecans. The flavor combo just says Christmas in our home, and I like that they freeze well.

—NANCY ROLLAG KEWASKUM, WISCONSIN

PREP: 30 MIN. + CHILLING **BAKE:** 10 MIN./BATCH **MAKES:** 4 DOZEN

- 1 **cup butter, softened**
- 1 **cup sugar**
- 1 **egg**
- 2 **tablespoons 2% milk**
- 1 **teaspoon vanilla extract**
- 3 **cups all-purpose flour**
- 1½ **teaspoons baking powder**
- 2 **teaspoons grated orange peel**
- ⅔ **cup chopped dried cranberries**
- ¼ **cup chopped pecans**
- 8 **to 10 drops red food coloring, optional**

1. In a large bowl, cream butter and sugar until light and fluffy. Beat in the egg, milk and vanilla. Combine flour and baking powder; gradually add to creamed mixture and mix well.

2. Transfer 1 cup of dough to a small bowl; stir in orange peel and set aside. Add the cranberries, pecans and, if desired, food coloring to remaining dough; divide in half.

3. Line an 8-in. x 4-in. loaf pan with waxed paper. Press one portion of cranberry dough evenly into pan; top with orange dough, then remaining cranberry dough. Cover and refrigerate for 2 hours or until firm.

4. Remove dough from pan; cut in half lengthwise. Cut each portion into ¼-in. slices. Place 1 in. apart on lightly greased baking sheets.

5. Bake at 375° for 8-10 minutes or until edges begin to brown. Remove to wire racks. Store in an airtight container.

Cherry-Orange Icebox Cookies: *Substitute dried cherries for the cranberries and almonds for the pecans.*

Peppermint Meltaways

For a festive-looking gift, I like to place these meltaways on a platter covered with red or green plastic wrap and a large bow. They're also fun served as a refreshing post-dinner treat.

—DENISE WHEELER NEWAYGO, MICHIGAN

PREP: 30 MIN. **BAKE:** 10 MIN./BATCH + COOLING **MAKES:** 3½ DOZEN

- 1 **cup butter, softened**
- ½ **cup confectioners' sugar**
- ½ **teaspoon peppermint extract**
- 1¼ **cups all-purpose flour**
- ½ **cup cornstarch**
- **FROSTING**
- 2 **tablespoons butter, softened**
- 1½ **cups confectioners' sugar**
- 2 **tablespoons 2% milk**
- ¼ **teaspoon peppermint extract**
- 2 **to 3 drops red food coloring, optional**
- ½ **cup crushed peppermint candies**

1. In a small bowl, cream butter and confectioners' sugar until light and fluffy. Beat in extract. Combine flour and cornstarch; gradually add to creamed mixture and mix well.

2. Shape into 1-in. balls. Place 2 in. apart on ungreased baking sheets. Bake at 350° for 10-12 minutes or until bottoms are lightly browned. Remove to wire racks to cool.

3. In a small bowl, beat butter until fluffy. Add the confectioners' sugar, milk, extract and, if desired, food coloring; beat until smooth. Spread over cooled cookies; sprinkle with crushed candies. Store in an airtight container.

A dear friend shared this recipe with me many years ago. These cookies quickly became a much-requested treat at my house, so it's a good thing the recipe makes a big batch! —**GLADYS MAURER** LARAMIE, WYOMING

Date Nut Icebox Cookies

PREP: 15 MIN. + CHILLING **BAKE:** 10 MIN./BATCH
MAKES: ABOUT 8 DOZEN

- 1 **cup butter, softened**
- 1 **cup shortening**
- 2½ **cups sugar**
- 2 **eggs**
- 1½ **teaspoons vanilla extract**
- 1 **tablespoon light corn syrup**
- 5 **cups all-purpose flour**
- 1 **teaspoon salt**
- 1 **teaspoon baking soda**
- 1 **cup finely chopped walnuts**
- 1 **cup finely chopped dates**

1. In a large bowl, cream the butter, shortening and sugar until light and fluffy. Add eggs, one at a time, beating well after each addition. Beat in vanilla and corn syrup. Combine the flour, salt and baking soda; gradually add to the creamed mixture and mix well. Stir in walnuts and dates.

2. Shape into four 6-in. rolls; wrap each in plastic wrap. Refrigerate overnight.

3. Unwrap and cut into ¼-in. slices. Place 2½ in. apart on ungreased baking sheets. Bake at 375° for 10-12 minutes or until lightly browned. Cool for 2-3 minutes before removing to wire racks.

top tip Nice & Round

To keep a nice round shape for refrigerated cookie dough, place each roll inside a tall glass and place the glass on its side in the refrigerator. This keeps the bottom of the dough from flattening out.

Gingerbread Cookies

The smell of these cookies reminds me of going to Grandma's house. My boys always linger around the kitchen when I make them, and my husband usually takes a batch to work to share with co-workers.

—CHRISTY THELEN KELLOGG, IOWA

PREP: 30 MIN. + CHILLING **BAKE:** 10 MIN./BATCH + COOLING
MAKES: 5 DOZEN

- ¾ **cup butter, softened**
- 1 **cup packed brown sugar**
- 1 **egg**
- ¾ **cup molasses**
- 4 **cups all-purpose flour**
- 2 **teaspoons ground ginger**
- 1½ **teaspoons baking soda**
- 1½ **teaspoons ground cinnamon**
- ¾ **teaspoon ground cloves**
- ¼ **teaspoon salt**
  Vanilla frosting of your choice
  Red and green paste food coloring

1. In a large bowl, cream butter and brown sugar until light and fluffy. Add egg and molasses. Combine the flour, ginger, baking soda, cinnamon, cloves and salt; gradually add to creamed mixture and mix well. Cover and refrigerate for 4 hours or overnight or until easy to handle.

2. On a lightly floured surface, roll dough to ⅛-in. thickness. Cut with floured 2½-in. cookie cutters. Place 1 in. apart on ungreased baking sheets.

3. Bake at 350° for 8-10 minutes or until edges are firm. Remove to wire racks to cool. Tint some of the frosting red and some green. Decorate cookies.

Hazelnut Crinkle Cookies

I enjoy trying new recipes, and I always have willing "taste testers" in my house. After sampling these sugar-dusted hazelnut goodies, my family's response was unanimous—an enthusiastic thumbs-up!

—JANEL ANDREWS JEROME, IDAHO

PREP: 30 MIN. + CHILLING **BAKE:** 10 MIN./BATCH **MAKES:** 7 DOZEN

- 1 jar (13 ounces) Nutella
- ¼ cup shortening
- 1⅓ cups sugar
- 2 eggs
- 1 teaspoon vanilla extract
- 3 cups all-purpose flour
- 2 teaspoons baking powder
- ½ teaspoon salt
- ⅓ cup 2% milk
- 2½ cups chopped hazelnuts, toasted, divided
- ½ cup confectioners' sugar

1. In a large bowl, cream the Nutella, shortening and sugar until light and fluffy, about 4 minutes. Beat in eggs and vanilla. Combine the flour, baking powder and salt; add to creamed mixture alternately with milk, mixing well after each addition. Fold in ½ cup hazelnuts. Cover and refrigerate for 30 minutes or until firm.

2. Finely chop the remaining hazelnuts. Place hazelnuts and confectioners' sugar in separate shallow bowls. Roll dough into 1-in. balls; roll in hazelnuts, then sugar.

3. Place 1 in. apart on ungreased baking sheets. Bake at 375° for 10-12 minutes or until set and surface is cracked. Cool for 1 minute before removing from pans to wire racks.

Jumbo Coconut Chocolate Chip Cookies

These gourmet cookies are my most-asked-for recipe. Chock-full of coconut and chocolate chips and dipped in white candy coating, they are truly a chocolate lover's delight.

—JACKIE RUCKWARDT COTTAGE GROVE, OREGON

PREP: 20 MIN. **BAKE:** 15 MIN. **MAKES:** ABOUT 2 DOZEN

- 1 cup butter, softened
- 1 cup sugar
- 1 cup packed brown sugar
- 2 eggs
- 2 teaspoons vanilla extract
- 2½ cups all-purpose flour
- 1 teaspoon baking soda
- 1 teaspoon baking powder
- 1 teaspoon salt
- 2⅔ cups flaked coconut
- 1 cup (6 ounces) semisweet chocolate chips
- ½ cup milk chocolate chips
- 5 ounces white candy coating, coarsely chopped, optional

1. In a large bowl, cream butter and sugars until light and fluffy. Add eggs, one at a time, beating well after each addition. Beat in vanilla. Combine the flour, baking soda, baking powder and salt; gradually add to the creamed mixture and mix well. Stir in the coconut and chips. Shape 3 tablespoonfuls of dough into a ball; repeat with remaining dough.

2. Place balls 3 in. apart on ungreased baking sheets. Bake at 350° for 12-18 minutes or until lightly browned. Remove to wire racks to cool.

3. If desired, melt candy coating in a microwave; stir until smooth. Dip one end of cooled cookies in candy coating. Allow excess to drip off. Place on waxed paper; let stand until set.

Eggnog-Filled Cookie Cups

Using a miniature muffin tin, I make little cookie cups, which can be filled with various puddings. My family loves the taste of eggnog, so I incorporated it into these fun treats.

—MELISSA JELINEK MENOMONEE FALLS, WISCONSIN

PREP: 45 MIN. **BAKE:** 10 MIN./BATCH + COOLING **MAKES:** 2½ DOZEN

- 1 package (3 ounces) cook-and-serve vanilla pudding mix
- 1½ cups eggnog
- ⅓ cup 2% milk
- 2 teaspoons rum extract, divided
- 1 cup butter, softened
- ½ cup packed brown sugar
- 2 egg yolks
- 2 cups all-purpose flour
- ⅛ teaspoon salt
- ¼ cup sugar
- ⅛ teaspoon ground allspice
- ¼ teaspoon ground nutmeg

1. In a small saucepan, combine the pudding mix, eggnog and milk. Cook and stir until mixture comes to a boil. Remove from the heat; stir in 1 teaspoon extract. Transfer to a small bowl. Cover surface of pudding with waxed paper; refrigerate until chilled.

2. In a large bowl, cream butter and brown sugar until light and fluffy. Beat in egg yolks and remaining extract. Combine flour and salt; gradually add to creamed mixture and mix well.

3. In a small bowl, combine sugar and allspice. Shape dough into 1-in. balls; roll in sugar mixture. With floured fingers, press onto the bottoms and up the sides of well-greased miniature muffin cups.

4. Bake at 350° for 10-15 minutes or until light golden brown. Immediately remove from pans to wire racks to cool.

5. Just before serving, pipe or spoon pudding into cups. Sprinkle with nutmeg. Store in an airtight container in the refrigerator.

Glazed Pfeffernuesse

Our version of the classic German cookie is nice to have on hand throughout the holiday season. They stay fresh—and become more intense in flavor—when stored in an airtight container.

—TASTE OF HOME TEST KITCHEN

PREP: 1¼ HOURS + CHILLING **BAKE:** 10 MIN./BATCH
MAKES: ABOUT 10 DOZEN

- 1¼ cups butter, softened
- 1¼ cups packed brown sugar
- ¾ cup molasses
- ½ cup water
- 1 teaspoon anise extract
- 6 cups cake flour
- ½ teaspoon baking soda
- ½ teaspoon salt
- 1½ teaspoons ground cinnamon
- ½ teaspoon ground allspice
- ½ teaspoon ground cloves
- ¼ teaspoon ground nutmeg
- ¼ teaspoon ground mace
- ⅛ teaspoon pepper
- ⅛ teaspoon ground cardamom
- 2 cups finely chopped nuts
GLAZE
- 1 cup confectioners' sugar
- 3 tablespoons 2% milk
- ¼ teaspoon vanilla extract
  Additional confectioners' sugar

1. In a large bowl, cream butter and brown sugar until light and fluffy. Beat in the molasses, water and extract. Combine the flour, baking soda, salt and spices; gradually add to creamed mixture and mix well. Stir in nuts. Cover and refrigerate for 1 hour.

2. Roll dough into 1-in. balls. Place 2 in. apart on greased baking sheets. Bake at 375° for 10-12 minutes or until golden.

1. In a large bowl, cream butter and sugar until light and fluffy. Beat in vanilla. Combine the flour, walnuts and cocoa; gradually add to creamed mixture and mix well. Cover and refrigerate for 1 hour or until easy to handle.

2. On a lightly floured surface, roll out dough to ¼-in. thickness. Using a floured, plain or finely scalloped 2-in. round cookie cutter, cut a semicircle off one corner of the dough, forming the inside of a crescent shape. Reposition cutter 1¼ in. from inside of crescent; cut cookie, forming a crescent 1¼ in. wide at its widest point. Repeat. Chill and reroll scraps if desired.

3. Place 1 in. apart on ungreased baking sheets. Bake at 350° for 9-11 minutes or until set. Cool for 1 minute before removing to wire racks to cool completely.

4. Sprinkle cookies with confectioners' sugar. In microwave, melt chocolate chips and shortening; stir until smooth. Drizzle over cookies; let stand until set. Store in an airtight container.

3. Meanwhile, in a shallow bowl, combine the confectioners' sugar, milk and vanilla. Place additional confectioners' sugar in another shallow bowl. Remove cookies to wire racks; cool 5 minutes. Dip tops of warm cookies in glaze and allow excess to drip off; dip in confectioners' sugar. Cool completely on wire racks. Store in an airtight container.

Chocolate Walnut Crescents

I use a round cookie cutter to form the crescent shapes for these nutty treats. They're so pretty sprinkled with sugar and drizzled with chocolate.

—TERRYANN MOORE VINELAND, NEW JERSEY

PREP: 40 MIN. + CHILLING **BAKE:** 10 MIN./BATCH + COOLING
MAKES: 10½ DOZEN

- 1　cup butter, softened
- ½　cup sugar
- 1　teaspoon vanilla extract
- 2　cups all-purpose flour
- 2　cups ground walnuts
- 3　tablespoons baking cocoa
- 2　to 3 tablespoons confectioners' sugar
- 1　package (12 ounces) semisweet chocolate chips
- 2　teaspoons shortening

Diamond Almond Bars

Making these chewy almond bars has been a tradition in our family for generations. They're especially popular at holidays. Just be sure to freeze a few dozen for later.

—LIZ GREEN TAMWORTH, ONTARIO

PREP: 20 MIN. **BAKE:** 25 MIN. + COOLING
MAKES: 5 DOZEN

 1 **cup butter, softened**
 1 **cup plus 1 tablespoon sugar, divided**
 1 **egg, separated**
 1 **teaspoon almond extract**
 2 **cups all-purpose flour**
 ½ **cup blanched sliced almonds**
 ¼ **teaspoon ground cinnamon**

1. In a large bowl, cream butter and 1 cup sugar until light and fluffy. Beat in egg yolk. Beat in extract. Gradually add flour to creamed mixture and mix well.
2. Press into a greased 15-in. x 10-in. x 1-in. baking pan. Beat egg white until foamy; brush over dough. Top with almonds. Combine cinnamon and remaining sugar; sprinkle over the top.
3. Bake at 350° for 25-30 minutes or until lightly browned (do not overbake). Cool on a wire rack for 10 minutes. Cut into diamond-shaped bars. Cool completely.

FAST FIX ▶ White Chocolate Holiday Cookies

At first glance, these treats look a bit like traditional chocolate chip cookies. But one bite quickly reveals white chocolate chunks with spicy dashes of ginger and cinnamon.

—BONNIE BAUMGARDNER SYLVA, NORTH CAROLINA

PREP/TOTAL TIME: 30 MIN. **MAKES:** 20 COOKIES

½	**cup butter, softened**	1	**teaspoon baking soda**
½	**cup shortening**	¼	**teaspoon salt**
¾	**cup packed brown sugar**	¼	**teaspoon ground cinnamon**
½	**cup sugar**	¼	**teaspoon ground ginger**
1	**egg**	6	**ounces white baking chocolate, coarsely chopped**
½	**teaspoon almond extract**		
2	**cups all-purpose flour**	1½	**cups chopped pecans**

1. In a large bowl, cream the butter, shortening and sugars until light and fluffy. Beat in egg and extract. Combine dry ingredients; gradually add to creamed mixture and mix well. Stir in white chocolate and pecans.
2. Drop by rounded teaspoonfuls 2 in. apart onto greased baking sheets. Bake at 350° for 8-10 minutes or until lightly browned. Remove to wire racks to cool.

> A number of years ago, I won first prize in a recipe contest with these yummy swirl cookies. The tastes of raspberries and walnuts really come through in each bite, and they're so much fun to make!
>
> **—PAT HABIGER** SPEARVILLE, KANSAS

Raspberry Nut Pinwheels

PREP: 20 MIN. + CHILLING
BAKE: 10 MIN./BATCH + COOLING
MAKES: ABOUT 3½ DOZEN

- ½ **cup butter, softened**
- 1 **cup sugar**
- 1 **egg**
- 1 **teaspoon vanilla extract**
- 2 **cups all-purpose flour**
- 1 **teaspoon baking powder**
- ¼ **cup seedless raspberry jam**
- ¾ **cup finely chopped walnuts**

1. In a large bowl, cream butter and sugar until light and fluffy. Beat in egg and vanilla. Combine flour and baking powder; gradually add to creamed mixture and mix well.

2. Roll out dough between waxed paper into a 12-in. square. Remove top piece of waxed paper. Spread dough with jam and sprinkle with nuts. Roll up tightly jelly-roll style; wrap in plastic wrap. Refrigerate for 2 hours or until firm.

3. Unwrap dough and cut into ¼-in. slices. Place 2 in. apart on ungreased baking sheets. Bake at 375° for 9-12 minutes or until edges are lightly browned. Remove to wire racks to cool.

top tip | Making the Slice

To make refrigerator cookie dough easier to slice, make sure the mix-ins, such as fruit and nuts, are finely chopped. If the pieces are too big, the dough may break apart. After each slice, rotate the roll to avoid having one side that's flat.

Caramel Tassies

Buttery cookie cups with a smooth caramel filling make a nice addition to a Christmas dessert tray. My family looks forward to these all year.

—**JANE BRICKER** SCOTTDALE, PENNSYLVANIA

PREP: 1 HOUR **BAKE:** 15 MIN./BATCH + COOLING **MAKES:** 4 DOZEN

- 1 **cup butter, softened**
- 2 **packages (3 ounces each) cream cheese, softened**
- 2 **cups all-purpose flour**

FILLING

- 1 **package (14 ounces) caramels**
- ¼ **cup plus 3 tablespoons evaporated milk**

FROSTING

- 2 **tablespoons shortening**
- 2 **tablespoons butter, softened**
- 1 **cup confectioners' sugar**
- 1 **tablespoon evaporated milk**

1. In a large bowl, cream butter and cream cheese until light and fluffy. Gradually add flour and mix well. Cover and refrigerate for 1 hour or until easy to handle.

2. Roll dough into 1-in. balls; press onto the bottoms and up the sides of ungreased miniature muffin cups. Prick bottoms with a fork. Bake at 375° for 15-17 minutes or until golden brown. Cool for 5 minutes before removing from pans to wire racks.

3. In a large heavy saucepan over low heat, melt caramels with milk. Remove from the heat; cool slightly. Transfer to a heavy-duty resealable plastic bag; cut a small hole in a corner of the bag. Pipe filling into pastry cups. Cool to room temperature.

4. For frosting, in a small bowl, beat shortening and butter until smooth. Gradually beat in confectioners' sugar and milk until fluffy. Pipe onto filling. Store in the refrigerator.

Butter Pecan Roll-Ups

Try my variation on traditional lace cookies by making them into golden brown curls. They go great alongside a scoop of ice cream.

—**STELLA WARTMANN** PORT CHARLOTTE, FLORIDA

PREP: 10 MIN. **BAKE:** 5 MIN./BATCH + COOLING **MAKES:** ABOUT 6 DOZEN

- 6 **tablespoons butter, softened**
- ½ **cup sugar**
- ½ **cup packed brown sugar**
- 1 **egg**
- ½ **teaspoon vanilla extract**
- 6 **tablespoons all-purpose flour**
- ⅛ **teaspoon salt**
- 1 **cup ground pecans**

1. In a small bowl, cream butter and sugars until light and fluffy. Beat in egg and vanilla. Combine flour and salt; gradually add to creamed mixture and mix well. Stir in pecans.

2. Drop six teaspoonfuls onto a well-greased baking sheet. Bake at 400° for 4-5 minutes or until edges begin to brown. Cool for 1 minute. Loosen each cookie and curl around a wooden spoon handle. Cool on a wire rack. Repeat with remaining dough.

Buttercups

I used to make these cookies as simple Christmas cutouts until I hit on the idea of adding a brown butter filling. Sometimes I'll fill the centers with melted chocolate.

—ALICE LE DUC CEDARBURG, WISCONSIN

PREP: 25 MIN. + CHILLING **BAKE:** 10 MIN./BATCH + COOLING
MAKES: 3 DOZEN

- 1 **cup butter, softened**
- 1½ **cups confectioners' sugar**
- 1 **egg**
- 1 **teaspoon vanilla extract**
- 2½ **cups all-purpose flour**
FILLING
- ¼ **cup butter, cubed**
- 1½ **cups confectioners' sugar**
- ¾ **teaspoon vanilla extract**
- 5 **tablespoons water**
- ¼ **cup raspberry preserves or fruit preserves of your choice**

1. In a large bowl, cream butter and sugar until light and fluffy. Beat in egg and vanilla. Gradually add flour and mix well. Divide dough in half; wrap each portion in plastic wrap. Refrigerate for 2 hours or until easy to handle.
2. On a lightly floured surface, roll out each portion of dough to ⅛-in. thickness. Cut with a floured 2½-in. scalloped cookie cutter. Cut a 1-in. hole in the centers of half of the cookies with a floured cutter.
3. Place 2 in. apart on ungreased baking sheets. Bake at 375° for 8-10 minutes or until lightly browned. Remove to wire racks to cool.
4. Heat butter in a small saucepan over medium heat until golden brown, about 7 minutes. Remove from the heat;

gradually add the confectioners' sugar, vanilla and enough water to achieve a spreading consistency.
5. Spread on the bottoms of the solid cookies; top with remaining cookies. Place ½ teaspoon preserves in the center of each.

Cinnamon Stars

My grandmother made these aromatic Cinnamon Stars every Christmas when I was a child. I have fond memories of helping her in the kitchen.

—JEAN JONES PEACHTREE CITY, GEORGIA

PREP: 15 MIN. + CHILLING **BAKE:** 15 MIN./BATCH **MAKES:** 5 DOZEN

- 1 **cup butter, softened**
- 2 **cups sugar**
- 2 **eggs**
- 2¾ **cups all-purpose flour**
- ⅓ **cup ground cinnamon**

1. In a large bowl, cream butter and sugar until light and fluffy. Add eggs, one at a time, beating well after each addition. Combine flour and cinnamon; gradually add to creamed mixture and mix well. Cover and refrigerate for 1 hour or until easy to handle.
2. On a lightly floured surface, roll out to ¼-in. thickness. Cut with a 2½-in. star-shaped cookie cutter dipped in flour. Place 1 in. apart on ungreased baking sheets.
3. Bake at 350° for 15-18 minutes or until edges are firm and bottoms of cookies are lightly browned. Remove to wire racks to cool.

Candied Cherry Nut Bars

PREP: 20 MIN. **BAKE:** 20 MIN. + COOLING
MAKES: 3 DOZEN

- 1¼ cups all-purpose flour
- ⅔ cup packed brown sugar, divided
- ¾ cup cold butter, cubed
- 1 egg
- ½ teaspoon salt
- 1½ cups salted mixed nuts
- 1½ cups halved green and red candied cherries
- 1 cup (6 ounces) semisweet chocolate chips

1. In a small bowl, combine the flour and ⅓ cup brown sugar; cut in butter until mixture resembles coarse crumbs. Press into a lightly greased 13-in. x 9-in. baking pan. Bake at 350° for 15-17 minutes or until set.

2. In a large bowl, beat the egg, salt and remaining brown sugar until blended. Stir in the nuts, cherries and chocolate chips. Spoon evenly over crust.

3. Bake 20-25 minutes longer or until topping is set. Cool on a wire rack before cutting.

Every year at Christmas, my mother and I would make dozens of cookies, including this one. Now all the women in my family get together for a baking bonanza, rotating houses each year.

—**BARBARA WILSON** THAMESVILLE, ONTARIO

top tip
Special Touch

For special holiday occasions and dinner parties, cut bars into small squares and serve them in colorful candy cups or cupcake wrappers.

Apple Walnut Bars

If you need a homespun snack that can be assembled in a hurry, try these nutty bars. The squares are sweet, flavorful and loaded with chopped apple and nuts.
—**JENNIFER DZUBINSKI** SAN ANTONIO, TEXAS

PREP: 15 MIN. **BAKE:** 35 MIN. **MAKES:** 16 SERVINGS

- ½ cup butter, softened
- 1 cup sugar
- 1 egg
- 1 cup all-purpose flour
- ½ teaspoon baking powder
- ½ teaspoon baking soda
- ½ teaspoon ground cinnamon
- 1 medium tart apple, peeled and chopped
- ¾ cup chopped walnuts

1. In a large bowl, cream butter and sugar until light and fluffy. Beat in egg. Combine the flour, baking powder, baking soda and cinnamon; gradually add to the creamed mixture, just until combined. Stir in apple and walnuts.

2. Pour into a greased 8-in. square baking dish. Bake at 350° for 35-40 minutes or until a toothpick inserted near the center comes out clean. Cool on a wire rack.

Brown Sugar Cutouts

I bake so many cookies for the holidays that I have one recipe box just for cookies alone! But of all of them, these simple cutouts are among my husband's favorites.
—**NORMA MUELLER** WAUWATOSA, WISCONSIN

PREP: 35 MIN. + CHILLING **BAKE:** 10 MIN./BATCH **MAKES:** ABOUT 6 DOZEN

- 1 cup butter, softened
- 2 cups packed brown sugar
- 3 eggs
- 2 teaspoons grated lemon peel
- 3 cups all-purpose flour
- 1 teaspoon baking soda
- 1 teaspoon ground ginger

FROSTING
- 1½ cups confectioners' sugar
- ½ teaspoon vanilla extract
- 2 to 3 tablespoons half-and-half cream
- Green food coloring, optional

1. In a large bowl, cream butter and brown sugar until light and fluffy. Beat in eggs and lemon peel. Combine the flour, baking soda and ginger; gradually add to creamed mixture and mix well. Divide dough in half. Shape each into a ball, then flatten into a disk. Wrap in plastic wrap and refrigerate for 2 hours or until easy to handle.

2. On a lightly floured surface, roll one portion of dough to ⅛-in. thickness. Cut with floured 2-in. cookie cutters. Place 2 in. apart on ungreased baking sheets. Repeat.

3. Bake at 350° for 8-10 minutes or until golden brown. Remove to wire racks to cool.

4. For frosting, in a small bowl, combine the confectioners' sugar, vanilla and enough cream to achieve spreading consistency. Add food coloring if desired to some or all of the frosting. Decorate cookies.

Cherry Bonbon Cookies

You'll see these red and green bonbon cookies in my home every yuletide. They're a traditional staple on my cookie tray.

—**LORI DANIELS** BEVERLY, WEST VIRGINIA

PREP: 20 MIN. **BAKE:** 15 MIN./BATCH + COOLING **MAKES:** 3 DOZEN

36	maraschino cherries	
1	cup butter, softened	
1½	cups confectioners' sugar	
1	tablespoon 2% milk	
3	teaspoons vanilla extract	
2¾	cups all-purpose flour	
¼	teaspoon salt	

CHRISTMAS GLAZE

1¼	cups confectioners' sugar
1	to 2 tablespoons water

Red and green liquid food coloring
Colored sprinkles

CHOCOLATE GLAZE

1	cup confectioners' sugar
1	to 2 tablespoons water
1	ounce unsweetened chocolate, melted
1	teaspoon vanilla extract
½	cup chopped pecans or walnuts

1. Pat cherries dry with paper towels; set aside. In a large bowl, cream butter and confectioner's sugar until light and fluffy. Beat in milk and vanilla. Combine flour and salt; gradually add to creamed mixture.

2. Shape a tablespoonful of dough around each cherry, forming a ball. Place 2 in. apart on ungreased baking sheets. Bake at 350° for 14-16 minutes or until bottoms are browned. Remove to wire racks to cool.

3. For Christmas glaze, in a small bowl, combine confectioners' sugar and enough water to achieve a dipping consistency. Transfer half of the glaze to another bowl; tint one bowl green and the other red. Dip the tops of nine cookies in green glaze and nine cookies in red glaze, then decorate with sprinkles. Let stand until set.

4. For chocolate glaze, in a small bowl, combine confectioners' sugar and enough water to achieve dipping consistency. Stir in chocolate and vanilla. Dip the tops of remaining cookies in glaze, then sprinkle with nuts. Let stand until set.

Candy Cane Cookies

A rich almond flavor and a pretty sprinkling of peppermint make these cookies so festive. The cute candy canes are a sure sign of Christmas!

—**TAMMY SCHENK** HARLOWTON, MONTANA

PREP: 25 MIN. **BAKE:** 10 MIN./BATCH + COOLING
MAKES: 3 DOZEN

1	cup butter, softened
1	cup confectioners' sugar
1	egg
1½	teaspoons almond extract
2½	cups all-purpose flour
1	teaspoon salt
	Red food coloring
½	cup crushed peppermint candy canes
½	cup sugar

1. In a large bowl, cream butter and confectioners' sugar until light and fluffy. Beat in egg and extract. Combine flour and salt; gradually add to creamed mixture and mix well.

2. Divide dough in half; add 6-7 drops of food coloring to one half. Shape tablespoonfuls of each color of dough into 4-in. ropes. Place ropes side by side; lightly press ends together and twist. Place on ungreased baking sheets; curve to form canes.

3. Bake at 375° for 9-12 minutes or until lightly browned. Combine crushed candy canes and sugar; immediately sprinkle over cookies. Cool for 2 minutes before removing from pans to wire racks to cool completely.

> 66 These whimsical little mice taste like truffles and have been a family favorite for years. We so enjoy the smiles and laughs they always get! Every Christmas, we make sure to have enough for friends, neighbors and get-togethers. 99

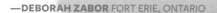

—**DEBORAH ZABOR** FORT ERIE, ONTARIO

Christmas Mice Cookies

PREP: 30 MIN. + CHILLING **MAKES:** 1½ DOZEN

- ⅔ **cup semisweet chocolate chips**
- 2 **cups chocolate wafer crumbs, divided**
- ⅓ **cup sour cream**
- 36 **red nonpareils**
- ¼ **cup sliced almonds**
- 18 **pieces black shoestring licorice (2 in. each)**

1. In a microwave, melt chocolate chips; stir until smooth. Stir in 1 cup crumbs and sour cream. Cover and refrigerate for 1 hour.
2. For each one, roll 1 tablespoon chocolate mixture into a ball, tapering one end to resemble a mouse. Roll in remaining chocolate crumbs. Position nonpareils for eyes, almond slices for ears and licorice pieces for tails.

Chocolate-Drizzled Cherry Bars

I bake for my church Christmas party every year, and I always get kudos on these bars.
—**JANICE HEIKKILA** DEER CREEK, MINNESOTA

PREP: 35 MIN. **BAKE:** 20 MIN. + COOLING **MAKES:** 3 DOZEN

- 2 **cups all-purpose flour**
- 2 **cups quick-cooking oats**
- 1½ **cups sugar**
- 1¼ **cups butter, softened**
- 1 **can (21 ounces) cherry pie filling**
- 1 **teaspoon almond extract**
- ¼ **cup semisweet chocolate chips**
- ¾ **teaspoon shortening**

1. In large bowl, combine the flour, oats, sugar and butter until crumbly. Set aside 1½ cups for topping. Press remaining crumb mixture into an ungreased 13-in. x 9-in. baking dish. Bake at 350° for 15-18 minutes or until edges begin to brown.
2. In small bowl, combine pie filling and extract; carefully spread on crust. Sprinkle with reserved crumb mixture. Bake 20-25 minutes longer or until edges are lightly browned.
3. In a microwave, melt chocolate chips and shortening; stir until smooth. Drizzle over bars. Cool on a wire rack.

CHRISTMAS MICE COOKIES

Mocha Sandwich Cookies

I've had cookies that melted in my mouth, but not like this! I love to make them into sandwiches with an almond-mocha filling.
—**ANNA SYLVESTER** SYLVANIA, OHIO

PREP: 20 MIN. + CHILLING   **BAKE:** 10 MIN./BATCH + COOLING
MAKES: 2 DOZEN

- ¾ cup butter, softened
- ½ cup confectioners' sugar
- 1 teaspoon vanilla extract
- 1 cup all-purpose flour
- ½ cup cornstarch

FILLING

- 2 tablespoons butter, softened
- ⅔ cup confectioners' sugar
- 1½ teaspoons heavy whipping cream
- ¼ teaspoon almond extract
- 2 tablespoons baking cocoa
- ½ teaspoon instant coffee granules
- 1 to 2 tablespoons boiling water
- 2 tablespoons sliced almonds, toasted and finely chopped

1. In a large bowl, cream butter and confectioners' sugar until light and fluffy. Beat in vanilla. Combine flour and cornstarch; gradually add to creamed mixture and mix well. Cover and refrigerate for 1 hour.

2. Shape dough into ¾-in. balls; press lightly to flatten. Place 1 in. apart on ungreased baking sheets. Bake at 375° for 10-12 minutes. Cool on wire racks.

3. For filling, in a small bowl, cream butter and confectioners' sugar. Beat in cream and extract. In a small bowl, combine the cocoa, coffee and boiling water; stir to dissolve coffee granules. Add to creamed mixture and mix well. Fold in almonds. Cover and refrigerate for 30 minutes.

4. Spread filling over the bottoms of half of the cookies; top with remaining cookies. Store in the refrigerator.

Snowcapped Brownies

Baking is one of my favorite hobbies, and my wife says these brownies with cream cheese frosting are outstanding. When you really want to impress, drizzle them with caramel sauce and sprinkle on chocolate curls.
—**LYLE BORCHERDING** JOHNSTOWN, PENNSYLVANIA

PREP: 20 MIN.   **BAKE:** 35 MIN. + COOLING   **MAKES:** 2½ DOZEN

- 1 cup butter, cubed
- ¾ cup baking cocoa
- 4 eggs
- 2 cups sugar
- 1 teaspoon vanilla extract
- 1 cup all-purpose flour
- ½ teaspoon salt
- 2 cups (12 ounces) semisweet chocolate chips
- 1 cup chopped nuts, optional

TOPPING

  4 **ounces cream cheese, softened**
1½ **cups cold 2% milk, divided**
  1 **package (3.4 ounces) instant vanilla pudding mix**
  ⅛ **teaspoon almond extract**
1½ **cups whipped topping**
      Caramel ice cream topping and chocolate curls, optional

1. In a small saucepan, melt butter; stir in cocoa until smooth. Remove from the heat. In a large bowl, beat the eggs, sugar and vanilla for 1 minute. Gradually add flour and salt. Stir in cocoa mixture. Fold in chocolate chips and, if desired, nuts.

2. Pour into a greased 13-in. x 9-in. baking dish. Bake at 350° for 30-35 minutes or until a toothpick inserted near the center comes out with moist crumbs (do not overbake). Cool on a wire rack.

3. In a large bowl, beat cream cheese and ½ cup milk until smooth. Add pudding mix and remaining milk; beat for 2 minutes or until thickened. Stir in extract; fold in whipped topping. Spread over cooled brownies. Refrigerate until set.

4. Just before serving, drizzle with caramel topping and garnish with chocolate curls if desired.

Peanut Butter Squares

I grew up in Lancaster County, Pennsylvania, and spent a lot of time in the kitchen with my mom and grandmother making Pennsylvania Dutch classics. This is one I adapted and just love.
—**RACHEL GREENAWALT KELLER** ROANOKE, VIRGINIA

PREP: 20 MIN. + CHILLING **MAKES:** 4 DOZEN

  ¾ **cup cold butter, cubed**
  2 **ounces semisweet chocolate**
1½ **cups graham cracker crumbs (about 24 squares)**
  1 **cup flaked coconut**
  ½ **cup chopped salted peanuts**
  ¼ **cup toasted wheat germ**

top tip

Li'l Chocolate Curls

For small curls, a 4-ounce chocolate bar can be left out in a warm place until warm but not melted. With a vegetable peeler, draw along the flat side of the chocolate bar, making a curl. Move each curl onto the dessert with a toothpick.

FILLING

  2 **packages (8 ounces each) cream cheese, softened**
  ¾ **cup sugar**
  ⅔ **cup chunky peanut butter**
  1 **teaspoon vanilla extract**
TOPPING
  4 **ounces semisweet chocolate, chopped**
  ¼ **cup butter, cubed**

1. In a microwave-safe bowl, melt butter and chocolate; stir until smooth. Stir in the cracker crumbs, coconut, peanuts and wheat germ. Press into a greased 13-in. x 9-in. pan. Cover and refrigerate for at least 30 minutes.

2. In a small bowl, combine filling ingredients. Spread over crust. Cover and refrigerate for at least 30 minutes.

3. In a microwave, melt chocolate and butter; stir until smooth. Pour over filling. Cover and refrigerate for at least 30 minutes or until topping is set. Cut into squares. Refrigerate leftovers.

Editor's Note: *This recipe was tested in a 1,100-watt microwave.*

Toffee Cranberry Crisps

PREP: 15 MIN. + CHILLING **BAKE:** 10 MIN./BATCH
MAKES: 5½ DOZEN

- 1 **cup butter, softened**
- ¾ **cup sugar**
- ¾ **cup packed brown sugar**
- 1 **egg**
- 1 **teaspoon vanilla extract**
- 1½ **cups all-purpose flour**
- 1½ **cups quick-cooking oats**
- 1 **teaspoon baking soda**
- ¼ **teaspoon salt**
- 1 **cup dried cranberries**
- 1 **cup miniature semisweet chocolate chips**
- 1 **cup milk chocolate English toffee bits**

1. In a large bowl, cream butter and sugars until light and fluffy. Beat in egg and vanilla. Combine the flour, oats, baking soda and salt; gradually add to creamed mixture and mix well. Stir in the cranberries, chocolate chips and toffee bits.

2. Shape into three 12-in. logs; wrap each in plastic wrap. Refrigerate for 2 hours or until firm. Unwrap and cut into ½-in. slices. Place 2 in. apart on lightly greased baking sheets.

3. Bake at 350° for 8-10 minutes or until golden brown. Remove to wire racks to cool.

top tip

How to Quickly Soften Butter

If you want to make cookies right now but the butter's still cold, simply microwave the sticks at 70 percent power in 10-second intervals from two to four times. The butter should be ready to use.
—PATRICIA WINN FREEVILLE, NEW YORK

Try my mos... ...ll
enjoy it. Th...
chips and t...
—ANN QUAERNA...

Soft Buttermilk Sugar Cookies

Family gatherings are very important to us, so we have lots of special recipes. My late grandma, Pauline Taylor, used to make these soft sugar cookies. They're one of our family's favorites.

—TRACI ROWLETT OLDENBURG, INDIANA

PREP: 20 MIN. **BAKE:** 10 MIN./BATCH
MAKES: ABOUT 2½ DOZEN

- ½ **cup shortening**
- 1¼ **cups sugar, divided**
- 2 **eggs**
- 2 **teaspoons vanilla extract**
- 2 **cups all-purpose flour**
- 2 **teaspoons baking powder**
- 1 **teaspoon salt**
- ½ **teaspoon baking soda**
- ½ **cup buttermilk**
- ¼ **teaspoon ground cinnamon**

1. In a large bowl, cream shortening and 1 cup sugar until light and fluffy. Beat in eggs and vanilla. Combine the flour, baking powder, salt and baking soda; add to creamed mixture alternately with buttermilk, beating well after each addition (batter will be moist).

2. Combine cinnamon and remaining sugar. Drop dough by tablespoonfuls onto greased baking sheets. Sprinkle with cinnamon-sugar.

3. Bake at 375° for 8-10 minutes or until edges begin to brown. Remove to wire racks. Store in an airtight container.

Raspberry Dreams

I made variations to my friend's recipe to come up with this treat. My family looks forward to these sensational jam-filled sandwich cookies for the holidays.

—LORI BROWN SIOUX FALLS, SOUTH DAKOTA

PREP: 25 MIN. + CHILLING **BAKE:** 10 MIN./BATCH + COOLING **MAKES:** ABOUT 4½ DOZEN

2 **cups butter, softened**	**FILLING**
1 **cup sugar**	1 **jar (12 ounces) raspberry**
4 **egg yolks**	**preserves**
2 **teaspoons vanilla extract**	**ICING**
1 **drop lemon juice**	1 **cup confectioners' sugar**
5⅓ **cups all-purpose flour**	1 **drop lemon juice**
¼ **teaspoon salt**	1 **drop red food coloring, optional**
	1 **to 2 tablespoons 2% milk**

1. In a large bowl, cream butter and sugar until light and fluffy. Add egg yolks, one at a time, beating well after each addition. Beat in vanilla and lemon juice. Combine flour and salt; gradually add to the creamed mixture and mix well. Refrigerate for 1 hour or until easy to handle.

2. Divide dough into three portions. On a lightly floured surface, roll out each portion to ¼-in. thickness. Cut with a 2-in. round cookie cutter. Place 1 in. apart on ungreased baking sheets.

3. Bake at 350° for 8-10 minutes or until edges are very lightly browned. Remove to wire racks to cool.

4. Spread the bottoms of half of the cookies with raspberry preserves; top with remaining cookies.

5. For icing, combine the sugar, lemon juice, food coloring if desired and enough milk to achieve a drizzling consistency. Drizzle over cookies.

Holiday Spritz

I tried substituting rum extract for vanilla in a classic spritz recipe, and the end result was a cookie that tasted a lot like eggnog.

—LISA VARNER EL PASO, TEXAS

PREP: 30 MIN. **BAKE:** 10 MIN./BATCH **MAKES:** 7 DOZEN

- 1 **cup butter, softened**
- 1 **cup confectioners' sugar**
- 1 **egg**
- 1½ **teaspoons rum extract**
- 2½ **cups all-purpose flour**
- ¼ **teaspoon salt**
  Colored sugar

1. In a large bowl, cream butter and confectioners' sugar until light and fluffy. Beat in egg and extract. Combine flour and salt; gradually add to creamed mixture and mix well.
2. Using a cookie press fitted with the disk of your choice, press cookies 1 in. apart onto ungreased baking sheets. Sprinkle with colored sugar.
3. Bake at 375° for 6-9 minutes or until lightly browned. Cool for 2 minutes before removing from pans to wire racks.

Raspberry Sandwich Spritz

I started baking these Christmas classics when I was in high school, and I still make them for my children and grandkids.

—JOAN O'BRIEN PUNTA GORDA, FLORIDA

PREP: 30 MIN. **BAKE:** 10 MIN./BATCH + STANDING **MAKES:** 2 DOZEN

- 1 **cup butter, softened**
- ¾ **cup sugar**
- 1 **egg**
- 1 **teaspoon vanilla extract**
- 2¼ **cups all-purpose flour**
- ½ **teaspoon salt**
- ¼ **teaspoon baking powder**
- 1 **cup seedless raspberry jam**
- 1 **cup (6 ounces) semisweet chocolate chips**
  Chocolate sprinkles

1. In a large bowl, cream butter and sugar until light and fluffy. Beat in egg and vanilla. Combine the flour, salt and baking powder; gradually add to creamed mixture and mix well.
2. Using a cookie press fitted with a ribbon disk, form dough into long strips on ungreased baking sheets. Cut each strip into 2-in. pieces (do not separate). Bake at 375° for 12-15 minutes or until edges are golden brown. Cut again if necessary. Remove to wire racks to cool.
3. Spread the bottoms of half of the cookies with jam; top with remaining cookies. In a microwave, melt chocolate chips; stir until smooth. Place chocolate sprinkles in a small bowl. Dip each end of cookies in melted chocolate; allow excess to drip off. Dip in sprinkles. Place on waxed paper; let stand until set.

Raspberry Truffle Brownies

Each rich, fudgelike brownie is bursting with fresh, plump red raspberries and topped with a dreamy, bittersweet ganache. I think it's true perfection for chocolate lovers.

—AGNES WARD STRATFORD, ONTARIO

PREP: 30 MIN. **BAKE:** 25 MIN. + CHILLING **MAKES:** 1 DOZEN

- 6 **ounces bittersweet chocolate, chopped**
- ½ **cup butter, cubed**
- 2 **eggs**
- 1 **cup sugar**
- 1 **teaspoon vanilla extract**
- 1 **cup all-purpose flour**
- ¼ **teaspoon baking soda**
- ¼ **teaspoon salt**
- 1 **cup fresh raspberries**

FROSTING

- 6 **ounces bittersweet chocolate, chopped**
- ¾ **cup heavy whipping cream**
- 2 **tablespoons seedless raspberry jam**
- 1 **teaspoon vanilla extract**
- 12 **fresh raspberries**

1. In a microwave, melt chocolate and butter; stir until smooth. In a large bowl, beat the eggs, sugar and vanilla. Stir in chocolate mixture. Combine the flour, baking soda and salt; gradually add to chocolate mixture just until combined. Gently fold in raspberries.

2. Spread into a greased 9-in. square baking pan. Bake at 350° for 25-30 minutes or until a toothpick inserted near the center comes out clean (do not overbake). Cool on a wire rack.

3. For frosting, in a microwave-safe bowl, combine the chocolate, cream and jam. Microwave at 50% power for 2-3 minutes or until smooth, stirring twice. Transfer to a small bowl; stir in vanilla. Place in a bowl of ice water; stir for 3-5 minutes. With a hand mixer, beat on medium speed until soft peaks form.

4. Cut a small hole in a corner of a heavy-duty resealable plastic bag; insert #825 star tip. Fill with ½ cup frosting. Spread remaining frosting over brownies. Cut into 12 bars. Pipe a chocolate rosette in the center of each brownie; top with a raspberry. Cover and refrigerate for 30 minutes or until frosting is set. Refrigerate leftovers.

Editor's Note: *This recipe was tested in a 1,100-watt microwave.*

Almond-Tipped Shortbread Fingers

My husband enjoys these cookies so much that he usually can't wait until they're set to start eating them. If you'd like, try dipping them into melted semisweet chocolate and chopped pecans instead of white chocolate and almonds.

—CINDY SIFFORD MOUNT ZION, ILLINOIS

PREP: 30 MIN. **BAKE:** 15 MIN./BATCH + COOLING **MAKES:** 4 DOZEN

- 1 **cup butter, softened**
- ¾ **cup packed brown sugar**
- 2 **teaspoons vanilla extract**
- 2 **cups all-purpose flour**
- 6 **ounces white baking chocolate, chopped**
- 1¼ **cups chopped almonds**

1. In a large bowl, cream butter and brown sugar until light and fluffy. Beat in vanilla. Gradually add flour and mix well. Shape ½ cupfuls of dough into ½-in. thick logs. Cut logs into 2-in. pieces.

2. Place 2 in. apart on ungreased baking sheets. Bake at 325° for 15-17 minutes or until lightly browned. Remove to wire racks to cool.

3. In a microwave, melt white chocolate; stir until smooth. Dip one end of each cookie into chocolate; allow excess to drip off. Then dip into almonds. Place on waxed paper; let stand until set.

FAST FIX Soft Lemon-Ginger Cookies

Loaded with old-fashioned flavor, this yummy cookie is hard to beat. Santa will love gobbling these up with a glass of ice-cold milk.

—**SHARON BRETZ** HAVRE DE GRACE, MARYLAND

PREP/TOTAL TIME: 30 MIN. **MAKES:** 2 DOZEN

- ½ cup butter, softened
- 1 cup packed brown sugar
- 1 egg
- 3 tablespoons sour cream
- ½ teaspoon lemon extract
- ½ teaspoon vanilla extract
- 1¾ cups all-purpose flour
- 1 teaspoon baking soda
- 1 teaspoon cream of tartar
- 1 teaspoon ground ginger
- ¼ teaspoon salt

1. In a large bowl, cream butter and brown sugar until light and fluffy. Beat in the egg, sour cream and extracts. Combine the flour, baking soda, cream of tartar, ginger and salt; gradually add to creamed mixture and mix well.

2. Drop by rounded teaspoonfuls 2 in. apart onto ungreased baking sheets. Bake at 350° for 10-12 minutes or until lightly browned. Immediately remove from pans to wire racks.

Caramel Brownies

My family can't possibly eat all of the sweets I whip up, so my co-workers are more than happy to sample them—particularly these rich, chewy brownies that are full of gooey caramel, chocolate chips and crunchy walnuts.

—**CLARA BAKKE** COON RAPIDS, MINNESOTA

PREP: 20 MIN. **BAKE:** 35 MIN. + COOLING **MAKES:** 2 DOZEN

- 2 cups sugar
- ¾ cup baking cocoa
- 1 cup canola oil
- 4 eggs
- ¼ cup 2% milk
- 1½ cups all-purpose flour
- 1 teaspoon salt
- 1 teaspoon baking powder
- 1 cup (6 ounces) semisweet chocolate chips
- 1 cup chopped walnuts, divided
- 14 ounces caramels
- 1 can (14 ounces) sweetened condensed milk

1. In a large bowl, beat sugar, cocoa, oil, eggs and milk. Combine the flour, salt and baking powder; gradually add to egg mixture until well blended. Fold in chocolate chips and ½ cup walnuts.

2. Spoon two-thirds of the batter into a greased 13-in. x 9-in. baking pan. Bake at 350° for 12 minutes.

3. Meanwhile, in a large saucepan, heat the caramels and condensed milk over low heat until caramels are melted. Pour over baked brownie layer. Sprinkle with remaining walnuts.

4. Drop remaining batter by teaspoonfuls over caramel layer; carefully swirl brownie batter with a knife.

5. Bake 35-40 minutes longer or until a toothpick inserted near the center comes out with moist crumbs (do not overbake). Cool on a wire rack.

> **Almond sugar cookies make an even better gift when hand-dipped in chocolate and drizzled with contrasting candy coating.**

—TASTE OF HOME TEST KITCHEN

Chocolate-Dipped Cookies

PREP: 25 MIN. + CHILLING
BAKE: 10 MIN./BATCH + COOLING **MAKES:** 4½ DOZEN

- ½ **cup butter, softened**
- ¾ **cup sugar**
- 1 **egg**
- 1 **teaspoon vanilla extract**
- 1 **cup all-purpose flour**
- ⅓ **cup baking cocoa**
- ½ **teaspoon baking soda**
- ¼ **teaspoon salt**
- ½ **cup chopped almonds**
- ½ **cup miniature semisweet chocolate chips**
- 12 **ounces white candy coating disks, melted**
- 12 **ounces dark chocolate candy coating disks, melted**
- 2 **ounces milk chocolate candy coating disks, melted**

1. In a large bowl, cream butter and sugar. Beat in egg and vanilla. Combine the flour, cocoa, baking soda and salt; gradually add to the creamed mixture. Stir in almonds and chocolate chips. Cover and refrigerate for 2 hours. Divide dough in half. Shape into two 8-in. rolls; wrap each in plastic wrap. Refrigerate for 3 hours or until firm.

2. Unwrap and cut into ¼-in. slices. Place 2 in. apart on greased baking sheets. Bake at 350° for 8-10 minutes or until set. Remove to wire racks to cool.

3. Dip half of the cookies in white coating; allow excess to drip off. Place on waxed paper. Repeat with remaining cookies in dark chocolate coating.

4. Place milk chocolate coating in a resealable plastic bag; cut a small hole in one corner of the bag. Pipe designs on cookies. Let stand for 30 minutes or until set.

Lebkuchen

PREP: 25 MIN. **BAKE:** 25 MIN. + COOLING
MAKES: 3 DOZEN

- ½ cup butter, softened
- ½ cup sugar
- ⅓ cup packed brown sugar
- 2 eggs
- 1 cup molasses
- ¼ cup buttermilk
- ½ teaspoon anise extract
- 4½ cups all-purpose flour
- 1½ teaspoons baking powder
- 1 teaspoon baking soda
- 1 teaspoon ground cinnamon
- ½ teaspoon salt
- ½ teaspoon each ground cloves, allspice and cardamom
- ½ cup ground walnuts
- ½ cup raisins
- ½ cup pitted dates
- ½ cup candied lemon peel
- ⅓ cup flaked coconut
- ¼ cup candied orange peel
- 3 tablespoons candied pineapple

GLAZE

- ½ cup sugar
- ¼ cup water
- 2 tablespoons confectioners' sugar

1. Line a 15-in. x 10-in. x 1-in. baking pan with foil; grease the foil and set aside.

2. In a large bowl, cream butter and sugars until light and fluffy. Add eggs, one at a time, beating well after each. Beat in the molasses, buttermilk and anise extract. Combine the flour, baking powder, baking soda, cinnamon, salt, cloves, allspice and cardamom; gradually add to creamed mixture and mix well. Stir in walnuts.

3. In a food processor, combine raisins, dates, lemon peel, coconut, orange peel and pineapple in batches; cover and process until chopped. Stir into batter. Press dough into prepared pan.

4. Bake at 350° for 25-28 minutes or until lightly browned. In a small saucepan, bring sugar and water to a boil. Boil for 1 minute. Whisk in confectioners' sugar. Spread over warm bars. Cool in pan on a wire rack.

It's tradition for my family to get together on Thanksgiving weekend and bake these spice-filled treats. The recipe is very old and was handed down from my great-grandmother.

—**ESTHER KEMPKER** JEFFERSON CITY, MISSOURI

No-Bake Cookie Balls

These quick bites are great when you're short on time or don't want to turn on the oven. I make them a day or two ahead to let the flavors blend.

—CARMELETTA DAILEY WINFIELD, TEXAS

PREP: 20 MIN. + STANDING **MAKES:** 5 DOZEN

- 1 cup (6 ounces) semisweet chocolate chips
- 3 cups confectioners' sugar
- 1¾ cups crushed vanilla wafers (about 55 wafers)
- 1 cup chopped walnuts, toasted
- ⅓ cup orange juice
- 3 tablespoons light corn syrup
  Additional confectioners' sugar

1. In a large microwave-safe bowl, melt chocolate chips; stir until smooth. Stir in the confectioners' sugar, vanilla wafers, walnuts, orange juice and corn syrup.
2. Roll into 1-in. balls; roll in additional confectioners' sugar. Store in an airtight container.

Viennese Cookies

When I worked at a medical clinic, I became known as the "Cookie Lady" because I love to cook and bake. This recipe was given to me by a Swedish friend. I often make three or four times the recipe so I have plenty to share and send.

—BEVERLY STIRRAT MISSION, BRITISH COLUMBIA

PREP: 35 MIN. + CHILLING **BAKE:** 10 MIN./BATCH + COOLING **MAKES:** ABOUT 3 DOZEN

- 1¼ cups butter, softened
- ⅔ cup sugar
- 2¼ cups all-purpose flour
- 1⅔ cups ground almonds
- 1 cup apricot preserves
- 2 cups (12 ounces) semisweet chocolate chips
- 2 tablespoons shortening

1. In a large bowl, cream butter and sugar until light and fluffy. Combine flour and ground almonds; gradually add to creamed mixture and mix well. Cover and refrigerate for 1 hour.
2. On a lightly floured surface, roll dough to ¼-in. thickness. Cut with a floured 2¼-in. round cookie cutter. Place 2 in. apart on ungreased baking sheets.
3. Bake at 350° for 7-9 minutes or until edges are lightly browned. Remove to wire racks to cool completely.
4. Spread jam on the bottoms of half of the cookies; top with remaining cookies. In a microwave, melt chocolate chips and shortening; stir until smooth. Dip half of each sandwich cookie into chocolate mixture; allow excess to drip off. Place on waxed paper until set. Store in an airtight container.

2. Shape into ¾-in. balls. Place 1 in. apart on ungreased baking sheets. Bake at 350° for 10-12 minutes or until bottoms are lightly browned. Remove to wire racks to cool completely.

3. Place remaining confectioners' sugar in a large resealable plastic bag. Add cookies, a few at a time, and shake to coat. Store in an airtight container.

Dark Chocolate Butterscotch Brownies

My daughters and I love homemade brownies. We experimented with many recipes and finally came up with what we think is the best-ever brownie. The rich, satiny frosting and butterscotch chips are irresistible.

—KIT CONCILUS MEADVILLE, PENNSYLVANIA

PREP: 25 MIN. **BAKE:** 25 MIN. + COOLING **MAKES:** ABOUT 5 DOZEN

- 4 **ounces unsweetened chocolate, chopped**
- ¾ **cup butter, cubed**
- 2 **cups sugar**
- 3 **egg whites**
- 1½ **teaspoons vanilla extract**
- 1 **cup all-purpose flour**
- 1 **cup 60% cocoa bittersweet chocolate baking chips**
- 1 **cup butterscotch chips**

GLAZE

- 1 **cup 60% cocoa bittersweet chocolate baking chips**
- ¼ **cup butter, cubed**

Nutty Orange Snowballs

These buttery cookies are an old recipe from my mom in North Dakota. They used to be reserved only for weddings and special occasions. But they're ideal for Christmas because they look just like snowballs!

—JUDITH WEIDNER SPEARFISH, SOUTH DAKOTA

PREP: 30 MIN. **BAKE:** 10 MIN./BATCH + COOLING **MAKES:** 3 DOZEN

- 1 **cup butter, softened**
- 1¼ **cups confectioners' sugar, divided**
- 1 **teaspoon grated orange peel**
- ½ **teaspoon orange extract**
- ½ **teaspoon vanilla extract**
- 2 **cups all-purpose flour**
- ¼ **teaspoon salt**
- ½ **cup finely chopped walnuts**
- ½ **cup finely chopped hazelnuts**

1. In a large bowl, cream butter and ¾ cup confectioners' sugar until light and fluffy. Beat in orange peel and extracts. Combine flour and salt; gradually add to creamed mixture and mix well. Stir in nuts.

1. In a microwave, melt unsweetened chocolate and butter; stir until smooth. Cool slightly. In a large bowl, combine sugar and chocolate mixture. Stir in egg whites and vanilla. Gradually add flour to chocolate mixture. Stir in chips.

2. Spread into a greased 13-in. x 9-in. baking pan. Bake at 350° for 25-30 minutes or until a toothpick inserted near the center comes out clean (do not overbake). Cool on a wire rack.

3. For glaze, in a microwave, melt chips and butter; stir until smooth. Immediately spread over brownies. Cool before cutting.

Editor's Note: *This recipe was tested using Ghirardelli 60% cocoa bittersweet chocolate baking chips. Semisweet chocolate chips may be substituted.*

Holiday Lace Cookies

Mother baked these every Thanksgiving. She passed the recipe down to me because my family liked them so much. We all cherish these addictive cranberry cookies; they taste almost like candy.

—MILDRED SHERRER FORT WORTH, TEXAS

PREP: 45 MIN. + CHILLING **BAKE:** 15 MIN./BATCH + COOLING
MAKES: 4 DOZEN

      1 cup butter, softened
    2¼ cups confectioners' sugar
      ¼ cup light corn syrup
    1¼ cups all-purpose flour
      1 cup chopped pecans
      ¼ cup dried cranberries

1. In a large bowl, cream butter and confectioners' sugar until light and fluffy. Beat in corn syrup. Gradually beat in flour and mix well. Fold in pecans and cranberries. Shape dough into two 6-in. logs; wrap each in plastic wrap. Chill for at least 2 hours or until firm.

2. Unwrap and cut into ¼-in. slices. Place 3 in. apart on ungreased foil-lined baking sheets. Bake at 350° for 11-12 minutes or until center and edges are browned and lacy. Allow cookies to cool completely before carefully removing from foil.

Chocolate Marshmallow Meltaways

Kids are thrilled to find a marshmallow hidden under this cookie's cocoa frosting. I enjoyed these cookies as a child, and now my own family loves them, too.

—JOANNA SWARTLEY HARRISONBURG, VIRGINIA

PREP/TOTAL TIME: 30 MIN. **MAKES:** 3 DOZEN

      ½ cup butter-flavored shortening
      ¾ cup sugar
      1 egg
      ¼ cup 2% milk
      1 teaspoon vanilla extract
    1¾ cups all-purpose flour
      ½ cup baking cocoa
      ½ teaspoon salt
      ½ teaspoon baking soda
    18 large marshmallows, halved

FROSTING

      3 tablespoons butter, softened
      3 cups confectioners' sugar
      3 tablespoons baking cocoa
      ⅛ teaspoon salt
      4 to 6 tablespoons 2% milk

1. In a large bowl, cream shortening and sugar until light and fluffy. Beat in egg, milk and vanilla. Combine flour, cocoa, salt and baking soda; gradually add to creamed mixture and mix well.

2. Drop by tablespoonfuls 2 in. apart onto ungreased baking sheets. Bake at 350° for 8 minutes. Press a marshmallow half, cut side down, onto each cookie; bake 2 minutes longer. Remove to wire racks to cool.

3. In a small bowl, beat the butter, confectioners' sugar, cocoa and salt until smooth. Add enough milk to achieve a spreading consistency. Frost cookies.

German Chocolate Toffee Cookies

When the folks at the hospital where I work as a cook first sampled my cookie treats, everyone commented on how much they enjoyed them! German sweet chocolate gives them a unique twist.

—JOYCE ROBB DILLON, MONTANA

PREP: 20 MIN. **BAKE:** 15 MIN./BATCH **MAKES:** 13 DOZEN

- 1 cup butter, softened
- 1 cup shortening
- 2½ cups sugar
- ½ cup packed brown sugar
- 4 ounces German sweet chocolate, melted
- 4 eggs
- 2 teaspoons water
- 2 teaspoons vanilla extract
- 6½ cups all-purpose flour
- 2 teaspoons baking soda
- 1½ teaspoons salt
- 1½ cups milk chocolate English toffee bits
- 1½ cups chopped walnuts

1. In a large bowl, cream the butter, shortening and sugars until light and fluffy. Beat in chocolate. Add eggs, one at a time, beating well after each addition. Beat in water and vanilla. Combine the flour, baking soda and salt; gradually add to the creamed mixture and mix well. Stir in toffee bits and walnuts.

2. Drop by tablespoonfuls 2 in. apart onto greased baking sheets. Bake at 350° for 12-15 minutes or until golden brown. Remove to wire racks to cool.

Frosted Poppy Seed Cookies

Poppy seed cookies are among my husband and daughters' favorite cookies. When I make them for Christmas, sometimes I cut them into holiday shapes and decorate them with red and green frosting.

—MARY JACKSON GERMANTOWN, WISCONSIN

PREP: 30 MIN. + CHILLING **BAKE:** 10 MIN./BATCH + COOLING **MAKES:** ABOUT 5½ DOZEN

- ½ cup butter, softened
- ½ cup shortening
- 1 cup sugar
- 1 egg
- 1 teaspoon vanilla extract
- 3 cups all-purpose flour
- 1 teaspoon baking soda
- 1 teaspoon salt
- 1 cup (8 ounces) sour cream
- ¼ cup poppy seeds

FROSTING
- 3 tablespoons butter, softened
- 1½ cups confectioners' sugar
- ½ teaspoon vanilla extract
- 2 to 3 tablespoons 2% milk
- Colored sprinkles and colored sugar, optional

1. In a large bowl, cream the butter, shortening and sugar until light and fluffy. Beat in egg and vanilla. Combine the flour, baking soda and salt; add to creamed mixture alternately with sour cream. Stir in poppy seeds. Cover and refrigerate for 8 hours or until easy to handle.

2. On a heavily floured surface, roll out dough to ⅛-in. thickness. Cut with floured 2½-in. cookie cutters. Place 2 in. apart on ungreased baking sheets.

3. Bake at 375° for 8-10 minutes or until set and edges are lightly browned. Cool for 2 minutes before removing to wire racks to cool completely.

4. For frosting, in a small bowl, beat the butter, confectioners' sugar, vanilla and enough milk to achieve desired consistency. Lightly frost centers of cookies; sprinkle with colored sprinkles or colored sugar if desired.

"I combined three recipes to come up with a crisp cookie topped with a sweet fudge center. Flaked coconut and coconut extract are what set the flavors apart from the rest."

—**KAREN BARTO** CHURCHVILLE, VIRGINIA

Fudge-Filled Toffee Cookies

PREP: 25 MIN. + CHILLING **BAKE:** 15 MIN./BATCH
MAKES: 5½ DOZEN

½ **cup butter, softened**
½ **cup sugar**
½ **cup confectioners' sugar**
½ **cup canola oil**
1 **egg**
½ **teaspoon almond extract**
¼ **teaspoon coconut extract**
1¾ **cups all-purpose flour**
½ **cup whole wheat flour**
½ **teaspoon salt**
½ **teaspoon baking soda**
½ **teaspoon cream of tartar**
¾ **cup milk chocolate English toffee bits**
⅔ **cup chopped pecans**
⅔ **cup flaked coconut**
   Additional sugar

FILLING

1½ **cups semisweet chocolate chips, melted**
¾ **cup sweetened condensed milk**
1½ **teaspoons vanilla extract**
1¼ **cups pecan halves**

1. In a large bowl, cream butter and sugars until light and fluffy. Beat in the oil, egg and extracts. Combine the flours, salt, baking soda and cream of tartar; gradually add to the creamed mixture and mix well. Stir in the toffee bits, pecans and coconut. Cover and refrigerate for 1 hour or until easy to handle.
2. Shape dough into 1-in. balls; roll in sugar. Place 2 in. apart on ungreased baking sheets. Using the end of a wooden spoon handle, make an indentation in the center of each.
3. In a large bowl, combine the melted chocolate, milk and vanilla until smooth. Spoon 1 teaspoon into the center of each cookie. Top with a pecan half.
4. Bake at 350° for 12-14 minutes or until lightly browned. Remove to wire racks to cool.

Frosted Peanut Butter Cookies

PREP/TOTAL TIME: 30 MIN.
MAKES: ABOUT 2 DOZEN

- 1 **package (17½ ounces) peanut butter cookie mix**
- 2 **cups confectioners' sugar**
- ¼ **cup baking cocoa**
- ¼ **cup hot water**
- 1 **teaspoon vanilla extract**
  Sliced almonds or pecan halves

1. In a large bowl, prepare cookie dough according to package directions. Shape into 1-in. balls. Place 2 in. apart on ungreased baking sheets.

2. Bake at 375° for 8-10 minutes or until edges are golden brown. Cool for 1 minute before removing to wire racks.

3. For frosting, in a large bowl, combine the confectioners' sugar, cocoa, water and vanilla. Spread over cookies; top with nuts.

Coffee Shortbread

Christmas morning coffee and cookies—with this recipe, it's a tradition worth embracing.
—DIXIE TERRY GOREVILLE, ILLINOIS

PREP: 15 MIN. **BAKE:** 20 MIN./BATCH + COOLING
MAKES: ABOUT 5 DOZEN

- 1 **cup butter, softened**
- ½ **cup packed brown sugar**
- ¼ **cup sugar**
- 2 **tablespoons instant coffee granules**
- 2 **cups all-purpose flour**
- ¼ **teaspoon salt**
- ½ **cup semisweet chocolate chips, melted**
- ½ **cup vanilla or white chips, melted**

1. In a large bowl, cream butter, sugars and coffee granules until light and fluffy. Combine flour and salt; gradually add to creamed mixture.

2. On lightly floured surface, roll dough to ¼-in. thickness. Cut with floured 3-in. cookie cutter. Place 2 in. apart on ungreased baking sheets.

3. Bake at 300° for 20-22 minutes or until set. Remove to wire racks to cool. Drizzle with melted chips.

This is our go-to chocolate frosting recipe for topping peanut butter, sugar or chocolate chip cookies. The chocolate dries with a glossy sheen that will make your cookies shine. —TASTE OF HOME TEST KITCHEN

FROSTED PEANUT BUTTER COOKIES

Chocolate Malted Cookies

Like good old-fashioned malted milk? Here's the next best thing! With malted milk powder, chocolate syrup plus chocolate chips and chunks, these are the yummiest cookies I've ever tasted...and with six kids, I've made a lot of them over the years.

—TERI LEE RASEY CADILLAC, MICHIGAN

PREP/TOTAL TIME: 30 MIN. **MAKES:** ABOUT 1½ DOZEN

- 1 cup butter-flavored shortening
- 1¼ cups packed brown sugar
- ½ cup malted milk powder
- 2 tablespoons chocolate syrup
- 1 tablespoon vanilla extract
- 1 egg
- 2 cups all-purpose flour
- 1 teaspoon baking soda
- ½ teaspoon salt
- 1½ cups semisweet chocolate chunks
- 1 cup milk chocolate chips

1. In a large bowl, beat the shortening, brown sugar, malted milk powder, chocolate syrup and vanilla for 2 minutes. Add egg.

2. Combine the flour, baking soda and salt; gradually add to creamed mixture, mixing well after each addition. Stir in chocolate chunks and chips.

3. Shape into 2-in. balls; place 3 in. apart on ungreased baking sheets. Bake at 375° for 12-14 minutes or until golden brown. Cool for 2 minutes before removing to a wire rack.

Thumbprint Cookies

The thumbprints in these festive cookies can hold a variety of fruity jams. They add beautiful color to a platter of holiday treats.

—TASTE OF HOME TEST KITCHEN

PREP: 15 MIN. **BAKE:** 10 MIN./BATCH **MAKES:** 2½ DOZEN

- 6 tablespoons butter, softened
- ½ cup sugar
- 1 egg
- 2 tablespoons canola oil
- 1 teaspoon vanilla extract
- ¼ teaspoon butter flavoring
- 1½ cups all-purpose flour
- ¼ cup cornstarch
- 1 teaspoon baking powder
- ¼ teaspoon salt
- Assorted jams and/or preserves

1. In a large bowl, cream butter and sugar until light and fluffy. Beat in the egg, oil, vanilla and butter flavoring. Combine the flour, cornstarch, baking powder and salt; gradually add to creamed mixture and mix well.

2. Roll into 1-in. balls. Place 2 in. apart on greased baking sheets. Using the end of a wooden spoon handle, make an indentation in the center of each.

3. Bake at 350° for 8-10 minutes or until the edges are lightly browned. Remove to wire racks. Fill each cookie with ¼ teaspoon jam and/or preserves; cool.

WHITE CHOCOLATE TORTE, PAGE 224

Heavenly Desserts

237
233
222

> **My mother-in-law got this recipe from an Italian friend many years ago. I added the chocolate-nut crust. It is our very favorite dessert.**
>
> —GLORIA A. WARCZAK CEDARBURG, WISCONSIN

Festive New York-Style Cheesecake

PREP: 20 MIN. **BAKE:** 45 MIN. + CHILLING
MAKES: 12 SERVINGS

- 1-¼ **cups crushed chocolate wafers**
- ½ **cup chopped walnuts**
- ⅓ **cup sugar**
- ½ **cup butter, melted**

FILLING
- 2 **packages (8 ounces each) cream cheese, softened**
- 3 **tablespoons sour cream**
- ⅓ **cup sugar**
- 2 **eggs, lightly beaten**
- ½ **cup evaporated milk**
- 1 **teaspoon lemon juice**

TOPPING
- 2 **cups (16 ounces each) sour cream**
- 5 **tablespoons sugar**
- 1 **teaspoon vanilla extract**
  Assorted candies and chocolate syrup

1. In a small bowl, combine the wafer crumbs, walnuts and sugar; stir in butter. Press onto the bottom and halfway up the sides of an ungreased 10-in. springform pan. Freeze for 15 minutes.

2. In a large bowl, beat the cream cheese, sour cream and sugar until smooth. Add eggs; beat on low speed just until combined. Combine milk and lemon juice; add to cream cheese mixture just until blended.

3. Pour into crust. Place pan on a baking sheet. Bake at 350° for 35-40 minutes or until center is almost set.

4. Combine the sour cream, sugar and vanilla; carefully spread over cheesecake. Bake 10 minutes longer. Cool on a wire rack for 10 minutes. Carefully run a knife around edge of pan to loosen; cool 1 hour longer. Refrigerate overnight. Garnish with candies and drizzle with chocolate syrup. Refrigerate leftovers.

Pumpkin Pound Cake

As a twist on traditional pound cake, this seasonal treat uses oil and canned pumpkin instead of butter. As it bakes, it fills my kitchen with a spicy aroma that smells like Christmas.

—VIRGINIA LOEW LEESBURG, FLORIDA

PREP: 10 MIN. **BAKE:** 1 HOUR + COOLING
MAKES: 12-16 SERVINGS

- 2½ cups sugar
- 1 cup canola oil
- 3 eggs
- 3 cups all-purpose flour
- 2 teaspoons baking soda
- 1 teaspoon ground cinnamon
- 1 teaspoon ground nutmeg
- ½ teaspoon salt
- ¼ teaspoon ground cloves
- 1 can (15 ounces) solid-pack pumpkin
  Confectioners' sugar

1. In a large bowl, combine sugar and oil until blended. Add eggs, one at a time, beating well after each addition. Combine the flour, baking soda, cinnamon, nutmeg, salt and cloves; add to egg mixture alternately with pumpkin, beating well after each addition.

2. Transfer to a greased 10-in. fluted tube pan. Bake at 350° for 60-65 minutes or until toothpick inserted near the center comes out clean. Cool for 10 minutes before inverting onto a wire rack. Remove pan and cool completely. Dust with confectioners' sugar.

Cranberry Layer Cake

I used a recipe that called for a fluted tube pan to create this layered version. Cranberries, walnuts and cream cheese frosting make it taste so homey and delicious that you'd never guess it starts with a convenient cake mix.

—SANDY BURKETT GALENA, OHIO

PREP: 20 MIN. **BAKE:** 30 MIN. + COOLING **MAKES:** 12 SERVINGS

- 1 package white cake mix (regular size)
- 1⅓ cups water
- ⅓ cup canola oil
- 3 eggs
- 1 tablespoon grated orange peel
- 1 cup fresh or frozen cranberries, thawed and coarsely chopped
- 1 cup finely chopped walnuts

CREAM CHEESE FROSTING

- 1 package (8 ounces) cream cheese, softened
- ½ cup butter, softened
- 3½ cups confectioners' sugar
- 1 teaspoon vanilla extract
- ½ teaspoon grated orange peel
- ¼ cup finely chopped walnuts

1. In a large bowl, combine the first five ingredients; beat on low speed for 30 seconds. Beat on medium for 2 minutes. Stir in cranberries and walnuts. Pour into two greased and floured 9-in. round baking pans.

2. Bake at 350° for 30-35 minutes or until a toothpick inserted near the center comes out clean. Cool for 10 minutes before removing from pans to wire racks to cool completely.

3. In a large bowl, beat cream cheese and butter until fluffy. Add the confectioners' sugar, vanilla and orange peel; beat until blended. Spread between layers and over top and sides of cake. Sprinkle with walnuts. Refrigerate leftovers.

Home-style Cran-Raspberry Pie

I'm a great-grandmother of 25 and love to bake and cook for family. This is a popular pie with folks in New Jersey. Here in the Garden State, fresh cranberries and raspberries are plentiful.

—VIVIAN GALLAGHER BERLIN, NEW JERSEY

PREP: 40 MIN. **BAKE:** 45 MIN. + COOLING **MAKES:** 8 SERVINGS

2¼ cups all-purpose flour	2¼ cups fresh or frozen raspberries
1 tablespoon sugar	1¼ cups plus 1 tablespoon sugar, divided
1 teaspoon salt	
¾ cup shortening	2 tablespoons quick-cooking tapioca
1 egg yolk, lightly beaten	
4 to 5 tablespoons cold water	¼ teaspoon almond extract
1 teaspoon almond extract	2 tablespoons butter
FILLING	1 egg white, lightly beaten
2¼ cups fresh or frozen cranberries, thawed and coarsely chopped	

1. In a bowl, combine the flour, sugar and salt; cut in shortening until crumbly. In a small bowl, combine the egg yolk, cold water and almond extract; gradually add to flour mixture, tossing with a fork until dough forms a ball.

2. Divide dough in half so that one ball is slightly larger than the other. On a lightly floured surface, roll out larger ball to fit a 9-in. pie plate. Transfer pastry to pie plate; trim even with edge of plate.

3. In a large bowl, combine the cranberries, raspberries, 1¼ cups sugar, tapioca and extract; stir gently and let stand for 15 minutes. Spoon filling into crust; dot with butter. Roll out remaining pastry; make a lattice crust. Trim, seal and flute edges. Brush with egg white; sprinkle with remaining sugar.

4. Bake at 425° for 15 minutes. Reduce heat to 350°; bake 30-35 minutes longer or until crust is golden brown and the filling is bubbly. Cool completely on a wire rack. Refrigerate until serving.

Peppermint Puff Pastry Sticks

I wanted to impress my husband's family with something you'd expect to find in a European bakery, and these chocolaty treats are what I came up with. The buttery, flaky pastry just melts in your mouth.

—DARLENE BRENDEN SALEM, OREGON

PREP: 15 MIN. **BAKE:** 15 MIN./BATCH + COOLING
MAKES: ABOUT 3 DOZEN

1 sheet frozen puff pastry, thawed
10 ounces milk chocolate candy coating, coarsely chopped
1½ cups crushed peppermint candies

1. Unfold pastry sheet onto a lightly floured surface. Cut into 4-in. x ½-in. strips. Place on greased baking sheets. Bake strips at 400° for 12-15 minutes or until golden brown. Remove to wire racks to cool.

2. In a microwave, melt candy coating; stir until smooth. Dip each cookie halfway, allowing excess to drip off. Sprinkle with crushed candies. Place on waxed paper; let stand until set. Store in an airtight container.

Chocolate, coconut and pecans triple the fun. Add to that layers of the best frosting you will ever taste and you're in for a slice of cake you won't soon forget. —**ABIGAIL RIDER** EAST POINT, KENTUCKY

Triple-Layer Chocolate Cake

PREP: 40 MIN. **BAKE:** 20 MIN. + COOLING
MAKES: 12 SERVINGS

- ½ **cup butter, softened**
- ½ **cup shortening**
- 2 **cups sugar**
- 5 **eggs**
- 1 **teaspoon vanilla extract**
- 2 **cups all-purpose flour**
- ¼ **cup baking cocoa**
- 1 **teaspoon baking soda**
- 1 **cup buttermilk**
- 1 **cup flaked coconut**
- 1 **cup chopped pecans**

CHOCOLATE CREAM CHEESE FROSTING

- 1 **package (8 ounces) cream cheese, softened**
- ½ **cup butter, softened**
- 4 **cups confectioners' sugar**
- ¼ **cup baking cocoa**
- 1 **teaspoon vanilla extract**
  Pinch salt

1. In a large bowl, cream the butter, shortening and sugar until light and fluffy. Add eggs, one at a time, beating well after ach addition. Stir in vanilla. Combine the flour, cocoa and baking soda; add to the creamed mixture alternately with buttermilk, beating well after each addition. Fold in coconut and pecans.

2. Pour batter into three greased and floured 9-in. round baking pans. Bake at 350° for 20-25 minutes or until a toothpick inserted near the center comes out clean. Cool for 10 minutes before removing from pans to wire racks to cool completely.

3. For frosting, in a large bowl, beat cream cheese and butter until fluffy. Add the confectioners' sugar, cocoa, vanilla and salt; beat until smooth. Spread frosting between layers and over top and sides of cake. Store in the refrigerator.

Chocolate Velvet Dessert

This velvety creation is the result of several attempts to duplicate a chocolate dessert I enjoyed on vacation. It looks so tempting on a holiday buffet table that I've seen people decide to forgo the main course and just go for this.

—MOLLY SEIDEL EDGEWOOD, NEW MEXICO

PREP: 20 MIN. **BAKE:** 45 MIN. + CHILLING **MAKES:** 16 SERVINGS

- 1½ **cups chocolate wafer crumbs**
- 2 **tablespoons sugar**
- ¼ **cup butter, melted**
- 2 **cups (12 ounces) semisweet chocolate chips**
- 6 **egg yolks**
- 1¾ **cups heavy whipping cream**
- 1 **teaspoon vanilla extract**

CHOCOLATE BUTTERCREAM FROSTING

- ½ **cup butter, softened**
- 3 **cups confectioners' sugar**
- 3 **tablespoons baking cocoa**
- 3 **to 4 tablespoons 2% milk**

1. In a small bowl, combine wafer crumbs and sugar; stir in butter. Press onto the bottom and 1½ in. up the sides of a greased 9-in. springform pan. Place on a baking sheet. Bake at 350° for 10 minutes. Cool on a wire rack.

2. In a large microwave-safe bowl, melt chocolate chips; stir until smooth. Cool. In a small bowl, combine the egg yolks, cream and vanilla. Gradually stir a small amount of mixture into melted chocolate until blended; gradually stir in remaining mixture. Pour into crust.

3. Place the pan on a baking sheet. Bake at 350° for 45-50 minutes or until center is almost set. Cool on a wire rack for 10 minutes. Carefully run a knife around edge of pan to loosen; cool 1 hour longer. Refrigerate overnight.

4. In a large bowl, combine the butter, confectioners' sugar, cocoa and enough milk to achieve a piping consistency. Using a large star tip, pipe frosting on dessert.

Maple-Mocha Brownie Torte

Instead of making regular brownies, I bake brownie mix in cake pans to make a quick torte topped with a fluffy maple frosting. This dessert is at the top of my list of speedy standbys.

—**AMY FLORY** CLEVELAND, GEORGIA

PREP: 30 MIN. **BAKE:** 20 MIN. + COOLING **MAKES:** 12 SERVINGS

- 1 **package brownie mix (13-in. x 9-in. pan size)**
- ½ **cup chopped walnuts**
- 2 **cups heavy whipping cream**
- 2 **teaspoons instant coffee granules**
- ½ **cup packed brown sugar**
- 1½ **teaspoons maple flavoring**
- 1 **teaspoon vanilla extract**
  Chocolate curls or additional walnuts, optional

1. Prepare batter for brownie mix according to package directions for cake-like brownies. Stir in walnuts. Pour into two greased 9-in. round baking pans.
2. Bake at 350° for 20-22 minutes or until a toothpick inserted 2 in. from the edge comes out clean. Cool for 10 minutes before removing from pans to wire racks to cool completely.
3. In a large bowl, beat cream and coffee granules until stiff peaks form. Gradually beat in the brown sugar, maple flavoring and vanilla.
4. Spread 1½ cups over one brownie layer; top with second layer. Spread remaining cream mixture over top and sides of torte. Garnish with chocolate curls or walnuts if desired. Store in the refrigerator.

Apple Pie in a Goblet

This dish is not only easy but very elegant. I got the recipe from a church cooking class, and now I fix it often. You can serve it in bowls, but I always get more oohs and aahs when I put it in goblets.

—**RENEE ZIMMER** GIG HARBOR, WASHINGTON

PREP: 10 MIN. **COOK:** 25 MIN. **MAKES:** 4 SERVINGS

- 3 **large tart apples, peeled and chopped**
- ¼ **cup sugar**
- ¼ **cup water**
- ¾ **teaspoon ground cinnamon**
- ¼ **teaspoon ground nutmeg**
- 12 **shortbread cookies, crushed**
- 2 **cups vanilla ice cream**
  Whipped cream

1. In a large saucepan, combine the apples, sugar, water, cinnamon and nutmeg. Bring to a boil. Reduce heat; cover and simmer for 10 minutes or until apples are tender. Uncover; cook 9-11 minutes longer or until most of the liquid has evaporated. Remove from the heat.
2. In each of four goblets or parfait glasses, layer 1 tablespoon cookie crumbs, the ice cream and the apple mixture. Top with remaining cookie crumbs and whipped cream. Serve immediately.

MAKE AHEAD ▸ Snowflake Pudding

PREP: 20 MIN. + CHILLING **MAKES:** 6 SERVINGS

- 1 envelope unflavored gelatin
- 1¼ cups cold 2% milk, divided
- ½ cup sugar
- ½ teaspoon salt
- 1 teaspoon vanilla extract
- 1⅓ cups flaked coconut, toasted
- 1 cup heavy whipping cream, whipped

SAUCE

- 1 package (10 ounces) frozen sweetened raspberries, thawed
- 1½ teaspoons cornstarch
- ½ cup red currant jelly

1. In a small saucepan, sprinkle gelatin over ¼ cup milk; let stand for 1 minute. Heat over low heat, stirring until gelatin is completely dissolved.

2. In a large saucepan, combine the sugar, salt and remaining milk; heat just until sugar is dissolved. Remove from the heat; stir in gelatin mixture and vanilla. Refrigerate until partially set. Fold in coconut and whipped cream. Pour into dessert dishes; refrigerate for at least 2 hours.

3. Meanwhile, strain raspberries to remove seeds. In a small saucepan, combine the cornstarch, raspberry pulp and currant jelly; stir until smooth. Bring to a boil; cook and stir for 2 minutes or until thickened. Chill for at least 1 hour. Serve with pudding.

I use coconut and whipped cream in my pudding to give it a flavor and snow-like texture I love. Topped with a crimson currant and berry sauce, this stunning dessert is dressed for the holidays.

—PATRICIA STRATTON MUSKEGON, MICHIGAN

MAKE AHEAD Coconut Angel Squares

I have many speedy dessert recipes, but this one is truly special. A friend shared it with me, and it immediately became my favorite; it tastes like a creamy coconut cream pie with only a fraction of the work.

—BETTY CLAYCOMB ALVERTON, PENNSYLVANIA

PREP: 15 MIN. + CHILLING **MAKES:** 12-15 SERVINGS

- 1 prepared angel food cake (8 to 10 ounces), cut into ½-inch cubes
- 1½ cups cold 2% milk
- 1 teaspoon coconut extract
- 2 packages (3.4 ounces each) instant vanilla pudding mix
- 1 quart vanilla ice cream, softened
- 1 cup flaked coconut, divided
- 1 carton (8 ounces) frozen whipped topping, thawed

1. Place cake cubes in a greased 13-in. x 9-in. dish. In a large bowl, whisk the milk, extract and pudding mixes for 2 minutes (mixture will be thick). Add ice cream and ¾ cup coconut; beat on low just until combined.

2. Spoon over cake cubes. Spread with whipped topping. Toast remaining coconut; sprinkle over top. Cover and chill for at least 1 hour. Refrigerate leftovers.

MAKE AHEAD Chocolate Dessert Delight

Some of my friends refer to this unbelievably rich ice cream dessert as death by chocolate...before they ask for seconds! It's a yummy, festive do-ahead treat.

—LEE ANN STIDMAN SPIRIT LAKE, IDAHO

PREP: 25 MIN. + FREEZING **MAKES:** 16-20 SERVINGS

- 2 cups chocolate graham cracker crumbs (about 32 squares)
- ½ cup butter, melted
- ½ cup chopped walnuts
- 1 tablespoon sugar

FILLING
- ½ gallon chocolate ice cream, softened
- 1 jar (12¼ ounces) caramel ice cream topping
- 1 jar (11¾ ounces) hot fudge ice cream topping
- ½ cup miniature semisweet chocolate chips
- ½ cup chopped walnuts

TOPPING
- 2 cups heavy whipping cream
- 3 tablespoons sugar
- 1 tablespoon baking cocoa
- 1 teaspoon vanilla extract
- ½ teaspoon instant coffee granules
    Additional miniature chocolate chips and chopped walnuts

1. For crust, combine crumbs, butter, walnuts and sugar; press into an ungreased 13-in. x 9-in. baking pan. Bake at 350° for 10 minutes; cool completely.

2. Spread half of the ice cream over crust; spoon caramel and hot fudge toppings over ice cream. Sprinkle with chocolate chips and walnuts; freeze until firm. Spread remaining ice cream over the top. Cover with plastic wrap. Freeze for at least 2 hours.

3. In a large bowl, beat cream until stiff peaks form. Fold in sugar, cocoa, vanilla and coffee granules. Pipe or spoon onto dessert. Sprinkle with additional chocolate chips and walnuts. Return to freezer until 10 minutes before serving.

Apple Dumplings with Sauce

Enjoy all the flavors of a caramel apple pie baked up into a comforting dumpling! I like a scoop of vanilla ice cream on the side, or you could drizzle the dumplings with a little milk.

—ROBIN LENDON CINCINNATI, OHIO

PREP: 1 HOUR + CHILLING **BAKE:** 50 MIN. **MAKES:** 8 SERVINGS

3 **cups all-purpose flour**	9 **teaspoons cinnamon-sugar, divided**
1 **teaspoon salt**	**SAUCE**
1 **cup shortening**	1½ **cups packed brown sugar**
⅓ **cup cold water**	1 **cup water**
8 **medium tart apples, peeled and cored**	½ **cup butter, cubed**
8 **teaspoons butter**	

1. In a bowl, combine flour and salt; cut in shortening until crumbly. Gradually add water, tossing with a fork until dough forms a ball. Divide into eight portions. Cover and refrigerate for at least 30 minutes or until easy to handle.

2. Roll each portion of dough between two lightly floured sheets of waxed paper into a 7-in. square. Place an apple on each square. Place 1 teaspoon butter and 1 teaspoon cinnamon-sugar in the center of each apple.

3. Gently bring up corners of pastry to each center; pinch edges to seal. If desired, cut out apple leaves and stems from dough scraps; attach to dumplings with water. Place in a greased 13-in. x 9-in. baking dish. Sprinkle with remaining cinnamon-sugar.

4. In a large saucepan, combine sauce ingredients. Bring just to a boil, stirring until blended. Pour over apples.

5. Bake at 350° for 50-55 minutes or until apples are tender and pastry is golden brown, basting occasionally with sauce. Serve warm.

Pomegranate Poached Pears

I enjoy listening to company as they try to guess the fresh flavors in my rosemary-infused pears. I love finding new ways to use the antioxidant-rich pomegranate juice.

—BEV JONES BRUNSWICK, MISSOURI

PREP: 20 MIN. **COOK:** 1 HOUR 25 MIN.
MAKES: 6 SERVINGS

3	**cups dry red wine or red grape juice**
1	**bottle (16 ounces) pomegranate juice**
1	**cup water**
½	**cup sugar**
¼	**cup orange juice**
2	**tablespoons grated orange peel**
3	**fresh rosemary sprigs (4 inches)**
1	**cinnamon stick (3 inches)**
6	**medium pears**
6	**orange slices**
6	**tablespoons Mascarpone cheese**

1. In a Dutch oven, combine the first eight ingredients. Core pears from the bottom, leaving stems intact. Peel pears; place on their sides in the pan. Bring to a boil. Reduce heat; cover and simmer for 25-30 minutes or until pears are almost tender. Remove with a slotted spoon; cool.

2. Strain poaching liquid and return to Dutch oven. Bring to a boil; cook until reduced to 1 cup, about 45 minutes. Discard rosemary and cinnamon. Place an orange slice on each serving plate; top with 1 tablespoon cheese and a pear. Drizzle with poaching liquid.

Chocolate Mint Cream Cake

I had a lot of fun dreaming this one up. It's easy, but very impressive when serving. The peppermint gives the cookies-and-cream flavor a cool holiday spin.

—**PATTY THOMPSON** JEFFERSON, IOWA

PREP: 30 MIN. **BAKE:** 20 MIN. + COOLING **MAKES:** 14 SERVINGS

- 1 **package white cake mix (regular size)**
- 1 **cup water**
- ½ **cup canola oil**
- 3 **eggs**
- ½ **teaspoon peppermint extract**
- 1 **cup crushed mint creme Oreo cookies**

TOPPING

- 2 **packages (3.9 ounces each) instant chocolate pudding mix**
- ⅓ **cup confectioners' sugar**
- 1½ **cups cold 2% milk**
- ½ **to 1 teaspoon peppermint extract**
- 1 **carton (12 ounces) frozen whipped topping, thawed**
- ½ **cup crushed mint creme Oreo cookies**
- 15 **mint Andes candies**

1. In a large bowl, combine the cake mix, water, oil, eggs and extract; beat on low speed for 30 seconds. Beat on medium speed for 2 minutes. Fold in crushed cookies.

2. Pour into three greased and floured 9-in. round baking pans. Bake at 350° for 18-24 minutes or until a toothpick inserted near the center comes out clean. Cool for 10 minutes before removing from pans to wire racks to cool completely.

3. For topping, combine the dry pudding mixes, confectioners'

sugar, milk and extract until thickened. Fold in whipped topping and crushed cookies.

4. Place one cake layer on a serving plate; spread with the topping. Repeat layers twice. Frost sides of cake with remaining topping.

5. Chop eight candies; sprinkle over center of cake. Cut remaining candies in half; garnish each serving with a half candy. Store in the refrigerator.

Banana Cream Meringue Pie

I grew up on a farm in Alberta, and I still remember my mom's pies, fresh from the oven for after supper. This creamy banana variety is so good, no store-bought version can compare!

—**CAROL MAERTZ** SPRUCE GROVE, ALBERTA

PREP: 30 MIN. **BAKE:** 15 MIN. + CHILLING **MAKES:** 8 SERVINGS

  Pastry for single-crust pie (9 inches)
- 1 **cup sugar, divided**
- ⅓ **cup cornstarch**
- ½ **teaspoon salt**
- 1 **can (12 ounces) evaporated milk**
- 1 **cup water**
- 3 **egg yolks, lightly beaten**
- 1 **teaspoon vanilla extract**
- 3 **egg whites**
- 1 **large firm banana**

1. Line a 9-in. pie plate with pastry; trim and flute edges. Line pastry shell with a double thickness of heavy-duty foil. Bake at 450° for 8 minutes. Remove foil; bake 5 minutes longer. Cool on a wire rack.

2. In a large saucepan, combine ⅔ cup sugar, cornstarch and salt. Stir in milk and water until smooth. Cook and stir over medium-high heat until thickened and bubbly. Reduce heat; cook and stir 2 minutes longer. Remove from the heat. Stir a small amount of hot filling into egg yolks; return all to pan, stirring constantly. Bring to a gentle boil; cook and stir 2 minutes longer. Remove from the heat. Gently stir in vanilla. Keep warm.

3. In a large bowl, beat egg whites on medium speed until soft peaks form. Gradually beat in remaining sugar, 1 tablespoon at a time, on high until stiff glossy peaks form and sugar is dissolved. Slice banana into the crust; pour filling over top. Spread meringue evenly over hot filling, sealing edges to crust.

4. Bake at 350° for 12-15 minutes or until golden brown. Cool on a wire rack for 1 hour. Refrigerate for at least 3 hours before serving.

MAKE AHEAD ▶ Berries with Champagne Cream

This recipe came from a cooking class I attended at a local department store. It's just the right dessert for Christmas or New Year's.

—MICHELE FEHRING FISHERS, INDIANA

PREP: 20 MIN. + CHILLING **MAKES:** 6 SERVINGS

- 8 **egg yolks**
- ½ **cup sugar**
- 1 **cup champagne**
- 1 **cup heavy whipping cream, whipped**
- 1 **pint fresh raspberries**
- 1 **pint fresh strawberries**

1. In a heavy saucepan, beat egg yolks and sugar with a portable mixer until thick and lemon-colored. Gradually beat in champagne. Place the saucepan over low heat. With a portable mixer, beat on low speed for 1 minute. Continue beating over low heat until mixture reaches 160°, about 5-6 minutes.

2. Cool quickly by placing pan in bowl of ice water; stir for 2 minutes. Press plastic wrap onto surface of custard. Refrigerate to chill.

3. Fold in whipped cream. Spoon three-quarters of the champagne cream into stemmed glasses. Top with berries. Spoon remaining champagne cream over berries.

MAKE AHEAD ▶ Pumpkin Cheesecake with Sour Cream Topping

Instead of making a traditional pie, I like to surprise holiday guests with a silky cheesecake. Make it a day ahead and let it chill overnight.

—DOROTHY SMITH EL DORADO, ARKANSAS

PREP: 15 MIN. + COOLING **BAKE:** 60 MIN. + CHILLING **MAKES:** 12-14 SERVINGS

- 1½ **cups graham cracker crumbs**
- ¼ **cup sugar**
- ⅓ **cup butter, melted**

FILLING

- 3 **packages (8 ounces each) cream cheese, softened**
- 1 **cup packed brown sugar**
- 1 **can (15 ounces) solid-pack pumpkin**
- 1 **can (5 ounces) evaporated milk**
- 2 **tablespoons cornstarch**
- 1¼ **teaspoons ground cinnamon**
- ½ **teaspoon ground nutmeg**
- 2 **eggs, lightly beaten**

TOPPING

- 2 **cups (16 ounces) sour cream**
- ⅓ **cup sugar**
- 1 **teaspoon vanilla extract**
  Additional ground cinnamon

1. In a small bowl, combine crumbs and sugar; stir in butter. Press onto the bottom and 1½ in. up the sides of a greased 9-in. springform pan. Bake at 350° for 5-7 minutes or until set. Cool for 10 minutes. In a large bowl, beat cream cheese and brown sugar until smooth. Beat in the pumpkin, milk, cornstarch, cinnamon and nutmeg. Add eggs; beat on low speed just until combined. Pour into crust.

2. Place pan on a baking sheet. Bake at 350° for 55-60 minutes or until center is almost set.

3. In a small bowl, combine the sour cream, sugar and vanilla; spread over filling. Bake 5 minutes longer. Cool on a wire rack for 10 minutes. Carefully run a knife around edge of pan to loosen; cool 1 hour longer. Chill overnight.

4. Remove sides of pan. Let stand at room temperature 30 minutes before slicing. Sprinkle with additional cinnamon.

> **❝I've been making this cake for years, and it's the most requested cake from my family and friends for coffee get-togethers. Now that I have two grandsons, I serve it at birthdays, too!❞**
>
> —**PENNY MCNEILL** KITCHENER, ONTARIO

Chocolate Toffee Cake

PREP: 25 MIN. **BAKE:** 55 MIN. + COOLING
MAKES: 12 SERVINGS

- 1 **package (8 ounces) milk chocolate English toffee bits**
- 1 **cup (6 ounces) semisweet chocolate chips**
- 2 **tablespoons brown sugar**

CAKE

- 1 **cup butter, softened**
- 1¼ **cups packed brown sugar**
- 4 **eggs**
- 1 **teaspoon vanilla extract**
- 3 **cups all-purpose flour**
- 1½ **teaspoons baking powder**
- ½ **teaspoon salt**
- ½ **teaspoon baking soda**
- 1¼ **cups buttermilk**

CARAMEL ICING

- ¼ **cup butter, cubed**
- 2 **teaspoons all-purpose flour**
- 1 **can (5 ounces) evaporated milk**
- 1 **cup packed brown sugar**

1. Combine the toffee bits, chips and brown sugar; set aside.

2. In a large bowl, cream butter and brown sugar until light and fluffy. Add eggs, one at a time, beating well after each addition (mixture will appear curdled). Beat in vanilla. Combine the flour, baking powder, salt and baking soda; add to the creamed mixture alternately with buttermilk, beating well after each addition.

3. Pour a third of the batter into a greased and floured 10-in. fluted tube pan. Sprinkle with a third of the toffee mixture. Repeat layers twice. Bake at 350° for 55-65 minutes or until a toothpick inserted near the center comes out clean.

4. Cool for 10 minutes before removing from pan to wire rack to cool completely. For icing, in a small saucepan, melt butter. Stir in flour until smooth; gradually add evaporated milk and brown sugar. Bring to a boil; cook and stir for 4-5 minutes or until thickened. Cool. Drizzle over cake.

Gingerbread Cupcakes

I love how the creamy maple frosting mellows the hearty ginger flavor. If you like gingerbread, you'll love this combination!

—**NANCY BECKMAN** HELENA, MONTANA

PREP: 25 MIN. **BAKE:** 20 MIN. + COOLING **MAKES:** 1 DOZEN

- ½ cup butter, softened
- ½ cup packed brown sugar
- 1 egg
- ½ cup water
- ½ cup molasses
- 1⅓ cups all-purpose flour
- ¾ teaspoon ground cinnamon
- ½ teaspoon baking powder
- ½ teaspoon baking soda
- ½ teaspoon salt
- ½ teaspoon ground ginger
- ½ teaspoon ground nutmeg
- ¼ teaspoon ground allspice

MAPLE FROSTING

- ⅓ cup butter, softened
- 1 ounce cream cheese, softened
- ¼ cup packed brown sugar
  Dash salt
- ¼ cup maple syrup
- ¼ teaspoon vanilla extract
- 1 cup confectioners' sugar

1. In a large bowl, cream butter and brown sugar until light and fluffy. Beat in egg. Beat in water and molasses. Combine the flour, cinnamon, baking powder, baking soda, salt, ginger, nutmeg and allspice; add to the creamed mixture. Beat on low speed until combined. Beat on medium for 2 minutes.
2. Fill paper-lined muffin cups two-thirds full. Bake at 350° for 20-25 min. or until toothpick inserted near center comes out clean. Cool 10 min., then move to wire rack to cool completely.
3. For frosting, in a small bowl, cream the butter, cream cheese, brown sugar and salt until light and fluffy. Beat in maple syrup and vanilla. Gradually beat in confectioners' sugar until smooth. Frost cupcakes. Store in the refrigerator.

Crumb-Topped Cherry Pie

This pie was my dad's favorite and one my mom made frequently for Sunday dinner. She often served it with homemade ice cream.

—**SANDY JENKINS** ELKHORN, WISCONSIN

PREP: 25 MIN. **BAKE:** 35 MIN. + COOLING **MAKES:** 6-8 SERVINGS

- 1¼ cups all-purpose flour
- ½ teaspoon salt
- ½ cup canola oil
- 2 tablespoons 2% milk

FILLING

- 1⅓ cups sugar
- ⅓ cup all-purpose flour
- 2 cans (14½ ounces each) pitted tart cherries, drained
- ¼ teaspoon almond extract

CRUMB TOPPING

- ½ cup all-purpose flour
- ½ cup sugar
- ¼ cup cold butter, cubed
- 1 cup heavy whipping cream
- 1 tablespoon confectioners' sugar
- ⅛ teaspoon vanilla extract

1. In a bowl, combine flour and salt. Combine oil and milk; stir into flour mixture with a fork just until blended. Pat evenly onto the bottom and up the sides of a 9-in. pie plate; set aside.
2. In a large bowl, combine filling ingredients; pour into crust. For topping, combine flour and sugar; cut in butter until crumbly. Sprinkle over filling.
3. Bake at 425° for 35-45 minutes or until crust is golden brown and filling is bubbly. Cool on a wire rack.
4. Just before serving, in a small bowl, beat cream until it begins to thicken. Add confectioners' sugar and vanilla; beat until soft peaks form. Serve with pie.

Mom served this as our traditional Christmas Day dessert. My kids are puzzled as to why we don't eat this steamed pudding on Christmas Eve!

—LOIS HERMAN WATERTOWN, NEW YORK

Eve Pudding

PREP: 35 MIN. **COOK:** 1½ HOURS + COOLING
MAKES: 12 SERVINGS

½ cup butter, softened
1 cup sugar
2 eggs
1½ cups all-purpose flour
1 teaspoon baking soda
¼ teaspoon salt
¼ teaspoon ground nutmeg
3 cups chopped peeled tart apples
1 cup chopped dates

SAUCE

2 eggs
½ cup sugar
2 tablespoons butter
1 cup heavy whipping cream
1 teaspoon vanilla extract

1. In a large bowl, cream butter and sugar until light and fluffy. Add eggs, one at a time, beating well after each addition. Combine the flour, baking soda, salt and nutmeg; add to creamed mixture. Fold in apples and dates.

2. Transfer to a well-greased 8-cup pudding mold; cover. Place mold on a rack in a deep pot; add 1 in. of hot water to pot.

3. Bring to a gentle boil; cover and steam for 1½ to 1¾ hours or until a toothpick inserted near the center comes out clean, adding more water as needed. Remove mold from pot; let stand for 10 minutes.

4. In a small heavy saucepan, combine the eggs, sugar and butter. Heat over low heat, whisking constantly, until mixture thickens and reaches 160°, about 4 minutes. Remove from the heat; cool to room temperature.

5. In a small bowl, beat cream until it begins to thicken. Add vanilla; beat until stiff peaks form. Fold into egg mixture.

6. Unmold pudding onto a serving plate; cut into wedges. Serve with sauce.

66 I've had this recipe for years and finally decided to make it for a friend's birthday. We all got together to celebrate with ice cream, snacks and this torte. Everyone loved it! Being a fan of white chocolate, I make it now for special occasions. 99

—NORMA VAN DEVANDER CALAIS, MAINE

White Chocolate Torte

PREP: 20 MIN. **BAKE:** 25 MIN. + COOLING
MAKES: 14-16 SERVINGS

- 1 cup butter, softened
- 2 cups sugar
- 4 ounces white baking chocolate, melted and cooled
- 4 eggs
- 1½ teaspoons clear vanilla extract
- 3 cups all-purpose flour
- 1 teaspoon baking soda
- 1 cup buttermilk
- ½ cup water
- ½ cup chopped pecans, toasted

FROSTING

- 2 packages (one 8 ounces, one 3 ounces) cream cheese, softened
- ⅓ cup butter, softened
- 4 ounces white baking chocolate, melted and cooled
- 1½ teaspoons clear vanilla extract
- 6½ cups confectioners' sugar
  Chocolate curls

1. Line three greased 9-in. round baking pans with waxed paper and grease the paper; set aside. In a large bowl, cream butter and sugar until light and fluffy. Beat in chocolate. Add eggs, one at a time, beating well after each addition. Beat in vanilla. Combine flour and baking soda; gradually add to creamed mixture alternately with buttermilk and water, beating well after each addition. Fold in pecans. Pour batter into prepared pans.

2. Bake at 350° for 23-27 minutes or until a toothpick inserted near the center comes out clean. Cool for 10 minutes before removing from pans to wire racks; discard waxed paper.

3. For frosting, in a large bowl, beat cream cheese and butter until fluffy. Beat in chocolate and vanilla. Gradually add confectioners' sugar until smooth. Spread frosting between layers and over top and sides of cake. Garnish with chocolate curls. Store in the refrigerator.

FAST FIX ▶ Raspberry Fondue Dip

I delight guests with this fun, nontraditional fondue. Creamy apple butter and cinnamon Red Hots are the secrets to giving it a holiday twist. I call it my apple-merry fondue.

—EDNA HOFFMAN HEBRON, INDIANA

PREP/TOTAL TIME: 25 MIN. **MAKES:** ABOUT 1 CUP

- 1 **package (10 ounces) frozen sweetened raspberries**
- 1 **cup apple butter**
- 1 **tablespoon Red Hots candies**
- 2 **teaspoons cornstarch**
  Assorted fresh fruit

1. Thaw and drain raspberries, reserving 1 tablespoon juice. Mash raspberries. Press through a fine-mesh strainer into a small saucepan; discard seeds.

2. Add apple butter and Red Hots to strained raspberries; cook over medium heat until candies are dissolved, stirring occasionally. Combine cornstarch and reserved juice until smooth; stir into berry mixture. Bring to a boil; cook and stir over medium heat for 1-2 minutes or until thickened.

3. To serve warm, transfer to a small fondue pot and keep warm. Or, to serve cold, refrigerate until chilled. Serve with fruit.

Peppermint Angel Roll

My husband and I love this ice cream roll. The angel food cake makes it lighter than other traditional Christmas desserts, but it's just as indulgent. Plus I appreciate how easy it is, especially during a hectic holiday season!

—HOLLY DICKE PLAIN CITY, OHIO

PREP: 30 MIN. **BAKE:** 15 MIN. + FREEZING **MAKES:** 10 SERVINGS

- 1 **package (16 ounces) angel food cake mix**
- 1 **tablespoon confectioners' sugar**
- ½ **gallon peppermint ice cream, softened**
- 1 **jar (11¾ ounces) hot fudge ice cream topping, warmed**
  Crushed peppermint candies and additional confectioners' sugar, optional

1. Prepare cake batter according to package directions. Line a greased 15-in. x 10-in. x 1-in. baking pan with waxed paper and grease the paper. Spread batter evenly into pan. Bake at 350° for 15-20 minutes or until cake springs back when lightly touched.

2. Cool for 5 minutes. Turn cake onto a kitchen towel dusted with confectioners' sugar. Gently peel off waxed paper. Roll up cake in the towel jelly-roll style, starting with a short side. Cool completely on a wire rack.

3. Unroll cake and spread ice cream over cake to within ½ in. of edges. Roll up again. Cover and freeze until firm.

4. Cut into slices; drizzle with hot fudge topping. If desired, garnish with crushed candies and dust with confectioners' sugar.

MAKE AHEAD ▶ White Chocolate-
Strawberry Tiramisu

My husband and I both love a traditional tiramisu,
but this recipe highlights another flavor combo
we crave—white chocolate and strawberries
with a hint of orange. I've also had good luck
using nondairy whipped topping and reduced-fat
cream cheese for lighter versions.

—ANNA GINSBERG AUSTIN, TEXAS

PREP/TOTAL TIME: 30 MIN. **MAKES:** 15 SERVINGS

- 2 **cups heavy whipping cream**
- 1 **package (8 ounces) cream cheese,
  softened**
- 4 **ounces Mascarpone cheese**
- 9 **ounces white baking chocolate, melted and
  cooled**
- 1 **cup confectioners' sugar, divided**
- 1 **teaspoon vanilla extract**
- 2 **packages (3 ounces each) ladyfingers, split**
- ⅔ **cup orange juice**
- 4 **cups sliced fresh strawberries
  Chocolate syrup, optional**

1. In a large bowl, beat cream until soft
peaks form; set aside. In another large bowl,
beat cheeses until light and fluffy. Beat in the
chocolate, ½ cup confectioners' sugar and
vanilla. Fold in 2 cups whipped cream.
2. Brush half the ladyfingers with half of the
orange juice; arrange in a 13-in. x 9-in. dish.
Spread with 2 cups cream cheese mixture;
top with 2 cups of berries. Brush remaining
ladyfingers with remaining orange juice;
arrange over berries.
3. In a large bowl, combine remaining cream
cheese mixture and confectioners' sugar;
fold in remaining whipped cream. Spread
over ladyfingers. Top with remaining berries.
Refrigerate until serving. Just before serving,
drizzle with chocolate syrup if desired.
Refrigerate leftovers.

MAKE AHEAD ▶ Eggnog Cream Pies

I created this recipe for my brother, who just happens to love eggnog. He was
delighted, to say the least, when he tasted this silky treat.

—ANNA LONG MODESTO, CALIFORNIA

PREP: 35 MIN. + CHILLING **MAKES:** 2 PIES (8 SERVINGS EACH)

- 2 **unbaked pastry shells (9 inches)**
- 4 **ounces cream cheese, softened**
- ½ **cup confectioners' sugar**
- 1 **teaspoon ground allspice**
- 1 **teaspoon ground nutmeg**
- 2 **cartons (one 8 ounces, one 12
  ounces) frozen whipped topping,
  thawed, divided**
- 3¾ **cups cold eggnog**
- 3 **packages (3.4 ounces each)
  instant cheesecake or vanilla
  pudding mix**
  Additional ground nutmeg

1. Line unpricked pastry shells with a double thickness of heavy-duty foil.
Bake at 450° for 8 minutes. Remove foil; bake 5 minutes longer. Cool on
wire racks.
2. In small bowl, beat cream cheese, sugar, allspice and nutmeg until
smooth. Fold in 8-oz. carton of whipped topping. Spoon into crusts.
3. In a large bowl, whisk eggnog and pudding mixes for 2 minutes. Let stand
for 2 minutes or until soft-set. Spread over cream cheese layer. Top with
remaining whipped topping; sprinkle with additional nutmeg. Cover and
refrigerate for 8 hours or overnight.

Snap Dessert Cups

PREP: 1 HOUR **BAKE:** 10 MIN./BATCH **MAKES:** 10 SERVINGS

- 3 **cups heavy whipping cream**
- 1 **cup sugar**
- 1 **package (12 ounces) fresh cranberries**
- ¼ **cup water**

BRANDY SNAP CUPS

- ½ **cup butter, cubed**
- ½ **cup sugar**
- ⅓ **cup molasses**
- 1 **teaspoon grated orange peel**
- ½ **teaspoon ground cinnamon**
- ¼ **teaspoon ground ginger**
- ¼ **cup all-purpose flour**
- 1 **teaspoon brandy extract**

CARAMEL SAUCE

- ½ **cup butter, cubed**
- ¼ **cup water**
- 1 **cup sugar**
- 1 **cup heavy whipping cream**
- 1 **teaspoon vanilla extract**

1. In a large heavy saucepan, combine cream and sugar. Cook and stir over medium heat until sugar is dissolved; set aside. In a small saucepan, combine cranberries and water. Cook over medium heat until the berries pop, about 15 minutes.

2. Press cranberry mixture through a sieve; discard skins and seeds. In a large bowl, combine cranberry pulp and cream mixture. Cover and refrigerate until chilled.

3. Fill cylinder of ice cream freezer two-thirds full; freeze according to the manufacturer's directions. Refrigerate remaining mixture until ready to freeze. When ice cream is frozen, transfer to a freezer container; freeze for 2-4 hours before serving.

4. In a large saucepan, combine the butter, sugar, molasses, orange peel, cinnamon and ginger. Bring to a boil. Remove from the heat. Quickly whisk in flour and extract until smooth. Place pan over a pan of boiling water to hold mixture at a spoonable consistency.

5. Prepare only two brandy snap cups at a time. Spoon 1 tablespoon of molasses mixture onto opposite ends of a greased baking sheet, forming two circles. Bake at 300° for 10 minutes or until bubbly and deep golden brown. Cool on pan on wire rack for 2 minutes.

6. Quickly loosen one at a time, and place each over an inverted greased 8-oz. custard cup, carefully shaping to the custard cup. Cool for 5 minutes. Carefully remove from custard cups. Repeat five times.

7. For caramel sauce, combine butter and water in a heavy saucepan. Cook and stir over medium-low heat until butter is melted; add sugar. Cook and stir until sugar is dissolved. Bring to a boil without stirring over medium-high heat. Boil and stir for 4 minutes longer or until mixture turns deep amber. Remove from the heat. Carefully stir in cream and vanilla.

8. To assemble, serve cranberry ice cream in brandy snap cups. Drizzle with caramel sauce.

> **"**For that wow factor, it's hard to top these extra-special treats. The homemade cranberry ice cream is served in edible cups and covered with a buttery caramel sauce.**"**

—**KAREN RUBIN** RAYMOND, NEW HAMPSHIRE

Maple Carrot Cupcakes

PREP: 15 MIN. **BAKE:** 20 MIN. + COOLING
MAKES: 1½ DOZEN

- 2 **cups all-purpose flour**
- 1 **cup sugar**
- 1 **teaspoon baking powder**
- 1 **teaspoon baking soda**
- 1 **teaspoon ground cinnamon**
- ½ **teaspoon salt**
- 4 **eggs**
- 1 **cup canola oil**
- ½ **cup maple syrup**
- 3 **cups grated carrots (about 6 medium)**

FROSTING
- 1 **package (8 ounces) cream cheese,
  softened**
- ¼ **cup butter, softened**
- ¼ **cup maple syrup**
- 1 **teaspoon vanilla extract**
  Chopped walnuts, optional

1. In a large bowl, combine the first six ingredients. In another bowl, beat eggs, oil and syrup. Stir into dry ingredients just until moistened. Fold in carrots.

2. Fill greased or paper-lined muffin cups two-thirds full. Bake at 350° for 20-25 minutes or until a toothpick inserted near the center comes out clean. Cool for 5 minutes before removing from pans to wire racks.

3. For frosting, combine the cream cheese, butter, syrup and vanilla in a bowl; beat until smooth. Frost cooled cupcakes. Sprinkle with nuts if desired. Store in the refrigerator.

top tip

Flour Facts

All-purpose flour is the most common flour used for cakes, but not all flour is created equal. Cake flour gives a more tender and delicate crumb. To substitute it for all-purpose flour, use 1 cup plus 2 tablespoons cake flour per cup of all-purpose flour.

I come from a family of cooks and was inspired to cook and bake ever since I was young. Mother and Grandmom were always in the kitchen cooking up something delicious. This is my Grandmom's recipe for Maple Carrot Cupcakes, which is always requested when we get together.

—LISA ANN PANZINO DINUNZIO VINELAND, NEW JERSEY

Steamed Cranberry-Molasses Pudding

This old-fashioned dessert has been a family tradition during the holidays for years. My children say it's just not Christmas without it!

—MILLICENT TILLY WATERTOWN, SOUTH DAKOTA

PREP: 15 MIN. **COOK:** 1 HOUR **MAKES:** 8-10 SERVINGS

- 1⅓ cups all-purpose flour
- 2 teaspoons baking soda
- 1 teaspoon baking powder
- ½ cup molasses
- ⅓ cup hot water
- 2 cups chopped fresh or frozen cranberries

BUTTER SAUCE
- ½ cup butter, cubed
- 1 cup sugar
- 1 cup heavy whipping cream

1. In a large bowl, combine the flour, baking soda and baking powder. Combine molasses and water; stir into dry ingredients. Fold in cranberries. Pour into a well-greased 4-cup pudding mold; cover.

2. Place mold on a rack in a deep stockpot; add 1 in. of hot water to pan. Bring to a gentle boil; cover and steam for 1 hour or until a toothpick inserted near the center comes out clean, adding water to pan as needed. Let stand for 5 minutes before removing from mold.

3. In a small saucepan, melt butter; stir in sugar and cream. Cook and stir over medium heat for 3-5 minutes or until heated through. Unmold pudding onto a serving plate; cut into wedges. Serve warm with sauce.

Decadent Brownie Swirl Cheesecake

This simple recipe uses brownie mix to prepare a fudgy crust and a clever trick for creating swirly designs on top. It's too easy and stunning not to try.

—TASTE OF HOME TEST KITCHEN

PREP: 50 MIN. + COOLING **BAKE:** 1½ HOURS + CHILLING **MAKES:** 16 SERVINGS

- 1 package fudge brownie mix (13-inch x 9-inch pan size)

FILLING
- 4 packages (8 ounces each) cream cheese, softened
- 1 cup sugar
- 4 eggs, lightly beaten
- 3 teaspoons vanilla extract or 1 teaspoon almond extract and 2 teaspoons vanilla extract
- Fresh raspberries and chocolate curls, optional

1. Prepare brownie mix according to package directions for chewy fudge brownies. Set aside ⅔ cup brownie batter; spread remaining batter into a greased 9-in. springform pan.

2. Place pan on a double thickness of heavy-duty foil (about 18 in. square). Securely wrap foil around pan. Bake at 350° for 25-28 minutes (brownies will barely test done). Cool for 10 minutes on a wire rack.

3. In a large bowl, beat cream cheese and sugar until smooth. Beat in eggs and vanilla on low speed just until combined. Stir ⅓ cup into reserved brownie batter; set aside. Spoon half of the cheesecake batter into crust; dollop with half of reserved chocolate cheesecake batter. Repeat layers. Cut through batter with a knife to swirl.

4. Place in a larger baking pan; add 1 in. of hot water to larger pan. Bake at 325° for 1½ hours or until surface is no longer shiny and center is almost set.

5. Remove pan from water bath and foil. Cool on a wire rack for 10 minutes. Carefully run a knife around the edge of pan to loosen; cool 1 hour longer. Refrigerate overnight. Remove sides of pan. Garnish with raspberries and chocolate curls if desired.

Miniature Napoleons

It can be a challenge to come up with an elegant sweet that works well for a cocktail party, but we found the perfect puffy treat.

—TASTE OF HOME TEST KITCHEN

PREP: 30 MIN. + CHILLING **BAKE:** 10 MIN. + FREEZING **MAKES:** 4½ DOZEN

- 6 **tablespoons sugar**
- 2 **tablespoons cornstarch**
- ¼ **teaspoon salt**
- 1 **cup 2% milk**
- 1 **egg yolk, beaten**
- 2 **tablespoons butter, divided**
- ½ **teaspoon vanilla extract**
- 1 **sheet frozen puff pastry, thawed**
- ½ **cup heavy whipping cream**
- 2 **ounces semisweet chocolate, chopped**

1. In small saucepan, combine sugar, cornstarch and salt. Stir in milk until smooth. Cook and stir over medium heat until thickened and bubbly. Reduce heat; cook and stir 1 min. longer.

2. Remove from the heat. Stir a small amount of hot mixture into egg yolk; return all to the pan, stirring constantly. Bring to a gentle boil; cook and stir 1 minute longer. Remove from the heat. Stir in 1 tablespoon butter and vanilla. Cool to room temperature without stirring. Refrigerate until chilled.

3. Unfold puff pastry; place on an ungreased baking sheet. Prick dough thoroughly with a fork. Bake according to package directions. Remove to a wire rack to cool

4. In a small bowl, beat cream until stiff peaks form. Fold into custard. Use a fork to split pastry in half horizontally. Spread filling over the bottom half; replace top. Cover and freeze for 4 hours or until firm.

5. Cut into 1½-in. x 1-in. rectangles. In a microwave, melt chocolate and remaining butter; stir until smooth. Drizzle over pastries. Freeze until serving.

Caramel Apple Cheesecake

This ooey-gooey dessert won the grand prize in an apple recipe contest. It was my first attempt at a cooking contest, but I learned that using the water bath method cooks the cake more gently so there's less cracking.

—LISA MORMAN MINOT, NORTH DAKOTA

PREP: 45 MIN. **BAKE:** 50 MIN. + CHILLING **MAKES:** 12 SERVINGS

- 1½ **cups cinnamon graham cracker crumbs (about 8 whole crackers)**
- ¾ **cup sugar, divided**
- ¼ **cup butter, melted**
- 1 **package (14 ounces) caramels**
- ⅔ **cup evaporated milk**
- ½ **cup chopped pecans, divided**
- 2 **packages (8 ounces each) cream cheese, softened**
- 2 **tablespoons all-purpose flour, divided**
- 2 **eggs, lightly beaten**
- 1½ **cups chopped peeled apples**
- ½ **teaspoon ground cinnamon**

1. Place a greased 9-in. springform pan on a double thickness of heavy-duty foil (about 18 in. square). Securely wrap foil around pan.

2. In a small bowl, combine the cracker crumbs, ¼ cup sugar and butter. Press onto the bottom and 1 in. up the sides of prepared pan. Place on a baking sheet. Bake at 350° for 10 minutes or until lightly browned. Cool on a wire rack.

3. In a heavy saucepan over medium-low heat, cook and stir caramels and milk until melted and smooth. Pour 1 cup over crust; sprinkle with ¼ cup pecans. Set remaining caramel mixture aside.

4. In a large bowl, beat the cream cheese, 1 tablespoon flour and remaining sugar until smooth. Add eggs; beat on low speed just until combined. Combine the apples, cinnamon and remaining flour; fold into cream cheese mixture. Pour into crust.

5. Place springform pan in a large baking pan; add 1 in. of hot water to larger pan. Bake for 40 minutes. Reheat reserved caramel mixture if necessary; gently spoon over cheesecake. Sprinkle with remaining pecans.

6. Bake 10-15 minutes longer or until center is just set. Remove pan from water bath. Cool on a wire rack for 10 minutes. Carefully run a knife around edge of pan to loosen; cool 1 hour longer. Refrigerate overnight. Remove sides of pan.

Shortbread Lemon Tart

PREP: 20 MIN. **BAKE:** 25 MIN. + COOLING
MAKES: 10-12 SERVINGS

- 3 **eggs**
- ¼ **cup lemon juice**
- 1¼ **cups sugar**
- 1 **tablespoon grated orange peel**
- ¼ **cup butter, melted**

CRUST
- 1 **cup all-purpose flour**
- ⅓ **cup confectioners' sugar**
- ½ **cup ground almonds**
- 1 **teaspoon grated lemon peel**
- 1 **teaspoon grated orange peel**
- ½ **cup cold butter, cubed**
  Additional confectioners' sugar

1. For filling, in blender, combine eggs, lemon juice, sugar and orange peel. Cover and blend on high until smooth. Add butter; cover and process on high just until smooth. Set aside.
2. In a food processor, combine the flour, confectioners' sugar, almonds, lemon peel, orange peel and butter; cover and process until mixture forms a ball. Press pastry onto the bottom and up the sides of an ungreased 9-in. tart pan with removable bottom.
3. Pour filling into crust. Bake at 350° for 25-30 minutes or until center is almost set. Cool on a wire rack. Just before serving, sprinkle with confectioners' sugar.

> **"**For a change from ordinary lemon bars, we added orange peel to the crust and filling and turned the recipe into a tart.**"**
>
> —**TASTE OF HOME TEST KITCHEN**

Walnut Apple Pie

I got this recipe from a friend after she served me a slice in her home. Now I serve it for special occasions and holidays. My family thinks it's a real treat; we call it our super apple pie.

—**WINIFRED ECKERLE** GERING, NEBRASKA

PREP: 25 MIN. **BAKE:** 1 HOUR + COOLING **MAKES:** 8 SERVINGS

Pastry for double-crust pie (9 inches)	1 **teaspoon ground cinnamon**
6 **cups thinly sliced peeled tart apples**	¼ **teaspoon salt**
⅓ **cup light corn syrup**	**TOPPING**
¼ **cup sugar**	¼ **cup finely chopped walnuts**
2 **tablespoons butter**	¼ **cup packed brown sugar**
1 **tablespoon cornstarch**	3 **tablespoons dark corn syrup**
	2 **tablespoons butter**

1. Line a 9-in. pie plate with bottom pastry; trim even with edge of plate. Arrange apples in crust; set aside.
2. In a small saucepan, combine the corn syrup, sugar, butter, cornstarch, cinnamon and salt. Cook and stir over low heat until butter is melted and sugar is dissolved. Pour over apples.
3. Roll out remaining pastry to fit top of pie; place over filling. Trim, seal and flute edges; cut slits in top.
4. Bake at 425° for 15 minutes. Reduce heat to 325°. Bake for 40-50 minutes or until crust is golden brown and filling is bubbly. Cover edges with foil during the last 15 minutes to prevent overbrowning if necessary.
5. Meanwhile, in a small saucepan, combine the topping ingredients. Cook and stir over low heat until butter is melted and sugar is dissolved.
6. Place the pie on a baking sheet. Pour topping over the top crust. Bake for 3-4 minutes or until bubbly. Cool on a wire rack.

Raspberry Chocolate Cheesecake

I am a farm wife, born and raised on a dairy farm. We have been blessed with three children who are grown and have embarked on agricultural careers. We all love to celebrate special occasions with this homemade cheesecake.

—ROBINNE HURT CROSSFIELD, ALBERTA

PREP: 40 MIN. + CHILLING **MAKES:** 12 SERVINGS

- 2 **cups chocolate wafer crumbs (about 38 wafers)**
- ⅓ **cup sugar**
- ½ **cup butter, melted**

FILLING
- 1 **envelope unflavored gelatin**
- ¾ **cup cold water**
- 2 **cups heavy whipping cream**
- 3 **packages (two 8 ounces, one 3 ounces) cream cheese, softened**
- ⅓ **cup sugar**
- 4 **ounces semisweet chocolate, melted and cooled**
- 1 **cup fresh or frozen raspberries**
  Fresh raspberries and mint, optional

1. Combine the wafer crumbs, sugar and butter. Press onto the bottom and 1 in. up the sides of a greased 9-in. springform pan; set aside.

2. In a small saucepan, sprinkle gelatin over cold water; let stand for 1 minute. Heat over low heat, stirring until gelatin is completely dissolved; cool slightly.

3. In a small bowl, beat cream until stiff peaks form; set aside. In a large bowl, beat cream cheese and sugar; stir in cooled gelatin. Transfer half of the mixture to another bowl.

4. To one bowl, fold in melted chocolate and half of the whipped cream. Pour over prepared crust. To the other bowl, carefully fold in the remaining whipped cream, then the raspberries. Pour over chocolate layer. Cover and refrigerate for 6 hours or overnight.

5. Carefully run a knife around edge of pan to loosen. Remove sides of pan. Garnish with berries and mint if desired. Refrigerate leftovers.

Strawberry White Chocolate Cheesecake: *Substitute white baking chocolate for the semisweet chocolate and sliced strawberries for the raspberries. Garnish with fresh strawberries and mint if desired.*

MAKE AHEAD ▶ ## Strawberry Angel Dessert

You can find fresh strawberries all year in the South. I think this is the most wonderful way to use them.

—THERESA MATHIS TUCKER, GEORGIA

PREP: 30 MIN. + CHILLING **MAKES:** 12-16 SERVINGS

- 1½ **cups sugar**
- 5 **tablespoons cornstarch**
- 1 **package (3 ounces) strawberry gelatin**
- 2 **cups water**
- 2 **pounds fresh strawberries, hulled, divided**
- 1 **package (8 ounces) cream cheese, softened**
- 1 **can (14 ounces) sweetened condensed milk**
- 1 **carton (12 ounces) frozen whipped topping, thawed**
- 1 **prepared angel food cake (8 to 10 ounces), cut into 1-inch cubes**

1. For glaze, in a large saucepan, combine the sugar, cornstarch and gelatin. Add water and stir until smooth. Cook and stir over medium-high heat until mixture begins to boil. Cook and stir 1-2 minutes longer or until thickened. Remove from the heat; cool completely. Cut half of the strawberries into quarters; fold into glaze.

2. In a small bowl, beat cream cheese until smooth. Beat in milk until blended. Fold in whipped topping.

3. In a 4-qt. clear glass bowl, layer half of the cake cubes, glaze and cream mixture. Repeat layers. Cut remaining strawberries in half and arrange over the top. Cover and refrigerate for at least 2 hours or overnight.

Working as a full-time psychologist, I've learned to appreciate quick desserts. This out-of-the-box recipe is a clever way to turn white cake mix into a beautiful pink ribbon showpiece.

—LISA VARNER EL PASO, TEXAS

Peppermint Ribbon Cake

PREP: 20 MIN.　**BAKE:** 35 MIN. + COOLING
MAKES: 12 SERVINGS

- 1　**package white cake mix (regular size)**
- ½　**teaspoon peppermint extract**
- ½　**teaspoon red food coloring**
- ½　**cup plus 2 tablespoons crushed peppermint candies, divided**
- 1　**cup confectioners' sugar**
- 1　**tablespoon 2% milk**

1. Prepare cake batter according to package directions. Transfer 1 cup to a small bowl; stir in the extract, food coloring and ½ cup crushed candies.

2. Spoon 2 cups of remaining batter into a greased and floured 10-in. fluted tube pan. Carefully top with peppermint batter; do not swirl. Top with remaining plain batter.

3. Bake at 350° for 35-45 minutes or until a toothpick inserted near the center comes out clean. Cool for 10 minutes before removing from pan to a wire rack to cool completely.

4. Combine confectioners' sugar and milk; drizzle over cake. Sprinkle with remaining crushed candies.

top tip　Fun With Extract

Try this ribbon cake with different extracts, such as strawberry, banana, coconut, lemon or hazelnut. Then select a hard candy that complements the flavor, crush it up and use it in the batter and topping as directed in the recipe above.

Holiday Walnut Torte

This torte is my grandma's best recipe. The soft layers of nut-filled cake with apricot glaze and cream cheese frosting are divine!
—EILEEN KORECKO HOT SPRINGS VILLAGE, ARKANSAS

PREP: 40 MIN. **BAKE:** 25 MIN. + COOLING **MAKES:** 10-12 SERVINGS

- 3 **eggs**
- 1½ **cups sugar**
- 3 **teaspoons vanilla extract**
- 1¾ **cups all-purpose flour**
- 1 **cup ground walnuts**
- 2 **teaspoons baking powder**
- ½ **teaspoon salt**
- 1½ **cups heavy whipping cream**

GLAZE
- ⅔ **cup apricot preserves**
- 1 **tablespoon sugar**

FROSTING
- ½ **cup butter, softened**
- 1 **package (3 ounces) cream cheese, softened**
- 2 **cups confectioners' sugar**
- 1 **teaspoon vanilla extract**
- ¾ **cup ground walnuts, divided**

1. In a large bowl, beat the eggs, sugar and vanilla on high speed for 5 minutes or until thick and lemon-colored. Combine the flour, walnuts, baking powder and salt; beat into egg mixture. Beat cream until stiff peaks form; fold into batter.
2. Pour into two greased and floured 9-in. round baking pans.

Bake at 350° for 25-30 minutes or until a toothpick inserted near the center comes out clean. Cool for 10 minutes before removing from pans to wire racks to cool completely.
3. In a small saucepan over medium heat, cook and stir preserves and sugar until sugar is dissolved. Set aside ½ cup. Brush remaining glaze over cake tops.
4. In a large bowl, beat butter and cream cheese until fluffy. Add confectioners' sugar and vanilla; beat until smooth. Spread ½ cup frosting over one cake; top with second cake and ¾ cup frosting. Sprinkle ½ cup walnuts over the top.
5. Spread reserved glaze over sides of cake; press remaining walnuts onto sides. Pipe remaining frosting around top edge of cake. Store in the refrigerator.

Linzertorte

My Austrian grandmother made this nutty jam-filled dessert only at Christmastime. So did my mother, and now I do, too.
—JEANNE SIEBERT SALT LAKE CITY, UTAH

PREP: 25 MIN. + CHILLING **BAKE:** 40 MIN.
MAKES: 2 TORTES (8 SERVINGS EACH)

- 2 **cups all-purpose flour**
- 2 **cups ground hazelnuts**
- ½ **cup sugar**
- ½ **cup packed brown sugar**
- 1 **teaspoon ground cinnamon**
- ⅛ **teaspoon salt**
  Dash ground cloves
- 1 **cup cold butter, cubed**
- 2 **eggs, lightly beaten**
- 1 **teaspoon grated lemon peel**
- 1⅓ **cups seedless raspberry jam**
  Confectioners' sugar, optional

1. In a large bowl, combine the first seven ingredients. Cut in butter until mixture resembles coarse crumbs. Add eggs and lemon peel; stir until mixture forms a ball. Divide into fourths. Cover and refrigerate for 3-4 hours or until chilled.
2. Remove two portions of dough from refrigerator; press each into an ungreased 9-in. fluted tart pan with removable bottom. Spread ⅔ cup jam over each.
3. Between two sheets of lightly floured waxed paper, roll one portion of remaining dough into 10-in. x 6-in. rectangle. Cut six 1-in.-wide strips; arrange in lattice design over jam. Repeat with remaining dough (return dough to the refrigerator if needed).
4. Bake at 350° for 40-45 minutes or until bubbly and crust is browned. Cool completely. Dust with confectioners' sugar.

Sweet Potato Pie & Maple Praline Sauce

Sweet potato pie is a tradition in the South, but the praline topping takes this one over the top!

—**ROSEMARY JOHNSON** IRONDALE, ALABAMA

PREP: 20 MIN. **BAKE:** 1 HOUR + COOLING
MAKES: 10 SERVINGS (1⅔ CUPS SAUCE)

> **Pastry for single-crust pie (9 inches)**
> 1¼ cups sugar, divided
> 1 cup chopped pecans
> 1 teaspoon ground cinnamon
> 4 eggs, lightly beaten
> 1 cup mashed sweet potatoes
> ¾ cup buttermilk
> ¼ cup butter, melted
> ¼ cup maple syrup
> 1 teaspoon maple flavoring
> ¼ teaspoon ground cloves
> **MAPLE PRALINE SAUCE**
> ½ cup butter, cubed
> ½ cup chopped pecans
> ½ cup sugar
> ½ cup maple syrup
> 1 teaspoon maple flavoring
> ¼ cup sour cream

1. Line a 9-in. deep-dish pie plate with pastry; trim and flute edges. In a small bowl, combine ¼ cup sugar, pecans and cinnamon; sprinkle evenly into pastry shell. Set aside.
2. In a large bowl, combine the eggs, sweet potatoes, buttermilk, butter, syrup, maple flavoring, cloves and remaining sugar. Pour over pecan layer.
3. Bake at 350° for 60-70 minutes or until a knife inserted near the center comes out clean. Cover edges with foil during the last 15 minutes to prevent overbrowning if necessary. Cool on a wire rack.
4. For sauce, in a small heavy skillet, melt butter. Add pecans; cook over medium heat until toasted, about 4 minutes. Add the sugar, syrup and maple flavoring; cook and stir for 2-4 minutes or until sugar is dissolved. Remove from the heat; stir in sour cream. Serve with pie.

Santa Cupcakes

My children decorate these cupcakes every year for Christmas. We use chocolate chips to make Santa's eyes and a Red Hot for his nose, but you can use any kind of candy you like.

—**SHARON SKILDUM** MAPLE GROVE, MINNESOTA

PREP: 25 MIN. **BAKE:** 20 MIN. + COOLING **MAKES:** ABOUT 1½ DOZEN

> 1 package white cake mix (regular size)
> 1 can (16 ounces) or 2 cups vanilla frosting, divided
>
> Red gel or paste food coloring
> Miniature marshmallows, chocolate chips, Red Hots candies and flaked coconut

1. Prepare and bake cake mix according to package directions for cupcakes. Cool for 10 minutes; remove from pans to wire racks to cool completely.
2. Place ⅔ cup frosting in a small bowl; tint with red food coloring. Set aside 3 tablespoons white frosting for decorating. Cover two-thirds of the top of each cupcake with remaining white frosting. Frost the rest of cupcake top with red frosting for hat. Place reserved white frosting in a small heavy-duty resealable plastic bag; cut a ¼-in. hole in one corner.
3. On each cupcake, pipe a line of frosting to create fur band of hat. Press a marshmallow on one side of hat for pompom. Under hat, place two chocolate chips for eyes and one Red Hot for nose. Gently press coconut onto face for beard.

Holiday Fruitcake

After some experimenting in the kitchen, I finally came up with my ideal fruitcake. I think it has just the right mix of nuts and fruit.

—**ALLENE SPENCE** DELBARTON, WEST VIRGINIA

PREP: 20 MIN. **BAKE:** 2 HOURS + COOLING
MAKES: 16 SERVINGS

- 3 **cups whole red and green candied cherries**
- 3 **cups diced candied pineapple**
- 1 **package (1 pound) shelled walnuts**
- 1 **package (10 ounces) golden raisins**
- 1 **cup shortening**
- 1 **cup sugar**
- 5 **eggs**
- 4 **tablespoons vanilla extract**
- 3 **cups all-purpose flour**
- 3 **teaspoons baking powder**
- 1 **teaspoon salt**

1. In a large bowl, combine the cherries, pineapple, walnuts and raisins; set aside.
2. In another large bowl, cream shortening and sugar until light and fluffy. Beat in eggs and vanilla. Combine the flour, baking powder and salt; add to creamed mixture and mix well. Pour over fruit mixture and stir to coat.
3. Transfer to a greased and floured 10-in. tube pan. Bake at 300° for 2 hours or until a toothpick inserted near the center comes out clean. Cool for 10 minutes before removing from pan to a wire rack to cool completely.
4. Wrap tightly and store in a cool place. Slice with a serrated knife; bring to room temperature before serving.

MAKE AHEAD ▶ Yule Log

When my husband's family is over for Christmas, I like to make something extra-special for dessert. We love the chocolate "bark" topping on this creamy cake.

—**VALERIE GEE** WEST SENECA, NEW YORK

PREP: 35 MIN. **BAKE:** 15 MIN. + FREEZING **MAKES:** 10 SERVINGS

- 3 **eggs**
- 1 **cup sugar**
- ⅓ **cup water**
- 1 **teaspoon vanilla extract**
- ¾ **cup all-purpose flour**
- 1 **teaspoon baking powder**
- ¼ **teaspoon salt**
- ¼ **cup confectioners' sugar**
- 3 **cups pistachio ice cream, softened**
- 12 **ounces bittersweet chocolate, divided**

1. Line a greased 15-in. x 10-in. x 1-in. baking pan with parchment paper; grease the paper and set aside.
2. In large bowl, beat eggs for 3 minutes. Gradually add sugar, beating for 2 minutes or until thick and lemon-colored. Stir in water and vanilla. Combine flour, baking powder and salt; add to egg mixture; beat until smooth.
3. Spread batter evenly into prepared pan. Bake at 350° for 12-15 minutes or until cake springs back when lightly touched. Cool for 5 minutes.
4. Invert cake on kitchen towel dusted with confectioners' sugar. Gently peel off parchment paper. Roll up cake in the towel jelly-roll style, starting with a short side. Cool completely on a wire rack.
5. Unroll cake; spread ice cream evenly over cake to within ½ in. of edges. Roll up again. Place seam side down on platter. Cover and freeze for 1 hour.
6. In a microwave, melt four ounces of chocolate; stir until smooth. Spread over a parchment paper-lined baking sheet. Refrigerate for 30 minutes.
7. Break chilled chocolate into 3-in. x 1-in. pieces. Melt remaining chocolate; spread over top, sides and ends of cake. Working quickly, place chocolate pieces on cake to resemble bark. Freeze until serving. Remove from the freezer 10 minutes before cutting.

"We went to California more than 20 years ago and had this amazing pie at a restaurant. When I got home, I learned how to make it for my family. It's been our favorite ever since."

—SANDRA ASHCRAFT PUEBLO, COLORADO

Mud Pie

PREP: 25 MIN. + FREEZING **MAKES:** 8 SERVINGS

- 1½ cups chocolate wafer crumbs
- ⅓ cup butter, melted
- 1 quart chocolate ice cream, softened
- 1 quart coffee ice cream, softened

CHOCOLATE SAUCE
- 2 tablespoons butter
- 2 ounces unsweetened chocolate
- 1 cup sugar
- ¼ teaspoon salt
- 1 can (5 ounces) evaporated milk
- ½ teaspoon vanilla extract

WHIPPED CREAM
- 1 cup heavy whipping cream
- 1 tablespoon sugar

1. In a small bowl, combine wafer crumbs and butter. Press onto the bottom and up the sides of an ungreased 9-in. deep-dish pie plate. Bake at 350° for 10 minutes. Cool on a wire rack.

2. In a large bowl, beat chocolate ice cream and coffee ice cream. Spoon into crust. Cover and freeze for 8 hours or overnight.

3. For chocolate sauce, in a small saucepan, melt butter and chocolate over low heat; stir until smooth. Stir in the sugar, salt and evaporated milk. Bring to a boil, stirring constantly. Remove from the heat; stir in vanilla. Set aside.

4. Remove pie from the freezer 15 minutes before serving. In a small bowl, beat cream until it begins to thicken. Gradually add sugar; beat until soft peaks form.

5. Drizzle three stripes of chocolate sauce into a pastry bag; carefully add whipped cream. Pipe onto each slice of pie. Serve with remaining chocolate sauce.

Toffee Almond Tart

PREP: 20 MIN. **BAKE:** 30 MIN. + COOLING **MAKES:** 14 SERVINGS

- 2 cups all-purpose flour
- 3 tablespoons plus 1½ cups sugar, divided
- ¾ cup cold butter, cubed
- 3 egg yolks
- 1½ cups heavy whipping cream
- ¼ teaspoon salt
- 2 cups sliced almonds
- 1 teaspoon vanilla extract

1. In a large bowl, combine flour and 3 tablespoons sugar; cut in butter until mixture resembles fine crumbs. Add egg yolks, tossing with a fork until combined.

2. Press onto the bottom and up the sides of an ungreased 11-in. fluted tart pan with removable bottom. Place the pan on a baking sheet. Bake at 375° for 10 minutes or until golden brown.

3. Meanwhile, in a large saucepan, combine the cream, salt and remaining sugar. Bring to a boil over medium heat, stirring constantly. Remove from the heat; stir in almonds and vanilla. Pour into crust.

4. Bake for 30-35 minutes or until golden brown. Cool on a wire rack. Store in the refrigerator.

❝My aunt passed this recipe on to my mother, who then shared it with me, so I knew it had to be a winner. It's a real treat for anyone who loves almonds.❞

—SHARLYN NICHOLS LIVINGSTON, CALIFORNIA

MAKE AHEAD ▶ Frozen Peppermint Delight

Pass the hot fudge, please! This frosty ice cream "cake" is refreshingly easy to make ahead, so it's ready when you are. Also try it with different flavors of ice cream.

—PAM LANCASTER WILLIS, VIRGINIA

PREP: 25 MIN. + FREEZING **MAKES:** 12-15 SERVINGS

- 1 package (15½ ounces) Oreo cookies, crushed
- ½ cup butter, melted
- 1 gallon peppermint ice cream, slightly softened
- 1 carton (12 ounces) frozen whipped topping, thawed
- 1 jar (11¾ ounces) hot fudge ice cream topping, warmed
  Crushed peppermint candy

1. In a large bowl, combine cookie crumbs and butter. Press into an ungreased 13-in. x 9-in. dish. Spread ice cream over crust; top with whipped topping. Cover and freeze until solid. May be frozen for up to 2 months.
2. Just before serving, drizzle with hot fudge topping and sprinkle with peppermint candy.

MAKE AHEAD ▶ Spiced Pumpkin Mousse

If your holidays wouldn't be complete without pumpkin desserts and you're looking for something other than pie, you've met your mousse. I can tell you that kids just love dipping into this treat with gingersnap cookies.

—LARA PENNELL MAULDIN, SOUTH CAROLINA

PREP: 30 MIN. + CHILLING **MAKES:** 6 SERVINGS

- 1½ teaspoons unflavored gelatin
- 4½ teaspoons cold water
- 3 egg yolks
- ¾ cup sugar
- 1½ cups canned pumpkin
- ¾ teaspoon ground cinnamon
- ¼ teaspoon ground ginger
- ⅛ teaspoon ground cloves
- 1½ cups heavy whipping cream
- 1½ teaspoons vanilla extract
- 18 gingersnap cookies, divided

1. In a small saucepan, sprinkle gelatin over water; let stand for 1 minute or until softened. Beat in egg yolks and sugar. Cook and stir over medium heat until a thermometer reads 160° and mixture has thickened, about 5 minutes.
2. Transfer to a small bowl; beat until cool and thickened, about 3 minutes. Beat in pumpkin and spices. Refrigerate for 1 hour or until set.
3. In a small bowl, beat cream and vanilla until stiff peaks form. Fold into pumpkin mixture.
4. Coarsely crumble 12 gingersnaps; sprinkle into six parfait or dessert dishes. Spoon or pipe mousse over the top. Cover and refrigerate for 1 hour or until set. Just before serving, garnish with remaining gingersnaps.

Almond Pistachio Baklava

I discovered the traditional baklava at a Greek cultural event and make it often, as friends and family tend to ask me for a batch. The original version called for walnuts, but I substituted almonds and pistachios.

—**JOAN LLOYD** BARRIE, ONTARIO

PREP: 1½ HOURS **BAKE:** 35 MIN. + STANDING **MAKES:** ABOUT 4 DOZEN

3¾ cups sugar, divided
2 cups water
¾ cup honey
2 tablespoons lemon juice
4 cups unsalted pistachios
3 cups unsalted unblanched almonds

1½ teaspoons ground cinnamon
½ teaspoon ground nutmeg
1¾ cups butter, melted
3 packages (16 ounces each, 14-inch x 9-inch sheet size) frozen phyllo dough, thawed

1. In a small saucepan, bring 2¾ cups sugar, water, honey and lemon juice to a boil. Reduce heat; simmer for 5 minutes. Cool.

2. In a food processor, combine pistachios and almonds; cover and process until finely chopped. Transfer to a large bowl. Stir in the cinnamon, nutmeg and remaining sugar; set aside. Brush a 15-in. x 10-in. x 1-in. baking pan with some of the butter. Unroll one package of phyllo dough; cut stack into a 10½-in. x 9-in. rectangle. Repeat with remaining phyllo. Discard scraps.

3. Line bottom of prepared pan with two sheets of phyllo dough (sheets will overlap slightly). Brush with butter. Repeat layers 14 times. (Keep dough covered with plastic wrap and a damp towel until ready to use to prevent it from drying out.) Sprinkle with a third of the nut mixture.

4. Top with 15 layers of buttered phyllo dough and a third of the nut mixture; repeat layers. Top with remaining phyllo dough, buttering each layer.

5. Using a sharp knife, cut into 1½-in. diamond shapes. Bake at 350° for 35-40 minutes or until golden brown. Place pan on a wire rack. Slowly pour cooled sugar syrup over baklava. Cover and let stand overnight.

MAKE AHEAD ▶ Gingersnap Pumpkin Pie

Butterscotch pudding and canned pumpkin make a fantastically fun combination in this rich and buttery pie.

—**TASTE OF HOME TEST KITCHEN**

PREP: 30 MIN. + CHILLING **MAKES:** 8 SERVINGS

1½ cups finely crushed gingersnaps (about 32 cookies)
¼ cup butter, melted
4 ounces cream cheese, softened
1 tablespoon sugar
1½ cups whipped topping
1 cup cold 2% milk
2 packages (3.4 ounces each) instant butterscotch pudding mix
½ cup canned pumpkin
½ teaspoon pumpkin pie spice
½ teaspoon vanilla extract
¼ teaspoon ground cinnamon
Additional whipped topping, optional

1. In a small bowl, combine cookie crumbs and butter. Press onto the bottom and up the sides of an ungreased 9-in. pie plate. Bake at 375° for 8-10 minutes or until crust is lightly browned. Cool on a wire rack.

2. For filling, in a small bowl, beat cream cheese and sugar until smooth. Fold in whipped topping. Spread over crust.

3. In a bowl, beat milk and pudding mixes for 1 minute. Stir in the pumpkin, pie spice, vanilla and cinnamon. Spread over cream cheese layer. Cover and refrigerate overnight. Garnish with additional whipped topping.

My mother-in-law gave this recipe to me the first year I was married. It's a holiday must at my husband's family Christmas dinners. We call it "white Christmas chiffon" and garnish it with coconut. —**KRISTINE FRY** FENNIMORE, WISCONSIN

MAKE AHEAD › Coconut Chiffon Pie

PREP: 30 MIN. + CHILLING **MAKES:** 6-8 SERVINGS

- 1 **unbaked pastry shell (9 inches)**
- 1 **envelope unflavored gelatin**
- ¼ **cup cold water**
- ½ **cup sugar**
- ¼ **cup all-purpose flour**
- ½ **teaspoon salt**
- 1½ **cups 2% milk**
- ¾ **teaspoon vanilla extract**
- ¼ **teaspoon almond extract**
- 1 **cup heavy whipping cream, whipped**
- 1 **cup flaked coconut**
  Shaved fresh coconut, optional

1. Line unpricked pastry shell with a double thickness of heavy-duty foil. Bake at 450° for 8 minutes. Remove foil; bake shell 5 minutes longer. Cool on a wire rack.

2. Sprinkle gelatin over cold water; let stand for 1 minute. In a small saucepan, combine the sugar, flour and salt. Gradually stir in milk until smooth. Cook and stir over medium-low heat until mixture comes to a boil; cook and stir 1 minute longer or until thickened.

3. Remove from the heat. Whisk in gelatin mixture until dissolved. Transfer to a large bowl. Refrigerate until slightly thickened, about 30 minutes.

4. Add extracts; beat on medium speed for 1 minute. Fold in whipped cream and flaked coconut. Spread into pie crust. Refrigerate for at least 3 hours before serving. Garnish with shaved fresh coconut if desired.

top tip › Saving Coconut

To soften shredded coconut that's turned hard, soak it in milk for 30 minutes. Drain and pat it dry on paper towels. The leftover coconut-flavored milk can be used within 5 days in baked goods and smoothies.

MAPLE GINGER FUDGE, PAGE 249

Candy Sampler

265

251

257

> **"**With everyone else making truffles and cookies, these salty-sweet goodies are a great way to round out a holiday candy tray, and they're especially popular at bake sales.**"**

—**VIRGINIA CHRONIC** ROBINSON, ILLINOIS

CHOCOLATE-COATED PRETZELS

Chocolate-Coated Pretzels

PREP: 15 MIN. + STANDING **MAKES:** 5-6 DOZEN

- 1 to 1¼ pounds white and/or milk chocolate candy coating, coarsely chopped
- 1 package (8 ounces) miniature pretzels Nonpariels, colored jimmies and colored sugar, optional

In a microwave, melt half of candy coating at a time; stir until smooth. Dip pretzels in candy coating; allow excess to drip off. Place on waxed paper; let stand until almost set. Garnish as desired; let stand until set.

Cookie Dough Truffles

The filling at the center of these yummy candies is genuine chocolate chip cookie dough—without the raw eggs.

—**LANITA DEDON** SLAUGHTER, LOUISIANA

PREP: 1 HOUR + CHILLING **MAKES:** 5½ DOZEN

- ½ cup butter, softened
- ¾ cup packed brown sugar
- 1 teaspoon vanilla extract
- 2 cups all-purpose flour
- 1 can (14 ounces) sweetened condensed milk
- ½ cup miniature semisweet chocolate chips
- ½ cup chopped walnuts
- 1½ pounds dark chocolate candy coating, coarsely chopped

1. In a large bowl, cream the butter and brown sugar until light and fluffy. Beat in vanilla. Gradually add flour alternately with milk, beating well after each addition. Stir in chocolate chips and walnuts.
2. Shape into 1-in. balls; place on waxed paper-lined baking sheets. Loosely cover and refrigerate for 1-2 hours or until firm.
3. In microwave, melt candy coating; stir until smooth. Dip balls in coating; allow excess to drip off. Place on waxed paper-lined baking sheets. Refrigerate until firm, about 15 min. If desired, remelt remaining candy coating and drizzle over candies. Store in the refrigerator.

Brandied Cherry Balls

These spiked bonbons are always cherry-picked from the box.

—**LINDA M.** GALAX, VIRGINIA

PREP: 45 MIN. + CHILLING **MAKES:** ABOUT 3½ DOZEN

- ½ cup dried cherries, finely chopped
- ½ cup cherry brandy
- 1 package (3 ounces) cream cheese, softened
- 1 tablespoon butter, softened
- 3¾ cups confectioners' sugar
- 6 ounces dark chocolate candy coating, chopped
- 1 tablespoon shortening

DRIZZLE
- White candy coating, chopped
- Pink paste food coloring

1. Place cherries in a small bowl. Cover with brandy; refrigerate overnight.
2. In a large bowl, beat cream cheese and butter until smooth. Add confectioners' sugar; beat until crumbly. Drain cherries, reserving 2 teaspoons brandy. Add cherries and reserved brandy to cream cheese mixture.
3. Roll into 1½-in. balls. Place balls on a waxed paper-lined baking sheet. Cover loosely and refrigerate for 1 hour.
4. In a microwave, melt dark chocolate candy coating and shortening; stir until smooth. Dip balls in chocolate; allow excess to drip off. Return to the baking sheet.
5. For drizzle, melt a small amount of white candy coating in a microwave; stir in food coloring until smooth. Drizzle over candies. Chill until set.

Angel Food Candy

Dipped in white and dark chocolate candy coating, this two-tone treat stands out on any dessert tray.

—**CARROL HOLLOWAY** HINDSVILLE, ARKANSAS

PREP: 40 MIN. + STANDING **COOK:** 45 MIN. + STANDING **MAKES:** 1½ POUNDS

- 1½ teaspoons butter, softened
- 1 cup sugar
- 1 cup dark corn syrup
- 1 tablespoon white vinegar
- 1 tablespoon baking soda
- ½ pound white candy coating, melted
- ½ pound dark chocolate candy coating, melted

1. Grease a 13-in. x 9-in. pan with butter; set aside. In a large heavy saucepan, combine the sugar, corn syrup and vinegar. Cook and stir over medium heat until sugar is dissolved. Cook, without stirring, until a candy thermometer reads 290° (soft-crack stage).
2. Remove from the heat; stir in baking soda. Pour into prepared pan but do not spread; cool. Break into pieces.
3. Dip each candy halfway into white candy coating; allow excess to drip off. Place on waxed paper-lined baking sheets until set. Dip plain half of candies into dark chocolate coating; allow excess to drip off. Return to waxed paper until set. Store in an airtight container.

Editor's Note: *We recommend that you test your candy thermometer before each use by bringing water to a boil; the thermometer should read 212°. Adjust your recipe temperature up or down based on your test.*

Butterscotch Fudge

I love to enter my fudge recipes at our county fairs. I have been doing it for years, and my entries always win a ribbon!

—**VIRGINIA HIPWELL** FENWICK, ONTARIO

PREP/TOTAL TIME: 25 MIN. **MAKES:** ABOUT 1½ POUNDS

- **1 teaspoon plus 2 tablespoons butter, divided**
- **1⅔ cups sugar**
- **⅔ cup evaporated milk**
- **½ teaspoon salt**
- **2 cups miniature marshmallows**
- **1 package (10 to 11 ounces) butterscotch chips**
- **½ cup chopped walnuts**
- **1 teaspoon maple flavoring**

1. Line an 8-in. square pan with foil and grease the foil with 1 teaspoon butter; set aside.

2. In a large saucepan, combine the sugar, milk, salt and remaining butter; cook and stir over medium heat until mixture comes to a boil. Boil for 5 minutes, stirring constantly.

3. Remove from the heat; add the marshmallows, chips, nuts and maple flavoring. Stir until marshmallows and chips are melted. Spoon into prepared pan. Let stand until set.

4. Using foil, lift fudge out of pan. Discard foil; cut fudge into 1-in squares. Store in an airtight container at room temperature.

Raisin Cashew Drops

During the holiday season, I serve these bite-size chocolates in festive paper cups decorated with snowmen or Santas. They're simple to make, and the combination of salty and sweet is a real crowd-pleaser.

—**CHERYL BUTLER** LAKE PLACID, FLORIDA

PREP: 20 MIN. + CHILLING **MAKES:** 2½ POUNDS

- **2 cups (12 ounces) semisweet chocolate chips**
- **1 can (14 ounces) sweetened condensed milk**
- **1 tablespoon light corn syrup**
- **1 teaspoon vanilla extract**
- **2 cups coarsely chopped cashews**
- **2 cups raisins**

1. In a heavy saucepan over low heat, melt chocolate chips with milk and corn syrup for 10-12 minutes, stirring occasionally. Remove from the heat; stir in vanilla until blended. Stir in cashews and raisins.

2. Drop by teaspoonfuls onto waxed paper-lined baking sheets. Refrigerate for 3 hours or until firm. Store in the refrigerator.

So-Easy Truffles

Don't expect these truffles to last long in your home. You'll need to hide them if you want to serve them for a special event.

—DENISE KUTCHKO ODESSA, MISSOURI

PREP: 45 MIN. **MAKES:** 4 DOZEN

- 1 **package (15½ ounces) Oreo cookies**
- 1 **package (8 ounces) cream cheese, cubed**
- 1 **cup chocolate wafer crumbs**

Place cookies in a food processor; cover and process until finely crushed. Add cream cheese; process until blended. Roll into 1-in. balls. Roll in wafer crumbs. Store in an airtight container in the refrigerator.

Peanut Butter Truffles: *Substitute a 16-oz. package of peanut butter cream-filled sandwich cookies for the chocolate sandwich cookies. Omit chocolate wafer crumbs. Melt 12 ounces of milk chocolate candy coating; stir until smooth. Dip balls in chocolate; place on waxed paper until set. Store in the refrigerator. Makes: 4 dozen.*

Vanilla Cookie Truffles: *Substitute a 16-oz. package of cream-filled vanilla sandwich cookies for the chocolate sandwich cookies. Melt 12 ounces of milk chocolate candy coating; stir until smooth. Dip balls in chocolate; sprinkle with ¼ cup chocolate crumbs. Place on waxed paper until set. Store in the refrigerator. Makes: 4 dozen.*

Snowball

I've been making these popular treats for more than 40 years, much to my family's delight. They look impressive with chocolate and coconut wrapped around a chewy marshmallow center, yet they're surprisingly simple to assemble.

—MURIEL WHITE BRAMPTON, ONTARIO

PREP: 20 MIN. + FREEZING **MAKES:** ABOUT 3 DOZEN

- ½ **cup butter, cubed**
- 1 **can (14 ounces) sweetened condensed milk**
- 3 **tablespoons baking cocoa**
- 1 **teaspoon vanilla extract**
- 2 **cups graham cracker crumbs (about 32 squares)**
- 3½ **cups flaked coconut, divided**
- 32 **to 35 large marshmallows**

1. Line a baking sheet with waxed paper; set aside.
2. In a large saucepan, combine the butter, milk, cocoa and vanilla. Cook and stir over medium heat until butter is melted and mixture is smooth. Remove from the heat; stir in cracker crumbs and 1½ cups coconut. Let stand until cool enough to handle.
3. Using moistened hands, wrap about 1 tablespoon of mixture around each marshmallow (dip hands in water often to prevent sticking). Roll in remaining coconut; place on prepared baking sheet. Cover and freeze until firm. Store in an airtight container in the refrigerator or freezer. May be frozen for up to 2 months.

White Christmas Fudge

Loaded with fruit and nuts, this smooth, sweet fudge is just right for a sweet bite at the end of a big meal.

—PAULA TRUSKA JEWETT, TEXAS

PREP: 20 MIN. + CHILLING   **MAKES:** ABOUT 2 POUNDS

- 1   teaspoon plus ¼ cup butter, divided
- 2½ cups confectioners' sugar
- ⅔   cup milk
- 12 ounces white baking chocolate, chopped
- ¼   teaspoon almond extract
- ¾   cup sliced almonds, toasted
- ¼   cup chopped dried apricots
- ¼   cup dried cherries
- ¼   cup dried cranberries

1. Line a 9-in. square pan with foil and grease the foil with 1 teaspoon butter; set aside.

2. In a large heavy saucepan, combine the confectioners' sugar, milk and remaining butter. Cook and stir over medium heat until combined. Bring to a boil; boil for 5 minutes without stirring. Reduce heat to low; stir in white chocolate. Cook and stir until chocolate is melted.

3. Remove from the heat; stir in extract. Fold in the almonds, apricots, cherries and cranberries. Immediately spread into prepared pan. Refrigerate for 2 hours or until set.

4. Using foil, lift fudge out of pan. Discard foil; cut fudge into 1-in. squares. Store in the refrigerator.

Pecan White Chocolate Fudge: *Use a 9-in. x 5-in. loaf pan; prepare as directed. Omit fruit. Substitute 1½ teaspoons vanilla extract for the almond extract. Substitute 1 cup toasted chopped pecans for the almonds.*

White Chocolate Peppermint Fudge: *Use a 9-in. x 5-in. loaf pan; prepare as directed. Omit almonds and fruit. Substitute ½ teaspoon peppermint extract for the almond extract. Fold ½ cup crushed peppermint candies into melted chocolate mixture.*

Maple Ginger Fudge

I combine my two fall favorites—maple and ginger—in this sweet, smooth fudge. One piece just isn't enough!

—STEVE WESTPHAL WIND LAKE, WISCONSIN

PREP: 10 MIN. **COOK:** 30 MIN. + CHILLING
MAKES: 1¼ POUNDS

- 2 teaspoons plus 2 tablespoons butter, divided
- 2 cups sugar
- ⅔ cup heavy whipping cream
- 2 tablespoons light corn syrup
- ¼ teaspoon ground ginger
- ½ teaspoon maple flavoring
- ½ cup chopped walnuts

1. Line a 9-in. x 5-in. loaf pan with foil and grease the foil with 1 teaspoon butter; set aside. Butter the sides of a small heavy saucepan with 1 teaspoon butter; add the sugar, cream, corn syrup and ginger. Bring to a boil over medium heat, stirring constantly. Reduce heat; cook mixture until a candy thermometer reads 238° (soft-ball stage), stirring occasionally.

2. Remove from the heat. Add maple flavoring and remaining butter (do not stir). Cool to 110° without stirring, about 1 hour. With a portable mixer, beat mixture on low speed for 1-2 minutes or until fudge begins to thicken. With a clean dry wooden spoon, stir in walnuts until fudge begins to lose its gloss, about 5 minutes.

3. Spread into prepared pan. Refrigerate until firm, about 30 minutes. Using foil, lift fudge out of pan. Discard foil; cut fudge into 1-in. squares. Store fudge in an airtight container in the refrigerator.

Editor's Note: *We recommend that you test your candy thermometer before each use by bringing water to a boil; the thermometer should read 212°. Adjust your recipe temperature up or down based on your test.*

Cinnamon Walnut Brittle

Seasoned with cinnamon, this spicy brittle is a great gift or family snack to munch while watching Christmas movies. Best of all, it goes together quick as a wink.

—JULIE RADCLIFFE BUTTE, MONTANA

PREP: 20 MIN. + COOLING **MAKES:** ¾ POUND

- 1 cup sugar
- ½ cup light corn syrup
- 1 cup chopped walnuts
- 1 teaspoon butter
- ½ teaspoon ground cinnamon
- 1 teaspoon baking soda
- 1 teaspoon vanilla extract

1. Butter a baking sheet; set aside. In a 2-qt. microwave-safe bowl, combine sugar and corn syrup. Microwave, uncovered, on high for 3 minutes; stir. Cook, uncovered, on high 2½ minutes longer. Stir in the walnuts, butter and cinnamon.

2. Microwave, uncovered, on high for 2 minutes longer or until mixture turns a light amber color (mixture will be very hot).

3. Quickly stir in baking soda and vanilla until light and foamy. Immediately pour onto prepared pan; spread with a metal spatula. Cool; break into pieces.

Editor's Note: *This recipe was tested in a 1,100-watt microwave.*

Toasted Coconut Truffles

Toasted coconut in the coating makes these truffles especially tempting for my husband. He thinks they are just fabulous. We like to include them in our Christmas gift packages.

—BETH NAGEL WEST LAFAYETTE, INDIANA

PREP: 30 MIN. + CHILLING   **MAKES:** ABOUT 5½ DOZEN

- **4 cups (24 ounces) semisweet chocolate chips**
- **1 package (8 ounces) cream cheese, softened and cubed**
- **¾ cup sweetened condensed milk**
- **3 teaspoons vanilla extract**
- **2 teaspoons water**
- **1 pound white candy coating, coarsely chopped**
- **2 tablespoons flaked coconut, finely chopped and toasted**

1. In a microwave-safe bowl, melt chocolate chips; stir until smooth. Add the cream cheese, milk, vanilla and water; beat with a hand mixer until blended. Cover and refrigerate until easy to handle, about 1½ hours.

2. Shape into 1-in. balls and place on waxed paper-lined baking sheets. Loosely cover and refrigerate for 1-2 hours or until firm.

3. In a microwave, melt candy coating, stir until smooth. Dip balls in coating; allow excess to drip off. Place on waxed paper-lined baking sheets. Sprinkle with coconut. Refrigerate until firm, about 15 minutes. Store in the refrigerator in an airtight container.

Holiday Divinity

I've been whipping up this Christmasy treat, with its jolly red and green candied cherries and scrumptious chopped nuts, since 1955. It's so light and meringue-like, it just melts in your mouth.

—HELEN WHITE KERRVILLE, TEXAS

PREP: 25 MIN.   **COOK:** 15 MIN.   **MAKES:** 1¼ POUNDS

- **2 cups sugar**
- **½ cup water**
- **⅓ cup light corn syrup**
- **2 egg whites**
- **1 teaspoon vanilla extract**
- **⅛ teaspoon salt**
- **1 cup chopped walnuts, toasted**
- **¼ cup diced candied cherries**
- **¼ cup diced candied pineapple**

1. In a heavy saucepan, combine the sugar, water and corn syrup; cook and stir until sugar is dissolved and mixture comes to a boil. Cook over medium heat, without stirring, until a candy thermometer reads 250° (hard-ball stage). Remove from the heat.

2. Meanwhile, in a stand mixer, beat the egg whites until stiff peaks form. With mixer running on high speed, carefully pour hot syrup in a slow, steady stream into the mixing bowl. Add vanilla and salt. Beat on high speed just until candy loses its gloss and holds its shape, about 10 minutes. Stir in nuts and fruit.

3. Drop by teaspoonfuls onto waxed paper. Store in airtight containers.

Editor's Note: *The use of a hand mixer is not recommended for this recipe.*

> **66** I get nothing but comments of delight when I make these candies, and usually have to prepare three batches. The refreshing orange flavor is a nice change from the usual chocolate holiday treats. **99**

—**BECKY BURCH** MARCELINE, MISSOURI

Orange Gumdrops

PREP: 10 MIN. **COOK:** 10 MIN. + STANDING
MAKES: ABOUT 6 DOZEN

- 1 **teaspoon plus 1 tablespoon butter, softened, divided**
- 1 **cup sugar**
- 1 **cup light corn syrup**
- ¾ **cup water**
- 1 **package (1¾ ounces) powdered fruit pectin**
- ½ **teaspoon baking soda**
- 1½ **teaspoons orange extract**
- 1 **teaspoon grated orange peel**
- 4 **drops yellow food coloring**
- 1 **drop red food coloring**
  Additional sugar, optional

1. Line the bottom and sides of a 9-in. x 5-in. loaf pan with foil. Grease the foil with 1 teaspoon butter; set aside.

2. Grease the bottom and sides of a large heavy saucepan with the remaining butter; add sugar and corn syrup. Cook and stir over medium heat until mixture comes to a boil, about 9 minutes. Cook over medium-high heat until a candy thermometer reads 280° (soft-crack stage), stirring occasionally.

3. Meanwhile, in another large saucepan, combine the water, pectin and baking soda (mixture will foam slightly). Cook and stir over high heat until mixture boils, about 2 minutes. Remove from the heat; set aside.

4. When corn syrup mixture reaches 280° (soft-crack stage), remove from the heat. Return pectin mixture to medium-high heat; cook until mixture begins to simmer. Carefully and slowly ladle corn syrup mixture in a very thin stream into pectin mixture, stirring constantly. Cook and stir 1 minute longer.

5. Remove from the heat; stir in the extract, peel and food coloring. Transfer to prepared pan. Let stand until firm, about 2 hours. Cut into squares. Roll gumdrops in additional sugar if desired.

Peppermint Taffy

This candy brings back many memories of my grandmother. I used to help her pull the taffy every Christmas Eve. It's a holiday tradition in my family.

—**SUZETTE JURY** KEENE, CALIFORNIA

PREP: 1½ HOURS **COOK:** 20 MIN. + COOLING **MAKES:** 1¾ POUNDS

- 1 tablespoon plus ¼ cup butter, cubed
- 2 cups light corn syrup
- 1½ cups sugar
- 2 teaspoons peppermint extract
- ½ teaspoon salt
- 6 drops red food coloring, optional

1. Grease a 15-in. x 10-in. x 1-in. pan with 1 tablespoon butter; set aside.

2. In a heavy small saucepan, combine corn syrup and sugar. Bring to a boil over medium heat. Add remaining butter; stir until melted. Cook and stir until a candy thermometer reads 250° (hard-ball stage).

3. Remove from the heat; stir in the extract, salt and food coloring if desired. Pour into prepared pan. Let stand for 5-10 minutes or until cool enough to handle. Divide into 4 portions.

4. With well-buttered fingers, quickly pull one portion of candy until firm but pliable (color will become light pink). Pull into a ½-in.-wide rope. Repeat with remaining candy. Cut into 1-in. pieces. Wrap each in waxed paper.

Editor's Note: *We recommend that you test your candy thermometer before each use by bringing water to a boil; the thermometer should read 212°. Adjust your recipe temperature up or down based on your test.*

Peanut Butter Chocolate Cups

PREP: 20 MIN. + CHILLING **MAKES:** 1 DOZEN

- 1 milk chocolate candy bar (7 ounces)
- ¼ cup butter
- 1 tablespoon shortening
- ¼ cup creamy peanut butter

1. In a microwave, melt the chocolate, butter and shortening; stir until smooth. Place foil or paper miniature baking cups in a miniature muffin tin. Place 1 tablespoon of chocolate mixture in each cup.

2. In a microwave, melt peanut butter; stir until smooth. Spoon into cups. Top with remaining chocolate mixture. Remelt chocolate mixture if necessary. Refrigerate for 30 minutes or until firm.

"Our children love these rich, creamy candies. I think they're better than the store-bought ones."

—**ALJENE WENDLING** SEATTLE, WASHINGTON

Marbled Orange Fudge

This decadent treat doesn't last long at our house. It reminds us of Creamsicles. Bright orange and marshmallow swirls make it the perfect take-along for holiday events and get-togethers.

—DIANE WAMPLER MORRISTOWN, TENNESSEE

PREP: 30 MIN. + CHILLING **MAKES:** ABOUT 2½ POUNDS

- 1½ teaspoons plus ¾ cup butter, divided
- 3 cups sugar
- ¾ cup heavy whipping cream
- 1 package white baking chips (10 to 12 ounces)
- 1 jar (7 ounces) marshmallow creme
- 3 teaspoons orange extract
- 12 drops yellow food coloring
- 5 drops red food coloring

1. Grease a 13-in. x 9-in. pan with 1½ teaspoons butter; set aside.

2. In a saucepan, combine the sugar, cream and remaining butter. Cook and stir over low heat until sugar is dissolved. Bring to a boil; cook and stir for 4 minutes. Remove from the heat; stir in chips and marshmallow creme until smooth.

3. Remove 1 cup and set aside. Add orange extract and food coloring to the remaining mixture; stir until blended. Pour into prepared pan. Drop reserved marshmallow mixture by tablespoonfuls over the top; cut through with a knife to swirl. Cover and refrigerate until set. Cut into squares.

Caramel Cashew Clusters

Several years ago, a co-worker came across candies like these in a store and asked if I could make them. After some trial and error, I came up with a winning recipe.

—KAREN DANIELS JEFFERSON CITY, MISSOURI

PREP: 25 MIN. + STANDING **MAKES:** 2½ DOZEN

- 2 pounds milk chocolate candy coating, coarsely chopped, divided
- 1 cup salted cashew halves
- 28 caramels
- 2 tablespoons heavy whipping cream

1. Line baking sheets with waxed paper and butter the paper; set aside.

2. In a microwave, melt 1 pound of candy coating; stir until smooth. Drop by scant tablespoonfuls onto prepared pans. Let stand until partially set, about 3 minutes. Top each with six or seven cashews. Let stand until completely set.

3. In a small heavy saucepan, combine caramels and cream. Cook and stir over low heat until melted; stir until smooth. Spoon over cashews. Reheat caramel over low heat if it thickens. Melt remaining candy coating; spoon over caramel. Let stand until set.

Peanut Butter Pretzel Bites

I come from a very large family, and my mother taught us all how to cook. This recipe is special to me because I was making candy with my own daughter when we came up with it.
—**LOIS FARMER** LOGAN, WEST VIRGINIA

PREP: 1½ HOURS + STANDING **MAKES:** 8½ DOZEN

- 1 **package (14 ounces) caramels**
- ¼ **cup butter, cubed**
- 2 **tablespoons water**
- 5 **cups miniature pretzels**
- 1 **jar (18 ounces) chunky peanut butter**
- 26 **ounces milk chocolate candy coating, melted**

1. In a microwave, melt caramels with butter and water; stir until smooth. Spread one side of each pretzel with 1 teaspoon peanut butter; top with ½ teaspoon caramel mixture. Place on waxed paper-lined baking sheets. Refrigerate until set.

2. Using a small fork, dip each pretzel into melted chocolate coating until completely covered; allow excess to drip off. Place on waxed paper. Let stand until set. Store in an airtight container in a cool dry place.

Editor's Note: *This recipe was tested in a 1,100-watt microwave.*

Chocolate Cream Bonbons

My grandmother gave me this recipe when I was a girl. Some of my fondest childhood memories are of her enormous kitchen and all the delicious treats.
—**JOAN LEWIS** RENO, NEVADA

PREP: 20 MIN. + CHILLING **MAKES:** ABOUT 6 DOZEN

- 4 **cups confectioners' sugar**
- 1 **cup ground pecans or walnuts**
- ½ **cup plus 2 tablespoons sweetened condensed milk**
- ¼ **cup butter, softened**
- 3 **cups (18 ounces) semisweet chocolate chips**
- 2 **tablespoons shortening**

1. In a large bowl, combine the confectioners' sugar, pecans, milk and butter. Roll into 1-in. balls. Place on waxed paper-lined baking sheets. Cover and refrigerate overnight.

2. In a microwave, melt chocolate chips and shortening; stir until smooth. Dip balls in chocolate; allow excess to drip off. Place on waxed paper; let stand until set. (If balls are too soft to dip, place in the freezer for a few minutes first.)

During the holiday season, I give these candies to teachers and friends. You don't need any fancy ingredients, and they're so simple to prepare.

—**DEBRA PEDRAZZI** AYER, MASSACHUSETTS

CHOCOLATE HAZELNUT TRUFFLES

Chocolate Hazelnut Truffles

PREP: 25 MIN. + CHILLING   **MAKES:** 2 DOZEN

- ¾ cup confectioners' sugar
- 2 tablespoons baking cocoa
- 4 milk chocolate candy bars (1.55 ounces each)
- 6 tablespoons butter
- ¼ cup heavy whipping cream
- 24 whole hazelnuts
- 1 cup ground hazelnuts, toasted

1. In a large bowl, sift together confectioners' sugar and cocoa; set aside.
2. In a saucepan, melt candy bars and butter. Add cream and reserved cocoa mixture. Cook and stir over medium-low heat until mixture is thickened and smooth. Pour into an 8-in. square dish. Cover and refrigerate overnight.
3. Using a melon baller or spoon, shape candy into 1-in. balls; press a hazelnut into each. Reshape balls and roll in ground hazelnuts. Store in an airtight container in the refrigerator.

Peppermint Patties

When I make these for Christmas, I like to add green food coloring with the extract.

—**MARY ESTER HOLLOWAY** BOWERSTON, OHIO

PREP: 25 MIN. + FREEZING   **MAKES:** ABOUT 12 DOZEN

- 3 pounds confectioners' sugar
- 1 can (14 ounces) sweetened condensed milk
- ½ cup butter, melted
- 3 teaspoons peppermint extract
- 3 pounds milk chocolate candy coating, coarsely chopped

1. In a large bowl, beat the confectioners' sugar, milk, butter and extract until smooth. Shape into ½-in. balls and flatten into patties. Freeze for 30 minutes.
2. In a microwave, melt half of candy coating at a time; dip patties into chocolate. Let excess drip off. Place on waxed-paper lined baking sheets until set. Store in airtight containers.

Pecan Toffee Fudge

My fudge is always popular wherever I take it and makes great gifts for loved ones and friends. The creaminess and toffee bits make it a hit with everyone. And it's so easy, even young children can help make it—with a little supervision!

—DIANE WILLEY BOZMAN, MARYLAND

PREP: 20 MIN. + CHILLING **MAKES:** 2½ POUNDS

- 1 teaspoon butter
- 1 package (8 ounces) cream cheese, softened
- 3¾ cups confectioners' sugar
- 6 ounces unsweetened chocolate, melted and cooled
- ¼ teaspoon almond extract
  Dash salt
- ¼ cup coarsely chopped pecans
- ¼ cup English toffee bits

1. Line a 9-in. square pan with foil and grease the foil with butter; set aside. In a large bowl, beat cream cheese until fluffy. Gradually beat in confectioners' sugar. Beat in the melted chocolate, extract and salt until smooth. Stir in pecans and toffee bits.

2. Spread into prepared pan. Cover and refrigerate overnight or until firm. Using foil, lift fudge out of pan. Gently peel off foil; cut fudge into 1-in. squares. Store in an airtight container in the refrigerator.

Nutty Caramels

A cousin passed this easy candy recipe on to me. We make it every Christmas and include the caramels in gift baskets.

—LYNN NELSON KASILOF, ALASKA

PREP: 5 MIN. **COOK:** 70 MIN. + COOLING **MAKES:** 1½ POUNDS

- 1 teaspoon plus ¼ cup butter, divided
- 1 cup sugar
- 1 cup light corn syrup
- 1 cup evaporated milk
- 1 cup chopped nuts
- 1 teaspoon vanilla extract
  Melted milk chocolate

1. Line a 9-in. square pan with foil and grease the foil with 1 teaspoon butter; set aside.
2. In a saucepan, combine the sugar, corn syrup, milk and remaining butter. Cook and stir over medium heat until sugar is dissolved. Bring to a rapid boil, stirring constantly, until a candy thermometer reads 248° (firm-ball stage).
3. Remove from the heat; stir in nuts and vanilla. Pour into prepared pan (do not scrape saucepan). Cool completely. Using foil, lift caramels out of pan; discard foil. Cut into small squares or diamonds. Drizzle each with chocolate if desired.
Editor's Note: *We recommend that you test your candy thermometer before each use by bringing water to a boil; the thermometer should read 212°. Adjust your recipe temperature up or down based on your test.*

Maple Cream Bonbons

My family will never forget one winter when I put trays of these candy centers on top of my van in the garage to freeze before dipping. Later, I drove off and was horrified to see the little balls rolling on the highway! Now when I make them, everyone giggles.

—**GINNY TRUWE** MANKATO, MINNESOTA

PREP: 30 MIN. + CHILLING **MAKES:** 5 DOZEN

- 1 **cup butter, softened**
- 3½ **cups confectioners' sugar**
- 3 **tablespoons maple flavoring**
- 2 **cups chopped walnuts**
- 2 **cups semisweet chocolate chips**
- 1 **cup butterscotch chips**

1. In a large bowl, cream the butter, sugar and maple flavoring until smooth. Stir in walnuts. Shape into 1-in. balls; place on waxed paper-lined baking sheets. Freeze until firm.

2. In a microwave, melt chips; stir until smooth. Dip balls in chocolate; allow excess to drip off. Place on waxed paper-lined baking sheets. Refrigerate until set. Store bonbons in the refrigerator.

Coconut Cashew Brittle

This rich, buttery brittle has always been part of our Christmas candy collection. Lots of coconut and cashews make it extra scrumptious.

—**DARLENE BRENDEN** SALEM, OREGON

PREP: 25 MIN. **BAKE:** 10 MIN. **MAKES:** ABOUT 3 POUNDS

- 2 **tablespoons plus 1 cup butter, divided**
- 2 **cups cashew halves**
- 2 **cups flaked coconut**
- 2 **cups sugar**
- 1 **cup light corn syrup**
- ½ **cup plus 1 teaspoon water, divided**
- 2 **teaspoons vanilla extract**
- 1½ **teaspoons baking soda**

1. Butter two 15-in. x 10-in. x 1-in. pans with 1 Tbsp. butter each; set aside.

2. Combine cashews and coconut on a third 15-in. x 10-in. x 1-in. baking pan. Bake at 350° for 8-10 minutes or until golden brown, stirring occasionally.

3. In a large heavy saucepan, combine the sugar, corn syrup and ½ cup water. Cook and stir over medium heat until mixture comes to a boil. Add remaining butter; cook and stir until butter is melted. Continue cooking, without stirring, until a candy thermometer reads 300° (hard-crack stage).

4. Meanwhile, combine the vanilla, baking soda and remaining water. Remove saucepan from the heat; add cashews and coconut. Add baking soda mixture; stir until light and foamy. Quickly pour onto prepared baking sheets. Spread with a buttered metal spatula to ¼-in. thickness. Cool before breaking into pieces. Store in an airtight container.

Editor's Note: *We recommend that you test your candy thermometer before each use by bringing water to a boil; the thermometer should read 212°. Adjust your recipe temperature up or down based on your test.*

Cherry Chocolate Bark

PREP: 20 MIN. + CHILLING **MAKES:** ABOUT 2 POUNDS

- 1 **tablespoon plus ½ cup butter, softened, divided**
- 2 **cups sugar**
- 12 **large marshmallows**
- 1 **can (5 ounces) evaporated milk**
  Dash salt
- 1 **cup vanilla or white chips**
- 1½ **teaspoons cherry extract**
- 1 **teaspoon vanilla extract**
- 1 **cup semisweet chocolate chips**
- ⅓ **cup creamy peanut butter**
- ¼ **cup finely chopped dry roasted peanuts**

1. Line a 15-in. x 10-in. x 1-in. pan with foil. Grease the foil with 1 tablespoon butter; set aside.

2. In a large heavy saucepan, combine the sugar, marshmallows, milk, salt and remaining butter. Bring to a boil; cook and stir mixture for 5 minutes. Remove from the heat. Stir in vanilla chips and extracts until smooth. Pour into prepared pan.

3. In a microwave-safe bowl, melt chocolate chips; stir until smooth. Stir in peanut butter and peanuts. Drop by tablespoonfuls over first layer; cut through with a knife to swirl. Chill until firm.

4. Using foil, lift candy out of pan. Discard foil. Break candy into pieces. Store in an airtight container in the refrigerator.

top tip

Chips vs. Baking Chocolate

Ounce for ounce, baking chocolate can be used in place of chocolate chips for melting. One cup of chips equals about 6 ounces. To melt, microwave semisweet chocolate at 50% power; use 30% power for milk and vanilla or white chocolate.

> **❝My daughter's candy bark caught my eye because it reminded me of a favorite candy bar I enjoyed as a child. I love the fudge-like texture.❞**
>
> —**JUDITH BATIUK** SAN LUIS OBISPO, CALIFORNIA

Raspberry Truffles

As everyone in my neighborhood knows, Christmas is my very favorite time of year. I make many cookies, cakes and candies, including these easy but elegant truffles. The aroma of the chocolate and raspberry is heavenly.

—HELEN VAIL GLENSIDE, PENNSYLVANIA

PREP: 40 MIN. + FREEZING **MAKES:** 4 DOZEN

- 1 tablespoon butter
- 2 tablespoons heavy whipping cream
- 1⅓ cups semisweet chocolate chips
- 7½ teaspoons seedless raspberry jam
- 6 ounces white candy coating or dark chocolate candy coating, coarsely chopped
- 2 tablespoons shortening

1. In a small heavy saucepan, combine butter, cream and chocolate chips. Cook over low heat for 4-5 minutes or until chocolate is melted. Remove from the heat; stir in jam until combined. Transfer to a small freezer container; cover and freeze for 20 minutes.

2. Drop by teaspoonfuls onto a foil-lined baking sheet. Freeze for 15 minutes. Roll into balls; freeze until very firm.

3. Place a wire rack over a large sheet of waxed paper. In a microwave, melt candy coating and shortening; stir until smooth. Cool slightly; spoon over balls. Place on the prepared wire rack. Let stand for 15 minutes or until set. Store in an airtight container in the refrigerator.

Pinwheel Mints

Both my grandmother and my mom used to make these candies as a replacement for ordinary mints at Christmas. When I offer them at parties, guests tell me they're wonderful, and then ask how I create the pretty swirl pattern.

—MARILOU ROTH MILFORD, NEBRASKA

PREP: 45 MIN. + CHILLING **MAKES:** ABOUT 3 DOZEN

- 1 package (8 ounces) cream cheese, softened
- ½ to 1 teaspoon mint extract
- 7½ to 8½ cups confectioners' sugar
- Red and green food coloring
- Additional confectioners' sugar

1. In a large bowl, beat cream cheese and mint extract until smooth. Gradually beat in as much confectioners' sugar as possible; knead in remaining confectioners' sugar until a firm mixture is achieved. Divide mixture in half; with food coloring, tint half pink and the other light green.

2. On waxed paper, lightly sprinkle remaining confectioners' sugar into a 12-in. x 5-in. rectangle. Divide pink portion in half; shape each portion into a 10-in. log.

3. Place one log on sugared waxed paper and flatten slightly. Cover with waxed paper; roll into a 12-in. x 5-in. rectangle. Repeat with remaining pink portion; set aside. Repeat with light green portion.

4. Remove top piece of waxed paper from one pink and one green rectangle. Place one over the other. Roll up jelly-roll style, starting with a long side. Wrap in waxed paper; twist ends. Repeat. Chill overnight.

5. To serve, cut into ½-in. slices. Store in an airtight container in the refrigerator for up to 1 week.

Almond Coconut Candies

I love the irresistible combination of coconut, almonds and dark chocolate. These special candies also make great gifts, if you can get yourself to part with any!

—**JANET LOOMIS** TERRY, MONTANA

PREP: 25 MIN. + CHILLING **MAKES:** 5 DOZEN

- 4½ cups confectioners' sugar
- 3 cups flaked coconut
- 1 cup sweetened condensed milk
- ½ cup butter, melted
- 1 teaspoon vanilla extract
- 60 whole unblanched almonds

FROSTING

- 1½ cups confectioners' sugar
- ½ cup baking cocoa
- ½ cup butter, melted
- 3 tablespoons hot coffee

1. In a large bowl, combine the first five ingredients. Shape into 1-in. balls; place on lightly greased baking sheets. Press an almond on top of each ball. Chill for 1 hour.

2. Combine frosting ingredients until smooth; immediately frost tops of candies. Chill until frosting is firm. Store in the refrigerator.

Pistachio Cranberry Bark

I first tasted this candy bark at a Bible study partner's home. I asked her for the recipe and made a few changes. Now my dad, who is not even a candy lover, raves about it!

—**SUSAN WACEK** PLEASANTON, CALIFORNIA

PREP: 20 MIN. + CHILLING **MAKES:** ABOUT 1 POUND

- 2 cups (12 ounces) semisweet chocolate chips
- 5 ounces white candy coating, chopped
- 1 cup chopped pistachios, toasted, divided
- ¾ cup dried cranberries, divided

1. In a microwave-safe bowl, melt semisweet chips; stir until smooth. Repeat with white candy coating.

2. Stir ¾ cup pistachios and half of the cranberries into semisweet chocolate. Thinly spread onto a waxed paper-lined baking sheet. Drizzle with candy coating.

3. Cut through with a knife to swirl. Sprinkle with remaining pistachios and cranberries. Chill until firm. Break into pieces. Store in an airtight container in the refrigerator.

Almond Cranberry Bark: *Substitute slivered almonds for the pistachios.*

Cherry Pretzel Bark: *Substitute ½ cup each slivered almonds and crushed pretzels for the pistachios and chopped dried cherries for the cranberries.*

Chocolate Peppermint Bark: *Omit pistachios and cranberries. Stir ½ cup crushed peppermint candies into melted chocolate. Sprinkle swirled chocolate with another ½ cup crushed peppermint candies.*

Peppermint Candy Candleholder

Need a simple but stylish holiday decoration? Try your hand at these peppermint candleholders. In just minutes, you can dress up any table setting, bookcase or mantel.

MATERIALS

Clear glass vase
Choice of candle or candles
Epsom salts
Round peppermint candies

DIRECTIONS

1. Clean glass vase and let dry.

2. Pour a layer of Epsom salts in the bottom of the vase about halfway to the top.

3. Place a layer of round peppermint candies, stopping about an inch from the top.

4. Center the candles in the vase. Slightly embed the candle bases in the peppermints.

5. Fill in around the candles with more peppermints until vase is full.

Crafter's Note: *You can also make these with green peppermint candies.*

Hawaiian Turtle Cups

PREP: 20 MIN. + CHILLING **MAKES:** 1 DOZEN

- 1½ cups white baking chips
- ½ cup macadamia nuts, chopped
- 18 caramels
- 2 teaspoons heavy whipping cream
- 12 dried pineapple pieces, chopped

1. In a microwave, melt white chips; stir until smooth. Pour by teaspoonfuls into greased miniature muffin cups; set aside remaining melted chips. Sprinkle the center of each muffin cup with nuts.

2. In a microwave, melt caramels and cream; stir until smooth. Pour over nuts. Reheat reserved chips if necessary; pour over caramel mixture. Top each with pineapple.

3. Chill for 30 minutes or until set. Run a knife around the edge of each cup to loosen.

Crispy Peanut Butter Balls

I make over 40 different types of cookies and candies during the holidays, including these.
—**LIZ DAVID** ST. CATHARINES, ONTARIO

PREP: 40 MIN. + CHILLING **MAKES:** 6 DOZEN

- 2 cups creamy peanut butter
- ½ cup butter, softened
- 3¾ cups confectioners' sugar
- 3 cups crisp rice cereal
- 4 cups (24 ounces) semisweet chocolate chips
- ¼ cup plus 1 teaspoon shortening, divided
- ⅓ cup white baking chips

1. In a bowl, beat peanut butter and butter until blended; gradually beat in confectioners' sugar until smooth. Stir in cereal. Shape into 1-in. balls. Refrigerate until chilled.

2. In a microwave, melt chocolate chips and ¼ cup shortening; stir until smooth. Dip balls into chocolate; allow excess to drip off. Place on a waxed paper-lined pan. Let stand until set.

3. In a microwave, melt white baking chips and remaining shortening. Stir until smooth. Drizzle over candies. Refrigerate until set.

Because my mother-in-law loves macadamia nuts and my daughter prefers white chocolate to milk chocolate, I came up with this fun twist on classic turtle candy. Now it's a family favorite.
—**LARISA SARVER** LASALLE, ILLINOIS

HAWAIIAN TURTLE CUPS

Easy Mint Chocolate Truffles

I make a lot of candy around the holidays. This is one recipe I turn to time and again, because the mixture isn't sticky or messy to work with, and I'm always happy with the results.
—**JEAN OLSON** WALLINGFORD, IOWA

PREP: 20 MIN. **COOK:** 10 MIN. + CHILLING **MAKES:** 70 TRUFFLES

- 1 tablespoon plus ¾ cup butter, divided
- 3 cups sugar
- 1 can (5 ounces) evaporated milk
- 2 cups (12 ounces) semisweet chocolate chips
- ½ teaspoon peppermint extract
- 1 jar (7 ounces) marshmallow creme
- 1 teaspoon vanilla extract
  Baking cocoa, finely chopped nuts or chocolate sprinkles

1. Line a 15-in. x 10-in. x 1-in. pan with foil. Grease the foil with 1 tablespoon butter; set aside.
2. In a heavy saucepan, combine the sugar, milk and remaining butter. Bring to a boil over medium heat. Cook, stirring constantly, until a candy thermometer reads 234° (soft-ball stage). Remove from the heat; stir in chips and peppermint extract until chocolate is melted. Stir in marshmallow creme and vanilla until smooth. Spread into prepared pan.
3. Refrigerate, uncovered, for 3 hours or until firm. Lift out of pan; cut into 1½-in. squares. Roll each into a ball. Roll truffles in cocoa, nuts or sprinkles. Refrigerate in an airtight container.
Editor's Note: *We recommend that you test your candy thermometer before each use by bringing water to a boil; the thermometer should read 212°. Adjust your recipe temperature up or down based on your test.*

Eggnog Truffle Cups

If you like homemade eggnog, you'll love these elegant truffle cups. They are a tasty way to say "cheers" to the holidays. I sometimes use small premade chocolate cups to save some time.
—**TERRIE MALSOM** VERMILLION, SOUTH DAKOTA

PREP: 30 MIN. + FREEZING **MAKES:** 3 DOZEN

- 1 cup (6 ounces) semisweet chocolate chips
- 2 teaspoons shortening
- 6 tablespoons eggnog
- 1 package (10 to 12 ounces) white baking chips
- ½ teaspoon rum extract
- ¼ to ¾ teaspoon ground nutmeg

1. In a microwave, melt semisweet chips and shortening; stir until smooth. Using a narrow pastry brush, brush the inside of 1-in. foil candy liners with ½ teaspoon melted chocolate. Freeze for 45 minutes or until firm.
2. Using ¼ teaspoon chocolate mixture for each cup, brush on another layer of chocolate. Freeze until firm.
3. In a small saucepan, bring eggnog to a boil over low heat. Remove from the heat; stir in vanilla chips until melted. Stir in extract. Refrigerate for 30 minutes or until filling begins to set.
4. Spoon or pipe 1½ teaspoons filling into each cup. Freeze until firm. Carefully remove and discard foil cups. Cover and store in an airtight container in the refrigerator. Just before serving, sprinkle with nutmeg.

Holiday Truffles

I like to lavish the chocolate lovers on my list with these sumptuous truffles. They always get enthusiastic reviews.

—JENNIFER LIPP LAUREL, NEBRASKA

PREP: 45 MIN. + CHILLING   **MAKES:** ABOUT 7 DOZEN

3 **packages (12 ounces each) semisweet chocolate chips, divided**	1½ **pounds white candy coating, melted**
2¼ **cups sweetened condensed milk, divided**	¾ **pound dark chocolate candy coating, melted**
½ **teaspoon orange extract**	⅓ **cup crushed peppermint candies**
½ **teaspoon peppermint extract**	½ **cup ground almonds**
½ **teaspoon almond extract**	⅓ **cup flaked coconut**
	Paste food coloring, optional

1. In a microwave-safe bowl, melt one package of chips; stir until smooth. Add ¾ cup milk and mix well. Stir in orange extract. Repeat twice, adding peppermint extract to one portion and almond extract to the other.

2. Cover and refrigerate for 45 minutes or until firm enough to shape into 1-in. balls.

3. Place on three separate waxed paper-lined baking sheets. Chill for 1-2 hours or until firm.

4. Dip orange-flavored truffles twice in white candy coating; allow excess to drip off. Place on waxed paper; let stand until set.

5. Dip peppermint-flavored truffles in dark chocolate coating; allow excess to drip off. Sprinkle with peppermint candies.

6. Dip almond-flavored truffles in dark chocolate; allow excess to drip off. Sprinkle with almonds or coconut. Tint white coating with food coloring; drizzle over white truffles if desired.

Nutty Chocolate Marshmallow Puffs

We like to do things big here in Texas, so don't expect a dainty little barely-a-bite truffle from me. Folks are delighted to discover a big fluffy marshmallow inside the chocolate coating.

—PAT BALL ABILENE, TEXAS

PREP: 20 MIN. + CHILLING   **MAKES:** 40 CANDIES

2 **cups milk chocolate chips**
1 **can (14 ounces) sweetened condensed milk**
1 **jar (7 ounces) marshmallow creme**
40 **large marshmallows**
4 **cups coarsely chopped pecans (about 1 pound)**

1. In a saucepan, heat chocolate chips, milk and marshmallow creme just until melted; stir until smooth (mixture will be thick).

2. With tongs, immediately dip the marshmallows, one at a time, in chocolate mixture; allow excess to drip off. Quickly roll in pecans. Place on waxed paper-lined baking sheets (Reheat chocolate mixture if necessary for easier coating.)

3. Refrigerate until firm. Store in the refrigerator in an airtight container.

People always want to know how I make my peanut butter fudge dipped in melted white chocolate. It's a nice contrast to typical chocolates on a candy platter. —**GLORIA JARRETT** LOVELAND, OHIO

White Chocolate Peanut Butter Squares

PREP: 20 MIN. + FREEZING **COOK:** 15 MIN.
MAKES: 3¼ POUNDS (ABOUT 9½ DOZEN)

- 1 **tablespoon plus ¾ cup butter, divided**
- 3 **cups sugar**
- ⅔ **cup evaporated milk**
- 1 **package (10 ounces) peanut butter chips**
- 1 **jar (7 ounces) marshmallow creme**
- 1 **cup chopped nuts**
- 1 **tablespoon vanilla extract**
- 1½ **pounds white candy coating, coarsely chopped**
- ½ **cup semisweet chocolate chips, optional**
- 1 **teaspoon shortening, optional**

1. Line a 13-in. x 9-in. pan with foil. Grease the foil with 1 tablespoon butter; set aside.
2. In a large heavy saucepan, combine the sugar, evaporated milk and remaining butter. Bring to a boil over medium heat; cook and stir for 5 minutes. Remove from the heat; stir in peanut butter chips until melted. Add the marshmallow creme, nuts and vanilla; stir until blended. Pour into prepared pan. Cool.
3. Remove from pan and cut into 1-in. squares. Place on waxed paper-lined baking sheets; freeze or refrigerate until firm.
4. In a microwave, melt candy coating; stir until smooth. Dip the squares into the coating; allow excess to drip off. Place on waxed paper-lined baking sheets until set.
5. In microwave, melt chocolate chips and shortening if desired; stir until smooth. Drizzle over the squares. Store in airtight container.

top tip
Leftover Milk?

To avoid wasting leftover evaporated milk, I pour it in ice cube trays. Once frozen, the cubes store nicely in a resealable freezer bag. Then I can pull out a few whenever I need some for mashed potatoes.

—**CAROL TOPPING** PAONIA, COLORADO

DO NOT OPEN
UNTIL
DECEMBER
25th

DO NOT O
UNTIL
DECEMBER
25th

MACADAMIA NUT MINI LOAVES, PAGE 283

Gifts From the Kitchen

Mild Tomato Salsa

After my sister gave me her salsa recipe, we had to try it right away. My children and I have been making batches of it ever since. We pair pint jars with packages of tortilla chips for neighborly gifts.

—PAMELA LUNDSTRUM BIRD ISLAND, MINNESOTA

PREP: 1½ HOURS **PROCESS:** 20 MIN. **MAKES:** 10 PINTS

- 36 **medium tomatoes, peeled and quartered**
- 4 **medium green peppers, chopped**
- 3 **large onions, chopped**
- 2 **cans (12 ounces each) tomato paste**
- 1¾ **cups white vinegar**
- ½ **cup sugar**
- 1 **medium sweet red pepper, chopped**
- 1 **celery rib, chopped**
- 15 **garlic cloves, minced**
- 4 **to 5 jalapeno peppers, seeded and chopped**
- ¼ **cup canning salt**
- ¼ **to ½ teaspoon hot pepper sauce**

1. In a large stockpot, cook tomatoes, uncovered, over medium heat for 20 minutes. Drain, reserving 2 cups liquid. Return tomatoes to the pot.

2. Stir in the green peppers, onions, tomato paste, vinegar, sugar, red pepper, celery, garlic, jalapenos, canning salt, hot pepper sauce and reserved tomato liquid. Bring to a boil. Reduce heat; simmer, uncovered, for 1 hour, stirring frequently.

3. Ladle hot mixture into hot jars, leaving ¼-in. headspace. Adjust caps. Process for 20 minutes in a boiling-water bath. **Editor's Note:** *Wear disposable gloves when cutting hot peppers; the oils can burn skin. Avoid touching your face.*

Susie's Hot Mustard

A similar recipe to this one was given to me many years ago. I changed it over time to come up with my own sweet-hot version. My father-in-law enjoys it with ham, and my husband enjoys it on any food that needs a punch of flavor.

—SUSIE GIBSON ALTA LOMA, CALIFORNIA

PREP: 15 MIN. + STANDING **COOK:** 20 MIN. + COOLING **MAKES:** 4 CUPS

- 1 **can (4 ounces) ground mustard**
- 1 **cup white wine vinegar**
- 3 **eggs**
- ¾ **cup sugar**
- 1 **tablespoon molasses**
- 1 **teaspoon honey**
- 2 **cups mayonnaise**
- 1 **tablespoon mustard seed, optional**

1. In a small bowl, combine mustard and vinegar. Cover and let stand at room temperature for 8 hours or overnight.

2. In a large saucepan, whisk the eggs, sugar, molasses, honey and mustard mixture. Cook and stir over low heat until mixture is thickened and a thermometer reads 160°, about 20 minutes. Cool. Stir in mayonnaise and mustard seed if desired. Cover and refrigerate for up to 3 weeks.

I like to dress up popcorn with corn chips and peanuts. The hot sauce adds a bit of kick that no one can resist. —**DEIRDRE DEE COX** KANSAS CITY, KANSAS

BUFFALO-STYLE SNACK MIX

FAST FIX▸ Buffalo-Style Snack Mix

PREP/TOTAL TIME: 25 MIN. **MAKES:** 2½ QUARTS

2½ quarts popped popcorn, divided
2 cups corn chips
1 cup dry roasted peanuts
¼ cup butter, cubed
2 tablespoons Louisiana-style hot sauce
1 teaspoon celery seed

1. In a large bowl, combine 2 cups popcorn, corn chips and peanuts. In a small saucepan, melt butter; add hot sauce and celery seed. Remove from the heat. Pour over popcorn mixture and toss to coat.
2. Transfer to a greased 15-in. x 10-in. x 1-in. baking pan. Bake at 350° for 10-15 minutes or until crisp. Place in a large bowl; add remaining popcorn and toss to coat. Store in an airtight container.

Sweet-Hot Spiced Nuts

There's just enough heat in these sugar and spiced almonds to make them addictive.
—**CARLA HUTTON** LAKESIDE, MONTANA

PREP: 10 MIN. **BAKE:** 20 MIN. + COOLING **MAKES:** 2 CUPS

1 egg white
2 cups unblanched almonds
2 teaspoons canola oil
⅓ cup sugar
¾ teaspoon cayenne pepper
½ teaspoon salt
½ teaspoon ground coriander
¼ teaspoon ground cinnamon
⅛ teaspoon ground allspice

1. In a large bowl, beat egg white until frothy. Add almonds and oil; stir gently to coat. Combine the remaining ingredients; add to egg white mixture and gently stir to coat.
2. Spread into a 15-in. x 10-in. x 1-in. baking pan coated with cooking spray. Bake at 300° for 18-22 minutes or until lightly browned, stirring once. Cool completely. Store in an airtight container.

Orange Pear Jam

I came up with this recipe when a neighbor gave me an armload of pears. Jam-packed with fruity flavor, it's a nice change of pace from strawberry.

—DELORES WARD DECATUR, INDIANA

PREP: 20 MIN. **COOK:** 20 MIN. + STANDING **MAKES:** ABOUT 7 CUPS

- 7 **cups sugar**
- 5 **cups chopped peeled fresh pears**
- 1 **cup crushed pineapple, drained**
- 2 **tablespoons lemon juice**
- 2 **packages (3 ounces each) orange gelatin**

1. In a Dutch oven, combine the sugar, pears, pineapple and lemon juice. Bring to a full rolling boil over high heat, stirring constantly. Reduce heat; simmer for 15 minutes, stirring frequently. Remove from the heat; stir in gelatin until dissolved.

2. Pour into jars or containers; cool to room temperature, about 1 hour. Cover and let stand overnight or until set, but no longer than 24 hours. Refrigerate for up to 3 weeks.

top tip | Fun Jam Jar

For a thoughtful presentation, wrap up a jar of jam in a vintage recipe box and include the recipe. You can find old recipe boxes at yard and garage sales, thrift shops and antique stores.

Peach Raspberry Jam

Back when my children were young, I put up about 100 jars of jams and jellies each summer, including this freezer version.

—DONN WHITE WOOSTER, OHIO

PREP: 10 MIN. **COOK:** 10 MIN. + STANDING **MAKES:** ABOUT 5 CUPS

- 1¼ **cups finely chopped peaches**
- 2 **cups fresh raspberries**
- 2 **tablespoons lemon juice**
- 4 **cups sugar**
- ¾ **cup water**
- 1 **package (1¾ ounces) powdered fruit pectin**

1. Place peaches in a large bowl. In a small bowl, mash the raspberries; strain to remove seeds if desired. Add raspberries and lemon juice to peaches. Stir in sugar. Let stand for 10 minutes. In a small saucepan, bring water and pectin to a full rolling boil. Boil for 1 minute, stirring constantly. Add to fruit mixture; stir for 2-3 minutes or until sugar is dissolved.

2. Pour into jars or freezer containers; cool to room temperature, about 30 minutes. Cover and let stand overnight or until set, but not longer than 24 hours. Refrigerate for up to 3 weeks or freeze for up to 1 year.

Apricot Pineapple Braid

Our family eagerly waits for Christmas morning, knowing this fruit-filled delight will be on the table. I make several extras for our friends' breakfasts, too.

—LORANELL NELSON GOODLAND, KANSAS

PREP: 55 MIN. + RISING **BAKE:** 25 MIN. **MAKES:** 2 LOAVES

- 4½ **to 5 cups all-purpose flour**
- ½ **cup sugar**
- 2 **packages (¼ ounce each) active dry yeast**
- 1½ **teaspoons salt**
- ½ **cup water**
- ½ **cup 2% milk**
- ¼ **cup butter, cubed**
- 2 **eggs, lightly beaten**

FILLING

- 2 **cups chopped dried apricots**
- 1 **can (8 ounces) crushed pineapple, undrained**
- 1 **cup packed brown sugar**
- ¾ **cup water**
- ¼ **cup orange juice**

GLAZE

- 1   **cup confectioners' sugar**
- ¼   **teaspoon vanilla extract**
- 1   **to 2 tablespoons 2% milk**

1. In a large bowl, combine 2 cups flour, sugar, yeast and salt. In a saucepan, heat the water, milk and butter to 120°-130°. Add to dry ingredients; beat until moistened. Beat in eggs until smooth. Stir in enough remaining flour to form a stiff dough.

2. Turn onto a floured surface; knead until smooth and elastic, about 6-8 minutes. Place in a greased bowl, turning once to grease top. Cover and let rise in a warm place until doubled, about 1 hour.

3. Meanwhile, combine the filling ingredients in a large saucepan. Bring to a boil. Reduce heat; simmer, uncovered, for 10-15 minutes or until thickened. Cool.

4. Punch dough down. Turn onto a lightly floured surface; divide in half. Roll each half into a 16-in. x 8-in. rectangle. Place on greased baking sheets.

5. Spoon filling down the center third of each rectangle. On each long side, cut 1-in.-wide strips about 2½ in. into center. Starting at one end, fold alternating strips at an angle across filling. Pinch ends to seal and tuck under. Cover and let rise until doubled, about 30 minutes.

6. Bake at 350° for 25-30 minutes or until golden brown. Remove from pans to wire racks to cool.

7. For glaze, combine the confectioners' sugar, vanilla and enough milk to achieve desired consistency. Drizzle over warm braids.

Cherry-Almond Balls

I have included this treat in my Christmas baking for years, much to the delight of my family. Instead of almonds, I'll sometimes use pecans, and they're equally loved.

—**ADA ROST** HERNANDO, FLORIDA

PREP: 15 MIN. **BAKE:** 15 MIN./BATCH + COOLING **MAKES:** 5 DOZEN

- ¾   **cup butter, softened**
- ⅓   **cup confectioners' sugar**
- 1   **teaspoon vanilla extract**
- 2   **cups all-purpose flour**
- ¼   **teaspoon salt**
- ½   **cup chopped almonds**
- 60 **red and/or green candied cherries**
     Additional confectioners' sugar

1. In a small bowl, cream butter and sugar until light and fluffy. Add vanilla. Combine flour and salt; gradually add to creamed mixture and mix well. Stir in almonds.

2. Roll 1 teaspoon of dough around each cherry. Place on greased baking sheets. Bake at 325° for 15-20 minutes or until lightly browned. Remove to wire racks to cool slightly; roll in confectioners' sugar.

Chocolate Peanut Butter Candy

With only three ingredients, these chocolate-swirl treats take just moments to whip up! Kids just love helping out with the stirring, swirling and drizzling.

—**HOLLY DEMERS** ABBOTSFORD, BRITISH COLUMBIA

PREP: 10 MIN. + CHILLING **MAKES:** ABOUT 2½ POUNDS

- 1 **pound white candy coating, coarsely chopped**
- 2 **cups (12 ounces) semisweet chocolate chips**
- 1½ **cups creamy peanut butter**

1. In a large microwave-safe bowl, melt candy coating; stir until smooth. Stir in peanut butter; thinly spread onto a waxed paper-lined baking sheet.

2. In another microwave-safe bowl, melt chocolate chips; stir until smooth. Drizzle over candy coating mixture; cut through with a knife to swirl the chocolate. Chill until firm.

3. Break into pieces. Store in an airtight container in the refrigerator.

Pretzel Cereal Crunch

A container of this treat was left in my mailbox several Christmases ago, and it disappeared in a heartbeat! My neighbor shared the recipe, and I've since added peanut butter because I love it so much.

—**CINDY LUND** VALLEY CENTER, CALIFORNIA

PREP: 20 MIN. + COOLING **MAKES:** ABOUT 9 CUPS

- 1¼ **cups Golden Grahams**
- 1¼ **cups Apple Cinnamon Cheerios**
- 1¼ **cups miniature pretzels**
- 1 **cup chopped pecans, toasted**
- 1 **package (10 to 12 ounces) white baking chips**
- 2 **tablespoons creamy peanut butter**

In a large bowl, combine the cereals, pretzels and pecans. In a microwave-safe bowl, melt chips; stir until smooth. Stir in peanut butter. Drizzle over cereal mixture; toss to coat. Spread evenly on a waxed paper-lined baking sheet. Cool completely; break into pieces. Store in an airtight container.

Holiday Cranberry Jam

I make this tangy seasonal treat to give to friends and family. I especially like serving it for brunch along with some muffins or toast and fruit.

—**SANDEE BERG** FORT SASKATCHEWAN, ALBERTA

PREP: 20 MIN. **PROCESS:** 10 MIN. **MAKES:** 5 HALF-PINTS

- 2 cups fresh or frozen cranberries
- 1 medium orange, peeled and broken into sections
- 1 carton (16 ounces) frozen sliced strawberries, thawed
- 3 cups sugar
- 1 pouch (3 ounces) liquid fruit pectin

1. In a food processor, coarsely process cranberries and orange sections. Place in a Dutch oven with strawberries and sugar. Bring to a full rolling boil over high heat, stirring constantly. Boil for 1 minute.

2. Remove from the heat and stir in the pectin. Skim off the foam. Carefully ladle into hot half-pint jars, leaving ¼-in. headspace. Remove air bubbles; wipe rims and adjust lids. Process for 10 minutes in a boiling-water canner.

Editor's Note: *The processing time listed is for altitudes of 1,000 feet or less. Add 1 minute to the processing time for each 1,000 feet of additional altitude.*

Friendship Brownies

Invite your buds over for brownies and send them home with the recipe—and the ingredients, too. With a little luck, when they whip up their batches, you'll be invited.

—**TRAVIS BURKHOLDER** MIDDLEBURG, PENNSYLVANIA

PREP: 15 MIN. **BAKE:** 35 MIN. + COOLING **MAKES:** 16 BROWNIES

BROWNIE MIX
- 1 cup plus 2 tablespoons all-purpose flour
- ⅔ cup packed brown sugar
- ¾ teaspoon salt
- ⅔ cup sugar
- 1 teaspoon baking powder
- ⅓ cup baking cocoa
- ½ cup semisweet chocolate chips
- ½ cup chopped walnuts

ADDITIONAL INGREDIENTS
- 3 eggs
- ⅔ cup canola oil
- 1 teaspoon vanilla extract

Pour the flour into a 1-qt. glass container with a tight-fitting lid. Layer with brown sugar, salt, sugar, baking powder, cocoa, chocolate chips and nuts (do not mix). Cover and store in a cool dry place for up to 6 months.

To prepare brownies: *In a large bowl, beat the eggs, oil and vanilla. Stir in the brownie mix until well combined. Spread into a greased 9-in. square baking pan. Bake at 350° for 34-38 minutes or until a toothpick inserted near the center comes out clean. Cool on a wire rack.*

Gingerbread Boy Cookies

Mom always used the same round-headed cookie cutter to make these boys. They always came out of the oven soft and chewy with plenty of traditional molasses-ginger flavor.

—DONNA SASSER HINDS MILWAUKIE, OREGON

PREP: 1 HOUR + CHILLING **BAKE:** 10 MIN./BATCH **MAKES:** 3-4 DOZEN

½ **cup butter, cubed**	½ **teaspoon ground ginger**
½ **cup sugar**	½ **teaspoon ground cinnamon**
½ **cup molasses**	¼ **teaspoon salt**
2 **teaspoons white vinegar**	**Decorating icing, nonpareils,**
1 **egg, lightly beaten**	**red-hot candies or candies**
3 **cups all-purpose flour**	**of your choice, optional**
½ **teaspoon baking soda**	

1. In a large saucepan, combine the butter, sugar, molasses and vinegar; bring to a boil, stirring constantly. Remove from the heat; cool to lukewarm. Stir in egg. Combine the flour, baking soda, ginger, cinnamon and salt; stir into molasses mixture to form a soft dough.

2. Divide dough into thirds. Shape each portion into a disk; wrap in plastic wrap. Refrigerate for at least 2 hours or until easy to handle.

3. On a lightly floured surface, roll dough to ¼-in. thickness. Cut with a floured 3-in. gingerbread boy cookie cutter. Place on greased baking sheets. Bake at 375° for 7-9 minutes or until edges are firm. Remove to wire racks; cool completely. Decorate as desired.

Kickin' Snack Mix

Ranch salad dressing mix, buttery pistachios and a hit of cayenne put a zesty spin on traditional snack mix. This is the gift that will have everyone reaching for more.

—KIM VOGT CREIGHTON, NEBRASKA

PREP: 20 MIN. **BAKE:** 45 MIN. + COOLING
MAKES: 3 QUARTS

- 3 **cups Crispix**
- 3 **cups Wheat Chex**
- 2 **cups cheddar-flavored snack crackers**
- 1 **cup pretzel sticks**
- 1 **cup almonds**
- 1 **cup mixed nuts**
- 1 **cup pistachios**
- ½ **cup butter-flavored popcorn oil**
- 1 **envelope ranch salad dressing mix**
- 1 **teaspoon dill weed**
- 1 **teaspoon garlic powder**
- 1 **teaspoon cayenne pepper**

1. In a large bowl, combine the first seven ingredients. In a small bowl, combine the oil, dressing mix, dill, garlic powder and cayenne. Drizzle over cereal mixture; toss to coat.

2. Transfer to two greased 15-in. x 10-in. x 1-in. baking pans. Bake at 250° for 45-55 minutes, stirring every 15 minutes. Cool on wire racks.

3. Store in an airtight container.

merry & bright

WHITE CHOCOLATE PEPPERMINT CRUNCH

White Chocolate Peppermint Crunch

PREP: 15 MIN. + CHILLING **MAKES:** ABOUT 1½ POUNDS

- 2 **tablespoons butter, divided**
- 1 **pound white candy coating, coarsely chopped**
- 1 **tablespoon canola oil**
- 1 **cup crushed peppermint candies or candy canes**

1. Line a baking sheet with foil and grease the foil with 1 tablespoon butter; set aside.

2. In a microwave-safe bowl, melt candy coating; stir until smooth. Stir in oil and remaining butter until smooth. Stir in peppermint candies.

3. Pour onto prepared baking sheet, spreading to desired thickness. Refrigerate for 30 minutes or until firm. Break into pieces. Store in an airtight container in the refrigerator.

Garlic Cheese Spread

Put a homemade touch on store-bought crackers or pita with a garlicky cream cheese spread. Packaged in an 8-ounce jar and wrapped with ribbon, this quick recipe also makes a tasty hostess gift.

—**TASTE OF HOME TEST KITCHEN**

PREP: 10 MIN. + CHILLING **MAKES:** 1 CUP

- 1 **package (8 ounces) cream cheese, softened**
- 1 **tablespoon olive oil**
- 3 **tablespoons grated Parmesan cheese**
- 2 **tablespoons minced green onion**
- 1 **garlic clove, minced**
- ¼ **teaspoon pepper**
  Flatbread, focaccia bread or assorted crackers

1. In a small bowl, beat cream cheese and oil until fluffy. Add the Parmesan cheese, onion, garlic and pepper; beat until well blended.

2. Spoon into a small container. Cover and refrigerate at least 1 hour. Serve with flatbread, focaccia or crackers. Store in the refrigerator.

FAST FIX ▶ Chocolate Sauce

I make different toppings to enjoy on our favorite dessert—ice cream sundaes. This smooth chocolate sauce is always a big hit and could easily be packaged in a cute squeeze bottle with a homemade label.

—**NANCY MCDONALD** BURNS, WYOMING

PREP/TOTAL TIME: 15 MIN. **MAKES:** ABOUT 3⅓ CUPS

- ½ cup butter
- 2 ounces unsweetened chocolate
- 2 cups sugar
- 1 cup half-and-half cream or evaporated milk
- ½ cup light corn syrup
- 1 teaspoon vanilla extract

1. In a large heavy saucepan, melt butter and chocolate; stir until smooth. Add the sugar, cream and corn syrup. Bring to a boil, stirring constantly. Boil for 1½ minutes. Remove from the heat.

2. Stir in vanilla. Serve warm or cold over ice cream or pound cake. Refrigerate leftovers.

Chocolate Chip Nougat

The rewards of homemade candy don't get much sweeter than these divine morsels. If you can bear to part with them, they make priceless holiday gifts.

—**SANDI FRIEST** PAYNESVILLE, MINNESOTA

PREP: 20 MIN. **COOK:** 55 MIN. + COOLING **MAKES:** 2½ POUNDS

- 1 teaspoon plus ¼ cup butter, softened, divided
- 3 cups sugar, divided
- ⅔ cup plus 1¼ cups light corn syrup, divided
- 2 tablespoons water
- 2 egg whites
- 2 cups chopped walnuts, toasted
- 2 teaspoons vanilla extract
- 1 cup (6 ounces) miniature semisweet chocolate chips
- 2 to 3 drops each red and/or green food coloring, optional

1. Line a 9-in. square pan with foil; grease foil with 1 teaspoon butter and set aside. In a small heavy saucepan, combine 1 cup sugar, ⅔ cup corn syrup and water. Bring to a boil over medium heat, stirring constantly. Reduce heat to medium-low. Cook, without stirring, until a candy thermometer reads 250°-266° (hard-ball stage).

2. Meanwhile, beat egg whites in a heat-proof large bowl until stiff peaks form. With mixer running on high speed, carefully add hot syrup in a slow steady stream, beating constantly at high speed until thickened; cover and set aside.

3. In a large heavy saucepan, combine remaining sugar and corn syrup. Bring to a boil over medium heat, stirring constantly. Reduce heat to medium-low; cook, without stirring, until a candy thermometer reads 275° (soft-crack stage).

4. Meanwhile, melt remaining butter. Pour hot syrup into reserved egg white mixture; stir with a wooden spoon. Stir in the walnuts, vanilla and melted butter.

5. Pour half of nougat mixture into prepared pan; press evenly. Sprinkle with chocolate chips. Tint remaining nougat mixture with red and/or green food coloring if desired; spread over chocolate chips. Press down evenly with buttered fingers. Let stand for several hours until set.

6. Using a knife coated with cooking spray, cut nougat into 1-in. squares. Wrap in plastic wrap or waxed paper if desired. Store at room temperature.

Editor's Note: *We recommend that you test your candy thermometer before each use by bringing water to a boil; the thermometer should read 212°. Adjust your recipe temperature up or down based on your test.*

Cream Cheese Raspberry Muffins

My raspberry-walnut muffins make a special holiday treat for neighbors. I wrap up a few on a plate for a fresh-from-the-oven gift.
—PHYLLIS EISMANN SCHMALZ KANSAS CITY, KANSAS

PREP: 25 MIN. **BAKE:** 25 MIN. + COOLING **MAKES:** 8 MUFFINS

- 1 package (3 ounces) cream cheese, softened
- 2 tablespoons butter, softened
- ½ cup sugar
- 1 egg
- 1 egg white
- 3 tablespoons buttermilk
- ½ teaspoon vanilla extract
- ¾ cup all-purpose flour
- ½ teaspoon baking powder
- ⅛ teaspoon baking soda
- ⅛ teaspoon salt
- ¾ cup fresh raspberries
- 2 tablespoons chopped walnuts, toasted
- ¼ cup confectioners' sugar
- 1 teaspoon 2% milk

1. In a small bowl, cream the cream cheese, butter and sugar until smooth. Beat in egg and egg white. Beat in buttermilk and vanilla. Combine the flour, baking powder, baking soda and salt; add to creamed mixture just until moistened. Fold in raspberries and walnuts.

2. Fill paper-lined muffin cups three-fourths full. Bake at 350° for 25-28 minutes or until a toothpick inserted in muffin comes out clean. Cool for 5 minutes before removing from pan to a wire rack to cool completely.

3. Combine confectioners' sugar and milk; drizzle over muffins.

Cream Cheese Dainties

Try using different flavors of spreadable fruit in these tender, melt-in-your-mouth cookies. They make a sensational gift paired with an herbal tea.
—LYNNE STEWART JULIAN, PENNSYLVANIA

PREP: 20 MIN. + CHILLING **BAKE:** 15 MIN./BATCH **MAKES:** 4 DOZEN

- 1 cup butter, softened
- 1 package (8 ounces) cream cheese, softened
- 2½ cups all-purpose flour
- ½ cup apricot spreadable fruit or seedless raspberry preserves

1. In a large bowl, cream butter and cream cheese until light and fluffy. Gradually add flour to the creamed mixture and mix well. Divide dough into four portions; cover and refrigerate until easy to handle.

2. On a lightly floured surface, roll one portion of dough at a time into a 10-in. x 7½-in. rectangle. Trim edges if necessary. Cut into 2½-in. squares.

3. Place ¼ teaspoon spreadable fruit or preserves near each end of two diagonal corners. Moisten the remaining two corners with water; fold over and press lightly.

4. Place on ungreased baking sheets. Bake at 350° for 12-15 minutes or until corners are lightly browned. Cool 2-3 minutes before removing to wire racks to cool.

Tarragon Vinegar

PREP: 10 MIN. + STANDING   **MAKES:** 2 CUPS

- **1   cup tarragon sprigs**
- **2   cups white wine vinegar**
-      **Additional fresh tarragon sprig**

1. Wash tarragon and pat dry. Place in a sterilized jar. Using a wooden spoon, gently bruise the tarragon. Add the vinegar. Cover and store in a cool, dark place for 2-3 weeks to let flavors develop.

2. Strain and discard tarragon. Pour into sterilized bottle. Add additional tarragon. Store in cool, dark place up to 6 months.

Apple Pie Jam

My husband and I love this jam so much because it tastes just like apple pie without the crust!
—AUDREY GODELL STANTON, MICHIGAN

PREP: 30 MIN.   **PROCESS:** 10 MIN.   **MAKES:** 7 HALF-PINTS

- **4   to 5 large Golden Delicious apples, peeled and sliced (about 2 pounds)**
- **1   cup water**
- **5   cups sugar**
- **½   teaspoon butter**
- **1   pouch (3 ounces) liquid fruit pectin**
- **1½   teaspoons ground cinnamon**
- **1   teaspoon ground nutmeg**
- **¼   teaspoon ground mace, optional**

1. In a Dutch oven, combine apples and water. Cover and cook slowly until tender. Measure 4½ cups apples; return to pan. (Save remaining apple mixture for another use or discard.)

2. Add sugar and butter to pan; bring to a full rolling boil, stirring constantly. Quickly stir in pectin; return to a full rolling boil. Boil 1 minute, stirring constantly.

3. Remove from the heat; skim off foam. Stir in spices. Carefully ladle hot mixture into hot half-pint jars, leaving ¼-in. headspace. Remove air bubbles; wipe rims and adjust lids. Process for 10 minutes in a boiling-water canner.

Editor's Note: *Processing time is for altitudes of 1,000 feet or less. See Editor's Note on p. 273.*

Add fresh tarragon sprigs to basic white wine vinegar in a decorative jar, and you'll have a lovely, contemporary gift for a cook on your Christmas list.
—**SUE GRONHOLZ** BEAVER DAM, WISCONSIN

TARRAGON VINEGAR

Slice & Bake Orange Spice Wafers

Thin and crispy, these ginger spice cookies stack well, making them a great gift to send to a loved one.
—TASTE OF HOME TEST KITCHEN

PREP: 45 MIN. + CHILLING **BAKE:** 5 MIN./BATCH
MAKES: 16 DOZEN

- 1 **cup butter, softened**
- ¾ **cup sugar**
- ¾ **cup packed brown sugar**
- 1 **egg**
- 2 **tablespoons light corn syrup**
- 3 **cups all-purpose flour**
- 2 **teaspoons baking soda**
- 2 **teaspoons ground ginger**
- 2 **teaspoons grated orange peel**
- ¼ **teaspoon each ground allspice, cloves and nutmeg**
  Additional sugar, optional

1. In a large bowl, cream butter and sugars until light and fluffy. Beat in egg and corn syrup. Combine the flour, baking soda, ginger, orange peel, allspice, cloves and nutmeg; gradually add to creamed mixture and mix well.
2. Shape into four 6-in. rolls; wrap in plastic wrap. Refrigerate overnight.
3. Unwrap and cut into ⅛-in. slices. Place 2 in. apart on ungreased baking sheets. Sprinkle with additional sugar if desired.
4. Bake at 400° for 5-6 minutes or until lightly browned. Remove to wire racks to cool.

Chocolate-Covered Praline Chews

Welcome a new candy-making tradition with these caramel-like praline chews. The black-and-white candy coating gives them a modern, eye-catching twist.
—CHRISTINA MITCHELL HAUGHTON, LOUISIANA

PREP: 40 MIN. **COOK:** 45 MIN. + CHILLING **MAKES:** ABOUT 3 DOZEN

- 1 **cup sugar**
- 1 **cup light corn syrup**
  Dash salt
- ¼ **cup butter, cubed**
- 2 **teaspoons milk**
- 2 **cups pecan halves**
- ½ **teaspoon vanilla extract**
- 6 **ounces white candy coating, coarsely chopped**
- 6 **ounces milk chocolate candy coating, coarsely chopped**

1. In a large heavy saucepan, combine the sugar, corn syrup and salt. Bring to a boil over medium heat; cook until a candy thermometer reads 245° (firm-ball stage), stirring occasionally. Gradually stir in the butter, milk and pecans. Continue cooking until temperature returns to 245°. Remove from the heat; stir in vanilla. Immediately drop by tablespoonfuls onto greased baking sheets. Cool.
2. In a microwave, melt white candy coating at 70% power for 1 minute; stir. Microwave at additional 10- to 20-second intervals, stirring until smooth.
3. Dip candies halfway into coating and allow excess to drip off. Place on waxed paper-lined baking sheets; refrigerate for 15 minutes or until set.
4. In a microwave, melt milk chocolate coating at 70% power for 1 minute; stir. Microwave at additional 10- to 20-second intervals, stirring until smooth.
5. Dip other half of each candy and allow excess to drip off. Return to baking sheets; refrigerate until set.
Editor's Note: *We recommend that you test your candy thermometer before each use by bringing water to a boil; the thermometer should read 212°. Adjust your recipe temperature up or down based on your test.*

FAST FIX Orange Caramel Ice Cream Sauce

We added a touch of orange extract to a creamy caramel sauce to make a rich, homemade ice cream topping you won't find in stores. Try it drizzled over butter pecan, vanilla or chocolate.

—TASTE OF HOME TEST KITCHEN

PREP/TOTAL TIME: 20 MIN. **MAKES:** 1⅓ CUPS

- 1 cup packed brown sugar
- 1 cup heavy whipping cream
- ½ cup sweetened condensed milk
- ½ teaspoon orange extract
    Butter pecan ice cream
    Orange spirals, optional

1. In a large saucepan, cook and stir brown sugar and cream over medium heat until sugar is dissolved. Bring to a boil; cook for 5 minutes or until mixture is reduced by half. Remove from the heat. Stir in milk and orange extract. Cover and refrigerate.
2. Just before serving, warm over low heat. Serve with ice cream. Garnish with orange spirals if desired.

Zesty Lemon Curd

There are lemon trees in our backyard, so I'm always on the prowl for new ways to use the fruit. When we shared some of our homegrown citrus with neighbors, they repaid us by giving us this recipe!

—JEAN GAINES BULLHEAD CITY, ARIZONA

PREP/TOTAL TIME: 25 MIN. **MAKES:** 3 CUPS

- 3 egg, lightly beaten
- 2 cups sugar
- ¾ cup lemon juice
- 2 teaspoons grated lemon peel
- 1 cup butter, cubed

1. In a large heavy saucepan over medium heat, whisk the eggs, sugar, lemon juice and peel until blended. Add butter; cook, whisking constantly, until mixture is thickened and coats the back of a metal spoon. Transfer to a small bowl; cool for 10 minutes. Cover and refrigerate until chilled.
2. Spread on muffins or rolls, or serve over waffles or ice cream.

Homemade Canned Spaghetti Sauce

This savory canned sauce is a tomato-grower's dream come true! Use up garden bounty and share it with neighbors year-round.

—TONYA BRANHAM MOUNT OLIVE, ALABAMA

PREP: 1½ HOURS + SIMMERING **PROCESS:** 40 MIN. **MAKES:** 9 QUARTS

- 25 pounds tomatoes
- 4 large green peppers, seeded
- 4 large onions, cut into wedges
- 4 cans (6 ounces each) tomato paste
- 1 cup canola oil
- ⅔ cup sugar
- ¼ cup salt
- 8 garlic cloves, minced
- 4 teaspoons dried oregano
- 2 teaspoons dried parsley flakes
- 2 teaspoons dried basil
- 2 teaspoons crushed red pepper flakes
- 2 teaspoons Worcestershire sauce
- 2 bay leaves
- 1 cup plus 2 tablespoons bottled lemon juice

1. In a Dutch oven, bring 8 cups water to a boil. Using a slotted spoon, place tomatoes, one at a time, in boiling water for 30-60 seconds. Remove each tomato and immediately plunge in ice water. Peel and quarter tomatoes.

2. In a food processor, cover and process green peppers and onions in batches until finely chopped.

3. In a stockpot, combine the tomatoes, green pepper mixture, tomato paste, oil, sugar, salt, garlic, oregano, parsley, basil, pepper flakes, Worcestershire sauce and bay leaves. Bring to a boil. Reduce heat; simmer, uncovered, for 4-5 hours, stirring occasionally. Discard bay leaves.

4. Add 2 tablespoons lemon juice to each of nine hot 1-qt. jars. Ladle hot mixture into jars, leaving ½-in. headspace. Remove air bubbles; wipe rims and adjust lids. Process for 40 minutes in a boiling-water canner.

Editor's Note: *The processing time listed is for altitudes of 1,000 feet or less. For altitudes up to 3,000 feet, add 5 minutes; 6,000 feet, add 10 minutes; 8,000 feet, add 15 minutes; 10,000 feet, add 20 minutes.*

Snowcapped Gingerbread Biscotti

These cookies are among my favorites to add to the holiday cookie trays I make. They have the traditional flavor of gingerbread cookies, the refinement of Italian biscotti and a playful, cheery "snow-dipped" decoration.

—TRISHA KRUSE EAGLE, IDAHO

PREP: 45 MIN. + CHILLING **BAKE:** 35 MIN. + COOLING **MAKES:** 2½ DOZEN

- ⅓ cup butter, softened
- 1 cup packed brown sugar
- ¼ cup molasses
- 3 eggs
- 3¼ cups all-purpose flour
- 3 teaspoons ground cinnamon
- 1 teaspoon ground nutmeg
- ½ teaspoon baking powder
- ½ teaspoon salt
- ½ teaspoon ground allspice
- ½ teaspoon ground cloves
- 1 cup hazelnuts, toasted and chopped
- ¼ cup finely chopped crystallized ginger
- 1 cup butterscotch chips, melted
- 1 cup vanilla or white chips, melted

1. In a large bowl, cream butter and brown sugar until light and fluffy. Beat in molasses. Add eggs, one at a time, beating well after each addition. Combine the flour, cinnamon, nutmeg, baking powder, salt, allspice and cloves; gradually add to creamed mixture and mix well. Stir in hazelnuts and ginger.

2. Divide dough in half. Cover and refrigerate for 30 minutes.

3. On a lightly floured surface, shape dough into two 10-in. x 3-in. logs. Transfer to greased baking sheets. Bake at 350° for 20-25 minutes or until lightly browned and firm to the touch.

4. Transfer to a cutting board; cut diagonally with a sharp knife into ½-in. slices. Place cut side down on greased baking sheets. Bake for 7-9 minutes on each side or until lightly browned. Remove to wire racks to cool.

5. Dip biscotti halfway into melted butterscotch chips; shake off excess. Place on waxed paper until set. Dip butterscotch-coated ends partially into melted vanilla chips; shake off excess. Place on waxed paper until set. Store in an airtight container.

Cranberry-Chocolate Chip Cookie Mix

I give this cookie mix in a jar on numerous occasions for teacher gifts and Christmas stocking stuffers. One teacher told me these were the best cookies she's ever made!

—SHELLEY FRIESEN LEDUC, ALBERTA

PREP: 15 MIN. **BAKE:** 10 MIN./BATCH **MAKES:** 2½ DOZEN

1¼ cups all-purpose flour	½ cup dried cranberries
1 teaspoon baking soda	½ cup chopped walnuts
½ teaspoon salt	½ cup quick-cooking oats
½ teaspoon ground cinnamon	**ADDITIONAL INGREDIENTS**
¾ cup packed brown sugar	⅔ cup butter, softened
1 cup (6 ounces) semisweet chocolate chips	1 egg
	¾ teaspoon vanilla extract

In a small bowl, combine the flour, baking soda, salt and cinnamon. In a 1-qt. glass container, layer the flour mixture, brown sugar, ½ cup chocolate chips, cranberries, walnuts, oats and remaining chips. Cover and store in a cool dry place for up to 6 months. Yield: 1 batch (about 4 cups total).

To prepare cookies: *In a large bowl, beat the butter, egg and vanilla until blended. Add cookie mix and mix well. Drop by rounded tablespoonfuls 2 in. apart onto ungreased baking sheets. Bake at 350° for 10-15 minutes or until golden brown. Remove to wire racks.*

Flavored Mocha Drink Mix

I rely on vanilla and almond extracts to get two wonderful flavors from one hot beverage mix. At Christmastime, you can package these fun mixes in pretty jars, decorative tins or holiday mugs to make great-tasting gifts.

—EDNA HOFFMAN HEBRON, INDIANA

PREP/TOTAL TIME: 5 MIN.
MAKES: 1 SERVING PER BATCH

1½ cups powdered nondairy creamer
1 cup sugar
½ cup instant coffee granules
½ cup baking cocoa
   Dash salt
¼ teaspoon vanilla extract
¼ teaspoon almond extract
ADDITIONAL INGREDIENTS
¾ cup boiling water
   Whipped cream, optional

In a large bowl, combine the first five ingredients. Divide mixture in half. Stir in vanilla to one portion and almond extract to the other. Store in airtight containers in a cool dry place for up to 1 year. Yield: 14-16 batches (7-8 batches vanilla mocha mix; 7-8 batches almond mocha mix), about 3 cups total.

To prepare beverage: *Dissolve about 3 tablespoons mix in water; stir well. Top with whipped cream if desired.*

On a cold-weather day, these mini loaves, loaded with rich macadamia nuts and topped with toasted coconut, offer a taste of the tropics.

—KIM GILLILAND SIMI VALLEY, CALIFORNIA

Macadamia Nut Mini Loaves

PREP: 20 MIN. **BAKE:** 40 MIN. + COOLING
MAKES: 5 LOAVES

- 1 jar (3½ ounces) macadamia nuts, divided
- ⅓ cup flaked coconut
- 1½ cups sugar, divided
- ¾ cup butter, softened
- 2 eggs
- 3 cups all-purpose flour
- 1 teaspoon baking powder
- ½ cup 2% milk
- 3 tablespoons lemon juice
- 2 teaspoons grated lemon peel
- 1½ teaspoons vanilla extract

1. Finely chop enough of the macadamia nuts to measure ⅓ cup; set aside. Coarsely chop remaining nuts; toss with coconut and 1 tablespoon sugar. Set aside.

2. In a large bowl, cream butter and remaining sugar until light and fluffy. Beat in eggs. Combine flour and baking powder; gradually add to creamed mixture alternately with milk, beating well after each addition. Stir in the lemon juice, lemon peel, vanilla and reserved finely chopped nuts.

3. Spoon into five greased 5¾-in. x 3-in. x 2-in. loaf pans. Sprinkle with reserved coconut mixture. Bake at 325° for 40-45 minutes or until a toothpick inserted near the center comes out clean (cover loosely with foil if top browns too quickly). Cool for 10 minutes before removing from pans to wire racks to cool completely.

Editor's Note: *If top begins to brown too quickly, cover loosely with heavy-duty aluminum foil.*

APRICOT-GLAZED TURKEY BREAST, PAGE 296

Thanksgiving Gathering

302

295

289

MAKE AHEAD ▶ Cherry Pineapple Salad

Dark cherries and cream cheese make a really pretty layered salad. My sister-in-law often brings it to our family get-togethers on holidays and special occasions.

—**LEONA LUECKING** WEST BURLINGTON, IOWA

PREP: 20 MIN. + CHILLING **MAKES:** 12-16 SERVINGS

- 3 packages (3 ounces each) cherry gelatin
- 2⅓ cups boiling water
- 2 cans (16½ ounces each) pitted dark sweet cherries
- 1 can (20 ounces) pineapple tidbits
- ⅓ cup lemon juice
- ⅓ cup heavy whipping cream
- ⅓ cup mayonnaise
- 2 packages (3 ounces each) cream cheese, softened
  Dash salt
- ½ cup coarsely chopped nuts

1. In a large bowl, dissolve gelatin in water. Drain and reserve enough cherry and pineapple juices to measure 2½ cups; add to gelatin with lemon juice. Set fruits aside.

2. Divide gelatin in half. Set aside one portion of gelatin at room temperature; chill the other portion until partially set. Fold pineapple into chilled gelatin; pour into a 13-in. x 9-in. dish. Chill until almost firm.

3. In a small bowl, beat the cream, mayonnaise, cream cheese and salt until light and fluffy. Spread over chilled gelatin layer. Refrigerate until firm. Chill reserved gelatin mixture until partially set. Fold in cherries and nuts; spread over cream cheese layer. Chill for at least 3 hours.

FAST FIX ▶ Creamy Broccoli with Cashews

I got this recipe from a friend I went to elementary school with in the '60s. The sour cream and honey sauce is different from most mayonnaise-based salads, and the cashews give it a nice crunch.

—**KAREN ANN BLAND** GOVE, KANSAS

PREP/TOTAL TIME: 20 MIN. **MAKES:** 6 SERVINGS

- 9 cups fresh broccoli florets
- ¼ cup chopped onion
- 2 tablespoons butter
- 1 cup (8 ounces) sour cream
- 2 teaspoons honey
- 1 teaspoon cider vinegar
- ½ teaspoon salt
- ½ teaspoon paprika
- ½ cup coarsely chopped cashews

1. Place broccoli in a steamer basket; place in a large saucepan over 1 in. of water. Bring to a boil; cover and steam for 3-4 minutes or until crisp-tender.

2. Meanwhile, in a small skillet, saute onion in butter until tender. Remove from the heat; stir in the sour cream, honey, vinegar, salt and paprika.

3. Transfer broccoli to a serving bowl. Add sour cream mixture and toss to coat. Sprinkle with cashews.

> **"Your holiday turkey will never turn out dry again if you reach for this recipe. Brining overnight and stuffing with apples result in juicy, tender meat."**
>
> **—MICHAEL WILLIAMS SR.** MORENO VALLEY, CALIFORNIA

Golden Roasted Turkey

PREP: 40 MIN. + MARINATING
BAKE: 2¾ HOURS + STANDING **MAKES:** 14 SERVINGS

- 4 cartons (32 ounces each) vegetable broth
- 1 cup kosher salt
- ½ cup packed brown sugar
- 1 tablespoon whole peppercorns
- 1½ teaspoons whole allspice
- 1½ teaspoons minced fresh gingerroot
- 4 quarts cold water
- 2 turkey-size oven roasting bags
- 1 turkey (14 to 16 pounds)
- 1 cup water
- 1 medium apple, sliced
- 1 small onion, sliced
- 1 cinnamon stick (3 inches)
- 4 fresh rosemary sprigs
- 6 fresh sage leaves
- 1 tablespoon canola oil
- ½ teaspoon pepper

1. In stockpot, combine first six ingredients. Bring to boil. Cook and stir until salt and brown sugar dissolve. Remove from heat. Add cold water to cool brine to room temperature.

2. Place a turkey-size oven roasting bag inside a second roasting bag; add turkey. Carefully pour cooled brine into bag. Squeeze out as much air as possible; seal bags and turn to coat. Place in a roasting pan. Refrigerate for 18-24 hours, turning occasionally.

3. In microwave-safe bowl, combine water, apple, onion and cinnamon. Microwave on high for 3-4 min. until tender; drain water.

4. Drain and discard brine. Rinse turkey under cold water; pat dry. Place cooked apple mixture, rosemary and sage in turkey cavity. Skewer turkey openings; tie drumsticks.

5. Place turkey breast side up on a rack in a roasting pan. Rub with oil and pepper. Bake, uncovered, at 325° for 2¾ to 3¼ hours or until a thermometer reads 180°. (Cover loosely with foil if turkey browns too quickly.) Cover and let stand for 15 minutes before carving; discard apple mixture and herbs.

Cinnamon Apple Crumb Pie

I use pecan Sandies to make a buttery, streusel-like topping. It browns nicely and gives the pie just the right amount of crunch.

—CAROLYN RUCH NEW LONDON, WISCONSIN

PREP: 15 MIN. **BAKE:** 50 MIN. + COOLING **MAKES:** 6-8 SERVINGS

> 1   can (21 ounces) apple pie filling
> 1   unbaked pastry shell (9 inches)
> ½   teaspoon ground cinnamon
> 4   tablespoons butter, divided
> 1½ to 2 cups crushed pecan shortbread cookies

1. Pour pie filling into pastry shell. Sprinkle with cinnamon and dot with 1 tablespoon butter. Melt remaining butter. Place cookie crumbs in a small bowl; stir in butter until coarse crumbs form. Sprinkle over filling. Cover edges of pastry loosely with foil.

2. Bake at 450° for 10 minutes. Reduce heat to 350°; remove foil and bake for 40-45 minutes or until crust is golden brown and filling is bubbly. Cool on a wire rack for at least 2 hours.

Artichoke Stuffing

Parmesan and artichokes make this stuffing stand out from the rest. It's so good with turkey! But I also use it when I bake a chicken by halving the recipe.

—LORIE VERKUYL RIDGECREST, CALIFORNIA

PREP: 30 MIN. **BAKE:** 35 MIN. **MAKES:** 14 CUPS

> 1   loaf (1 pound) sourdough bread, cut into 1-inch cubes
> ½   pound sliced fresh mushrooms
> 2   celery ribs, chopped
> 1   medium onion, chopped
> 2   tablespoons butter
> 3   to 4 garlic cloves, minced
> 2   jars (6½ ounces each) marinated artichoke hearts, drained and chopped
> ½   cup grated Parmesan cheese
> 1   teaspoon poultry seasoning
> 1   egg
> 1   can (14½ ounces) chicken broth

1. Place bread cubes in two ungreased 15-in. x 10-in. x 1-in. baking pans. Bake at 350° for 15 minutes or until lightly browned.

2. In a large skillet, saute the mushrooms, celery and onion in butter until tender. Add garlic; cook 1 minute longer. Stir in the artichokes, cheese and poultry seasoning. Transfer to a large bowl; stir in bread cubes.

3. In a small bowl, whisk egg and broth until blended. Pour over bread mixture and mix well.

4. Transfer to a greased 3-qt. baking dish (dish will be full). Cover and bake at 350° for 30 minutes. Uncover; bake 5-15 minutes longer or until a thermometer reads 165°.

Chocolate Pumpkin Bread

It never hurts to have several loaves of pumpkin bread in the freezer to send home with friends and family. Use this as a go-to recipe and adjust the mix-ins to your liking.
—TASTE OF HOME TEST KITCHEN

PREP: 15 MIN. **BAKE:** 70 MIN. + COOLING
MAKES: 2 LOAVES (16 SLICES EACH)

3⅓ cups all-purpose flour
3 cups sugar
4 teaspoons pumpkin pie spice
2 teaspoons baking soda
1 teaspoon salt
½ teaspoon baking powder
4 eggs
1 can (15 ounces) solid-pack pumpkin
⅔ cup water
⅔ cup canola oil
2 cups (12 ounces) semisweet chocolate chips
1 cup sliced almonds, toasted

1. In a large bowl, combine the first six ingredients. In another bowl, whisk the eggs, pumpkin, water and oil; stir into dry ingredients just until moistened. Stir in chocolate chips and almonds.
2. Pour into two greased 9-in. x 5-in. loaf pans. Bake at 350° for 70-75 minutes or until a toothpick inserted near the center comes out clean. Cool for 10 minutes before removing from pans to wire racks to cool completely.
Make Ahead Note: *Wrap cooled loaves in foil and freeze up to 3 months.*

Brie with Apricot Topping

One of our favorite quick appetizers is baked brie. This one features a dried apricot topping, but don't be shy when it comes to experimenting with other dried fruits, such as cherries or figs.
—TASTE OF HOME TEST KITCHEN

PREP/TOTAL TIME: 25 MIN. **MAKES:** 6-8 SERVINGS

½ cup chopped dried apricots
2 tablespoons brown sugar
2 tablespoons water
1 teaspoon balsamic vinegar
   Dash salt
½ to 1 teaspoon minced fresh rosemary or ¼ teaspoon dried rosemary, crushed
1 round Brie cheese (8 ounces)
   Assorted crackers

1. In a small saucepan, combine the apricots, brown sugar, water, vinegar and salt. Bring to a boil. Reduce heat to medium; cook and stir until slightly thickened. Remove from the heat; stir in rosemary.
2. Remove rind from top of cheese. Place in an ungreased ovenproof serving dish. Spread apricot mixture over cheese. Bake, uncovered, at 400° for 10-12 minutes or until cheese is softened. Serve with crackers.

FAST FIX Pork with Gorgonzola Sauce

PREP: 15 MIN. **BAKE:** 10 MIN. **MAKES:** 6 SERVINGS

- ¼ cup Dijon mustard
- 1 tablespoon olive oil
- 1 tablespoon dried thyme
- 2 pork tenderloins (¾ pound each)
  Salt and pepper to taste
- 1 garlic clove, minced
- 1 tablespoon butter
- 1 tablespoon all-purpose flour
- 1 cup heavy whipping cream
- ¼ cup dry white wine
- ¼ cup chicken broth
- 1 cup (4 ounces) crumbled Gorgonzola cheese
  Additional Gorgonzola cheese crumbles, optional

1. In a small bowl, whisk the Dijon mustard, olive oil and thyme until blended; set aside. Sprinkle pork with salt and pepper. In a large nonstick skillet over high heat, brown pork on all sides, about 10 minutes.

2. Transfer pork to a foil-lined roasting pan that has been coated with cooking spray. Spread Dijon mustard mixture over all sides of pork. Bake at 425° for 10-20 minutes or until a thermometer reads 145°. Remove from oven and let stand 5 minutes.

3. Meanwhile, in a small saucepan, over medium heat, saute garlic in butter for 30 seconds. Stir in flour until well blended. Gradually whisk in the cream, wine and chicken broth. Bring to a boil; cook and stir for 1 minute or until thickened. Add cheese. Cook and stir until sauce is reduced to desired consistency, about 5 minutes.

4. Slice pork and transfer to serving plates. Spoon sauce over pork. Sprinkle pork with additional cheese if desired.

Our pick for a quick-fix alternative to turkey is pork. And instead of gravy, a tangy Gorgonzola cheese is melted into a creamy broth, giving this sauce a rich, unforgettable flavor.

—TASTE OF HOME COOKING SCHOOL

FAST FIX ▶ Honey-Thyme Butternut Squash

Instead of potatoes, try whipping up mashed butternut squash with honey, butter and thyme. More than a festive Thanksgiving side, this 30-minute dish will be a new fall favorite for weeknight meals, too.

—BIANCA NOISEUX BRISTOL, CONNECTICUT

PREP/TOTAL TIME: 30 MIN. **MAKES:** 10 SERVINGS

- 1 large butternut squash (about 5 pounds), peeled and cubed
- ¼ cup butter, cubed
- 3 tablespoons half-and-half cream
- 2 tablespoons honey
- 2 teaspoons dried parsley flakes
- ½ teaspoon salt
- ⅛ teaspoon dried thyme
- ⅛ teaspoon coarsely ground pepper

1. In a large saucepan, bring 1 in. of water to a boil. Add squash; cover and cook for 10-15 minutes or until tender.

2. Drain. Mash squash with the remaining ingredients.

Roasted Fall Vegetables

I love serving this tender veggie side dish as part of a comforting dinner on a chilly night. The cayenne pepper gives it a zippy flavor that's not overpowering.

—JULI MEYERS HINESVILLE, GEORGIA

PREP: 30 MIN. **BAKE:** 40 MIN. **MAKES:** 14 SERVINGS

- 1 large acorn squash, peeled and cut into 1½-inch cubes
- 1 large rutabaga, peeled and cut into 1-inch cubes
- 1 medium pie pumpkin or butternut squash, peeled and cut into 1-inch cubes
- 3 large carrots, peeled and cut into 1½-inch pieces
- 1 medium parsnip, peeled and cut into 1-inch cubes
- ¼ cup grated Parmesan cheese
- ¼ cup canola oil
- 3 tablespoons minced fresh parsley
- 2 tablespoons paprika
- 2 teaspoons salt
- 1 teaspoon garlic powder
- ½ teaspoon cayenne pepper

1. In a large bowl, combine the first five ingredients. In a small bowl, combine the remaining ingredients. Pour over vegetables; toss to coat.

2. Transfer to two greased 15-in. x 10-in. x 1-in. baking pans. Bake, uncovered, at 425° for 40-50 minutes or until tender, stirring occasionally.

Maui-Inspired Turkey Breast Roll

I came up with this because my family loves macadamia nuts, and we think the sage-garlic butter rub gives the turkey a lovely taste.

—**LEIMOMI LEAR** WAKEFIELD, NEW HAMPSHIRE

PREP: 40 MIN. **BAKE:** 2¼ HOURS **MAKES:** 12 SERVINGS

- 2 **boneless turkey breast halves (2 to 2½ pounds each)**
- ¾ **cup butter, softened, divided**
- 4 **garlic cloves, minced**
- 1 **tablespoon fresh sage or 1 teaspoon dried sage leaves**
- 2 **celery ribs, chopped**
- 1 **small onion, chopped**
- 3 **cups reduced-sodium chicken broth**
- ½ **cup chopped macadamia nuts, toasted**
- 2 **teaspoons poultry seasoning**
- ¼ **teaspoon salt**
- ¼ **teaspoon pepper**
- 1 **package (12 ounces) unseasoned stuffing cubes**
- ½ **cup unsweetened pineapple juice**
- 1 **tablespoon olive oil**

GRAVY

- 1¾ **cups reduced-sodium chicken broth**
- 2 **tablespoons cornstarch**
- 2 **tablespoons unsweetened pineapple juice**

1. Remove skin from the turkey breasts; set aside. Flatten turkey breasts to ⅜-in. thickness. Place breasts side by side so that they are overlapping slightly. Combine ½ cup butter, garlic and sage; rub over turkey.

2. In a large skillet, melt remaining butter. Add celery and onion; saute until tender. Add the broth, nuts and seasonings. Bring to a boil. Reduce heat; simmer, uncovered, for 2 minutes. Stir in stuffing cubes.

3. Spread stuffing mixture over turkey to within 1 in. of edges. Roll up jelly-roll style, rolling turkey away from you; arrange skin over top of roll. Tie with kitchen string at 2-in. intervals.

4. Place on a rack in a large roasting pan. Combine pineapple juice and olive oil; set aside.

5. Bake turkey at 325° for 2¼ to 2¾ hours or until a thermometer reads 170°, basting occasionally with pineapple juice mixture.

6. Remove meat to a serving platter and keep warm. For gravy, add broth to the pan, scraping to loosen browned bits. Pour into a small saucepan and bring to a boil. Combine cornstarch and pineapple juice until smooth; gradually stir into the pan. Bring to a boil; cook and stir for 2 minutes or until thickened. Serve with turkey.

Pine Nut and Cranberry Rice Pilaf

Stock up on dried cranberries and rice—once you try this pilaf, you'll want to make it again and again.

—**CARMEL PATRONE** LONGPORT, NEW JERSEY

PREP: 15 MIN. **COOK:** 25 MIN. **MAKES:** 4-5 SERVINGS

- ¾ cup chopped celery
- ½ cup chopped onion
- 2 tablespoons butter
- 1 tablespoon olive oil
- 1 cup uncooked long grain rice
- 2½ cups chicken broth
- ½ cup chopped fresh mushrooms
- ½ cup dried cranberries
- ½ teaspoon garlic powder
- ½ teaspoon curry powder
  Salt and pepper to taste
- 2 tablespoons minced fresh parsley
- 3 tablespoons pine nuts, toasted

1. In a large saucepan, saute celery and onion in butter and oil until tender. Add rice; cook and stir for 5 minutes or until lightly browned.
2. Add the broth, mushrooms, cranberries, garlic powder, curry powder, salt and pepper. Bring to a boil. Reduce heat; cover and simmer for 20 minutes or until liquid is absorbed and rice is tender.
3. Remove from the heat. Stir in parsley; sprinkle with pine nuts.

Maple-Oat Dinner Rolls

Even though I'm in my 80s, I still love to bake for our children, grandchildren and great-grandchildren. These hearty rolls are one of our favorites.

—**HELEN DAVIS** WATERBURY, VERMONT

PREP: 25 MIN. + RISING **BAKE:** 25 MIN. **MAKES:** 2 DOZEN

- 1 package (¼ ounce) active dry yeast
- ½ cup warm water (110° to 115°), divided
- ½ cup warm strong brewed coffee (110° to 115°)
- ½ cup old-fashioned oats
- ¼ cup sugar
- ¼ cup maple syrup
- 1 egg
- 3 tablespoons shortening
- 1 teaspoon salt
- 3 to 3½ cups bread flour
- 1 tablespoon butter, melted

1. In a large bowl, dissolve yeast in ¼ cup warm water. Add the coffee, oats, sugar, syrup, egg, shortening, salt, remaining water and 2 cups flour. Beat until smooth. Stir in enough remaining flour to form a soft dough.
2. Turn onto a floured surface; knead until smooth and elastic, about 6-8 minutes. Place in a greased bowl, turning once to grease top. Cover and let rise in a warm place until doubled, about 1 hour.
3. Punch down dough. Turn onto a floured surface; divide into four portions. Divide each portion into six pieces; shape each into a ball. Place in a greased 13-in. x 9-in. baking pan. Cover and let rise until doubled, about 30 minutes.
4. Bake at 350° for 25-30 minutes or until golden brown. Brush rolls with butter. Remove from pan to a wire rack. Serve warm.

> **“**Ginger, turmeric, cinnamon and a little sherry do an incredible job of seasoning this slightly sweet soup. The recipe was given to me by a friend from South Africa. I made some adjustments to lighten it up and now it's a family favorite.**”**

—**SHELLY SNYDER** LAFAYETTE, COLORADO

Cream of Butternut Soup

PREP: 35 MIN. **COOK:** 30 MIN. **MAKES:** 8 SERVINGS

- 1 **cup chopped onion**
- 2 **celery ribs, chopped**
- 2 **tablespoons butter**
- 2 **cans (14½ ounces each) reduced-sodium chicken broth**
- 1 **teaspoon sugar**
- 1 **bay leaf**
- ½ **teaspoon salt**
- ½ **teaspoon ground ginger**
- ½ **teaspoon ground turmeric**
- ¼ **teaspoon ground cinnamon**
- 1 **butternut squash (2½ pounds), peeled and cubed**
- 3 **medium potatoes, peeled and cubed**
- 1½ **cups 1% milk**
- 2 **tablespoons sherry or additional reduced-sodium chicken broth**

1. In a large saucepan coated with cooking spray, cook onion and celery in butter until tender. Stir in the broth, sugar, bay leaf, salt, ginger, turmeric and cinnamon. Add the squash and potatoes. Bring to a boil. Reduce heat; cover and simmer for 15-20 minutes or until vegetables are tender.

2. Remove from the heat; cool slightly. Discard bay leaf. In a blender, puree vegetable mixture in batches. Return to the pan. Stir in milk and sherry; heat through (do not boil).

FAST FIX Green Beans in Yellow Pepper Butter

Colorful, crunchy and buttery beans will be all the rage at your holiday table. For a variation, sprinkle pine nuts over the top before serving.

—JUDIE WHITE FLORIEN, LOUISIANA

PREP/TOTAL TIME: 30 MIN. **MAKES:** 8 SERVINGS

- 2 **medium sweet yellow peppers, divided**
- 7 **tablespoons butter, softened, divided**
- ¼ **cup pine nuts**
- 1 **tablespoon lemon juice**
- ¼ **teaspoon salt**
- ⅛ **teaspoon pepper**
- 1½ **pounds fresh green beans, trimmed**

1. Finely chop one yellow pepper. In a small skillet, saute pepper in 1 tablespoon butter until tender. Set aside.

2. Place the pine nuts, lemon juice, salt, pepper and remaining butter in a food processor; cover and process until blended. Add cooked pepper; cover and process until blended. Set butter mixture aside.

3. Place beans in a large saucepan and cover with water. Cut remaining pepper into thin strips; add to beans. Bring to a boil. Cover and cook for 5-7 minutes or until crisp-tender; drain. Place vegetables in a large bowl; add butter mixture and toss to coat.

Traditional Holiday Stuffing

Sausage and sage add a gourmet taste to this stuffing, but I like the zesty addition of mayonnaise and mustard. This recipe serves two dozen people, perfect for large family or church gatherings.

—LORRAINE BRAUCKHOFF ZOLFO SPRINGS, FLORIDA

PREP: 35 MIN. **BAKE:** 45 MIN. **MAKES:** 24 SERVINGS

- 1 **package (12 ounces) reduced-fat bulk pork sausage or breakfast turkey sausage links, casings removed**
- 3 **celery ribs, chopped**
- 1 **large onion, chopped**
- 2 **tablespoons reduced-fat mayonnaise**
- 2 **tablespoons prepared mustard**
- 4 **teaspoons rubbed sage**
- 1 **tablespoon poultry seasoning**
- 2 **loaves (16 ounces each) day-old white bread, cubed**
- 1 **loaf (16 ounces) day-old whole wheat bread, cubed**
- 3 **eggs, lightly beaten**
- 2 **cans (14½ ounces each) reduced-sodium chicken broth**

1. In a large nonstick skillet coated with cooking spray, cook the sausage, celery and onion over medium heat until meat is no longer pink; drain. Remove from the heat; stir in the mayonnaise, mustard, sage and the poultry seasoning.

2. Place bread cubes in a large bowl; add sausage mixture. Combine eggs and broth; pour over bread cubes and stir gently to combine. Transfer to two 3-qt. baking dishes coated with cooking spray.

3. Cover and bake at 350° for 30 minutes. Uncover; bake 12-18 minutes longer or until a thermometer reads 165°.

Editor's Note: *If using this recipe to stuff poultry, replace the eggs with ¾ cup egg substitute. Bake until a meat thermometer reads 180° for poultry and 165° for stuffing. Allow ¾ cup stuffing per pound of turkey. Bake remaining stuffing as directed in the recipe.*

Apricot-Glazed Turkey Breast

Turkey takes center stage in this dish paired with several interesting flavors. Garlic, ginger and apricot enhance this traditional entree without loading on calories.

—**JANET SPRUTE** LEWISTON, IDAHO

PREP: 15 MIN. + MARINATING **BAKE:** 2 HOURS + STANDING **MAKES:** 12 SERVINGS

1 bone-in turkey breast (5 to 6 pounds)	½ cup white wine or reduced-sodium chicken broth
2 garlic cloves, peeled and thinly sliced	⅓ cup reduced-sugar apricot preserves
1 tablespoon sliced fresh gingerroot	1 tablespoon spicy brown mustard
	2 teaspoons reduced-sodium soy sauce

1. With fingers, carefully loosen skin from turkey breast. With a sharp knife, cut ten 2-in.-long slits in meat under the skin; insert a garlic clove slice and a ginger slice into each slit.

2. Place turkey in a large bowl; pour ¼ cup wine under the skin. Secure skin to underside of breast with toothpicks. Pour remaining wine over turkey. Cover and refrigerate for 6 hours or overnight.

3. In a small bowl, combine the preserves, mustard and soy sauce; set aside. Drain and discard marinade; place turkey on a rack in a foil-lined roasting pan.

4. Bake at 325° for 2 to 2½ hours or until a thermometer reads 170°, basting with apricot mixture every 30 minutes (cover loosely with foil if turkey browns too quickly). Cover and let stand for 15 minutes before carving.

FAST FIX Fruit & Nut Salad

Make salad fun. Bananas, peanuts and marshmallows give this dish a whimsical taste that will have everyone reaching for seconds. Kids, especially, will love this fruity combination.

—**KAREN ANN BLAND** GOVE, KANSAS

PREP/TOTAL TIME: 15 MIN. **MAKES:** 9 SERVINGS

- 4 medium firm bananas, sliced
- 1 medium green apple, chopped
- 1 medium red apple, chopped
- ½ cup miniature marshmallows
- ½ cup dried cranberries
- 1 carton (8 ounces) frozen whipped topping, thawed
- ½ cup dry roasted peanuts, coarsely chopped, divided

In a large bowl, gently stir the bananas, apples, marshmallows, cranberries and whipped topping. Fold in ¼ cup peanuts. Refrigerate until serving. Sprinkle with remaining peanuts just before serving.

During the winter we make brimming bowls of savory Chicken Wild Rice Soup. It has a lot of substance, and the men in my family especially love it. —**VIRGINIA MONTMARQUET** RIVERSIDE, CALIFORNIA

Chicken Wild Rice Soup

PREP: 10 MIN. **COOK:** 40 MIN.
MAKES: 14 SERVINGS (3½ QUARTS)

- 2 quarts chicken broth
- ½ pound fresh mushrooms, chopped
- 1 cup finely chopped celery
- 1 cup shredded carrots
- ½ cup finely chopped onion
- 1 teaspoon chicken bouillon granules
- 1 teaspoon dried parsley flakes
- ¼ teaspoon garlic powder
- ¼ teaspoon dried thyme
- ¼ cup butter, cubed
- ¼ cup all-purpose flour
- 1 can (10¾ ounces) condensed cream of mushroom soup, undiluted
- ½ cup dry white wine or additional chicken broth
- 3 cups cooked wild rice
- 2 cups cubed cooked chicken

1. In a large saucepan, combine the first nine ingredients. Bring to a boil. Reduce heat; cover and simmer for 30 minutes.

2. In a Dutch oven, melt butter; stir in flour until smooth. Gradually whisk in broth mixture. Bring to a boil; cook and stir for 2 minutes or until thickened. Whisk in soup and wine. Add rice and chicken; heat through.

top tip — Perfect Portions

I like to make a big batch of soup, then freeze individual servings. I line bowls with plastic wrap, pour in soup and freeze. Once frozen, the soup can be popped out of the bowls and stored in large freezer bags. This also makes a nice gift for an ill friend or someone living alone.

—**SHIRLEY P.** REDMOND, WASHINGTON

Golden Au Gratin Potatoes

I call this a gratin from heaven. Horseradish and nutmeg are my secret ingredients for giving it such a special flavor.
—JANICE ELDER CHARLOTTE, NORTH CAROLINA

PREP: 35 MIN. **BAKE:** 1½ HOURS **MAKES:** 15 SERVINGS

- 2 **large onions, thinly sliced**
- 2 **tablespoons butter**
- 1 **cup half-and-half cream**
- 1 **cup canned pumpkin**
- 1 **tablespoon prepared horseradish**
- ½ **teaspoon ground nutmeg**
- 1 **teaspoon salt**
- ½ **teaspoon pepper**
- 2¼ **pounds potatoes, peeled and cut into ¼-inch slices**
- 2 **cups soft bread crumbs**
- 8 **ounces Gruyere or Swiss cheese, shredded**
- 2 **tablespoons chopped fresh sage**

1. In a large skillet, cook onions in butter over medium heat for 15-20 minutes or until onions are golden brown, stirring frequently.

2. In a large bowl, combine the cream, pumpkin, horseradish, nutmeg, salt and pepper. In a greased 13-in. x 9-in. baking pan, layer potato slices and onions. Spread with pumpkin mixture. Cover and bake at 350° for 1¼ hours.

3. Increase temperature to 400°. In a large bowl, combine the bread crumbs, cheese and sage. Sprinkle over top. Bake, uncovered, 15-20 minutes longer or until golden brown.

FAST FIX Hazelnut and Pear Salad

My husband, daughter and I raise hazelnuts in the Willamette Valley—so this salad is a family favorite. Since pears and cherries are in an abundance in our area, too, I included them in the recipe.
—KAREN KIRSCH ST. PAUL, OREGON

PREP/TOTAL TIME: 25 MIN. **MAKES:** 6 SERVINGS

- ⅓ **cup plus ½ cup chopped hazelnuts, toasted, divided**
- 2 **tablespoons plus ½ cup chopped red onion, divided**
- 2 **tablespoons water**
- 4½ **teaspoons balsamic vinegar**
- 4½ **teaspoons sugar**
- ½ **teaspoon salt**
- 1 **garlic clove, halved**
- ⅛ **teaspoon paprika**
- ¼ **cup olive oil**
- 1 **package (5 ounces) spring mix salad greens**
- 1 **medium pear, thinly sliced**
- ½ **cup crumbled Gorgonzola cheese**
- ¼ **cup dried cherries**

1. For dressing, place ⅓ cup hazelnuts, 2 tablespoons onion, water, vinegar, sugar, salt, garlic and paprika in a food processor; cover and process until blended. While processing, gradually add oil in a steady stream.

2. In a large bowl, combine salad greens and the remaining onion; add ½ cup dressing and toss to coat. Divide among six salad plates.

3. Top each salad with pear, cheese, cherries and remaining hazelnuts; drizzle with the remaining dressing.

Sausage Raisin Dressing

My mother was looking through a cookbook when a clipping with this recipe fell to the floor. Mom, who's 80, told me the recipe came from her mother. We cherish this heirloom recipe and hope others will too.

—BRENDA LIZ PARKINSON PRINCE GEORGE, BRITISH COLUMBIA

PREP: 20 MIN. **BAKE:** 50 MIN. **MAKES:** 10 SERVINGS

- 1 pound bulk pork sausage
- ¾ cup each chopped celery, green pepper and onion
- 6 cups cubed day-old bread (½-inch cubes), crusts removed
- 1 can (8 ounces) sliced water chestnuts, drained and chopped
- ½ cup raisins
- 1 teaspoon salt
- ⅛ teaspoon pepper
- 2 eggs
- ½ cup chicken broth

1. In a large skillet, cook the sausage, celery, green pepper and onion over medium heat until meat is no longer pink; drain.
2. In a bowl, combine the bread cubes, water chestnuts, raisins, salt and pepper. Add sausage mixture and toss to coat. Whisk eggs and broth; pour over bread mixture and toss to coat.
3. Transfer to a greased shallow 2½-qt. baking dish. Cover and bake at 350° for 35 minutes. Uncover; bake 15-20 minutes longer or until a thermometer reads 165°.

Smoked Salmon New Potatoes

Give twice-baked potatoes a rest this year and try these stuffed spuds. Smoked salmon and cream cheese blended with lemon juice and dill are simply piped into small red potatoes. Leftovers are even good with eggs for breakfast.

—TASTE OF HOME TEST KITCHEN

PREP: 20 MIN. **COOK:** 20 MIN. **MAKES:** 3 DOZEN

- 36 small red potatoes (about 1½ pounds)
- 1 package (8 ounces) reduced-fat cream cheese, cubed
- 2 packages (3 ounces each) smoked salmon or lox
- 2 tablespoons chopped green onion
- 2 teaspoons dill weed
- 2 teaspoons lemon juice
- ⅛ teaspoon salt
- ⅛ teaspoon pepper
  Fresh dill sprigs

1. Place the potatoes in a large saucepan and cover with water. Bring to a boil. Cook, covered, for 15-20 minutes or until tender.
2. Meanwhile, in a food processor, combine the cream cheese, salmon, onion, dill, lemon juice, salt and pepper. Cover and process until smooth; set aside.
3. Drain potatoes and immediately place in ice water. Drain and pat dry with paper towels. Cut a thin slice off the bottom of each potato to allow it to sit flat. With a melon baller, scoop out a small amount of potato (discard or save for another use).
4. Pipe or spoon salmon mixture into potatoes. Garnish with dill sprigs.

Herbed Roast Chicken

Not a fan of turkey? Here's a sure family-pleaser. I've been using this easy recipe for years. Marinating the chicken before roasting gives it a mild citrus tang and an attractive look.

—SAMUEL ONIZUK ELKTON, MARYLAND

PREP: 15 MIN. + MARINATING   **BAKE:** 2¼ HOURS + STANDING
MAKES: 8 SERVINGS

	One 2-gallon resealable plastic bag
½	cup orange juice
⅓	cup olive oil
2	tablespoons butter, melted
1	tablespoon balsamic vinegar
1	tablespoon Worcestershire sauce
6	garlic cloves, minced
1	tablespoon minced chives
1	tablespoon dried parsley flakes

1	tablespoon dried basil
1	teaspoon salt
1	teaspoon pepper
½	teaspoon dried marjoram
½	teaspoon dried rosemary, crushed
¼	teaspoon dried tarragon
1	roasting chicken (6 to 7 pounds)

1. In the 2-gallon resealable plastic bag, combine the orange juice, oil, butter, vinegar, Worcestershire sauce, garlic, chives and seasonings. Add the chicken; seal bag and turn to coat. Refrigerate for 8 hours or overnight, turning occasionally.

2. Drain and discard marinade. Place chicken on a rack in a shallow roasting pan. Bake, uncovered, at 350º for 2¼ to 2¾ hours or until a thermometer reads 180º. Cover loosely with foil if chicken browns too quickly. Cover and let stand for 15 minutes before carving.

FAST FIX Cauliflower with Buttered Crumbs

Add home-style flavor and interest to steamed cauliflower with a few ingredients you probably have in your kitchen.
—TASTE OF HOME TEST KITCHEN

PREP/TOTAL TIME: 20 MIN. **MAKES:** 6 SERVINGS

- 1 large head cauliflower, broken into florets
- ⅓ cup butter, cubed
- 1 tablespoon lemon juice
- ¼ cup dry bread crumbs
- ¼ cup grated Parmesan cheese
- 2 tablespoons minced fresh parsley
- ⅛ teaspoon salt
- ⅛ teaspoon pepper

1. Place 1 in. of water in a large saucepan; add cauliflower. Bring to a boil. Reduce heat; cover and simmer for 10-12 minutes or until crisp-tender.
2. Meanwhile, in a small heavy saucepan, cook butter over medium heat for 5 minutes or until golden brown, stirring frequently. Remove from the heat; stir in lemon juice. In a small bowl, combine the bread crumbs, cheese, parsley, salt and pepper; stir in 3 tablespoons browned butter.
3. Drain cauliflower and place in a serving dish. Drizzle with the remaining browned butter; sprinkle with bread crumb mixture.

Seasoned Rib Roast

I like to make gravy with the drippings of this roast. It's exceptional. And it's perfect for serving with mashed potatoes.
—EVELYN GEBHARDT KASILOF, ALASKA

PREP: 10 MIN. **BAKE:** 1¾ HOURS + STANDING **MAKES:** 6-8 SERVINGS

1½ teaspoons lemon-pepper seasoning	½ teaspoon dried rosemary, crushed
1½ teaspoons paprika	¼ teaspoon cayenne pepper
¾ teaspoon garlic salt	1 beef ribeye roast (3 to 4 pounds)

1. In a small bowl, combine the seasonings; rub over roast. Place roast fat side up on a rack in a shallow roasting pan.
2. Bake, uncovered, at 350° for 1¾ to 2½ hours or until meat reaches desired doneness (for medium-rare, a thermometer should read 145°; medium, 160°; well-done, 170°). Remove to a warm serving platter. Let stand for 10 minutes before carving.

Crunchy Sweet Potato Bake

This is our all-time favorite! We love the nutty crunch against the smooth, gingery sweet potatoes underneath.

—DAWN RIGGESTAD NEW BERN, NORTH CAROLINA

PREP: 30 MIN. **BAKE:** 25 MIN. **MAKES:** 8 SERVINGS

- 3 pounds sweet potatoes (about 7 medium), peeled and quartered
- ⅔ cup sugar
- ½ cup 2% milk
- ⅓ cup butter, softened
- 1 tablespoon finely chopped crystallized ginger
- 1 teaspoon ground cinnamon
- ¼ teaspoon ground nutmeg

TOPPING

- ¾ cup cornflakes, lightly crushed
- ¼ cup packed brown sugar
- ¼ cup chopped pecans
- ¼ cup butter, melted

1. Place sweet potatoes in a large saucepan and cover with water. Bring to a boil. Reduce heat; cover and simmer for 12-18 minutes or until tender. Drain. Mash the sweet potatoes with the sugar, milk, butter, ginger, cinnamon and nutmeg.

2. Transfer to a greased 2-qt. baking dish. Cover and bake at 350° for 20 minutes or until heated through.

3. Combine the topping ingredients; sprinkle over potatoes. Bake, uncovered, for 5-10 minutes or until topping is lightly browned.

Texas Garlic Mashed Potatoes

In Texas, you gotta go big on tasty combinations. These Lone Star State mashed potatoes get their flavor burst from sweet roasted garlic and caramelized onions.

—RICHARD MARKLE MIDLOTHIAN, TEXAS

PREP: 30 MIN. **BAKE:** 30 MIN. **MAKES:** 6 SERVINGS

- 1 whole garlic bulb
- 1 teaspoon plus 1 tablespoon olive oil, divided
- 1 medium white onion, chopped
- 4 medium potatoes, peeled and quartered
- ¼ cup butter, softened
- ¼ cup sour cream
- ¼ cup grated Parmesan cheese
- ¼ cup 2% milk
- ½ teaspoon salt
- ¼ teaspoon pepper

1. Remove papery outer skin from garlic (do not peel or separate cloves). Cut top off of garlic bulb. Brush with 1 teaspoon oil. Wrap bulb in heavy-duty foil. Bake at 425° for 30-35 minutes or until softened.

2. Meanwhile, in a large skillet over low heat, cook onion in remaining oil for 15-20 minutes or until golden brown, stirring occasionally. Transfer to a food processor. Cover and process until blended; set aside.

3. Place potatoes in a large saucepan and cover with water. Bring to a boil. Reduce heat; cover and cook for 15-20 minutes or until tender. Drain. Place potatoes in a large bowl. Squeeze softened garlic into bowl; add the butter, sour cream, cheese, milk, salt, pepper and onion. Beat until mashed.

Warm or cold? Take your choice of how to serve this colorful autumn beverage. It's such a pretty color, and the spicy sweet-tart flavor is delightful with a Thanksgiving meal. —DIXIE TERRY GOREVILLE, ILLINOIS

FESTIVE CRANBERRY DRINK

MAKE AHEAD ▸ Festive Cranberry Drink

PREP: 25 MIN. **COOK:** 20 MIN. **MAKES:** 3 QUARTS

- 4 cups fresh or frozen cranberries
- 3 quarts water, divided
- 1¾ cups sugar
- 1 cup orange juice
- ⅔ cup lemon juice
- ½ cup red-hot candies
- 12 whole cloves

1. In a Dutch oven, combine cranberries and 1 qt. water. Cook over medium heat until berries pop, about 15 minutes. Remove from the heat. Strain through a fine strainer, pressing mixture with a spoon; discard skins. Return cranberry pulp and juice to the pan.

2. Stir in the sugar, juices, red-hots and remaining water. Place cloves on a double thickness of cheesecloth. Bring up corners of cloth and tie with kitchen string to form a bag; add to juice mixture. Bring to a boil; cook and stir until sugar and red-hots are dissolved.

3. Remove from the heat. Strain through a fine mesh sieve or cheesecloth. Discard spice bag. Serve drink warm or cold.

Glazed Orange Carrots

With a sweet, buttery, orangey coating, this is an easy way to get kids to eat carrots.
—**MARILYN HASH** ENUMCLAW, WASHINGTON

PREP/TOTAL TIME: 25 MIN. **MAKES:** 6 SERVINGS

- 2 pounds fresh carrots, sliced
- 2 tablespoons butter
- ¼ cup thawed orange juice concentrate
- 2 tablespoons brown sugar
- 2 tablespoons minced fresh parsley

1. Place 1 in. of water in saucepan; add carrots. Bring to boil. Reduce heat; cover and simmer for 7-9 minutes until crisp-tender. Drain.

2. Melt butter in a large skillet; stir in orange juice concentrate and brown sugar. Add carrots and parsley; stir to coat. Cook and stir for 1-2 minutes or until glaze is thickened.

General Index

This handy index lists every recipe by food category and/or major ingredient, so you can easily locate recipes to suit your needs. Recipes marked with * are ready in 30 minutes or less.

PAGE 9

PAGE 42

PAGE 26

PAGE 176

PAGE 23

PAGE 63

PAGE 127

PAGE 270

PAGE 240

PAGE 115

CRAFT INDEX

PAGE 261

Alphabetical Index

Recipes marked with * are ready in 30 minutes or less.

PAGE 292

PAGE 12